GW01454533

Our Family Business takes us on a personal journey into Śrīla Prabhupāda's timeless legacy of love, wherein we can all have an intimate role. With every page I read, I can feel the contagious spirit of gratitude and compassion that springs from the heart of Vaiśeṣika Dāsa.

Radhanath Swami

Forty years ago I watched in wonder as people became enchanted by Vaiśeṣika Prabhu at O'Hare International Airport and bought books. The consciousness, philosophy, and technique behind that enchantment has appeared as words in this book. Reader, be enchanted!

Śivarāma Swami

In *Our Family Business,* Vaiśeṣika Prabhu has brilliantly captured the spirit that drove Śrīla Prabhupāda's disciples beyond all limits to please His Divine Grace by publishing and distributing his books by the millions all over the world. Reader beware! This book has the potential to not only rekindle that same spirit in the hearts of those who live only to elicit Śrīla Prabhupāda's smile, but to ignite that same spirit in the hearts of those who were not even aware that that's what this life is all about. Thank you Vaiśeṣika Prabhu for keeping this spirit alive!

Nirañjana Swami

Śrīla Prabhupāda once said, "One day historians will note how this Kṛṣṇa consciousness movement saved the world in its darkest hours." Surely such historians will recount the major role that the distribution of Śrīla Prabhupāda's books played in delivering the world from the darkness of ignorance that so much characterizes this age. Their task has now been made all that easier with the publication of *Our Family Business,* by Vaiśeṣika Dāsa. His monumental work covers the entire period of book distribution in the Hare Kṛṣṇa movement, from its inception in the early 1970s down to the present

Praise for Our Family Business

Our Family Business takes one through the Hare Kṛṣṇa explosion in book distribution in a most compelling and thrilling manner from one who was a key player in it. This book also takes one into the modern day in which not only temple devotees but devotees in the congregation can participate in the family business of distributing transcendental literature. This book reveals how His Divine Grace A. C. Bhaktivedanta Swami Prabhupāda, ISKCON's founder-*ācārya,* led and inspired the devotees to distribute ancient spiritual classics of India to a Western audience seeking a higher purpose in life. From the very first pages of this book, you will not want to put it down. It's surely a must-have.

Jayapatāka Swami

Our Family Business: The Great Art of Distributing Śrīla Prabhupāda's Books is a must-read *saṅkīrtana* story. This book is for those who distribute Śrīla Prabhupāda's books, who want to distribute them but don't yet feel sufficiently inspired to, or who have never been exposed to the service. Vaiśeṣika Prabhu has been distributing Śrīla Prabhupāda's books for over forty years, and he has inspired devotees around the world to perform this valuable service to Śrīla Prabhupāda.

Gopal Krishna Goswami

Just as Śrīla Prabhupāda's books about Kṛṣṇa *are* Kṛṣṇa, so Vaiśeṣika Prabhu's masterful offering is also Kṛṣṇa in a most approachable, relishable, relevant, personal form that will educate, enlighten, and empower devotees to publish and distribute – and read and apply – Śrīla Prabhupāda's books now and in the future.

Giriraj Swami

day. What's more, it gives practical guidelines how this most important contribution to the salvation of humanity can go on for centuries or even longer. *Our Family Business* is a great milestone in the history of the Hare Kṛṣṇa movement.

Indradyumna Swami

Gather around, young and old, and you will hear of the book distribution epidemic – well, just a relic of yesteryear? The *saṅkīrtana* that mesmerized the ISKCON world in the '70s – was it just an exceptional comet, blazing in a unique social period? *Our Family Business* absolutely, positively confirms that reading and distributing Śrīla Prabhupāda's books is always the core spirit of ISKCON.

Amid fluctuations of enthusiasm to read and distribute Prabhupāda's books as ISKCON's life and soul, *Our Family Business* pulls us all up straight – reinfecting and reinjecting us with genuine Hare Kṛṣṇa dharma.

Devamrita Swami

Vaiśeṣika Prabhu's *Our Family Business* first encompasses the background and history of Śrīla Prabhupāda and the explosion of His Divine Grace's book distribution in the 1970s, then shifts that same dynamic energy forward, with highly practical tips for igniting a new blast of transcendental knowledge for a new millennium. Each page demonstrates, with notes, quotes, and anecdotes, how the compassionate heart of a single Vaiṣṇava invokes compassion in others, who then, as a team, reach out to share their good fortune with others, creating a sublime wave of kindness, intelligence, and light that washes gently but unmistakably over the grinding, dejected, dark lives of all in its path.

Kalakaṇṭha Dāsa

The essential realizations in *Our Family Business* are highly addictive. Buy it! Read it! Live it!

Navīna Nīrada Dāsa

OUR FAMILY BUSINESS

"The highest truth is reality
distinguished from illusion
for the welfare of all."

ŚRĪMAD-BHĀGAVATAM 1.1.2

OUR FAMILY BUSINESS

The Great Art of Distributing Śrīla Prabhupāda's Books

Vaiśeṣika Dāsa

THE BHAKTIVEDANTA BOOK TRUST

For more information, please visit:

www.ourfamilybusiness.info
www.fanthespark.com
www.distributebooks.com

Set in 10-point Baskerville Original
Book design by Govinda Cordua

Copyright © 2016 The Bhaktivedanta Book Trust International, Inc.

Published by The Bhaktivedanta Book Trust

www.bbt.se
www.bbtmedia.com
www.bbt.org

ISBN 978-91-7149-900-4

DEDICATION

Our Family Business is dedicated
to all those who help Śrīla Prabhupāda
publish and distribute his books,
as well as to all those who read them
and apply their principles.

Contents

REALIZATIONS

Foreword

The gratitude I feel toward the author of this work, Vaiśeṣika Prabhu, surpasses the ability of my words to do it proper justice. And yet that gratitude becomes enhanced, in quantity and quality, when I consider the joy and satisfaction *Our Family Business* is unquestionably providing to Śrīla Prabhupāda, in whose eternal divine service this work has been written. Śrīla Prabhupāda surely sees what even I can see: that this book is a kind of potent seed, which, being broadcast and cultivated in the fertile fields of ISKCON, will produce its superabundant fruit all over the world.

The primordial originator of our *sampradāya* – the extended family indicated by the title of this work – is Lord Brahmā. He is also the deputed creator of our universe. The knowledge, theoretical and practical, enabling him to create had been instilled in him prenatally by the Supreme Brahman. Consequently, Brahmā is known as *veda-garbha,* "impregnated with the Vedic knowledge from his very birth," or "a Vedāntist from the embryo."[1] Iconographically, Lord Brahmā's inviolable possession of Vedic knowledge is signified by the book grasped in one of his hands.

However, *Śrīmad-Bhāgavatam* relates, Brahmā felt unfulfilled with merely creating the cosmos. After all, it is just a big prison, a penitential dwelling for the numberless fallen souls. Lord Brahmā didn't want to be a mere jailer. He knew that the prison was meant for its inmates' rehabilitation and release, and he was eager to participate in that effort. Receiving further empowerment from Lord Kṛṣṇa, Brahmā inaugurated his special project by imparting potent knowledge to his son Nārada Muni, who set out to distribute that knowledge throughout his father's vast creation. This is how our family business got started: Endlessly traveling everywhere, Nārada Muni, "the eternal spaceman," went out on *saṅkīrtana*.

More recently, Nārada's disciple Vyāsadeva, foreseeing the moral and cognitive debilitations soon to afflict the human race in Kali-yuga, edited that body of knowledge and committed it to writing. One portion of it, however, he withheld, judging it too lofty for liberal distribution. Yet after Nārada's prodding, he made even that accessible – that highest and most confidential knowledge of divinity: the Vṛndāvana pastimes recently enacted on earth by Kṛṣṇa Himself. This supreme revelation discloses the private life of God – the Lord's most unceremonious diversions with intimate associates, in which Kṛṣṇa's exquisite sweetness and charm eclipses His awesome majesty.

This rare and priceless revelation is offered only once within a day of Brahmā, that is, once every 8,600,000,000 of our earthly years. And Vyāsadeva wrote it down. He realized that only a rare soul would have the qualifications to grasp what he had set down – an open secret, but still a secret. However, both Vyāsa and Nārada knew what Brahmā knew: that in the same *yuga* cycle in the day that Vṛndāvana-Kṛṣṇa descends, the Lord descends once more, and this time not as the Supreme Lord but as the Lord's supreme devotee – as Śrī Caitanya Mahāprabhu.

So exceptional is the revelation of *vṛndāvana-līlā* that the Lord himself comes as His own devotee to practice and teach the equally exceptional method that qualifies a devotee to receive that revelation. Descending with His eternal expansions and associates, Śrī Kṛṣṇa Caitanya undertakes His mission: to institute the *yuga-dharma, saṅkīrtana,* the dispensation for this age. This is the method by which we, the highly unfit souls of our time, can be rendered fit to receive the supreme secret. This is explained by Kṛṣṇadāsa Kavirāja Gosvāmī in *Śrī Caitanya-caritāmṛta* (*Ādi-līlā* 7.20–28):

> The characteristics of Kṛṣṇa are understood to be a storehouse of transcendental love. Although that storehouse of love certainly came with Kṛṣṇa when He was present, it was sealed. But when Śrī Caitanya Mahāprabhu came with His associates of the Pañca-tattva, they broke the seal and plundered the storehouse to taste transcendental love of Kṛṣṇa. The more they tasted it, the more their thirst for it grew. Śrī Pañca-tattva themselves danced again and again and thus made it easier to drink nectarean love of Godhead. They danced, cried, laughed, and chanted like madmen, and in this way they distributed love of Godhead. In distributing love of Godhead, Caitanya Mahāprabhu and His associates did not consider who was a fit candidate and who was not, nor where such distribution should or should not take place. They made no conditions. Wherever they got the opportunity, the members of the Pañca-tattva distributed love of Godhead.
>
> Although the members of the Pañca-tattva plundered the storehouse of love of Godhead and ate and distributed its contents, there was no scarcity, for this wonderful storehouse is so complete that as the love is distributed, the supply increases hundreds of times. The flood of love of Godhead swelled in all directions, and thus young men, old men, women, and children were all immersed in that inundation. The Kṛṣṇa consciousness movement will inundate the entire world and drown everyone, whether one be a gentleman, a rogue, or even lame, invalid, or blind. When the five members of the Pañca-tattva saw the entire world drowned in love of Godhead and the seed of material enjoyment in the living entities completely destroyed, they all became exceedingly happy. The more the five members of the Pañca-tattva cause the rains of love of Godhead to fall, the more the inundation increases and spreads all over the world.

Significantly, Lord Caitanya elected to receive Vaiṣṇava initiation into the Brahma-sampradāya, whose originator displays a book as his distinctive attribute, and whose *ācāryas* became so distinguished for literary production that their lineage became known as "the *sampradāya* of the book." Book production and distribution – as Vaiśeṣika Prabhu so nicely explains – is "literary *saṅkīrtana*," and as such was greatly appreciated by Mahāprabhu. Lord Caitanya specifically engaged His highly cultured successors, the Six Gosvāmīs of Vṛndāvana, in literary production, and they brought into the world an immortal library of superb devotional works. Others, like Viśvanātha Cakravartī Ṭhākura and Śrīla Baladeva Vidyābhūṣaṇa, followed.

Writing at the end of the sixteenth century, Kṛṣṇadāsa Kavirāja foresaw that the flood of *prema* let loose by Lord Caitanya would one day inundate the whole world. That global flood began with Śrīla Bhaktivinoda Ṭhākura who, in the final decades of the nineteenth century, came out with a torrent of books and periodicals to present Lord Caitanya's teaching to an urban, modernizing, "English-knowing," Indian middle class. In 1896, his English-language essay "Śrī Caitanya Mahāprabhu: His Life and Precepts" went out to university libraries in the West.

His son Śrīla Bhaktisiddhānta Sarasvatī Ṭhākura continued his father's work in the same spirit. Writings poured from his press. Śrīla Sarasvatī Ṭhākura's ambition was global. In 1927 he refashioned his father's Bengali-language journal *Sajjanatoṣaṇī* into the English-language *The Harmonist,* and, having established over sixty Gauḍīya Maṭha temples through the length and breadth of India in record time, dispatched three disciples to London in 1933. They were armed with a 762-page English-language tome entitled *Sree Krishna Chaitanya,* the first of three projected volumes. They delayed their voyage until they had some of the just-printed books in hand.

These first waves of *prema* were harbingers of the flood to come. There was a pause: The Gauḍīya Maṭha became debilitated and distracted by internal strife. And the whole globe became engulfed by modern, high-tech warfare, producing eighty million fatalities – a testimony of sorts to "progress."

Animated by the order and by the example of his spiritual master, Śrīla Prabhupāda began the English-language *Back to Godhead* magazine in 1944, as war raged around him. By 1960, preparing to go to the West, he took *sannyāsa* and began work on the three volumes of *Śrīmad-Bhāgavatam* he would take with him on the *Jaladuta* in 1965. His mission to the West was thus carefully modeled after Śrīla Bhaktisiddhānta Sarasvatī Ṭhākura's mission of 1933. That 1933 effort had been conducted with the concerted force and resources of the entire Gauḍīya Maṭha behind it; this 1965 effort was undertaken by one old man, alone and unsupported. Lacking money, health, and youthful energy, Śrīla Prabhupāda ignited in America and then Europe "the Hare Kṛṣṇa explosion," releasing the flood of *prema* that would cover the world.

What was his secret? How did he do it?

Our Family Business tells us, quite methodically, how Śrīla Prabhupāda did it. Not only does Vaiśeṣika Prabhu know how Śrīla Prabhupāda did it, he teaches us how we can do it too.

Can *we* be like Śrīla Prabhupāda? I vividly remember when I learned the answer, in the fall of 1971, when I was a brand-new temple president in Philadelphia. I received a photocopied newsletter mailed out by Śyāmasundara Dāsa, Śrīla Prabhupāda's secretary, then traveling with him in Africa. Śyāmasundara recounts a particular occasion when Śrīla Prabhupāda was reflecting on his accomplishments. They had just come from London, where Śrīla Prabhupāda had defeated in debate the secretary of Mensa, the high IQ society. After recalling this, Prabhupāda went on to say: "I am one person, and just see what I have done. Now we are five hundred [initiated disciples]. *So each of you become just like me and see what can be done.*"

To be sure, *Our Family Business* is written specifically as an instruction manual for book distribution, yet the work covers its subject so thoroughly and deeply that it simultaneously serves as a superb instruction manual for Kṛṣṇa bhakti itself. Even if book distribution is not your primary service, you will still find yourself enlightened, encouraged, and enlivened by reading and rereading *Our Family Business*. It will inspire and guide any and every devotee to improve *any* service he or she may undertake for Kṛṣṇa: cook, *pūjārī*, farm worker, yard worker, manager, teacher, editor, or writer – it doesn't matter. Moreover, every devotee should, in one fashion or another, share Kṛṣṇa consciousness with others. *Saṅkīrtana* is everyone's *dharma*.

The radiant thread running throughout this work is the elucidation of the inseparable bond between effective book distribution and the effective execution of *sādhana,* that is, the regular performance of the foundational spiritual practices of Kṛṣṇa consciousness – following the four regulative principles, chanting *japa* attentively, and attentive and regular reading of *Bhagavad-gītā, Śrīmad-Bhāgavatam,* and similar works.

For example, in the section of chapter thirteen entitled "Devotees Who Practice Strong Sādhana Are Attractive," Vaiśeṣika Prabhu sets forth a compelling case, replete with particular experiences and astute observations, that steadiness and purity in performance of *sādhana* will automatically invest a devotee with a particular aura, a liminal, subtle sort of effulgence, so that on *saṅkīrtana,* people will spontaneously become attracted – drawn simply by the devotee's *presence.*

Those who had proximate association with Śrīla Prabhupāda's person became acutely aware of such an aura. Although his bearing was typically unassuming, even modest, there was something around him that made his presence captivating.

"Purity is the force," Śrīla Prabhupāda said. (This also was memorably recorded in Śyāmasundara's newsletter, part of a complete epigram: "Preaching is the essence; books are the basis; utility is the principle; and purity is the force.")

When purity declines, we may find something else happening in the guise of *saṅkīrtana.* I encountered a dramatic instance of this in 1987, when, as a new member of the Governing Body Commission, I began to receive some unpleasant surprises.

One summer's day in a major American temple, I stood in the ornate lobby absorbed in discussion with the new temple president when a young *brahmacārī* approached us. A dedicated book distributor, the *brahmacārī* had taken charge of the small group that went out with *Gītās* and *Bhāgavatams* to the city's international airport. He had already confided in me that his main frustration was a persistent difficulty in getting the devotees and transport freed up to do this service. Now he approached us and asked the temple president: "Can I take the van to go to the airport for book distribution?" The president looked annoyed, and grimaced. "No!" He said, "No!" Clearly the *brahmacārī's* quest was something of a chronic vexation. The next words were delivered machine-gun style: "We need the van for *saṅkīrtana*!"

I knew what he meant by that word. A good number of devotees were already making ready to head out to the baseball stadium. Spreading out through the parking lots, invoking the need for humanitarian relief, they would sell ball caps and pennants displaying the logo of the local major league team to its fans. It was an important source of income for the temple. With a sinking heart, I realized that the meaning of "*saṅkīrtana*" had changed.

Now, thanks to Vaiśeṣika Prabhu, I can confidently proclaim, "Never again!"

"There are two kinds of strength," Śrīla Prabhupāda writes, "*daiva* and *puruṣākāra. Daiva* refers to the strength achieved from the transcendence, and *puruṣākāra* refers to the strength organized by one's own intelligence and power. Transcendental power is always superior."[2]

Our Family Business is clearly a product of that *daiva* power, and it can invest that same *daiva* power on those who are prepared to receive it. Not only will this book protect *saṅkīrtana* from any *dharmasya glāni,* but I am convinced it will so enliven *saṅkīrtana* that it will pour its benedictions more and more profusely on this tormented world.

With gratitude, I bow to the feet of Vaiśeṣika Prabhu and to all those who follow in his footsteps.

paraṁ vijayate śrī-kṛṣṇa-saṅkīrtanam

Ravīndra Svarūpa Dāsa

Preface

Dear Reader,

Even though you've just picked up this book and it's possible that we're meeting for the first time, I want to reveal my heart to you about why I wrote this book before you go any further.

Śrīla Prabhupāda's books rescued me from the material world. I never wanted to be a normal high school kid. I wanted to know more about life and truth than the mundane subjects they teach you. I wanted to know what death is and why I have to die. As educated and well meaning as my teachers and parents were, however, they couldn't answer such questions.

I was sixteen when I set out on my spiritual quest. I gave away most of my possessions and stopped wearing shoes and riding in cars. I fasted, prayed, and meditated. In my quest for answers to life's troubling mysteries, I read any book that looked spiritual. Because I was able to formulate questions, I believed there must also be answers to them, so I kept looking. My persistence paid off the day I received one of Śrīla Prabhupāda's *Back to Godhead* magazines. As I read and reread it, I found myself touched to the core by Śrīla Prabhupāda's clear, confident, authoritative voice. Reading him was different from reading anyone else. He answered the questions that were haunting me, but he also answered questions I hadn't known to ask.

I took complete shelter of Śrīla Prabhupāda and his books in the summer of 1973. Studying and distributing them have been my life's mission ever since, and in this book I share some of the things I've learned over four decades of performing this service for Śrīla Prabhupāda's pleasure.

I called this book *Our Family Business* because Kṛṣṇa's devotees are a family and it has always been the business of that family to share Kṛṣṇa's glories with as many people as possible. Śrīla Prabhupāda, as a good son of his spiritual master, considered every sincere member of his spiritual family and every service rendered as important and equally valuable. Still, anyone who served directly under Śrīla Prabhupāda, or anyone who has made a careful study of his writings, can't help but notice that Śrīla Prabhupāda was especially pleased when his devotees went out to teach Kṛṣṇa consciousness to others, especially by distributing his books. On October 27, 1976, for example, Śrīla Prabhupāda wrote to Jayatīrtha Dāsa, "Kṛṣṇa becomes more and more pleased by seeing the increment of book distribution. Devotional service is absolute, but one who preaches His message becomes very dear to Lord Kṛṣṇa."

May this book remind us of Śrīla Prabhupāda's penchant for printing and distributing his books. May it instill in future generations of workers in Śrīla Prabhupāda's family business, no matter what service they may perform, that distributing his books has a special place in Śrīla Prabhupāda's heart and in the hearts of our previous *ācāryas,* and that pleasing the guru is the active principle that allows advancement in Kṛṣṇa consciousness.

In these pages I have mostly written about the history of book distribution from Śrīla Prabhupāda's arrival in the US in 1965 until his departure from this world in 1977, for these histories clearly show the direct correlation between the rapid growth of book distribution and the astonishing expansion of the Hare Kṛṣṇa movement. Śrīla Prabhupāda confirmed this correlation in an arrival address given in Los Angeles on June 20, 1975: "Print as many books in as many languages and distribute throughout the whole world. Then [the] Kṛṣṇa consciousness movement will automatically increase." But although I mainly stayed within those years when discussing the

His Divine Grace A. C. Bhaktivedanta Swami Prabhupāda

Founder-*Ācārya* of the International Society for Krishna Consciousness

history of book distribution, I don't want to give the impression that the story ends there or that those years are all that matter. So I have set up a wiki page – ourfamilybusiness.info – where devotees can continue telling this very important story. Please visit, tell us of your own history and realizations and of all the accomplishments you or others have had regarding book distribution that don't appear in the pages of this book.

People often suggest that despite ISKCON's earlier success in expanding book distribution, many things could have been done better. I agree. Aspiring to improve one's service is an eternal principal. Success in the service of distributing Śrīla Prabhupāda's books depends particularly on the quality of one's consciousness. Book distribution is a special service in that Kṛṣṇa arranges for devotees to meet a wide variety of souls in order to plant the seed of bhakti in their hearts. During that intense endeavor, distributors are tested in unique ways, and they may make the mistake of putting off the very persons they are trying to benefit. While representing the Supreme, for example, devotees can easily develop a condescending attitude and, losing track of their own compassion and humility, mistreat or disrespect the people they are approaching. Disrespecting others is not only forbidden in scripture, it is counterproductive in the spreading of Kṛṣṇa consciousness. The world doesn't need a new group of fanatics. Rather, it needs compassionate, well-adjusted devotees who genuinely care about each person they meet. It is not only vital that people receive Śrīla Prabhupāda's books but that we also deliver those books in ways that endear us to their recipients.

What's more, those entrusted with management positions in the *saṅkīrtana* movement must always remember that it is their sacred duty to care for the devotees in their charge. Unfortunately, we didn't always have that understanding in the past. Managers who put money and bricks before the spiritual advancement and practical necessities of the devotees under their care do more harm than good. Managers must remember that purity is the force. Learning to distribute Śrīla

Prabhupāda's books on their own merit and thus allowing the distributors to feel the joy and spiritual depth that comes from sharing Kṛṣṇa consciousness with others is very different from engaging devotees in selling stickers, candles, paintings, and who knows what else. Many of the anomalies some of us now attribute to book distribution were actually caused by ill-advised diversions into selling anything *but* books in the name of *saṅkīrtana.*

In his purport to *Śrī Caitanya-caritāmṛta, Ādi-līlā* 7.91, Śrīla Prabhupāda states that the real goal of our mission is not to simply collect money; rather, we want to see that the devotees in our movement, and people in general, advance in Kṛṣṇa consciousness:

> According to the revealed scriptures, if a spiritual master can convert even one soul into a perfectly pure devotee, his mission in life is fulfilled. Śrīla Bhaktisiddhānta Sarasvatī Ṭhākura always used to say, "Even at the expense of all the properties, temples, and *maṭhas* that I have, if I could convert even one person into a pure devotee, my mission would be fulfilled." It is very difficult, however, to understand the science of Kṛṣṇa, what to speak of developing love of Godhead. Therefore if by the grace of Lord Caitanya and the spiritual master a disciple attains the standard of pure devotional service, the spiritual master is very happy. The spiritual master is not actually happy if the disciple brings him money, but when he sees that a disciple is following the regulative principles and advancing in spiritual life, he is very glad and feels obliged to such an advanced disciple.

To neglect the spiritual, emotional, and physical needs of the devotees who are pushing on Lord Caitanya's mission is immoral. Mature or enlightened leaders understand that devotees who come to the Kṛṣṇa consciousness movement are not only special souls but volunteers. Such surrendered souls must be protected and encouraged, never exploited or coerced. In *Our Family Business,* I emphasize empowerment over bureaucracy and encouragement over coercion.

In ISKCON's early days, devotees were sometimes sent out on book distribution without proper training, encouragement, or consideration of their physical or mental capabilities. Discouraged (and in some cases traumatized), some still cringe whenever book distribution is discussed. I feel their pain. I hope the recent developments in the great art of distributing Śrīla Prabhupāda's books presented in *Our Family Business* help those devotees heal from their earlier experiences. May our past mistakes be pillars to a healthier approach to how we interact with the public and how we support the devotees who go out to meet it.

Śrīla Prabhupāda taught us that ISKCON's success is based on the love and trust we share. ISKCON leaders must create an environment in which the body of devotees will feel enlivened to perform devotional service that is, in Śrīla Prabhupāda's words, "individual, spontaneous, and voluntary." In the spiritually surcharged atmosphere that will result if we follow this mood, devotees will naturally feel inspired to reach for ever higher goals both in their service and in their spiritual relationships. It's so much easier to sacrifice and work hard when one's heart is filled with gratitude for what one has and what one is becoming. This is a basic theme of *Our Family Business.*

The good news is that by systematic training in the art of distributing Śrīla Prabhupāda's books, as well as by reading those books with like-minded devotees, we can raise our consciousness, overcome our shortcomings, and continually improve our service. Where there's a will, there's a way! Keeping our prime directive to leave each person we meet with a good impression, and emphasizing that book distributors must be exemplars of the principles contained in the books they distribute, we can both increase the distribution of Śrīla Prabhupāda's books and act in ways that will win the hearts of the public. Therefore I stress in this book the importance of being strict, serious, and sincere in one's daily practices of devotional service. This is a prerequisite for book distributors, and it's a prerequisite for those who have positions of authority in the *saṅkīrtana* movement, whether those persons be managers, parents, teachers, or *saṅkīrtana* leaders.

Because Śrīla Prabhupāda emphasized that failure is the pillar of success, another reason I wrote this book – and perhaps it's the most *important* reason – is to identify what we did and are still doing right so that we can concentrate on our successes and continue to perfect the ways and means by which Śrīla Prabhupāda's books are distributed.

I am often asked what we have to show for all the books we've distributed. I answer this question in the last chapter, but here's one small example of how Śrīla Prabhupāda's books had a dramatic effect on an entire nation:

In the summer of 1989, the Bhaktivedanta Book Trust took advantage of a new law allowing religious books to enter the Soviet Union and printed 200,000 Russian-language books in Germany. The Soviet customs officials were not yet informed about this new law, however, and the truck drivers were held up at the border. After two weeks of intense negotiations with Soviet government officials, the trucks were finally allowed to cross. But the books were confiscated and stored in a customs warehouse in Moscow. For two months the Soviet devotees organized massive protests in the streets of Moscow. They chanted, "Give us our books!" The protest banners they carried read "We don't want vodka! We want our books!" The books were finally released in October of 1989. In an interview, Bhakti Vijñāna Goswami describes the results:

> The entire community of Russian devotees – actually, the entire community of devotees from all over the Soviet Union – participated in those demonstrations. At that time there were altogether only about a hundred devotees. Everything started from those books. The temples started from those books. The new devotees came from those books. The millions and millions of books that were distributed after that – everything started from these two hundred thousand books.

No less important are the effects that Śrīla Prabhupāda's books have had on millions of individual lives throughout the world. Each book distributed has an effect, even if we can't immediately see it.

As we carry on the distribution of Śrīla Prabhupāda's books all over the world, we will see such miraculous victories again and again.

Our Family Business is a humble offering to the lotus feet of my spiritual master His Divine Grace A. C. Bhaktivedanta Swami Prabhupāda, and his faithful servants. Several senior devotees urged me to write this book. By their mercy, I have diligently researched Śrīla Prabhupāda's teachings to bring out the deep affection he had for book distribution and for the devotees who distribute his books. My research also points to the fact that he considered the service of distributing his books foundational to ISKCON, even as he promoted so many other vital preaching projects, including temples, schools, restaurants, farm projects, and more.

Any shortcomings or mistakes you find in this book are mine. I pray for your mercy, understanding, and forgiveness. Please feel free to correct me where necessary. I live to be corrected.

Humbly in your service,
Vaiśeṣika Dāsa

Completed on November 15, 2015
in the month of Kārttika
at ISKCON Bhaktivedanta Ashram
at the foot of Govardhana Hill
on the occasion of the disappearance day of
His Divine Grace A. C. Bhaktivedanta Swami Prabhupāda

Oṁ Tat Sat

Acknowledgments

Keśava Bhāratī Dāsa Goswami, my dearest friend and confidant, was not only the chief editor for this book but also my constant companion as I brainstormed, strategized, and wrote it. He made important suggestions and substantive contributions to the text and encouraged me at every step, dropping everything else he was doing to assist me in more ways than I can count. His expert editing pervades this book. Were it not for his unceasing mantra, "Vaish, we've got to get this book out," and his insistence that I suspend my other services to complete the book, I would still be chipping away at writing it even now.

I thank my dear wife **Nirakula Devī Dāsī,** who formed a protective ring around me to give me the space and time I needed and took on many of my services on top of her already heavy workload just so I could write. She eagerly listened to numerous drafts of the chapters and offered honest feedback. Her cooking kept me healthy and enlivened during what felt like a writing marathon.

Kaiśorī Devī Dāsī, our project manager, babysat this project from the day I began writing it until the book was published and hit the streets. Her faith in both the project and in my ability to complete it was a constant source of inspiration. Even though I missed many self-imposed deadlines, she never complained; rather, she continued to patiently check in with me about my progress. Her polish edits greatly improved the quality of this book. There may be a harder working devotee in ISKCON, but I have yet to meet him or her.

My deep gratitude to **Ravīndra Svarūpa Dāsa** for his foreword. He also gave of his valuable time to go through the manuscript with an editor's eye and to give me his heartfelt encouragement.

Special thanks to **Jayādvaita Swami** for going over the entire manuscript with his unique editing ability. His detailed suggestions and encouraging words have uplifted my writing.

Rāmeśvara Dāsa generously shared his time and resources to piece together a number of the important historical aspects of book distribution. He had an intimate service connection with Śrīla Prabhupāda during the expansion of book distribution in the 1970s, so his insights were invaluable.

Thanks to **Bhāgavata Āśraya Dāsa,** who constantly checked in on the project and gave us game-changing suggestions and advice.

Navīna Nīrada Dāsa gave me important feedback and suggestions from his perspective as a lifelong book distributor and a strict practitioner of bhakti.

Dayānidhi Dāsa, a long-time participant at ISKCON Silicon Valley (ISV), gave a significant financial contribution out of the goodness of his heart to help support the project.

Thanks to the following devotees who gave of their valuable time to be interviewed for this book: Balāi Dāsī, Bhīma Dāsa, Bhūmi Devī Dāsī, Brahmā Dāsa, Brahmānanda Dāsa, Cāru Dāsa, Gargamuni Dāsa, Gopavṛndapāla Dāsa, Guṇagrāhi Goswami, Haridāsa Ṭhākura Dāsa, Harikeśa Dāsa, Hridayānanda Dāsa Goswami, Jāmbavān Dāsa, Labaṅgalatikā Devī Dāsī, Madhudviṣa Dāsa (Śrīla Prabhupāda's disciple), Mahārha Devī Dāsī, Mahātmā Dāsa (who allowed me to quote extensively from his memoirs), Maṇidhara Dāsa, Nidrā Devī Dāsī, Praghoṣa Dāsa, Premārṇava Dāsa, Rohiṇī Sūta Dāsa, Satyanārāyaṇa Dāsa, Śrutadeva Dāsa, Sura Dāsa, Tejīyas Dāsa, Trai Dāsa, Tripurāri Swami, Yogeśvara Dāsa. I know I've inevitably left devotees off this list. But your help has been valuable and I thank you deeply for it.

A heartfelt thanks to Giriraj Swami, Dhanurdhara Swami, and Bhūrijana Dāsa for their sage advice on various sections of the book. Dhanurdhara Mahārāja gave especially important feedback on the "Thoughtfulness Principle." Bhūrijana Dāsa advised me to write at least one sentence a day without fail – advice that helped me find the momentum to finish the book, but helped me in many other ways as well.

I thank all the devotees at ISV who have made distributing Śrīla Prabhupāda's books their life and soul. ISV is the laboratory where we test various new methods for distributing Śrīla Prabhupāda's books. The members of Team ISV have selflessly given their lives to this experiment. May Lord Caitanya continue to shower them with His blessings.

I thank the many *saṅkīrtana* leaders, book distributors, and ISKCON leaders around the world – my heroes – who have embraced the distribution of Śrīla Prabhupāda's books as their life and soul. I thank them for their help in proving the efficacy of The Four Laws of Book Distribution, the Monthly *Saṅkīrtana* Festival, and other ideas presented in *Our Family Business.*

My thanks to the BBT team – Nareśvara Dāsa, Brahma Muhūrta Dāsa, and Govinda Dāsa – for their expert feedback, suggestions, fact-checking, and production of my book.

And my thanks and gratitude to my many book distribution mentors over the years.

Note: While writing *Our Family Business,* I was faced with a conundrum. How could I adequately glorify all the devotees who helped expand book distribution all over the world? When I finally understood that it would impossible to include everyone who has served Śrīla Prabhupāda's mission by translating, publishing, or distributing his books, I resolved to choose devotees who exemplified particular points I intended to make and those who were readily available to interview. I ask the forgiveness of the many luminaries I have not mentioned in these pages.

Introduction

WHITE CASTLE IS A POPULAR American fast-food chain known for its stark-white castlelike buildings and cheap burgers. Nationally, franchises like these move millions of tons of product: the meat of cows systematically slaughtered to satisfy the whims of people's tongues. After reading *Śrīmad-Bhāgavatam,* who could not easily identify these eateries as fortresses from which Kali personified dispenses sin – wholesale?

It was by design, then, that my dear godbrother Divyāṅga Dāsa and I regularly stormed the gates of the White Castle in St. Louis, Missouri, in order to distribute Śrīla Prabhupāda's books to its customers inside.

During the early 1980s, every Saturday afternoon, after a day of distributing books at Lambert Field (St. Louis's international airport) and on our way back to the temple, we'd make a detour through the poverty-stricken inner city of St. Louis. Divyāṅga would pull up his silver Chevy Caprice Classic outside the White Castle there and keep the engine running while

I ran in, cradling a stack of bright blue First Canto *Śrīmad-Bhāgavatams,* and handed one to every customer.

After a week of selling books at the airport, we usually had an excess of donations. We wanted to share the wealth by distributing extra books as charity. Although some people in the White Castle donated for their book, those who didn't still got to keep it if they wanted to.

After these excursions Divyāṅga and I would marvel – and we still do today – at how the sublime *Śrīmad-Bhāgavatam,* which "rejects all religious activities that are materially motived," ended up in the trunk of his Chevy and traveled all the way to the inner city of St. Louis, Missouri, where illiteracy rates were said to run high and even those who *did* read books would never have dreamed of buying a book like *Śrīmad-Bhāgavatam.*

We wondered at it, but we knew how this miracle had happened: Śrīla Prabhupāda had performed it. Following the words of Nārada Muni – "This *Śrīmad-Bhāgavatam* is meant to create a revolution in the impious lives of the world's misdirected civilization" – Śrīla Prabhupāda had loaded two hundred sets of these hardbound Vaikuṇṭha deities into trunks, brought them to the shores of America, and launched a full-scale spiritual revolution with them.

Before that, he had been based at his Rādhā-Dāmodara sanctuary in Vṛndāvana painstakingly drafting and assembling in three volumes the First Canto of *Śrīmad-Bhāgavatam,* a work containing the world's most detailed knowledge of God. These books first hit the humming streets of Manhattan before being launched onto the streets of cities around the world.

By extreme good fortune Divyāṅga and I were among the thousands whose lives were transformed by these books and who had joined Śrīla Prabhupāda's spiritual revolution. Now, as card-carrying members of this insurgency, we ran everywhere to distribute these books to everyone we met.

In the material world, every soul feels unbearable stress.

The pure spiritual being encased in a gross body and subtle mind takes a beating life after life, suffering dearly. Śrīla Prabhupāda writes about an "ocean of tears" in his purport to *Śrīmad-Bhāgavatam* 3.28.32, created by the accumulated tears shed by souls disappointed and confounded by life's reverses. To avoid the distress built into the hard struggle for existence, some people numb themselves with intoxication; others take to philosophical speculation to justify and sidestep the gloom.

But in *Śrīmad-Bhāgavatam* 1.5.32, Nārada Muni explains to Śrīla Vyāsadeva the real cure: "O Brāhmaṇa Vyāsadeva, it is decided by the learned that the best remedial measure for removing all troubles and miseries is to dedicate one's activities to the service of the Supreme Lord Personality of Godhead [Śrī Kṛṣṇa]."

Page by page, Śrīla Prabhupāda's writing dispenses medicine to the materially distressed mind: hearing about Lord Kṛṣṇa from the mouths of His pure, unmotivated devotees. Ultimately, the cause of all suffering is ignorance, and ignorance leads to sinful deeds and the karmic reactions for them. In Lord Kṛṣṇa's own words, spoken in *Bhagavad-gītā* 4.37, transcendental knowledge burns to ashes all the karmic reactions of a living being, just as a fire burns to ashes unlimited fuel supplied to it. Rūpa Gosvāmī therefore says that the greatest charity work one can do is to distribute transcendental knowledge. Transcendental knowledge relieves people's suffering, and those who receive such knowledge learn not only why they are suffering but how to stop it forever.

During an epidemic, can those who hold the cure not feel responsible for dispensing it? Those who possess a vaccine must take all risks to distribute it. In *Śrīmad-Bhāgavatam* 8.7.39 Lord Śiva states, "People in general, being bewildered by the illusory energy of the Supreme Personality of Godhead, are always engaged in animosity toward one another. But devotees, even at the risk of their own temporary lives, try to save them." Therefore Lord Caitanya directs: "Distribute this Kṛṣṇa consciousness movement all over the world. Let people eat these fruits [of love of God] and ultimately become free from old age and death." (*Śrī Caitanya-caritāmṛta, Ādi-līlā* 9.39)

Following this order, the Vaiṣṇavas sacrifice their own peace of mind and move into the cities to distribute this medicine to the needy. Śrīla Prabhupāda, for example, despite every conceivable obstacle – old age, declining health, no money, and no connections – left the holy land of Vṛndāvana and daringly boarded a freighter bound for America, bringing with him only a few meager personal effects yet trunks of First Canto *Śrīmad-Bhāgavatams*. The *Śrīmad-Bhāgavatam* is pregnant with the words of Lord Kṛṣṇa and pure devotee saints such as Uddhava, Maitreya, Vidura, Brahmā, Nārada, Śukadeva, Parīkṣit, and Prahlāda, and the books Śrīla Prabhupāda brought were further embellished with his own sublime purports, the fruits of his lifelong practice of hearing with rapt attention the words of his spiritual master, Śrīla Bhaktisiddhānta Sarasvatī Ṭhākura. As it turned out, people everywhere were ready to hear this spiritual message.

They still are.

I have therefore written *Our Family Business* to encourage devotees everywhere to distribute transcendental knowledge, most particularly in the form of Śrīla Prabhupāda's books. This book is meant not only to help devotees in their quest to learn or perfect the art of distributing Śrīla Prabhupāda's books, but also to inspire and assist those who are organizing this great transcendental sacrifice. The aim is to create a culture that will live and breathe book distribution, an atmosphere in which devotees can find true happiness in meeting people and introducing them to Kṛṣṇa consciousness. Through hearing, chanting, and relishing what's in the books, and through organizing in a systematic way the distributors and the devotees who back up the distributors, my hope is that Śrīla Prabhupāda's movement will be reinvigorated with the spirit Śrīla Prabhupāda himself breathed into it: "Distribute books, distribute books, distribute books."[1] Nothing will please His Divine Grace more.

Śrīla Prabhupāda not only asked that his books be widely and profusely distributed, but he also encouraged his followers to become expert in presenting them. In a letter to Bali Mardana Dāsa dated December 31, 1972, Śrīla Prabhupāda calls book distribution a "great art":

> I am convinced that if you simply glorify Kṛṣṇa and our books in the best descriptive manner, that anyone and everyone, no matter even atheist or otherwise, they can be convinced to purchase. Of course that is a great art and not everyone can do it, but gradually by practice of preaching in this way, striving to so much present a wonderful picture of our books to the people, gradually you will master the trick how to do it.

Moreover, Śrīla Prabhupāda recommended distributing his books as a practice for advancing in spiritual life (*sādhana*). In his purport to *Śrīmad-Bhāgavatam* 10.2.37, for example, he writes: "By fully concentrating on distributing books for Kṛṣṇa, one is fully absorbed in Kṛṣṇa. This is *samādhi.*"

And in another letter typical of his fire for spreading Kṛṣṇa consciousness, he calls on his followers: "Whenever possible, try to talk about Kṛṣṇa consciousness to your friends or whomever you may meet. Simply by this attempt you will get superior strength and knowledge about Kṛṣṇa consciousness."[2]

In *Our Family Business* we look into not only how distributing Śrīla Prabhupāda's books is important to individual ISKCON devotees as *sādhana,* but also how and why it is vital to the natural, organic growth and health of our ISKCON Society as a whole. Many devotees already regularly distribute books, and a growing number of other devotees are eager to get involved. Experts, newcomers, well-wishers, retirees in need of a refresher course – all will find something in this book to inspire them. Finally, this book is meant to give a fresh and favorable second look at distributing books for those who, for whatever reason, now think of it disparagingly.

Our Family Business also discusses the history of book distribution in ISKCON, and includes foundational principles for building a successful book distribution program, the paramount importance of proper conduct in public, illustrative and inspirational first-person stories with dialogue, new methods of book distribution, secrets of highly effective book distributors, and more.

How did Śrīla Prabhupāda feel about the need for such an intense endeavor to organize the distribution of his books? He wrote this in a letter to Tejīyas Dāsa on January 5, 1973: "Tax your brain for finding new ways and better ways for distributing our books widely."

In writing this book I have sincerely tried to do just that. If on account of taxing my brain one more devotee is inspired to take up this art or one extra book is distributed, I will consider the book a success. And if *Our Family Business* helps spark a second wave of massive book distribution in my lifetime, I will die a happy soul.

CHRONICLES

"Yes. It is a revolution.
That is what I think as I write on and on –
a revolution to change
the entire course of human history."

ŚRĪLA PRABHUPĀDA, 1977

CHAPTER ONE

The Ambassador of Goodwill

A SIXTEEN-YEAR-OLD JUNIOR in high school, I sat cross-legged, transfixed in meditation before a candle flame and a small golden statue of the Buddha. Locked in my room that fine spring day in suburban Lafayette, California, I had been fasting and praying to God to reveal my true path in life.

I was also staunchly observing a vow of silence that day, when my high school friend Richie Corsa knocked on my bedroom door. Even though he sounded annoyed, I didn't answer. I reasoned that because he and I were ultimately "one" – a concept I had gleaned from the books I had been reading – he would know why I wasn't responding to his loud knocking and repeated requests to let him in.

Finally he gave up and through the keyhole yelled, "Willy, I know you're in there. I'm leaving you a magazine I bought from a Hare Kṛṣṇa on Telegraph Avenue. He took my last fifty cents. I have no interest in this stuff, but I know you're into it, so here it is."

I waited until he'd gone before coming out of my room to see what kind of magazine he'd left me. It was propped against the wall next to my door. The shiny cover illustration of Lord Caitanya immediately caught my eye. Arms raised in the air, He danced through a tropical landscape, followed by a group of other dancers. The masthead read, "Back to Godhead. Godhead is Light. Nescience is Darkness. Where There Is Godhead There Is No Nescience." Richie was spot on. I *was* interested in this stuff. I carried it into my room to have a closer look.

As soon as I turned to the inside front cover my eyes locked onto a painting of a golden-brown–complexioned guru. His head was cleanly shaven and he sat cross-legged on an ornate seat. He wore flowing saffron robes, and piles of lush flower garlands encircled his neck, cascading in layers down to his knees. Below the painting the caption read: "His Divine Grace A.C. Bhaktivedanta Swami Prabhupāda."

I had been searching for a guide and had studied the countenance of many a spiritual teacher, sometimes putting their pictures in front of me when I meditated in the hope that I might commune with them. Until that moment, however, I had never felt a strong connection to any of them.

Now suddenly I felt exhilarated. A singular thought entered my mind: *This is my teacher.* How and why I felt this so completely was not clear to me. Never before had I been gripped with such absolute conviction. I stared at the portrait for several minutes, and it occurred to me that it was utterly mystical for this magazine to have appeared at my door. Entranced, I turned the pages.

My Prayers Are Answered

It was obvious that someone had heard my prayers, for on each page of the magazine were answers to my deepest inquiries: Why do I have to die? Is God a person? What is the best way to know God?

One article – "Liberation of the Cave Dwellers," by Hayagrīva Dāsa – was based on a famous analogy in Plato's *Republic*. The article pointed out that people living in material consciousness are ignorant of the spiritual world. The author compared them to cave dwellers who have never stepped out of their cave and seen the sun. "How could they understand the world of light?" he asked. Someone would have to come from outside the cave, explain the power and magnificence of the sun, and somehow demonstrate what it was like. To do so the teacher might have to let in a beam of light and project it on the wall of the cave. The cave dwellers' education would have to begin slowly, because they might not even believe in something so fantastical as the sun.

"My room is the cave!" I thought, "and this magazine is the light. Someone's come to rescue me and show me the way out, back to the source of the light!"

Scouring each page I studied the photographs of devotees who were working for God: cooking, printing books, talking to groups of people. Their neck beads, shaved heads, and *tilaka* fascinated me. They looked so happy and determined. They became my heroes.

This was 1973, when millions of young Americans were clamoring for peace in the face of the controversial Vietnam War. The Beatles' lyrics called us to explore the inner world of our minds, and our status quo among our peers was maintained by rejecting the status quo of society at large.

At school, some of my friends talked about doing something noble with their lives, like joining the Peace Corps or working to preserve the environment. Others followed their parents' advice and worked hard to get good grades so they could get into a prestigious university. Like me, still others were confused about their place in the world. In such a turbulent and uncertain environment as the United States in the early 1970s, I often questioned the value of my dry high school studies. When a buddy of mine disappeared while hiking in the mountains, never to be found again, I felt even more desperate to discover the purpose of life.

The devotees didn't look confused at all. Reading their faces I felt they were going somewhere important and wonderful – and they seemed to know it. One article in the magazine was entitled, "We're Going to the Land of Kṛṣṇa, the Land Beyond Birth and Death." I desperately wanted to go with them.

I gave no thought at the time to the enormous effort that had gone into getting that *Back to Godhead* magazine to my door. It had appeared magically, and I had grabbed on to it like a lifeline, not fully considering who had made the line or who had thrown it. It wouldn't take long, however, for me to meet the devotees and find out who was behind it all.

My New Home

My mother dropped me off for my first visit to the San Francisco temple at 455 Valencia Street, where I met Janakīnātha Dāsa, an outwardly dour but sweet-hearted devotee who sat quietly chanting on his *japa* beads as he leaned casually on the front steps of the temple. Unsure of the etiquette, I greeted him with a "Hare Kṛṣṇa" and asked him if I could meet the guru, Śrīla Prabhupāda. Naively, I had assumed he'd be there. But Janakīnātha Dāsa summarily informed me that ISKCON was an international society and that Śrīla Prabhupāda had to travel all over the world to maintain it and was presently in India. When he saw my disappointment, however, he quickly added that Śrīla Prabhupāda's association could be perfectly had by reading his books. Janakīnātha's answer satisfied me, because to some degree I had already perceived this for myself. I happily followed him into the fragrant atmosphere of the San Francisco temple, which was soon to become my home.

I found out that my homecoming experience was not unique. Sharing stories with the devotees who had joined the temple before me, I found that they all had stories about receiving Śrīla Prabhupāda's books. Apparently, we had all heard the same clarion call.

One devotee who soon would become my fast friend and mentor, Keśava Bhāratī Dāsa (now Keśava Bhāratī Dāsa Goswami), had been searching for God through study and meditation when his landlady brought a *Śrī Īśopaniṣad* and a *Back to Godhead* magazine to his door, leaving them with him because "she had no interest, but thought he might."

A few days later, his wife Lynne (the late Kaulinī Devī Dāsī), returned from vacation with a copy of *Bhagavad-gītā As It Is* she had found in a used bookstore in central Mexico. Neither his landlord nor his wife knew the contents of the books; nor had they any idea that they had gifted him with books by the same author. Keśava Bhāratī Dāsa (then Kenneth Beck) also had no idea. He had put both books in a bag, unaware of the coincidence, and taken them the next evening to the gas station where he was working the midnight shift to make ends meet. On his break, just before sunrise, he took out both books to examine them. Incredulous, he at once noticed that they were from the same author. His eyes filled with tears, and he was soon weeping, certain that God had answered his prayers and intervened to show him the way to reach Him. A few days later he jumped into his Volkswagen van with his childhood friend Clint and hurried off to find the San Francisco temple. Inconceivably, Śrīla Prabhupāda had just arrived, and that very evening Ken found himself sitting in front of His Divine Grace at an evening program. His material life was finished.

Ask any assembly of devotees how they came to Kṛṣṇa consciousness and you will hear a montage of similarly miraculous sagas, each one precipitated by contact with Śrīla Prabhupāda's books.

God Reveals Himself Through Scripture

The reason for such miracles is that God appears in the form of literature. The Vedic scriptures confirm this truth. The *Brahma-sūtra* (1.1.3) says that God reveals Himself through scripture (*śāstra-yonitvāt*). And *Śrīmad-Bhāgavatam* (1.3.40) declares itself a direct incarnation of Kṛṣṇa: *idaṁ bhāgavataṁ nāma purāṇaṁ brahma-sammitam,* "This scripture named *Śrīmad-Bhāgavatam* is the literary incarnation of God."

Just as Kṛṣṇa makes His divine appearance in forms made of marble, wood, and paint, He similarly descends as an incarnation in paper and ink. The author, Vedavyāsa, is described as an empowered incarnation of Kṛṣṇa because he wrote down the eternal Vedic knowledge.

Śrīla Prabhupāda's Labor of Love

The enormous effort Śrīla Prabhupāda and his followers made to get that *Back to Godhead* (BTG) to my door was gradually disclosed to me. It was through an intense labor of pure devotion empowered by the order of his spiritual master that Śrīla Prabhupāda caused these beautiful incarnations of the Lord to appear in the various languages of the world. Then, as a master conductor directs an orchestra, Śrīla Prabhupāda inspired his young followers to illustrate, edit, publish, and distribute more than fifty million copies of the eighty books he had written in little more than a decade. He needed editors, and editors appeared. He needed Sanskritists, and they emerged. He encouraged fledgling artists, and they flourished. Young people – unfamiliar with publishing, shipping, warehousing, or sales – found themselves managing millions of dollars worth of books and seeing to their distribution, all of this arranged by His Divine Grace after he had reached his seventieth year.

Śrīla Prabhupāda had begun to write in earnest as early as 1944, publishing and distributing his single-sheet "Back to Godhead" leaflets. After finally retiring from his business and family life in 1954, moving to the Vaṁśī-gopālajī temple at Vṛndāvana's Keśī-ghāṭa in 1956, and accepting the renounced order of life in 1959, he had conceived of his multivolume presentation of *Śrīmad-Bhāgavatam.*

He traveled to and from Delhi, beginning the work on his

magnum opus in the Chippiwada district in Delhi, where he had been given a room at a Rādhā-Kṛṣṇa temple by an acquaintance, Krishna Pandit. In 1960 he moved into his tiny quarters at the famous Rādhā-Dāmodara temple in Vṛndāvana, where he would reside for nearly a decade, publishing and distributing "Back to Godhead" and preparing his *Śrīmad-Bhāgavatam* purports and a series of other writings. There he incubated his plan to carry out the request his spiritual master had made of him that he write and preach in English and take Kṛṣṇa consciousness to the West.

Print Books

Śrīla Bhaktisiddhānta's request was not new, for book printing and distribution has always been the "family business" of the Brahma-Madhva-Gauḍīya-sampradāya. Śrīla Bhaktivinoda Ṭhākura, wrote over one hundred books, and before him the Six Gosvāmīs of Vṛndāvana, on the order of Śrī Caitanya Mahāprabhu, had published hundreds of books. In fact, most great Vaiṣṇava spiritual masters have made literary contributions.

Mahāprabhu Himself had rediscovered and then with His own hand distributed copies of *Śrī Brahma-saṁhitā* and *Śrī Kṛṣṇa-karṇāmṛta* to His closest disciples. Śrīla Bhaktisiddhānta Ṭhākura, to highlight the prominence of literature in his Gauḍīya Maṭha mission, included an image of the printing press in its logo and often preached that distributing books was better than building opulent temples. Passing on the tradition of the previous great teachers of pure devotional service, Śrīla Bhaktisiddhānta Ṭhākura personally told our Śrīla Prabhupāda that if he ever got money, he should print books.

Śrīla Prabhupāda Begins Publishing

In Jhansi, before Śrīla Prabhupāda had gone to Vṛndāvana, he had founded the League of Devotees, an organization meant to respiritualize human society, and at the request of a godbrother he had worked on the magazine *Sajjana-toṣaṇi.* Neither of these projects worked out the way Śrīla Prabhupāda had wanted, but both reveal his ambitious vision. When he was handed the *Sajjana-toṣaṇi* project, for example, it was a simple publication with a small circulation. He soon developed a plan to expand it into a world-class publication, as popular and polished as India's *Illustrated Weekly.* But the godbrother who had asked for his help, overwhelmed by Śrīla Prabhupāda's enterprising approach, released him from the project.

Land disputes and a lack of local interest had foiled Śrīla Prabhupāda's League of Devotees in Jhansi, but his plans for the project there had not been small either. He had intended to recruit and train members to teach the *Bhagavad-gītā* and to perform *nāma-saṅkīrtana* throughout the world. Undeterred by the lack of response in Jhansi and the conflicts he had endured while editing *Sajjana-toṣaṇi,* with no fixed income or residence and only a couple of dhotis and kurtas, Śrīla Prabhupāda soon launched his "Back to Godhead" as a magazine.

The printer of Śrīla Prabhupāda's first BTG, Kumar Jain in New Delhi, remembers that Śrīla Prabhupāda was so poor that he usually arrived at his shop without having had breakfast. Śrīla Prabhupāda saved money for printing his magazine by skipping meals and walking instead of riding, hiring a rickshaw only when it was absolutely necessary in order to carry heavy rolls of paper for printing.

Alone in New Delhi, he wrote, edited, published, and distributed BTG. In the scorching heat he personally visited government offices, shopping areas, and tea stalls to sell his magazine. Sometimes he mailed out free copies, both within India and abroad.

After living and preaching in Delhi for some time, Śrīla Prabhupāda moved back to Vṛndāvana. But unlike other *sādhus,* who out of fear of being contaminated vow never to leave the holy *dhāma,* Śrīla Prabhupāda came and went, venturing to Delhi, Bombay, and Kanpur to raise funds for publishing his BTG.

As with *Sajjana-toṣaṇi,* Śrīla Prabhupāda's dream for BTG was grand. He eventually wanted printings of BTG sent to fifty countries around the world. In the midst of printing and distributing the small magazine, several people suggested that he also produce and distribute books, because they were more permanent. He took this advice as coming from Kṛṣṇa and wrote his first booklet, *Easy Journey to Other Planets.* Soon after, he began work on his *Śrīmad-Bhāgavatam* translations and purports.

Commuting from Vṛndāvana to Delhi to promote his cause, Śrīla Prabhupāda stayed in the homes of pious Hindu hosts. Sri Krishna Pandit gave him a room in Chippiwada, near Chandni Chowk, and also volunteered to do some secretarial work for him. From those Chippiwada days, Sri Krishna Pandit remembers that Śrīla Prabhupāda was engrossed in translating and writing his commentaries on *Śrīmad-Bhāgavatam.* He cooked for himself and typed and checked the proofs for BTG. "Every day he was typing ... His main activity was typing many hours a day," Sri Krishna Pandit recalls.[1]

Śrīla Prabhupāda had practically no financial means while living in Vṛndāvana at the Rādhā-Dāmodara Mandir. Still, he had every intention of spreading the message of *Śrīmad-Bhāgavatam* all over the world. His intense desire to do so became especially clear when he received an invitation to join the Congress for Cultivating the Human Spirit in Japan.

In preparation for the event he suspended his other projects and worked exclusively on a book he called *Light of the Bhāgavata,* a manuscript tailor-made for the Japanese event. Simultaneously he wrote a volley of letters appealing to potential patrons, including India's Prime Minister, beseeching them to pay his fare to Japan so that he might attend the Congress and bring knowledge of the *Bhāgavata* to Japan and the rest of the world. In the end, he was forced to cancel his trip, for no one gave him the money he needed; but he now had the manuscript for *Light of the Bhāgavata* completed.

Characteristically undeterred, Śrīla Prabhupāda continued to pray to the Lord, "When will the day come when a temple will be established in every house in every corner of the world?" Prahlāda Mahārāja, in his prayers to Lord Nṛsiṁhadeva, expresses his desire to live near big cities and towns – unlike most transcendentalists who prefer solitude – to deliver the fallen souls who are working hard "making elaborate plans for material happiness by maintaining their families, societies, and countries."[2]

Similarly, although Śrīla Prabhupāda referred to Vṛndāvana as his home, it was also the base from which, out of compassion for the fallen souls of the world, he planned his campaign to distribute *Śrīmad-Bhāgavatam* and the holy names of Kṛṣṇa to every continent on the globe. He created a pamphlet to promote sales of his first publication of *Śrīmad-Bhāgavatam.* The headline of that pamphlet said "*Śrīmad-Bhāgavatam:* India's Message of Peace and Goodwill." Soon Śrīla Prabhupāda would become the world's greatest ambassador of this message.

A careful study of this pamphlet reveals much about His Divine Grace's indomitable spirit. He had produced only three volumes of *Śrīmad-Bhāgavatam,* but the pamphlet advertised "sixty volumes of the elaborate English version." Although he would arrive in America with no support, no connections, and no money, his pamphlet includes the words, "all over the world for scientific knowledge of God."

A Representative from the Spiritual World

The dictionary meaning of ambassador is "an accredited diplomat sent by a country as its official representative to a foreign country." The word ambassador derives from the Latin *ambactus,* "servant." As the servant of his spiritual master, Śrīla Prabhupāda knew he was connected to the current of transcendental sound flowing from the spiritual world. He explained this principle to his disciple Yāmunācārya Dāsa in a letter dated October 21, 1969:

> When the Lord appeared on this earth 5,000 years ago, He instructed *Bhagavad-gītā* to Arjuna, and this purely transcendental message of Kṛṣṇa has been passed down for the past 5,000 years by the media of sincere disciples giving submissive aural reception to the words of Kṛṣṇa via the medium of the bona fide spiritual master. This acts like electricity, and if you touch a wire anywhere which is connected to the powerhouse, then you will be in contact with the electric current.

As an ambassador Śrīla Prabhupāda knew the unlimited power of his actual home country, Goloka Vṛndāvana, and its leader, Kṛṣṇa, the Supreme Personality of Godhead. He was connected and he knew it. Therefore in his prayer to Kṛṣṇa, penned aboard the freighter *Jaladuta,* Śrīla Prabhupāda wrote, *tabe yadi tava kṛpā ahaitukī/ sakala-i sambhava haya tumi se kautukī:* "But I know Your causeless mercy can make everything possible, because You are the most expert mystic."[3]

This same mood appears repeatedly throughout his teachings. In his purport to *Śrīmad-Bhāgavatam* 2.9.36, for example, Śrīla Prabhupāda writes:

> There is no need to seek properly qualified candidates for discharging devotional service to the Lord. Let them be either well behaved or ill trained, let them be either learned or fools, let them be either grossly attached or in the renounced order of life, let them be liberated souls or desirous of salvation, let them be inexpert in the discharge of devotional service or expert in the same, all of them can be elevated to the supreme position by discharging devotional service under the proper guidance.

The *Bhāgavatam* also states that its very purpose is "to create a revolution in the impious lives of this world's misdirected civilization." As the person *bhāgavata,* His Divine Grace Śrīla Prabhupāda repeatedly and urgently called for a worldwide, massive campaign to respiritualize humanity by distributing transcendental sound. This was his plan all along. Decades before coming to America he had drawn up a blueprint for a society that would train pure devotees who would then go out to save others.

In India, many persons warned him of the perils of leaving his motherland to cross the ocean. Some even argued that not only were Westerners incapable of being purified, but they would also profane the Hindu religion. Śrīla Prabhupāda knew well the power of *Śrīmad-Bhāgavatam,* the literary incarnation of Lord Kṛṣṇa, the most merciful Lord who had given liberation to the demon Pūtanā even after she had tried to poison Him.

Unlike most people who cross the ocean to find fame, money, or a better way of life, Śrīla Prabhupāda traveled as an ambassador of goodwill to distribute the fruits of love for God to the spiritually-impoverished masses, just as the most merciful form of Kṛṣṇa, Śrī Caitanya Mahāprabhu, had done and ordered everyone else to do five hundred years before:

ataeva saba phala deha' yāre tāre
khāiyā ha-uk loka ajara amare

> Distribute this Kṛṣṇa consciousness movement all over the world. Let people eat these fruits and ultimately become free from old age and death.

ataeva āmi ājñā diluṅ sabākāre
yāhāṅ tāhāṅ prema-phala deha' yāre tāre

> Therefore I order every man within this universe to accept this Kṛṣṇa consciousness movement and distribute it everywhere.[4]

Those who give others the opportunity to go back to Godhead

are by far the most charitable. About these magnanimous souls Narottama Dāsa Ṭhākura sings, *ebe yaśa ghuṣuk tribhuvana:* they are famous all over the three worlds.

The effect of Lord Caitanya's unlimited goodwill, delivered through the grand vision of His pure devotee, Śrīla Prabhupāda, to distribute transcendental literature throughout the world, touched me that day in unlikely suburban Lafayette, California. Is it any wonder that Śrīla Prabhupāda's sacrifice and determined campaign to bring the fruits of love of Godhead to the people of the world have made him the most famous? No one can compare. Therefore he is the greatest ambassador of goodwill the world has ever seen.

CHAPTER TWO

Becoming an Ambassador of Goodwill

MY SPIRITUAL MASTER and ISKCON's founder-*ācārya* Śrīla A.C. Bhaktivedanta Swami Prabhupāda was born on September 1, 1896 as Abhay Charan De. He first met his spiritual master in 1922. It was at that first meeting that Śrīla Bhaktisiddhānta Sarasvatī Ṭhākura asked him to go to the West to preach in English the message of Śrī Caitanya Mahāprabhu. Convinced that Śrī Caitanya Mahāprabhu's message was the panacea for suffering humanity, he took his guru's request seriously. From that day on, he later told us, he always thought of how to execute his spiritual master's order.[1]

Later, during Kārttika in 1935, Abhay received further confirmation of his lifetime service at a meeting with his guru at Rādhā-kuṇḍa. This time Śrīla Bhaktisiddhānta told him that if he ever got money he should print books.

In December 1936 Śrīla Prabhupāda wrote his guru a letter asking how he could best serve him. Śrīla Bhaktisiddhānta's response, dated December 13, 1936, just two weeks before he passed away, reconfirmed his initial request that Śrīla Prabhupāda preach Kṛṣṇa consciousness in the West.

In 1956 Śrīla Prabhupāda formally retired from his business and family life, then took *sannyāsa* in 1959. Throughout all these phases of his life, he kept his spiritual master's order in his heart until he was finally able to act on it. Śrīla Prabhupāda recalls, "With no companion, I loitered here and there until 1959, when I took *sannyāsa*. Then I was completely ready to discharge the order of my spiritual master."

Filled with sincere humility, Śrīla Prabhupāda writes that from the day he first received his spiritual master's order he desired to fulfill it, yet felt "quite unfit to do so."[2] Nonetheless, he fixed his life's goal on fulfilling that order. On a number of occasions he explained to his disciples how his having adhered to his guru's order was the key to his success in spreading Kṛṣṇa consciousness all over the world. In a letter to Bṛhaspati Dāsa, written on November 17, 1971, Śrīla Prabhupāda said, "I am successful in my teaching work because I have not deviated one inch from my spiritual master's instruction. This is my only qualification."

A Line of Unselfish Servants

With this comment, His Divine Grace evinces his fidelity to his spiritual master as well as the essential mood of a true ambassador of goodwill. An ambassador is a person who acts as an official representative of a country or specified activity. Everyone in this world works for someone else, but it's rare to find someone who works without a profit motive. As difficult as it is to find someone serving purely out of goodwill, Nārada Muni encourages us each to strive for such unselfish service, for it is "the eternal duty of the living entity."[3]

Every soul is by nature a servant. The only question is what type of service one should perform. In his manual of pure devotional service, the *Bhakti-rasāmṛta-sindhu,* Śrīla Rūpa Gosvāmī quotes a verse in which an aspiring devotee expresses remorse for having blindly followed the bad masters of his worldly desires, which never give him relief. The Gosvāmī prays that he may break off his service to these bad masters and instead engage in service to Kṛṣṇa, the Supreme Personality of Godhead, and His internal energy.[4] This full engagement of the mind and senses in selfless spiritual service is the only way to attract Kṛṣṇa. Such service exempts one from mundane worldly obligations and brings full satisfaction to the self.[5] Sincere desire for transcendental service is a sign that one's spiritual intelligence has awakened. A person who receives instruction for divine service from Kṛṣṇa's authorized representative and then takes it up wholeheartedly invokes the blessings of his spiritual master and the previous teachers in the line of pure devotion.

In a handwritten letter to the "boys and girls" who were distributing books in the Los Angeles ISKCON community, Śrīla Prabhupāda wrote: "You are working so hard for broadcasting the glories of Lord Kṛṣṇa's lotus feet and thus my Guru Mahārāja will be so pleased upon you. Certainly my Guru Mahārāja will bestow His blessings thousands [of] times more than me and that is my satisfaction."[6]

On hearing from scripture that only unmotivated, uninterrupted service to God can completely satisfy the self, the wise aspire to render such service. The previous masters in the line of devotional service all agree that such a person will not be disappointed. Even neophytes who follow the authorized previous masters and catch the spirit of pure devotion to Kṛṣṇa at once become effective ambassadors of goodwill and gradually become flawless servants of the Supreme Lord, despite their present shortcomings. Śrīla Prabhupāda confirms this eternal truth in his purport to *Śrī Caitanya-caritāmṛta, Madhya-līlā* 15.106:

> [W]hen the novice engages in devotional service ... and follows the order of a bona fide spiritual master, he is a pure devotee. Anyone can take advantage of hearing about Kṛṣṇa consciousness from such a devotee and thus gradually become purified. In other words, any devotee who believes that the

> holy name of the Lord is identical with the Lord is a pure devotee, even though he may be in the neophyte stage. By his association, others may also become Vaiṣṇavas.

Śrī Nārada Muni thus declares:

> Pure devotional service rendered to the Supreme Lord is spiritually so potent that simply by hearing about such transcendental service, by chanting its glories in response, by meditating on it, by respectfully and faithfully accepting it, or by praising the devotional service of others, even persons who hate the demigods and all other living beings can be immediately purified.[7]

"Become Guru!"

Remarkably, Lord Caitanya offers any willing person this topmost service: Become a guru by carrying Kṛṣṇa's message, and in this way deliver everyone you meet (*yare dekha, tāre kaha 'kṛṣṇa'-upadeśa āmāra ājñāya guru hañā tāra' ei deśa*).[8] Within this simple order lies the seed of perfection. In his purport to *Śrīmad-Bhāgavatam* 2.9.34, Śrīla Prabhupāda explains the power of the Supreme Personality of Godhead's direct orders: "This direct order of the Lord is a manifestation of His internal energy, and this particular energy is the means of seeing the Lord face to face."

Even a simple person who embraces the order of Śrī Caitanya Mahāprabhu and carries it out despite all obstacles rises to the highest position of bhakti by divine grace. Nārada Muni, for example, was elevated from an obscure birth to the topmost authority in pure devotional service by following the instructions of advanced devotees. By the same principle he was able in turn to elevate Mṛgāri the hunter to the status of a pure Vaiṣṇava. Nārada told Mṛgāri: "If you listen to my instructions, I shall find the way you can be liberated."[9] Mṛgāri had been raised by his father not only to hunt but also to enjoy torturing animals, but after accepting Nārada's instructions,

Mṛgāri became famous as a soft-hearted Vaiṣṇava who refused to harm even an ant.

Śrīla Prabhupāda points out the urgent need for ambassadors to carry Lord Caitanya's message of spiritual service to the people of the world, who are desperate for relief from material misery.

> Human society, at the present moment, is not in the darkness of oblivion. It has made rapid progress in the field of material comforts, education, and economic development throughout the entire world. But there is a pinprick somewhere in the social body at large, and therefore there are large-scale quarrels, even over less important issues. There is need of a clue as to how humanity can become one in peace, friendship, and prosperity with a common cause. *Śrīmad-Bhāgavatam* will fill this need, for it is a cultural presentation for the respiritualization of the entire human society.[10]

Government leaders are anxious about rising levels of unemployment, and people everywhere are eager for the dignity that comes from an honest livelihood. But Lord Caitanya is offering full employment in the most exalted livelihood of all. Why should anyone be worried? "Distribute this Kṛṣṇa consciousness movement all over the world. Let people eat these fruits and ultimately become free from old age and death."[11]

Service Inherited

A devotee who has embraced the *saṅkīrtana* service of distributing Śrīla Prabhupāda's books and realized its value wants to share that good fortune of expanding Lord Caitanya's mission to as many people as possible. Lord Caitanya Himself says: "I am the only gardener. How many places can I go? How many fruits can I pick and distribute?"[12]

Śrīla Prabhupāda writes in his purport to *Śrīmad-Bhāgavatam* 3.21.31:

> One's energy should be utilized for one's self-interest. That is the perfection of the energy. This energy can be utilized for real self-interest if one is compassionate. A person in Kṛṣṇa consciousness, a devotee of the Lord, is always compassionate. He is not satisfied that only he himself is a devotee, but he tries to distribute the knowledge of devotional service to everyone. There are many devotees of the Lord who faced many risks in distributing the devotional service of the Lord to people in general. That should be done.

By serving the devotees fervently engaged in spreading the *saṅkīrtana* movement, one catches the spillover from their service, a single drop of which gives one the invaluable gift of placement in Mahāprabhu's transcendental family of devotees who assist Him in spreading the *saṅkīrtana* movement. Śrīla Prabhupāda writes about this in his purport to *Śrīmad-Bhāgavatam* 3.22.5:

> Thus it is actually a fact that if one meets a saintly person completely engaged in transcendental duties and achieves his favor, then one's life mission becomes complete. What is not possible to achieve in thousands of lives can be achieved in one moment if there is an opportunity to meet a saintly person.

To his own spiritual master Śrīla Prabhupāda writes:

Message of service
thou has brought
A meaningful life
as Caitanya wrought
Unknown to all,
it is full of brace.
That's your gift,
Your Divine Grace.

My first inkling about the life of divine service came via the mercy of the devotee whose identity remains unknown to me – the devotee who sold a copy of *Back to Godhead* magazine to Richie Corsa, my unsuspecting high school friend, on Telegraph Avenue in Berkeley, California. Richie was wholly uninterested in Kṛṣṇa consciousness, but he had dutifully brought me the magazine because he knew I was an avid spiritual seeker. The very second I held that magazine in my hands I knew that my prayers for spiritual guidance had been answered. With one-pointed attention I studied the magazine, practically inhaling the words and pictures. Its contents seemed familiar to me, like meeting a best friend after a long separation.

Nārada Muni explains the significance of such an event: "My dear friend, even though you cannot immediately recognize Me, can't you remember that in the past you had a very intimate friend? Unfortunately, you gave up My company and accepted a position as enjoyer of this material world."[13]

After reading that publication dozens of times, I fixed my plan to move in with the devotees at 455 Valencia Street as soon as possible. By the kindness of my parents I succeeded. As a baby elephant lost in the jungle attaches itself to its mother, I grabbed on tightly to the devotees at the San Francisco temple. Kindred souls, they understood my cheerfulness on finding a life of devotional service. On my second day in the temple, my revered temple commander Kṛtakarmā Dāsa entrusted me with a most enjoyable service – washing the Lord's pots. He taught me how to make every single inch of a pot so shiny that I could see my reflection in it. He told me that the cleaner I made the pot, the cleaner my heart would become. I scrubbed very hard.

My pot-washing service ended abruptly one day three months later when Kṛtakarmā pulled me aside for a talk. "Listen, Bhakta William," he said, "pot washing is great, but how would you like to try a service that is especially pleasing to Śrīla Prabhupāda, a service that will put you in closer touch with him?" I said I was interested. In anticipation of his suggestion I felt as if I were about to hear the amount of the payout after winning a state lottery. Delighted by my response, Kṛtakarmā said, "Śrīla Prabhupāda has asked that we distribute his books. If you go out and try, not only will you quickly attract his attention, you'll also be following in his footsteps and those of the previous teachers in our line. You can start tomorrow." Without asking for details I agreed, and I spent the rest of that day and night wondering what book distribution would be like.

The Best Job in the Universe

The next day after breakfast, a jovial Kṛtakarmā handed me a canvas bag full of *Back to Godhead* magazines, a collection can, and a fistful of incense sticks. He then introduced me to my tutor, Bhakta Roberto – a happy-go-lucky devotee who spoke fluent Spanish but only a few words of English – and ushered us out the front door of our cozy temple.

Roberto led me on a fifteen-minute walk north on Valencia Street, through the seedy Mission District, into the clamorous downtown business district at Market and Powell, bustling with cable cars, tourists, and shoppers. Standing outside a Woolworth's department store, Bhakta Roberto began his work. Wearing a permanent smile, he approached passersby and methodically offered each a stick of incense. When someone took one, Roberto would hold out his collection can and say in his Latino accent, "Please, to give a donation for the temple." Whenever a charitable person dug into his or her pocket, extracted some change, and dropped it in the collection can, Roberto quickly handed the donor a BTG and then said thank you and a cheerful "Hare Kṛṣṇa!"

After watching for a while, I got the idea. Roberto taught me to fix my mind on how we were helping people to start their journey back to Godhead. He told me that anyone who gave even a penny would get permanent spiritual benefit. Roberto's mood of doing good for others had been passed down to him through the devotees who had heard it from

Śrīla Prabhupāda, who had imbibed it from his own spiritual master. In fact, all the Vaiṣṇavas in the line of devotion are famous for their mood of generosity. Rāmānujācārya, for example, in order to give mercy, is known to have publicly distributed his confidential initiation mantra, even though his guru told him that if he did so he would have to see hell. Śukadeva Gosvāmī, even though completely self-satisfied, spoke the *Bhāgavatam* out of his compassion for others. And Nityānanda Prabhu and His associates, the most intimate servants of Lord Caitanya, went door to door throughout Bengal to distribute Lord Caitanya's teachings.

Bhakta Roberto worked with the same big-hearted mood. He would nod at me after someone had taken a magazine and say, "Kṛṣṇa's mercy!" I liked Roberto's happy, openhearted mood. As we became comrades on that windy street, I thought back to only a few months before when indirectly a devotee had done *me* the same favor by distributing a *Back to Godhead* to my friend, Richie. Now I was on the giving end, with an opportunity to pass the favor on to someone else.

To onlookers at Market and Powell, my newly assumed service might have looked trivial, even lowly. Certainly my approach was awkward at first; in fact, on that first day, a thirty year-old tie-wearing man said to me, "Why don't you get a job?" I immediately thought, "I have the best job in the universe – following in the footsteps of my spiritual master and all the great bhakti masters before him."

Promoted

When we got back to the temple in the evening of that first day, Kṛtakarmā and a few other devotees greeted us enthusiastically at the front door. With his hand on my shoulder, Kṛtakarmā asked me how I liked my new service. From his question I could understand that I had been given a promotion.

About advancing in devotional life Śrīla Prabhupāda writes: "Advancement in spiritual life is exactly like advancement in service in a government office. If the supervisor of the department is satisfied with the service of a particular person, a promotion and increase in pay will automatically come."[14]

As the Ganges River descends from the spiritual world, passing through the different planets of the universe to sanctify whomever touches her waters, pure devotional service descends through generations of Kṛṣṇa's unalloyed devotees to cleanse the hearts of whomever it touches. Anuttama Dāsa, one of Śrīla Prabhupāda's distinguished disciples and ISKCON's International Director of Communications, wrote in his 1986 Vyāsa-pūjā offering:

> To serve you by becoming a dedicated preacher and servant of your mission is actually the most intimate service to you, Śrīla Prabhupāda. And it is available to all your disciples, granddisciples, and all future generations. It is available to me, and it will always be available to me. This is how I will realize your smile, your chastisements, your gentleness, guidance, and love. This is how we all can come to know you and feel you with us most intimately at every moment.

The realization that distributing Śrīla Prabhupāda's books was to be my lifetime service came to me incidentally in 1975 aboard a flight en route to the annual Māyāpur festival. A flight attendant handed me the disembarkation card I needed to fill out in order to clear immigration in India. On the card was a box that asked me to state my occupation. Since my only occupation was distributing Śrīla Prabhupāda's books, I thought of the word "messenger."

As I looked out the plane window I thought, "Who can argue with that? After all, everyone is *some* kind of messenger." Some are professional messengers, like the bicycle couriers who tear through New York City traffic to deliver time-sensitive letters to corporate managers. Others, like US postal carriers, earn a living by lugging and delivering mail. Professional or not, everyone is busy dispatching some kind of message. Politicians, poets, and parrots – all have a message to deliver.

Kṛṣṇa Himself acted as a messenger for the Pāṇḍavas when he pleaded for peace at the Kuru court.

Looking down again at the immigration form, I was struck anew by my assumed title "messenger." I was truly fortunate to be a messenger for my spiritual master, the great general in Lord Caitanya's *saṅkīrtana* movement. My fate could have had me carrying messages for the government or for a corporation run for ill-motivated profit. Instead, officially, it seemed, and by the special mercy of a pure Vaiṣṇava, I was an authorized agent carrying *Śrīmad-Bhāgavatam, Bhagavad-gītā,* and *Caitanya-caritāmṛta,* each enhanced with Śrīla Prabhupāda's divine purports and adorned with stunning paintings that opened a window to the spiritual world.

Saved By Service

Now decades have passed since Bhakta Roberto took me to Market and Powell, and I can see how it was my tight grip on the rope of distributing books that has pulled me past the many dangerous whirlpools that might otherwise have drowned me. In maintaining my vow of celibacy during my passionate youth, meeting my responsibilities in my married and business life, facing the death of my parents, making the inevitable hard decisions that come in life, my service was my savior. As my beloved friend Sura Dāsa once told me, "Vaish, your *sevā* will save ya." He was right. And I pray that my grip may remain tightly around this rope of distributing Śrīla Prabhupāda's books as I enter the last phase of my life.

This service is open to all! Anyone from any social stratum may voluntarily accept this service and become a messenger for Kṛṣṇa, thus rising to the exalted status of ambassador of goodwill. Śrīla Prabhupāda gives a practical example of how this happens in a letter to Uttamaśloka Dāsa dated December 11, 1975: "The *saṅkīrtana* devotees are very, very dear to Kṛṣṇa. Because [they] are doing the fieldwork of book distribution, Kṛṣṇa has immediately recognized them as true servants. Just like during wartime a farm boy or ordinary clerk who goes to fight for his country on the front immediately becomes a national hero for his sincere effort. So Kṛṣṇa immediately recognizes a preacher of Kṛṣṇa consciousness who takes all risks to deliver His message." About those who deliver His message Kṛṣṇa says in the *Gītā* (18.69), "There is no servant in this world more dear to Me than he, nor will there ever be one more dear."

Millions of so-called good causes abound in this world, but according to Śrī Caitanya Mahāprabhu, only one cause is truly great: delivering Kṛṣṇa's message to the forgetful conditioned souls suffering from ignorance of their true selves.

Anyone who feels thrilled upon hearing Kṛṣṇa's statement in the *Gītā,* or Mahāprabhu's order to deliver the *Gītā's* message, and who takes up that order, becomes a fortunate soul and the noblest of messengers; such a person becomes an ambassador of goodwill, tastes the sweetness of giving others the greatest gift, and feels the protection of Kṛṣṇa's internal energy.

"Higher-Class Propaganda Work"

Distributing Śrīla Prabhupāda's transcendental books, canvassing for Kṛṣṇa, going door to door to deliver *kṛṣṇa-kathā,* inviting people to chant the holy names – all these methods are authorized, practical, and standard ways to give Kṛṣṇa and His message to others. The exemplars in our spiritual line are particularly fond of these methods, and they bless anyone who engages in such devotional service. Śrīla Bhaktisiddhānta Sarasvatī verifies this truth:

> We do not belittle the importance of the *pāñcarātrika* process [the rules and rituals of Deity worship], of having representatives in theistic institutions, or establishing temples with Deities, yet we are of the opinion that the duty of the better or higher class is propaganda work. Mahāprabhu's *mano-'bhīṣṭa*

> [heart's desire] is that Vaikuṇṭha-nāma be proclaimed everywhere, and to that end many pamphlets need be printed.[15]

Fully absorbed in the mood of his guru even before coming to America, Śrīla Prabhupāda sat in his room at the Rādhā-Dāmodara temple in Vṛndāvana and wrote:

> Just preach the Lord's message to the fallen souls,
> going continuously from door to door
> By the grace of that preaching
> your life will become truly successful.[16]

After arriving in the West and launching his campaign on American shores, Śrīla Prabhupāda wrote this to Madhudviṣa Dāsa on March 26, 1970: "You are trying for the new temple, but our main business is *saṅkīrtana* and distribution of literature. If Kṛṣṇa gives us a better place, that is all right. Otherwise, we can remain at any place never mind hell or heaven; but we shall be only very cautious about propagating our *saṅkīrtana* movement."

Those who risk their lives to distribute transcendental knowledge through books, magazines, and other media get unusually high spiritual returns. The motivational speaker Jim Rohn once said: "If you are not willing to risk the unusual, you will have to settle for the ordinary." One need not hesitate to distribute transcendental books on the mandate of Mahāprabhu and His followers, for anyone who takes up this mission to any extent will be empowered to do so by the Lord's internal energy – an empowerment that resides eternally in Mahāprabhu's fully potent order. Such a fortunate soul becomes recognized as a true ambassador of goodwill.

CHAPTER THREE

Apply the Order

IN THIS CHAPTER I recount how Śrīla Prabhupāda applied his spiritual master's order to print and distribute transcendental books. I also tell how he gave the same order to his own disciples, and how his disciples and their disciples, by applying and passing down this order, become eligible for Kṛṣṇa's full mercy – in perpetuity.

Lord Kṛṣṇa's order descends directly from Him through the unbroken medium of disciplic succession (*paramparā*); thus one who applies the order is at once connected to Kṛṣṇa's internal energy. In this Kali-yuga, Lord Kṛṣṇa appears in the form of His own devotee (*bhakta-rūpa*), Śrī Kṛṣṇa Caitanya Mahāprabhu. Mahāprabhu ordered everyone to become guru and spread Kṛṣṇa's teachings to others. By applying the order received from one's guru in the line of Mahāprabhu, one attains the spiritual potency to achieve uncommon success in this life and the next.

Śrīla Prabhupāda points to the profound result he attained by applying his spiritual master's order:

> The present Kṛṣṇa consciousness movement was started with belief in the words of our spiritual master. He wanted to preach, we believed in his words and tried somehow or other to fulfill them, and now this movement has become successful all over the world.[1]

> So I think sometimes that "Why this wonderful thing has happened to me?" So I search out. I search out only that I had cent percent belief in the words of my spiritual master. That's all, nothing else.... Don't think of any nonsense. Simply execute what your guru has said. That is success.[2]

Śrīla Prabhupāda also records the explicit reasoning behind his guru's order in a letter to Śrutadeva Dāsa dated October 24, 1974:

> He personally instructed me that books are more important than big temples. At Rādhā-kuṇḍa, he told me that since constructing the big marble temple at Bagh Bazaar, there have been so many difficulties. Our men are envious over who will live in which room. I think it would be better to take off all the marbles and sell them and print books. He told me this personally. So I am always emphasizing book distribution.

What's more, Śrīla Prabhupāda wrote in a letter to Keśava Dāsa on January 1, 1972, that anyone who takes up the order to distribute his transcendental literature receives the special mercy of Kṛṣṇa: "And you are all helping me to fulfill the order which Guru Mahārāja gave me. So I am so much grateful to you, and I am sure Kṛṣṇa will bless you a million times over, for doing this work."

Commitment Empowers Action

Applying oneself to any endeavor requires commitment, and if we want to apply ourselves fully, we'll have to make an absolute commitment. Commitment empowers action. Even the secular world appreciates the power of absolute commitment. The Scottish mountaineer William Murray, for example, after fully committing himself to accomplishing his childhood dream of climbing Mount Everest, found the energy and resources to attempt it. He never made it to the summit, but only because his body would not acclimatize to the height of the last stage. Murray writes:

> Until one is committed, there is hesitancy, the chance to draw back, always ineffectiveness. Concerning all acts of initiative (and creation), there is one elementary truth, the ignorance of which kills countless ideas and splendid plans: that the moment one definitely commits oneself, then Providence moves too. All sorts of things occur to help one that would never otherwise have occurred. A whole stream of events issues from the decision, raising in one's favour all manner of unforeseen incidents and meetings and material assistance, which no man could have dreamt would have come his way. I learned a deep respect for one of Goethe's couplets:
>
> Whatever you can do or dream you can, begin it. Boldness has genius, power, and magic in it!

If boldly applying oneself to a mundane task has such power and magic, imagine what those who fully commit themselves to do the work ordered by the Supreme Personality of Godhead achieve. Such persons can perform wonderful feats. Lord Brahmā created a universe. The commitment to create was Brahmā's, but the Supersoul gave him the intelligence to succeed. Śrīla Prabhupāda writes in his purport to *Śrīmad-Bhāgavatam* 3.9.30:

> The mercy the Lord bestows upon a particular person engaged in executing the responsible work entrusted unto him is beyond imagination. But His mercy is received due to our penance and perseverance in executing devotional service. Brahmā was entrusted with the work of creating the planetary systems. The Lord instructed him that when he meditated he would very easily know where and how the planetary systems

> must be arranged. The directions were to come from within, and there was no necessity for anxiety in that task. Such instructions of *buddhi-yoga* are directly imparted by the Lord from within, as confirmed in the *Bhagavad-gītā* (10.10).

Since it is well known that Kṛṣṇa is pleased by even a small effort made on His behalf, what blessings and empowerment must come to those who dedicate their whole lives to applying His order.

For some, the goal of bhakti-yoga may seem far away, but even beginners at once taste sweet success simply by starting to do Kṛṣṇa's bidding, just as Murray tasted success even as he began his ascent of Mount Everest.

Doing the Impossible

Śrīla Prabhupāda sometimes gave orders that required incredible commitment even to *attempt* to execute. For example, in Los Angeles during the summer of 1975, he gave two of his disciples the seemingly impossible task of publishing seventeen books from raw manuscripts in just two months. Fifteen volumes of *Śrī Caitanya-caritāmṛta* had to go through editing, typesetting, proofreading, and layout. Paintings had to be drafted and completed to illustrate them. Add to that the two volumes of the Fifth Canto of *Śrīmad-Bhāgavatam* already in the works, and you get a total of seventeen volumes.

Rāmeśvara and Rādhāballabha – in charge of printing Śrīla Prabhupāda's books at that time – were shocked to hear Śrīla Prabhupāda's order. Before Śrīla Prabhupāda's arrival in Los Angeles they had invested in state-of-the-art production equipment and meticulously organized the publishing department. Having given their full attention and energy to maximizing efficiency, they had been proud to report to Śrīla Prabhupāda that they would be able to complete the printing of *Śrī Caitanya-caritāmṛta* at what they considered the swiftest pace possible: one volume every two months. Now, without warning, and before the devotees, Śrīla Prabhupāda gave them the unequivocal order to publish all seventeen volumes in only two months.

On hearing his spiritual master's instruction, Rāmeśvara made what he thought a sincere and reasonable response: "But Śrīla Prabhupāda, that's impossible!"

Śrīla Prabhupāda replied, "Impossible is a word found only in a fool's dictionary." Making Napoleon's famous dictum his own, Śrīla Prabhupāda infused it with spiritual power. For him there would be no retreats from Russia, no Waterloos.

As Śrīla Prabhupāda turned to finish his morning walk, the stunned Rāmeśvara and Rādhāballabha dropped behind. They realized they couldn't refuse, so instead, they began to consider how to apply the order.

The instant they accepted this seemingly impossible task, the power and magic inherent in commitment descended on them. As He did for Brahmā, the Supersoul provided the spiritual intelligence from within, and creative ideas flowed into their minds. The complexity of the task was mind-boggling, but in the following two months Rāmeśvara, Rādhāballabha, and the entire ISKCON Los Angeles community realized not only how the spiritual master's unrestricted blessings flow to those who apply his order but how, by his grace, the impossible can become possible.

The sacrifice the devotees made to execute this particular order is legendary. They gave up all comforts and worked tirelessly with single-minded resolve to achieve the goal, often waking in the morning slumped over desks or easels. After the goal was achieved, they received a letter from Śrīla Prabhupāda dated September 1, 1975: "You have taken seriously this work and I know that my Guru Mahārāja is pleased with you because he wanted this. So by this endeavor you will all go back home, back to Godhead."

Note Śrīla Prabhupāda's statement that his disciples' devotional sacrifice had pleased *his* guru, showing how a disciple's service is passed up through the chain of disciplic succession.

About the power of applying the pure devotee's order, Śrīla Prabhupāda recalls in his purport to *Śrīmad-Bhāgavatam* 3.22.5 his guru's first sacred order to him and how it affected his life:

> Once we had the opportunity to meet Viṣṇupāda Śrī Śrīmad Bhaktisiddhānta Sarasvatī Gosvāmī Mahārāja, and on first sight he requested this humble self to preach his message in the Western countries. There was no preparation for this, but somehow or other he desired it, and by his grace we are now engaged in executing his order, which has given us a transcendental occupation and has saved and liberated us from the occupation of material activities.

Śrīla Prabhupāda too worked with one-pointed attention. He applied his guru's order throughout his life against seemingly impossible odds, and just look at what he accomplished.

After Śrīla Prabhupāda arrived in America, in a lecture dated December 21, 1966, he explained to his disciples the power of applying the guru's order: "If you cannot do, if you simply think, 'How can I do? How can I do? How can I do?' Simply this – if you practically cannot do, but if you simply think that 'How can I do?' oh, then also you become liberated. Then also you become liberated. And what to speak of when we actually serve."

In Śrīla Prabhupāda's case, he never begrudged the paltry facility he had in India before traveling to the West; he used whatever was available, whatever he could afford, in order to execute his guru's order to preach Kṛṣṇa consciousness. Many people thought it unlikely that Prabhupāda could succeed given his advanced age and lack of resources, but with faith in his spiritual master's order and his diligence in applying it, by 1944 Śrīla Prabhupāda had conceived, written, edited, and typed the manuscript, as well as designed the logo for *Back to Godhead,* and after writing and printing BTG, he moved about the cities and towns of India to sell it.[3]

Soon Prabhupāda was publishing and distributing not

only magazines but also small books like *Easy Journey to Other Planets.* Next, he began his translation and commentary on *Śrīmad-Bhāgavatam* – a monumental task he would work on for the rest of his life. Immediately after publishing the *Bhāgavatam's* First Canto in three volumes, he personally showed the books around and sold the sets to bookstores, libraries, and academic institutions across India.

On March 2, 1975, in a room conversation in Atlanta, Śrīla Prabhupāda spoke to an assembly of book distributors about his days distributing books and magazines in India:

> The first stage I used to publish and distribute as *gṛhastha,* I did not mind whether one page or not. I was distributing. So spending about four hundred, five hundred rupees, I did not care if one page or not, but I'll distribute. Then, when I retired, left home, I was publishing and distributing myself to get subscription. The subscription was very cheap, two rupees, four *annas,* I think, for the year. Two copies per month ... Then I published *Bhāgavatam.* So I was going to libraries, schools, colleges, and everyone was purchasing. My *Bhāgavata* was being purchased by your Congress Library. In Delhi they have got office. So there was standing order, eighteen copies of my book as soon as they are published. The head librarian in India, New Delhi, he gave me standing order.

Guaranteed Success

What magic there is in setting out into the vast, unpredictable world to carry out the order of one's guru! A disciple on such a mission becomes fearless, because he or she knows that success is already guaranteed simply by setting out. Since life in the material world is fraught with challenges, the devotees who catch hold of their guru's order and face all challenges as opportunities to prove their devotion meet with uncanny success. How could it be otherwise?

Even before Śrīla Prabhupāda journeyed to America, the methodical way in which he carried out his guru's order brought unanticipated success time and again. In New Delhi, he sold eighteen sets of his newly published First Canto to the acquisitions librarian at Library of Congress office, the national library of the United States. The Library's representative in Delhi also agreed to buy future volumes, and then dispatched some of the three-volume sets to America, one of which ended up in the New York Public Library a year before Śrīla Prabhupāda's own arrival in America.

Śrīla Prabhupāda seemed both surprised and delighted by the success of his visit to the Delhi office of the Library of Congress. During Prabhupāda's first year in New York City, Brahmānanda Dāsa remembers him regularly taking several buses from his downtown flat to 42nd Street in Manhattan just to see his *Śrīmad-Bhāgavatams* in the library there.

After arriving in America and on his way from Butler, Pennsylvania, to New York City, Śrīla Prabhupāda stopped at the University of Pennsylvania in Philadelphia to meet with Professor W. Norman Brown, a distinguished Sanskrit scholar, who had booked Śrīla Prabhupāda as a speaker in one of his classes. While there, Śrīla Prabhupāda discovered that the Library of Congress had also placed a set of his *Śrīmad-Bhāgavatams* in the university's Van Pelt Library.

His guru's order always on his mind, Śrīla Prabhupāda had even sold a set of *Śrīmad-Bhāgavatams* to the captain of the *Jaladuta* before touching American soil for the first time.

Śrīla Prabhupāda's life in service wasn't easy, and finances were especially difficult. He had brought only two hundred sets of books with him, which he sold to support himself and his preaching. He had no other source of income. Śrīla Prabhupāda remembers:

> So some way or other, in 1965, I went to America, with great difficulty. But I took about two hundred sets of books. The customs clearance was done, I told them that "Oh, I am taking these books for distribution. Not for sale." Anyway, they passed, and with these books I reached America. And I was maintaining myself by selling these books for one year.[4]

Although Śrīla Prabhupāda was maintaining himself by selling his books during that first year in America, he once risked two hundred dollars from the sales of some sets to pay an advance on the apartment and storefront at 26 Second Avenue. When he signed the lease he had no idea how he would pay his next month's rent.[5]

Why did Śrīla Prabhupāda go through such hard endeavor to publish transcendental books and carry them to sell abroad? The primary reason is that Śrīla Bhaktisiddhānta had taught him that giving others transcendental literature is the most practical way to spread Lord Caitanya's movement.

The Agent of Divine Mercy

Śrīla Bhaktisiddhānta Sarasvatī Ṭhākura emphasized book distribution in his own preaching. In 1936 he founded the Paramarthi Printing Works in his Bhag Bazaar temple in Calcutta in order to publish Vaiṣṇava literature for mass distribution. To underscore the fact that the printing press was spiritual, he installed it next to the temple Deities. "Everything here," he later wrote, "including the building, printing machine, and supplies ... even the bricks and pillars, is *aprakṛta* and non-different from Kṛṣṇa."[6]

As Śrīla Bhaktisiddhānta put the printing press at the heart of his Gauḍīya mission, so did Śrīla Prabhupāda, establishing a printing press almost as soon as he incorporated ISKCON in July 1966. In fact, as early as 1969, before ISKCON owned any real estate or had much money to spend, Śrīla Prabhupāda asked his followers to purchase a building somewhere in the United States that could better facilitate his printing operations. His disciples in Boston were the first to oblige with a house on North Beacon Street. Boston thus became the home of ISKCON's first publishing house.

Balāi Dāsī, an eyewitness to the inauguration of ISKCON Press in Boston, recounts:

> When ISKCON Boston set up a full-scale printing operation, including a printing press, folding machine, stitching equipment, and photo lab, His Divine Grace came to visit especially for the occasion. When he arrived at the Boston temple, he went first to see the new press. As soon as he entered the doorway of the pressroom he glorified his spiritual master by chanting, "*Jaya oṁ viṣṇupāda paramahaṁsa parivrājakācārya* Śrī Śrīmad Bhaktisiddhānta Sarasvatī Gosvāmī Mahārāja, Śrīla Prabhupāda *kī jaya*!" After these prayers he said, "My Guru Mahārāja would be very pleased."

Śrīla Prabhupāda then turned to Balāi Dāsī's husband, Advaita Dāsa, the press operations manager, and said, "[T]he press is not only the heart of the Society, it is also my heart, and therefore it must be properly cleaned and maintained."

In an essay entitled "Madhva-Gauḍīya Literature," Śrīla Bhaktisiddhānta writes: "As soon as a single person will have conceived the sincere desire of undertaking the promulgation of the tidings of the Gauḍīya literature to the peoples of this world, he is thereby enrolled among the agents of divine mercy with power to forward the fulfillment of this expressed wish of the Supreme Lord."[7]

Not only did Śrīla Prabhupāda take to heart his guru's directive to promulgate Gauḍīya literature, but he also enrolled his fledging followers among the "agents of divine mercy." In this way Śrīla Prabhupāda became empowered and empowering.

In what became manifest as his signature style, Śrīla Prabhupāda wanted to carry out his guru's wishes in a big way, as shown by the following statement written to an early American disciple on June 12, 1968: "Therefore in future if there is money sufficient I wish to print each volume of my book, 5,000 copies. Now, very soon we shall get 5,000 copies of TLC [*Teachings of Lord Caitanya*] and we have to organize the sales propaganda. If there is sale, then there is no scarcity of matter for printing."

Concerning the sales of BTG, Śrīla Prabhupāda writes about how his disciples can help him:

> There are at least three hundred big cities in your country, and if we can appoint one selling agent only in each city, consuming an average of one hundred copies only, the total quantity comes to thirty thousand copies. This is not a Utopian idea. It is completely practical. Simply we have to arrange and organize.... So expecting on this calculation that in the near future we shall be able to distribute at least thirty thousand copies of *Back to Godhead,* you can immediately take quotations from Dai Nippon for regular twenty thousand copies minimum per month.[8]

The Power is in the Instruction

The instruction of the spiritual master is nondifferent from the spiritual master himself. How is that? Lord Caitanya ordered everyone to spread the *saṅkīrtana* movement. The Lord, being absolute, is nondifferent from His words. In this way, the order of Mahāprabhu – imbued with His own spiritual power – is effectively transferred through the sound of His words from the heart of the Lord to the hearts of His sincere followers. Those who take those orders seriously become the Lord's representatives, the spiritual masters, who then pass these words down to their disciples. In this way the order remains alive and vital. Śrīla Bhaktisiddhānta took the order he had himself received from his father and guru to preach Kṛṣṇa consciousness through the publishing and distributing of books and enrolled his own disciple in the same task. Śrīla Prabhupāda accepted and cherished that direction in turn and passed it on to his own disciples. Such instructions, received as a priceless legacy, become the pride of a progressive disciple.

Śrīla Prabhupāda confirms this in his purport to *Śrī Caitanya-caritāmṛta* (*Ādi-līlā* 1.35):

> The service of the spiritual master is essential. If there is no chance to serve the spiritual master directly, a devotee should serve him by remembering his instructions. There is no difference between the spiritual master's instructions and the

spiritual master himself. In his absence, therefore, his words of direction should be the pride of the disciple.

When Śrīla Prabhupāda penned his Seven Purposes of ISKCON, marking the official inauguration of his movement in the West, he included as the seventh and final purpose the way to achieve all the Society's other purposes: "With a view towards achieving aforementioned Purposes, to publish and distribute periodicals, magazines, books, and other writings."

Those among Śrīla Prabhupāda's disciples and followers who have embraced his instruction to distribute his books are now passing that same order on to the next generation. By accepting the order, ISKCON members are benefiting both themselves and the world.

So it was to keep his spiritual master's order alive that even before he had ample quantities of books or the facility or manpower to sell them or print more, Śrīla Prabhupāda concentrated the attention of the earliest members of his newly formed Society on his books. Śyāmasundara Dāsa, who joined ISKCON in 1967, tells how even before ISKCON's presses started rolling, Śrīla Prabhupāda publicly read from his books every day and painstakingly explained their contents:

> We just had the early *Śrīmad-Bhāgavatam* edition that Śrīla Prabhupāda brought with him on the *Jaladuta* for our personal reading. We would read something from that and try to understand it. Also, Prabhupāda's early lectures were packed with philosophy, because he had only those few books for us to read and he didn't know if he would live or die.
>
> We were just there listening deeply to his lectures; and after hearing them, we went out to try to spread Kṛṣṇa consciousness all over the world. We were total hippies, accustomed to taking LSD for breakfast. But Śrīla Prabhupāda went on reading his books aloud and speaking from them. This powerful vibration grabbed even the criminals and draft dodgers among us, and soon we were engaged in Kṛṣṇa's service.

Our family business began at creation: Lord Kṛṣṇa, by the transcendental sound of his flute, enlightened Brahmā – the *ādi-guru* of the Brahma-Madhva-Gauḍīya-sampradāya – with Vedic knowledge, symbolized here by the book in Brahmā's hand. Brahmā's sons and disciples, especially Śrī Nārada Muni, disseminated that knowledge throughout the universe.

Five hundred years before all these young devotees in America, India, and Europe hit the road to spread the teachings of Lord Caitanya and the chanting of the Hare Kṛṣṇa mantra, Śrī Caitanya Mahāprabhu had issued an order: "Everywhere you go, impart the teachings of Lord Kṛṣṇa to everyone you meet. In this way become a guru and deliver everyone in the land."

Great masters in bhakti-yoga like Śrīla Bhaktivinoda Ṭhākura, Śrīla Bhaktisiddhānta Sarasvatī Ṭhākura, and Śrīla A. C. Bhaktivedanta Swami Prabhupāda took Lord Caitanya's order to heart. They then taught others by their example how to follow the same order by organizing large numbers of devotees, each doing their part, to publicly chant the holy names, publish and distribute books, and systematically delineate the teachings of Śrī Caitanya Mahāprabhu both by speaking to large audiences and counseling individuals.

Dive In

Śrīla Prabhupāda brought this transcendental current across the Atlantic Ocean from India, carrying with him trunkloads of *Śrīmad-Bhāgavatams.* His followers rode that current across the land, going from door to door and town to town. By distributing Kṛṣṇa conscious books throughout America, Europe, Australia, Africa, and beyond, Śrīla Prabhupāda's young followers ushered into the world an unprecedented stream of refreshing water from the spiritual realm. That current is still flowing, and anyone with a little enthusiasm can swim in it.

Any simple soul who humbly applies Mahāprabhu's order to promote His *saṅkīrtana* movement has a better product and a bigger field of engagement than any well-placed entrepreneur of the material world. But unlike an entrepreneur driven by the desire for personal enrichment and all its attendant status and power, one who strives to advance the cause of Lord Caitanya magnanimously benefits all living beings and attains the eternal profit of returning to the spiritual world, Śrī Vṛndāvana-*dhāma,* at the end of life. Lord Brahmā states that from Lord Indra to the tiny germ, all living beings are bound by inexorable karma. Kṛṣṇa cuts the bonds of karma for those who engage in devotional service: *karmāṇi nirdahati kintu ca bhakti-bhājām.*[9]

The highest form of devotional service, according to Śukadeva Gosvāmī in his remarks about the mood and method of the preeminent Vaiṣṇava Lord Śiva, is to perform austerity for the sake of alleviating the suffering of others. Śrī Caitanya's order grants us this opportunity to practice the highest form of devotional service. Śukadeva Gosvāmī says, "It is said that great personalities almost always accept voluntary suffering because of the suffering of people in general. This is considered the highest method of worshiping the Supreme Personality of Godhead, who is present in everyone's heart.[10]

To encourage his followers to apply Lord Śiva's principle, Śrīla Prabhupāda wrote hundreds of letters like this one:

> You have taken seriously the publishing and also the distribution of these books, and that is the success of our mission. You have taken seriously this work and I know that my Guru Mahārāja is pleased with you because he wanted this. So by this your endeavor you will all go back home, back to Godhead.[11]

This noble service is now available to all. One simply has to apply the order and begin.

CHAPTER FOUR

Press On

IN HIS PURPORT to *Śrīmad-Bhāgavatam* 4.24.15, Śrīla Prabhupāda writes about "the secret of success":

> After being initiated and receiving the orders of the spiritual master, the disciple should unhesitatingly think about the instructions or orders of the spiritual master and should not allow himself to be disturbed by anything else. This is also the verdict of Śrīla Viśvanātha Cakravartī Ṭhākura, who, while explaining a verse of *Bhagavad-gītā* (2.41) beginning *vyavasāyātmikā buddhir ekeha kuru-nandana,* points out that the order of the spiritual master is the life substance of the disciple. The disciple should not consider whether he is going back home, back to Godhead; his first business should be to execute the order of his spiritual master. Thus a disciple should always meditate on the order of the spiritual master, and that is perfectional meditation. Not only should he meditate upon that order, but he should find out the means by which he can perfectly worship and execute it.

By his strict adherence to his spiritual master's order to print books, for the first time in history people all over the world would come to know and see Kṛṣṇa, the Supreme Personality of Godhead. Śrīla Prabhupāda writes in his purport to *Caitanya-caritāmṛta, Ādi-līlā* 7.95–96, "We believed in the words of our spiritual master and started in a humble way – in a helpless way – but due to the spiritual force of the order of the supreme authority, this movement has become successful."

Śrīla Prabhupāda started with no facility, yet he let loose an unprecedented deluge of transcendental knowledge on the world through his books. The volume and quality of literature that poured from Śrīla Prabhupāda's pen, typewriter, and dictating machine in the twelve short years after he arrived in America is historic and astounding. In fact, the number of his books that sold within that period place him as one the best-selling authors of all time. Taking fiction writers away from that short list, he is likely one of the best-selling nonfiction authors of all time.

In his concluding words to *Śrī Caitanya-caritāmṛta,* Śrīla Prabhupāda summarizes some of the ways in which he carried out his spiritual master's order to print and distribute books:

> After [Śrīla Bhaktisiddhānta Sarasvatī Ṭhākura] passed away, I started the fortnightly magazine *Back to Godhead* sometime in 1944 and tried to spread the cult of Śrī Caitanya Mahāprabhu through this magazine. After I took *sannyāsa,* a well-wishing friend suggested that I write books instead of magazines. Magazines, he said, might be thrown away, but books remain perpetually. Then I attempted to write *Śrīmad-Bhāgavatam.* Before that, when I was a householder, I had written on *Śrīmad Bhagavad-gītā* and had completed about eleven hundred pages, but somehow or other the manuscript was stolen. In any case, when I had published *Śrīmad-Bhāgavatam,* First Canto, in three volumes in India, I thought of going to the USA. By the mercy of His Divine Grace, I was able to come to New York on September 17, 1965. Since then, I have translated many books, including *Śrīmad-Bhāgavatam,* the *Bhakti-rasāmṛta-sindhu, Teachings of Lord Caitanya* (a summary), and many others.

In America Śrīla Prabhupāda continued the writing he had started in India, despite living alone in a foreign environment with barely enough money to survive. During those lean days, he once returned to his rented room only to find that someone had stolen his typewriter, tape recorder, and books. Undaunted, he pressed on, using whatever means he could to continue his writing and the distribution of the books he had brought from India.

As a testament to his faith in his spiritual master's order to print and distribute books, Śrīla Prabhupāda maintained himself that first year in New York solely by selling his sets of *Śrīmad-Bhāgavatam*. As young people, attracted by his public *kīrtana* and lectures, gradually joined him, he also engaged them in selling the books. When his followers became more committed, he inspired them to revive BTG. By 1966, his followers were printing and distributing a simple, black-and-white edition of the magazine.

Satsvarūpa Dāsa Goswami describes the printing of the first American BTG:

> It was an off night – no public *kīrtana* and lecture – and Swamiji was up in his room working on his translation of *Śrīmad-Bhāgavatam*. Downstairs, the printing of the first issue had been going on for hours. Rāyarāma had typed the stencils, and during the printing he had stood nervously over the machine, examining the printing quality of each page, stroking his beard, and murmuring, "Hmmmmm." Now it was time to collate and staple each magazine. The stencils had lasted for one hundred copies, and one hundred copies of each of the twenty-eight pages and the front and back cover were now lined up along two of the unvarnished benches Raphael had made that summer. A few devotees collated and stapled the magazine in an assembly line, walking along the stacks of pages, taking one page under another until they reached the end of the bench and gave the assembled stack of pages to Gargamuni, who stood brushing his long hair out of his eyes, stapling each magazine with the stapler and staples Brahmānanda had brought from his Board of Education office.

> Even Hayagrīva, who usually didn't volunteer for menial duties, was there, walking down the line, collating. Suddenly the side door opened, and to their surprise they saw Swamiji looking in at them. Then he opened the door wide and entered the room. He had never come down like this on an off night before. They felt an unexpected flush of emotion and love for him, and they dropped down on their knees, bowing their heads to the floor. "No, no," he said, raising his hand to stop them as some were still bowing and others already rising to their feet. "Continue what you are doing." When they stood up and saw him standing with them, they weren't sure what to do. But obviously he had come down to see them producing his *Back to Godhead* magazine, so they continued working, silently and efficiently. Prabhupāda walked down the row of pages, his hand and wrist extending gracefully from the folds of his shawl as he touched a stack of pages and then a finished magazine. "ISKCON Press," he said.[1]

After this first historic printing, Greg Scharf, now initiated as Gargamuni Dāsa, had given Śrīla Prabhupāda a dictating machine. Instead of typing his English translations and commentaries, Śrīla Prabhupāda could speak them into the dictating machine. Gargamuni had also found two old mimeograph machines for sale, and Śrīla Prabhupāda had negotiated a good price for them and bought them from the seller. The devotees would go on to use these machines to print the first dozen issues of BTG. He used the dictating machine to record his translations and commentaries. The recordings were then usually handed over to Satsvarūpa – or one summer, to Neal, a young college student who did the typing as part of a school project – who would transcribe them. Satsvarūpa would do some rough editing on the transcripts and give the manuscript for final editing to Hayagrīva, who would then give the edited text to Pradyumna for Sanskrit editing. This procedure was slow and cumbersome, and Śrīla Prabhupāda was constantly looking for ways to centralize the process and make it more efficient.

In 1967 Śrīla Prabhupāda had his third heart attack and spent time in both America and India recovering his health. But even while he was convalescing he went on with his translating, thinking constantly about his books and staying in regular communication with his disciples about them. On August 2, 1967, for example, Śrīla Prabhupāda wrote to his disciples from Vṛndāvana, informing them that he had taken a six-month leave to recover his health and that they should continue their activities with great vigor. He wrote a second letter on the same day, to Brahmānanda, encouraging him to push on with his efforts to get his books printed. Śrīla Prabhupāda added that he "will be glad to see that the books are being read by hundreds and thousands of men."

By 1968, after Śrīla Prabhupāda had returned to America, he began looking seriously into new ways to print BTG. He even considered printing in India. BTG looked unpolished; Śrīla Prabhupāda wanted it to have a professional look. Meanwhile, because sales were slow, Gargamuni, Brahmānanda, and others, investigated alternative ways to sell BTG. They even considered using professional marketers to boost sales.

By this time, Śrīla Prabhupāda had also finished writing *Teachings of Lord Caitanya* (TLC). Jayānanda Dāsa gave $5,000 toward the printing, but Śrīla Prabhupāda had no place to print it or a solid plan how to sell it. It was at this juncture that Śrīla Prabhupāda began to consider getting a press beyond the two small mimeograph machines. He needed a full service operation – devotees who could do layout, photo finishing, typesetting, folding, and binding. Into 1968, however, the idea of ISKCON starting its own full-scale press and possibly printing the TLC remained on hold. Śrīla Prabhupāda and his disciples continued to weigh their options.

The 1968 Macmillan Bhagavad-gītā As It Is

Then, in early 1968, there was a major breakthrough. Śrīla Prabhupāda had completed his new manuscript for *Bhagavad-*

gītā As It Is and was eager to see it published and distributed. He had developed a friendly relationship with the famous Beat Generation poet Allen Ginsberg, and had asked him to use his contacts to find a publisher for the *Gītā*. But Ginsberg's associates felt that Śrīla Prabhupāda's *Gītā* was not commercially viable. Next Śrīla Prabhupāda gave the manuscript to Rāyarāma. Rāyarāma took the manuscript to various publishers, but gave up trying after receiving negative responses similar to those of Ginsberg's men.

Then Śrīla Prabhupāda gave the job of finding the *Gītā* a publisher to Brahmānanda. Brahmānanda told me in an interview that he guessed only a Kṛṣṇa conscious publisher would be interested, because on every page of Śrīla Prabhupāda's commentary was something about devotional service to Kṛṣṇa. Nondevotee publishers would never find that saleable. Brahmānanda said, "I had absolutely no faith, therefore, that any publisher would take it. It had no commercial value." Nevertheless, he followed Śrīla Prabhupāda's order and sifted through bookstores and the library to find books on how to get a book like Śrīla Prabhupāda's *Gītā* published. Even after all that, however, he still had no idea what to do.

Meanwhile, ISKCON produced a record, and orders for it were coming in daily. Brahmānanda would collect ISKCON's mail at the New York temple storefront and take it upstairs to Śrīla Prabhupāda's room for his review. One day, a letter arrived from an employee at the Macmillan Company. It contained an order for the Hare Kṛṣṇa record and a check in payment. Śrīla Prabhupāda told Brahmānanda to deliver the record personally to the Macmillan employee and to inform him that he had a *Bhagavad-gītā* manuscript to publish.

Brahmānanda donned shirt and tie and went off to the Macmillan building, thirty-one stories high, to deliver the record. The man who had ordered the record turned out to be an accountant who had nothing to do with the company's publishing decisions, but just as Brahmānanda finished talking to him and was wondering what to do next, Macmillan's senior editor, James Wade, walked into the accounting office. The accountant was kind enough to introduce Mr. Wade to Brahmānanda, who summarily informed the editor that he had a *Gītā* by an Indian swami to publish. Mr. Wade asked if it was a complete *Bhagavad-gītā,* and when Brahmānanda said it was, the editor replied, "Great, our religion department has everything but a *Bhagavad-gītā.* We'll publish it."

Brahmānanda was stunned. This senior editor had just agreed to publish Śrīla Prabhupāda's *Gītā* sight unseen. Brahmānanda remembers racing back to the temple to tell Śrīla Prabhupāda. "When Śrīla Prabhupāda heard the news," Brahmānanda recounts, "he reacted as if he were expecting it."

So in February 1968, on the Vyāsa-pūjā day of Śrīla Bhaktisiddhānta Sarasvatī Ṭhākura, Brahmānanda delivered the manuscript of *Bhagavad-gītā As It Is* to the Macmillan Company.

ISKCON Press

By 1967, Śrīla Prabhupāda had heard of the respected Japanese publishing company Dai Nippon, and in 1968 he published the TLC with them. The Macmillan abridged edition of *Bhagavad-gītā As It Is* was finally available in 1969. The devotees not only read these two books but also sold them to bookstores wherever they could. Still, sales were slow.

Sales of the BTG were also slow, so to cover BTG's monthly printing costs, Śrīla Prabhupāda approved Rāyarāma's suggestion that they sell ad space in the magazine. However, after seeing the "hippie ads" Rāyarāma was running, Śrīla Prabhupāda withdrew his approval. He had already considered printing BTG with Dai Nippon to increase the professional standard of the magazine, but this meant that ISKCON would have to purchase a minimum of 20,000 BTGs per month. ISKCON was at that time selling only 500 copies a month. On February 15, 1969 Śrīla Prabhupāda wrote Rāyarāma a letter revealing his plan for a wider distribution of BTG:

> I can induce Los Angeles to pay $750, and we can deliver them 5,000 copies of *Back to Godhead.* Similarly, if San Francisco contributes $750 we can deliver them 5,000 copies. So far as Los Angeles and San Francisco are concerned, I can ask the boys to work and pay $750 positively every month. Similarly, if New York is agreed to work and pay $750, then the whole question is solved, and we can print 20,000 copies immediately from Dai Nippon. I do not know if it is practical, but to my mind, if New York, San Francisco, and Los Angeles agree to pay $750 each month, there is no problem.

After extensive correspondence between Śrīla Prabhupāda, Brahmānanda, and Dai Nippon, Śrīla Prabhupāda finally contracted with Dai Nippon to print his TLC as well as BTG. As per his plan, he asked each ISKCON center to submit a fixed amount of money to a BTG printing fund. In return, the temples received a proportionate number of BTGs, which they could give away or sell as they wished. Brahmānanda was responsible for collecting the money from each temple and paying Dai Nippon each month. The cost? $3,000 for 20,000 BTGs. This continued throughout 1969.

Even after Śrīla Prabhupāda signed with Dai Nippon, though, he continued to think about how to set up an ISKCON press in order to print less expensively and more efficiently. And it didn't take long for him to become slightly disenchanted with Dai Nippon, because they took longer than promised to deliver the TLC.

On March 16, 1969, Śrīla Prabhupāda wrote to Advaita Dāsa:

> My Dear Advaita,
>
> Please accept my blessings. I thank you very much for your letter of March 6, 1969, and I am so glad to know that you are feeling the Lord's mercy being given your engagement of printing Kṛṣṇa consciousness propaganda literature. I think we shall have to open the press immediately because the business transaction with Dai Nippon is not very prospective. If we have our own press we become completely independent in

> the matter of printing. The difficulty of printing in your country has increased on account of higher wages of the workers. But as we are now training our own men, I think we shall be able to print our books and magazines in lesser cost than in Japan. Now the practical experience is that for printing one book, TLC, this Dai Nippon has delayed so much. So I do not find any good prospect of printing our books in the Dai Nippon. So if you are confident our press can now be successfully run; if you are confident that now you can conduct our press, just to print our books and magazines with the help of your other godbrothers, just try to think over the matter very seriously. And when we meet together next in April, we shall finally decide about this. If we have got our own press then we shall print at least four books yearly, and 50,000 magazines every month. Then you will have ample opportunity for printing Kṛṣṇa consciousness literature. So we have now fully equipped staff, editorial, printers, binders, and managers, and Kṛṣṇa will be financier. So I think there is no more scarcity of anything and let us begin the job as soon as possible. You just consult amongst your godbrothers and I shall be glad to know how much money you can spare for the purchase of a nice press and other equipments.

On March 19, 1969, Śrīla Prabhupāda wrote to Brahmānanda with even more energy for ISKCON to start its own press: "Regarding Macmillan Company, if they have not replied your letter, then forget. We shall publish our own books. You organize the sales promotion. Neither I want to shorten the *Śrīmad-Bhāgavatam.* We should not count on them – let us try for our own publications."

And yet again, on March 20, 1969, Śrīla Prabhupāda wrote to Rāyarāma about ISKCON establishing its own press:

> I would have immediately developed a colony for press operation, but unfortunately there is no facility for conducting a press here at present. But so far I can think, your editorial staff must be situated where we have got our own press. I do not know whether it is Kṛṣṇa's desire that we should start our

> press immediately – but the circumstances give me to understand that we must start our press immediately. Because the negotiations with Dai Nippon are very much prolonging. I am thinking very seriously if we can print the 20,000 or more copies of BTG in our own press, as well as at least 4 books (the size of my *Śrīmad-Bhāgavatam*) in a year. That should be our future program, backed by our *saṅkīrtana* parties moving all over the world.

With ISKCON's own press in mind, Śrīla Prabhupāda put out the word that he would stay wherever the devotees were able to purchase a building that could house a press and publishing crew. Immediately devotees all over North America began looking for a building to house a full-scale press. In anticipation of their success, Śrīla Prabhupāda told several devotees – Vaikuṇṭhanātha, Patita Pāvana, Uddhava, and Advaita – to learn the publishing trade, including typesetting, binding, folding, and printing. He encouraged these devotees to find apprenticeships in the printing industry so they could learn the skills they would need to run the press machines when they arrived.

ISKCON Boston was the first to successfully purchase a house, on North Beacon Street, and Śrīla Prabhupāda asked the devotees connected with publishing to move there. To pay for the printing equipment he had devotees across North America pool the money they had collected to buy their own press houses in their areas. Tamal Krishna, for example, had collected $5,000 in Los Angeles in hopes of drawing Śrīla Prabhupāda out there with his own press house. But when the Boston devotees found their house first, Tamal Krishna gave that $5,000 to help finance the press in Boston. Those whom Śrīla Prabhupāda had asked to find apprenticeships also turned over their earnings, and then Śrīla Prabhupāda put in money from his own bank account. By pooling all these resources, Śrīla Prabhupāda was able to start ISKCON Press.

That all this happened at a time when money was tight in

ISKCON sheds light on Śrīla Prabhupāda's priorities. He had come to America intending to print his books and was ready to put all of his resources into it. His spiritual master had told him, "If you ever get money, print books." He was following this instruction to the letter.

But How Will We Sell These Books?

With the new TLCs finally on their way to America from Dai Nippon, Śrīla Prabhupāda began thinking of ways to market them. In a letter to Brahmānanda (May 6, 1969) he wrote:

> There are about 1,000 stores in New York at least. So if they take 3 copies each, we immediately distribute 3,000 copies. Similarly, in the other big cities we can distribute at least 1,000 in each city. There are at least 25 important cities in your country so in each city, if we distribute at least 1,000 copies there is potency of distributing 25,000 copies in your country only, what to speak of other countries, like England or any other part of the world where English is spoken. So it requires only organization.

Brahmānanda recounts how he and other devotees during ISKCON's early days carried out Śrīla Prabhupāda's request to organize the sales of his books and magazines:

> When the shipment of *Bhagavad-gītās* arrived from Macmillan, I sent pallets to the temples in Los Angeles, San Francisco, Montreal, Buffalo, Seattle, Santa Fe, Boston, and London, and I personally sold copies to various bookstores in New York; and when the TLC arrived we did the same. At that time there was no street distribution of books, only BTGs. The only exception was that in 1966 Gargamuni had sold a few sets of Śrīla Prabhupāda's Delhi edition of *Śrīmad-Bhāgavatam* and several *Easy Journey to Other Planets* from a mobile bookstand he had constructed and wheeled around the West and East Village in New York City. Śrīla Prabhupāda named Gargamuni's invention, "Kṛṣṇa's Chariot."

With book printing starting to happen, Śrīla Prabhupāda turned his attention more and more to distribution. He wrote to Brahmānanda on February 17, 1969:

> So you and Gargamuni take charge of distributing the books, and you study other methods of how to do this. If distribution of my books is fixed up then my life is fixed up in your country for the remaining days of my present body. Please therefore do it seriously. I am pleased that you are willing to take charge of the printing of my books. Kṛṣṇa has desired like that, so you try to execute this implicit order of Kṛṣṇa. Actually, by your grace, these two publications are already in the light, so your service in this connection is approved by Kṛṣṇa and naturally by me also.

Śrīla Prabhupāda's initial plan to sell 20,000 Dai Nippon BTGs to the ISKCON temples wasn't practical for a number of the temples. Many of the temples, try as they might, regularly fell behind in paying their portions to the BTG fund. Svarūpa Dāsa, Brahmānanda's secretary at that time, recalls that most ISKCON temples in North America were struggling just to pay the rent. "Collecting their dues for the BTG was tough," Svarūpa says, "what to speak of our keeping track of the accounts and shipping the BTGs to ISKCON centers in America and Canada, and paying Dai Nippon in a timely manner."

Informed of these shortfalls, Śrīla Prabhupāda wrote letters to ISKCON leaders reiterating his instruction that they must send their monthly payments to Brahmānanda so ISKCON could keep its commitment to Dai Nippon. ISKCON had yet to master the art of book and magazine sales, however, so despite Śrīla Prabhupāda's urging, the devotees continued to default on their monthly remittances.

Kṛṣṇa Book Is Published

At the beginning of 1969, Śrīla Prabhupāda decided to summarize the Tenth Canto of *Śrīmad-Bhāgavatam*. Concerned about his age and health, and determined that the people of the world hear about Kṛṣṇa's pastimes and see His beautiful form, Śrīla Prabhupāda suspended his work on the *Bhāgavatam's* Third Canto and gave his full attention to *Kṛṣṇa, The Supreme Personality of Godhead,* a book that would include fifty color reproductions of original paintings depicting Kṛṣṇa pastimes. Śrīla Prabhupāda assembled the artists in Boston along with the devotees trained in presswork, then patiently and lovingly guided the artists, empowering them to paint, one by one, the pastimes of Kṛṣṇa. The building that housed ISKCON Press in Boston wasn't well heated, and Boston winters can be brutal, but still, the press workers toiled unceasingly.

As Śrīla Prabhupāda spoke the *Kṛṣṇa Book* into his dictating machine and instructed his artists how to illustrate the book, devotees throughout ISKCON slowly began to learn about more of Kṛṣṇa's pastimes. Hearing of many of these pastimes for the first time, the devotees became spellbound.

By the time Śrīla Prabhupāda's *Kṛṣṇa Book* manuscript was ready, at the end of 1969, for layout and then printing, ISKCON's BTG account at Dai Nippon was deeply in arrears. Dai Nippon refused to print the *Kṛṣṇa Book* on credit. So Śrīla Prabhupāda contacted Śyāmasundara in London and asked him to approach George Harrison for a donation of $18,000 to pay the printing costs. Śyāmasundara was worried that asking George for money would spoil their relationship, but because the request had come from Śrīla Prabhupāda himself Śyāmasundara dutifully asked George what he thought. George was inspired by the project, and wrote out a check. With Śyāmasundara's coaching, he also wrote a short foreword to the book, making the book irresistible to young people of his generation. The payment arranged, Dai Nippon printed *Kṛṣṇa Book* by March 1970.

At that same time, Śrīla Prabhupāda also skillfully negotiated with Dai Nippon a separation between ISKCON's BTG account and its book printing account. The Dai Nippon executives accepted this agreement, and did not use any of the *Kṛṣṇa Book* money to pay off ISKCON's delinquent BTG account.

Eventually, ISKCON Press moved from Boston's North Beacon Street house to New York because Advaita found a two-story building that would be perfect for ISKCON's printing operations on Brooklyn's Tiffany Place, only four blocks from the Henry Street ISKCON temple. In New York the devotees purchased more press equipment.

Still, printing big books at ISKCON Press was proving more trouble than it was worth. Binding was a difficult skill to master. For instance, when the Press was still in Boston, the devotees had bound the first printing of *The Nectar of Devotion,* but it had fallen apart. Their skills at binding were not easy to improve after the Press moved, and there were other technical challenges. Clearly, both Dai Nippon and Macmillan produced a superior product at a price ISKCON could now afford. Hence, a year after moving to Tiffany Place, with Śrīla Prabhupāda's approval and guidance, the ISKCON Press team abandoned printing and concentrated solely on the prepress work for his books.

Books Arrive in Waves

After the 1968 *Bhagavad-gītā As It Is* was printed by Macmillan Company in 1969, Śrīla Prabhupāda released *Teachings of Lord Caitanya,* printed at Dai Nippon. These books, along with the monthly print run of 20,000 BTGs, were the beginning of an explosion in both the printing and distribution of Śrīla Prabhupāda's books. ISKCON Press published *Kṛṣṇa Consciousness: The Topmost Yoga System, Śrī Īśopaniṣad, The Nectar of Devotion,* and an updated edition of *Easy Journey to Other Planets.* The first volume of *Kṛṣṇa, the Supreme Personality of Godhead* (chapters 1–37) was also printed around this time.

In 1971, ISKCON prepared the manuscript and Dai

Nippon printed the second volume of *Kṛṣṇa Book* (chapters 38–90). Then, after officially forming the Bhaktivedanta Book Trust (BBT) in 1972, Śrīla Prabhupāda published the unabridged edition of his *Bhagavad-gītā As It Is* with the Macmillan Company. Other books followed – the first three cantos of *Śrīmad-Bhāgavatam, Kṛṣṇa Consciousness: The Topmost Yoga System* (1972), *On the Way to Kṛṣṇa* (1973), *Rāja-vidyā: The King of Knowledge* (1973), *Elevation to Kṛṣṇa Consciousness* (1973), *Śrīmad-Bhāgavatam*, cantos Four through Nine (1974–1977), *Śrī Caitanya-caritāmṛta* (1975), *The Nectar of Instruction* (1975), *Perfect Questions, Perfect Answers* (1977), *Teachings of Lord Kapila* (1977), and *The Science of Self-Realization* (1977) – altogether, sixty-four volumes.

These new books arrived in waves in the US, Canada, India, the UK, South Africa, and Europe, and Śrīla Prabhupāda encouraged his young disciples to read them, and also enlightened them about the spiritual value of distributing them. He expressed this in a letter to Kulaśekhara Dāsa, written on January 10, 1972:

> I am glad to hear that you are distributing nicely books and magazines. The more we sell books, the more we advance in Kṛṣṇa consciousness, and the more we help others to have solid information how they may take advantage of their human form of life and achieve the supreme perfection. So I want that you should now increase very greatly this selling of books and literatures.

Free from Errors

To assure that *Kṛṣṇa Book* would be of the topmost quality, Śrīla Prabhupāda sent Brahmānanda to Japan to oversee the printing at Dai Nippon. Brahmānanda spent three months in Tokyo, daily visiting Dai Nippon to oversee the book's design and layout and to check galley proofs.

As Śrīla Prabhupāda urged his disciples to increase the distribution of his books, he also guided them on how to improve the quality of their editing and prepress. And after the first shipments of *Kṛṣṇa Book* were dispatched, Śrīla Prabhupāda continued to write more books – persistently trying to improve the quality of each. He had already engaged a team of editors to improve the text, asking them from the beginning to make "grammatical correction, and phrasing for force and clarity."[2] He also worked further with the artists, recruiting more of his disciples for this service and teaching them either directly or through those he had already taught how to paint transcendental scenes depicting Kṛṣṇa's pastimes or philosophical points from the books.

On June 21, 1970, Śrīla Prabhupāda's senior Sanskrit editor, Pradyumna Dāsa, passed on an order, just conveyed to him by His Divine Grace, to editing teammate Jayādvaita Dāsa, by way of this memo:

> Prabhupāda said that if there is one mistake in one book, then you spoil the whole book. Murder the whole book. So also besides Sanskrit errors, there have been many, many English errors also, which are very obvious, just like these two abovementioned errors. So Prabhupāda has been emphasizing lately about the great need for making our books free from errors. "What's done has been done," but now we should try to do two things: make sure that errors like these won't occur again, and start a listing of past mistakes in each book so that we can correct them when they are reprinted. Concerning these two Sanskrit errors, one was not noted down before the new reprint was made. I think there should be a blueprint made of each book before it goes to press because then the editors will know for sure that there weren't any errors made in layout or that something fell off.

From that time on, under Śrīla Prabhupāda's guidance, Pradyumna collected errors reported by the devotees and kept them in a book for correcting in future editions.

Kṛṣṇa Book Saves the Day

Throughout Brahmānanda's stay in Tokyo, the executives at Dai Nippon kept telling him that they couldn't guarantee him advance copies before his scheduled return to America. Sure enough, the day before his flight, Dai Nippon confirmed that they could not give him even one advance copy to take back.

But just as he was climbing the airstairs at the Tokyo airport to board his San Francisco-bound flight, several Dai Nippon limousines, one carrying a top executive from the firm, pulled up on the tarmac to deliver one carton of the newly printed *Kṛṣṇa Book*. With dramatic flair, and the plane's passengers looking on from their windows, the carton of books was handed over to Brahmānanda. Brahmānanda opened the case of twenty-four newly printed books during the flight and sold one to the businessman sitting next to him.

When Brahmānanda arrived in San Francisco and showed Śrīla Prabhupāda the books, Śrīla Prabhupāda was especially pleased to hear how Brahmānanda had sold a copy on the plane. Brahmānanda remembers how Śrīla Prabhupāda then gave the carton to Gargamuni to distribute at the Ratha-yātrā:

> He gave the books over to Gargamuni, who had set up a book table. As Gargamuni got up to leave with the carton, Śrīla Prabhupāda said, "This one also." And he handed over his personal copy lying on his desk. We were stunned. Śrīla Prabhupāda had just expressed so much satisfaction in receiving this gorgeous production, but instead of relishing his own copy, he was more satisfied to have it distributed to the public. The books were quickly snapped up from the tables; the debut of the *Kṛṣṇa Books* was the sensation of the festival. It was a marvelous book launching.

A few months later, Dai Nippon dispatched to India and America huge shipments of *Kṛṣṇa Books*. Cāṇakya Paṇḍita writes that debt, fire, and disease are so dangerous that they must be attended to immediately. As it turns out, just as Lord Kṛṣṇa had saved His friends in Vṛndāvana by swallowing a forest fire, He was now appearing in ISKCON in the form of the *Kṛṣṇa Book* to save His devotees from the fire of their debts and to raise Śrīla Prabhupāda's Society to heights no one could have imagined.

CHAPTER FIVE

The Rest Is History

WHEN THE PALLETS containing thousands of shiny new hardbound copies of *Kṛṣṇa, the Supreme Personality of Godhead* arrived from Japan, the devotees who received them wondered how they would sell so many big books. They had been selling BTG for twenty-five cents; they would have to sell the new hardbound *Kṛṣṇa Book* for eight dollars.

Although the devotees in San Francisco were struggling with this thought, Keśava Dāsa, their temple president, kept a team of distributors, who were selling record numbers of BTGs around the Bay Area, going out. About nine months after Dai Nippon shipped the *Kṛṣṇa Books,* the San Francisco temple ran out of BTGs and began to go broke – a condition shared by a number of ISKCON temples at that time. Keśava Dāsa, desperate to keep the temple open, purchased some begging bowls from a local Buddhist shop along with a quantity of incense. He handed these out to the temple devotees and asked them to give the incense to people while they were out on *harināma* to help increase the collections.

Meanwhile, the new *Kṛṣṇa Books* were sitting in the basement of the San Francisco temple. Keśava had stockpiled the dozens of cases that had been sent to San Francisco by his brother Karandhara Dāsa, the temple president of ISKCON Los Angeles. Karandhara had received and warehoused the huge shipment of books sent by Brahmānanda from Japan and had sent portions of them to various temples, including to his brother in San Francisco. But the books simply sat in the basement because no one could imagine how to sell them.

As fire purifies gold, however, the intense heat created by the devotees' desire to distribute the new *Kṛṣṇa Books* fire4d their urgency to increase collections and purified their intelligence. Thus, one day a breakthrough idea came to Premārṇava Dāsa and Buddhimanta Dāsa. On their way home from a *harināma* party, they stopped at a gas station to refuel the temple van. When the time came to pay, they brought out a *Kṛṣṇa Book* and showed it to the attendant.

As the two devotees enthusiastically told the man about the book, they noticed he was actually interested. Gathering their courage, they suggested to the attendant that he take the book instead of cash in payment for the gas, and he agreed.

The very next day, inspired by their unexpected success, the spirited Buddhimanta asked Keśava for permission to take out some *Kṛṣṇa Books* to sell on the street. According to Jāmbavān Dāsa, one of the temple residents at the time, Keśava allowed Buddhimanta to do so, but was doubtful he could succeed. Buddhimanta came back to the temple beaming, however. He had sold three *Kṛṣṇa Books*! The next day, he sold another five.

Soon Buddhimanta, Premārṇava, Viśvareta, Jāmbavān, Yogeścandra, Trai Dāsa, and other members of the crack San Francisco BTG distribution party set out in a converted school bus across the northwest United States. They traveled town to town, going door to door, presenting *Kṛṣṇa Book*. They used the same systematic discipline they were using to sell BTGs to now sell scores of *Kṛṣṇa Books,* with Buddhimanta setting the pace. An elated Keśava wrote to Śrīla Prabhupāda to tell him about this breakthrough, and Śrīla Prabhupāda replied on January 1, 1972:

> I have been receiving so many reports about how my disciples of the San Francisco Temple cannot be surpassed by anyone in distributing my books. Sometimes they are selling as many as 70 Kṛṣṇa Books daily. So if this is true then certainly when I return to the US I must come and stay in your Temple. By distributing my books profusely you are giving me great encouragement to translate. And you are all helping me to fulfill the order, which Guru Mahārāja gave me. So I am so much grateful to you, and I am sure Kṛṣṇa will bless you a million times over, for doing this work.

Keśava read Śrīla Prabhupāda's letter to all the devotees in the San Francisco temple during the morning *Bhāgavatam* class. He emphasized how Śrīla Prabhupāda was especially pleased when his big books were distributed in mass quantities. Word got out about this letter and a fire to distribute books was ignited in devotees' hearts that spread throughout ISKCON.

Śrīla Prabhupāda's prolific writing, publishing, and frequent entreaties to his disciples to distribute his books built a momentum that eventually resulted in a powerful reaction among his followers who wanted to help him with his mission. The distribution of big books began slowly at first, but inspired by each new success, more and more devotees went out to distribute them. As the success stories made their way around the world, the results steadily grew until finally there was a veritable epidemic. The devotees practically went mad to distribute *Kṛṣṇa Book.*

Fortune Favors the Bold

Here's what happened to one of the devotees who caught the fever. At nearly the same time the San Francisco devotees were having their breakthrough in 1971, Mahātmā Dāsa, temple president of ISKCON Vancouver, was constantly meditating on how his *saṅkīrtana* team might distribute the volumes of *Kṛṣṇa Book* stored at *his* temple. Even for a natural innovator like Mahātmā, the idea of selling *Kṛṣṇa Book* to the Canadian public seemed a stretch. Until that time in November of 1971, no one in his community or anywhere else, as far as he knew, had ever done it.

Mahātmā and the Vancouver devotees, like ISKCON devotees elsewhere, had grown accustomed to selling BTGs for a quarter. They had also sold a smattering of *Easy Journey to Other Planets* for fifty cents, which at the time seemed like a lot to ask from the public. Getting *Kṛṣṇa Book* out of storage and into the hands of the Canadians would be a challenge for sure.

But Mahātmā's penchant for thinking big was strong, and his desire to please Śrīla Prabhupāda even stronger. These two urges were enough to overcome whatever hesitancy he felt, so on Thanksgiving Day 1971 he asked his team of six *saṅkīrtana* devotees to take some *Kṛṣṇa Books* out with them along with their usual BTGs. His team members thought the prospect of anyone buying a hardbound book was remote, but they all agreed that it wouldn't hurt to try. As Virgil once said, "Fortune favors the bold."

Calling fortune near, Mahātmā's team of twenty-something-year-olds boldly drove away from the temple that Thanksgiving Day with *Kṛṣṇa Books* alongside their BTGs in their cloth *saṅkīrtana* bags. Mahātmā wanted to inspire the devotees to aim high. Invoking the Bengali proverb Śrīla Prabhupāda often used to inspire his disciples to do something wonderful, Mahātmā called out, "Shoot for the rhinoceros!" And off they went.

Leap, and the Net Will Appear

To succeed in any venture, one must have the grit to begin. Naturalist John Burroughs encourages us to "Leap, and the net will appear." Spontaneously, both the Vancouver and San Francisco devotees had applied this secret of success: they had dared to execute the order of their guru. What better way to please the Supreme Lord Kṛṣṇa, who says to His *brāhmaṇa* friend Sudāmā, "I, the Soul of all beings, am not as satisfied by ritual worship, brahminical initiation, penances or self-discipline as I am by faithful service rendered to one's spiritual master."[1]

Śrīla Prabhupāda asked his novice followers to distribute his books, and they found the way forward by bravely jumping in and trying. Without a handbook or someone else's example to follow, with only their fixed determination to apply the order of their spiritual master, these youngsters took up a practical service, the process that would eventually allow them to see Kṛṣṇa face to face. Śrīla Prabhupāda had taught them, "Instead of being eager to see the Lord in some bush of Vṛndāvana while at the same time engaging in sense gratification, if one instead sticks to the principle of following the words of the spiritual master, he will see the Supreme Lord without difficulty."[2]

True, Mahātmā's team members, and others like them around the world, were being showered with profound spiritual benefit; but they were themselves creating a soothing rain of transcendental literature to descend on the dry, thirsty hearts of the world's inhabitants. Willing to take up what their spiritual master had asked them to do, they became spiritually intoxicated and felt the guiding touch of Kṛṣṇa's lotus hand.

While going door to door to distribute BTGs that Thanksgiving Day, Mahātmā's crew methodically showed the hardbound *Kṛṣṇa Book* alongside the BTG. Thinking it improbable that a stranger would agree to buy such an expensive religious book, they tried nonetheless. As expected, there were no takers – or so most of them thought.

At the end of the day, as the members of Mahātmā's team made their way back to the *saṅkīrtana* van, one of the devotees excitedly blurted out, "I had a major unforeseen accident!"

They were puzzled by his outburst until he shouted, "I sold a *Kṛṣṇa Book*!"

Mahātmā remembers:

> When we heard this, we were in total shock. Our whole world was turned upside down. All the devotees went crazy and were banging on the walls of the *saṅkīrtana* van, laughing and yelling and pouring congratulations on the first devotee on our team to sell a *Kṛṣṇa Book* outside the temple. We sensed that the impossible had just happened and that this was something big. It was a breakthrough for ISKCON.

A Life-Changing Expedition

A serendipitous event occurred the very next day. Haridāsa Ṭhākura Dāsa, a stalwart from the San Francisco book distribution team, arrived in Vancouver just in time to join Mahātmā and his team for their next adventure: their first *saṅkīrtana* road trip – a journey that would take them from Vancouver on a life-changing expedition to Edmonton, over seven hundred miles away.

Haridāsa Ṭhākura carried a secret in his heart: he had been at a temple where the devotees were already distributing big books both on the street and door to door. In fact, he had done it himself in San Francisco and was ready to do more. In my interview with Haridāsa Ṭhākura, he remembers:

> Those early days in 1971, we were all about distributing BTGs. BTG was not a newsstand magazine like *Time* or *Newsweek*. Rather, BTG gave the reader the spiritual world for just twenty-five cents. We'd go out in the morning to distribute BTGs, and at the end of the day we'd carefully count up to see which temple had done more, Berkeley or San Francisco. So you see, transcendental competition was alive and well even back then.
>
> As all the old devotees will tell you, Śrīla Prabhupāda required us to read from four different *śāstras* each day, and this made the devotees very attracted and attached to *śāstra*. It was

unheard of for any devotee to miss any of these classes. If you stayed in the temple, you attended these *śāstra* classes. We'd read *Kṛṣṇa Book* before taking rest at night, and by simply listening we felt that liquid honey was being poured on our souls. In the morning we held *Śrīmad-Bhāgavatam* class with commentary from one of the devotees, and then after the evening *ārati,* we'd have a *Bhagavad-gītā* class followed by a reading of *The Nectar of Devotion.*

So, from all the hearing at the temple, I was making some good progress in bhakti-yoga. As devotees might say, I was "fired up." One Friday, a beautiful spring night in April 1971, our leaders told us that we would be going door to door to distribute magazines. So after the evening *ārati* we all loaded into the temple van and drove off into the welcoming San Francisco night. That night, I had brought along my personal big books, a *Kṛṣṇa Book* and a *Bhagavad-gītā As It Is.*

Suddenly our driver let us all off in one of these typical San Francisco neighborhoods lined with brownstones, and said, "See you later!"

I remember knocking on one door and a couple answered – a young man and his girlfriend – and they kindly let me in. In talking to them, I went from calm to nuts and began saying, "You see this book?" pointing to the big silver *Kṛṣṇa Book.* "This book will prevent you from getting any serious disease and will make you wildly happy." I kept going on and on and on about the beautiful *Kṛṣṇa Book.* I thought, "This is my chance to really please Lord Kṛṣṇa and make two devotees right here and now!"

I must have talked, ranted, and raved for twelve minutes straight. At the end of it all, the two of them were sitting at the end of their couch clutching each other and looking at me with their mouths open. Suddenly I heard the man say, in a soft but determined voice: "Well, how much do you want for the big silver book?" I said, "How about ten dollars?" They gave it!

Soon I left for the next apartment in another building and the same thing happened! Only this time I sold my personal copy of the Macmillan softcover *Bhagavad-gītā.* In both apartments the people had been very pleased with their purchases. I walked back to meet the other devotees, feeling that Lord

> Kṛṣṇa was slapping me on the back the whole way, saying, "Way to go, Dāsa! Way to go!"
>
> When I finally returned to the *saṅkīrtana* van and told the devotees that I had sold two books, at first they thought I meant that I had sold two magazines. So, they said, "So what?" But when I explained how I had sold two *big* books, they all cheered.

Haridāsa's joining Mahātmā's team in Vancouver after his San Francisco epiphany was Kṛṣṇa's arrangement, the kind of special arrangement He makes for His devotees when they apply the order of their spiritual master. And now, setting off together into the Canadian countryside, the group was about to witness an even bigger breakthrough in book distribution.

Depending on Kṛṣṇa Totally

Mahātmā describes how the next breakthrough took place:

> We had received a letter from Śyāmasundara, Prabhupāda's secretary at the time, quoting Śrīla Prabhupāda as saying that "for anyone who goes anywhere and everywhere to preach without caring about where they stay or how they will eat or sleep, I take the dust from their feet and place it on my head."
>
> Prabhupāda's statement sparked a revolution in our hearts and we became determined to do something to put ourselves on the line. In fact, we nearly went crazy. We loaded our van with books and magazines and drove in the middle of winter through Canada with just some uncooked rice and *dāl,* with no money and without knowing where we would stay or how we would get gas for the van. But we were ecstatic because we were totally depending on Kṛṣṇa.
>
> We had never traveled town to town selling magazines before. And now we also brought along big books. We were going to new cities where no one knew us. We felt like pioneers. We were the first ones there. We were so young and we felt unqualified, so we just tried.

> We knew that it was at least possible to sell a big book to a stranger, and when Haridāsa Ṭhākura showed up and joined our traveling party, he broke the big book distribution wide open.
>
> We hit the road out of Vancouver in the late afternoon and arrived at some small town at eight in the evening. Not knowing exactly what to do, we just did *harināma* on the street there, because that is what we were used to doing. The problem was, it was winter and nobody was on the street except for the town drunk.
>
> As our chanting party started to sing on that empty street, Haridāsa Ṭhākura approached the drunk and began showing him the *Kṛṣṇa Book*. The rest of us watched Haridāsa, thinking that his attempt was ridiculous. But Haridāsa enthusiastically continued, talking away, showing this drunk every single picture in the *Kṛṣṇa Book*.

A First Big Book on the Street

Suddenly, to the amazement of Mahātmā and the other devotees, the drunk began to rummage through his pockets (which took him a while). Finally, he pulled out eight dollars and gave it to Haridāsa Ṭhākura for the book. No one had ever seen a book sold during *harināma* before, and now, amazingly, Haridāsa Ṭhākura had sold one to the only person on the street – the local drunk – and during a winter storm.

Mahātmā recalls:

> This event set the mood for the rest of the trip. The devotees now felt that they could distribute a *Kṛṣṇa Book* to anyone, anywhere, at anytime.
>
> But that night, as the euphoria wore off, we suddenly realized that it was late, it was freezing cold, and we had no place to stay. We drove around town looking for a place, and by Kṛṣṇa's grace we found a hostel. When we knocked on the door, a man welcomed us in and gave us our own quarters with a private bath. It looked like an ideal *brahmacārī āśrama,* and we had it all to ourselves. "Okay," we thought, "this depending on Kṛṣṇa stuff really works."

I'm Just Doing It

Mahātmā tells how during the rest of the journey Haridāsa Ṭhākura continued to set the pace for selling big books while the rest of the devotees were still trying to figure out how to do it:

> Sometimes, after breakfast, while we were still getting ready to go out on *saṅkīrtana,* Haridāsa Ṭhākura would run out the door for fifteen minutes, go door to door and come back, having sold a few books. As we were getting ready for bed he'd often do the same thing.
>
> When we asked him, "Haridāsa, what are you telling them?" He'd say, "I'm telling them that I'm in ecstasy!" Other times he'd say, "I don't know, I'm just doing it!" We soon understood that he was selling so many books due to his internal fire.
>
> Because of Haridāsa Ṭhākura's zeal, everyone on our traveling team started selling big books. As we did we became like people who had gambled for the first time and won big money. We all felt like this. As we went door to door to sell big books, we completely lost track of time. I remember that after I sold my first *Kṛṣṇa Book* I got lost and couldn't find my way back to the van because I felt so intoxicated with happiness. I was so excited that it was going on.
>
> On our traveling party our anticipation was so great – that someone else might take a book – we became completely absorbed. Anyone who was breathing became a good prospect. Most of the time we felt, "How can we go back?" So we'd knock on just one more door, until it became late. Even then, I remember the devotees, while driving back after a long day, seeing a person on the street and saying, "Let's stop. He might take a book."
>
> We thought, "This is exciting, and the whole movement needs to know about it." We were also excited to tell Śrīla Prabhupāda, which we did, and he wrote back to us: "An advanced devotee takes every opportunity to spread Kṛṣṇa consciousness."
>
> We never thought, "We need qualification to do this." We just did it. Only afterwards would we think, "Did we do this right?"

As the Vancouver devotees were trekking across Canada, selling their first big books, Śrīla Prabhupāda consistently wrote letters like this to his leaders:

> But even more important than the knowledge of Kṛṣṇa is the acting upon that knowledge, or devotional service. By the acting he realizes his knowledge and becomes complete. So I am very much encouraged that all you young boys and girls are working so hard to please Kṛṣṇa, and even I cannot give you any nice thing, still, because you have got some love for Kṛṣṇa and your Spiritual Master, therefore you have given up everything for selling books door to door and working very hard in every way just to push on this movement. For your sincere helping me I thank you all very very much.[3]

A Meteoric Rise

Following Śrīla Prabhupāda's directives, the devotees wanted to sell more and more books. No longer satisfied with what they now considered sporadic success, they began to organize and systematically sell larger quantities of books. In Los Angeles, for example, an enthusiastic new leader, Rāmeśvara Dāsa, went on to become Śrīla Prabhupāda's leading commander in organizing the advance of book distribution that would soon sweep the world.

Organization Begins

Rāmeśvara Dāsa recalls the immediate progress that came from better organizing the book distribution:

> The rise of book distribution was meteoric. From the early days in 1971, the first discovery and pioneering, to the accidental discovery of the Christmas marathon at the end of 1972, the enthusiasm and the inspiration was there, but the large-scale distribution did not begin until 1973. From the humble beginnings of ISKCON Press until 1972, when the BBT was first

formed, the income to the book and magazine funds, which were soon to be the BBT, grew from $50,000 up to $300,000 per year. But after the 1972 Christmas marathon there was a quantum leap, and throughout 1973, the BBT sold more than 4,100,000 pieces of literature for over $1,000,000, a tenfold increase. And thus the pattern was set.

In 1970, the daily life of a devotee consisted of going to the morning program, which had just been introduced by Śrīla Prabhupāda, eating a sumptuous *prasāda* breakfast, and then going out with the chanting party for the next six to eight hours, usually to one of the city's busiest downtown areas. Someone would bring *prasāda* to the chanters for lunch. In between chanting, the devotees would read among themselves from Śrīla Prabhupāda's books, and during the chanting they would distribute BTGs whenever a crowd formed to watch them. They returned to the temple for *Bhagavad-gītā* class, and to go to sleep.

But with the beginning of door-to-door book distribution in 1971 the pattern began to change. There was a new concept of *saṅkīrtana* and a new position called *saṅkīrtana* leader. We'd send out four or five cars with three devotees in each car. Gradually book distribution expanded from door to door to shopping centers, and from there to state fairs, concerts, malls, and airports. With this expansion the *saṅkīrtana* leader's job became more and more demanding and sophisticated. He had to purchase and maintain a whole fleet of vehicles, direct his *saṅkīrtana* party, keep track of inventory, and plot areas of the city where distributors could go. It became a part of temple life that when new devotees joined, as soon as possible after they were trained and had become a little steady, they would go out with one of the book distribution parties.

In 1972, Karandhara, the GBC of the western US, established this system in every temple in his zone. Keśava, the temple president of San Francisco, Bhakta Dāsa, the temple president of San Diego, Mahātmā Dāsa, temple president of Vancouver, and devotees in New York and elsewhere established traveling parties. Soon temples everywhere in America had them. *Brahmacārīs* would be sleeping in vans just to get away from the temple atmosphere, where the sense of urgency and the priority of distributing books was not universally felt.

Karandhara knew the importance of book distribution and therefore facilitated us and let us freely organize *saṅkīrtana*. As Karandhara gave us a free rein in 1973, we sent our best book distributor, Tripurāri, to New York and then Chicago to teach the art of book distribution. This had a tremendous influence on the whole Society. After being informed of this plan, Śrīla Prabhupāda wrote back:

> I approve your program of sending out your best men to train others, this is the process of Kṛṣṇa consciousness. Do it so that every devotee in this movement learns the art of distributing my books.

When this letter made its way around ISKCON, many temples lined up to have devotees come and train their members in the art of book distribution. Śrīla Prabhupāda's instruction endorsed a whole new era in our movement. We were transplanting all of the ideas, techniques, and systems developed on the West Coast to the other regions of America by sending out representatives all over North America as well as Europe, Australia, Mexico, and South America. It was taking on the shape of a very mature and sophisticated expansion, a transcendental version of a giant company springing to life and opening franchises all over the world.

In the pre-computer, pre-social-media world, devotees would read the BBT monthly newsletter. The newsletter started with Śyāmasundara's reports about Śrīla Prabhupāda's travels and instructions. After this Karandhara started the BBT newsletter; and in 1972, he handed the task over to me. In the newsletters, we were including quotes from Śrīla Prabhupāda's letters to devotees about book distribution. It had a huge impact.

On a personal note, I joined the Kṛṣṇa consciousness movement just as this "springing to life" was taking hold. The intensity of the devotees' desire to please Śrīla Prabhupāda by increasing book distribution created a sense of mission that energized ISKCON communities everywhere. The atmosphere was electrified.

Rāmeśvara remembers:

We had all known for some time that Śrīla Prabhupāda's main work was to translate, print, and distribute his books. And the conception in the Society had been that the magazine, *Back to Godhead,* could be distributed on the street chanting party, the *harināma saṅkīrtana* party, but that books were mostly sold through bookstores or to libraries or colleges. So the only book distribution that had been going on in those early days – 1969 through 1970 – was the type of *saṅkīrtana* in which one person was designated in the temple to make appointments and visit libraries and bookstores. No one had thought that you could take a book out on the street the way you take *Back to Godhead* out. So this was going on for a couple of years. Actually, my service during the first year and a half I was in the temple was to organize this type of book distribution.

I began working with Karandhara in 1971, but my direct correspondence with Śrīla Prabhupāda and his personal training for BBT work began immediately after the first book distribution Christmas marathon of 1972. After that marathon His Divine Grace wrote:

> So I am so much pleased upon all of the boys and girls in Los Angeles and all over the world who are understanding and appreciating this unique quality of our transcendental literature and voluntarily they are going out to distribute despite all circumstances of difficulty. By this effort alone they are assured to go back to home, back to Godhead.[4]

"The Only Solace in My Life"

Rāmeśvara continues:

Through his letters, morning walks, and room conversations, and sometimes in his classes, Śrīla Prabhupāda was building the BBT by expanding worldwide book distribution. The orders all came from him. He writes, for example:

> I have faith in your words that next year the figures will be far beyond what they were last year. It is the nature of the spiritual energy, it is always increasing if we just apply our energy.[5]

> Regarding sales figures, please endeavor in this way. The sales figures – this is the only solace in my life. When I hear that my books are selling so nicely, I become energetic like a young man. It is very good that printers are surprised at our sales figures.[6]

> Over the course of more than ninety letters and numerous personal conversations, I listened, watched, and served as Śrīla Prabhupāda personally managed the expansion of the Hare Kṛṣṇa movement throughout the world, all centered on and made possible by the BBT and the service of the first book distributors ... He knew exactly what he wanted – new centers, temples, farms, new BBT offices, giant India projects – long before any of us could imagine such things. As Śrīla Prabhupāda was building book distribution and the North American BBT, he was simultaneously loaning BBT funds to build ISKCON projects throughout the world. He built this movement through the BBT.

Spontaneous Attraction for Book Distribution

As soon as book distribution was better organized and the numbers of books going out began to increase, correspondingly, new devotees poured into the temple *āśramas* – among them some who were seemingly destined to help increase the book distribution. One such person who was spontaneously attracted to distributing books was Tom Beaudry.

Satsvarūpa Dāsa Gosvāmī explains in his *Śrīla Prabhupāda-līlāmṛta* (vol. 2, pp. 269, 272):

> Tom Beaudry was living with his wife in Santa Cruz, California. After attending a festival in Berkeley celebrating Lord Caitanya's appearance, where he chanted all day, and after reading

> Śrīla Prabhupāda's *Bhagavad-gītā,* he felt he should become Śrīla Prabhupāda's disciple. He began chanting and trying to interest his wife and friends in Kṛṣṇa consciousness. When a traveling party of *brahmacārīs* arrived to start a center in Santa Cruz, he told them he wanted to join. But they were skeptical. Then one day he showed up with a shaved head and dhoti. Tom Beaudry [then] moved from Santa Cruz to Los Angeles, and by associating with devotees like Rāmeśvara and other book distributors, he soon became a leader. He was initiated in June 1972 and received the name Tripurāri Dāsa. Every day he would go to a supermarket parking lot near the temple and sell a couple hundred copies of *Easy Journey to Other Planets.*

Soon Tripurāri Dāsa became a leader in the efforts to organize and increase the distribution of Śrīla Prabhupāda's books, and in 1975 Śrīla Prabhupāda gave him *sannyāsa*. Tripurāri Swami recalls the development of book distribution at the Los Angeles temple:

> Upon arriving in Los Angeles, I found out how much Śrīla Prabhupāda desired book distribution. Then I knew that book distribution was not only something that I could do but also something that Śrīla Prabhupāda really wanted. I didn't have an education, but I could talk to others about my good fortune of meeting the devotees. So I went out and sold BTG and other small books like *Easy Journey to Other Planets* and *Kṛṣṇa Consciousness, the Topmost Yoga System*.
>
> One day, Sārvabhauma Dāsa, one of our leading door-to-door *saṅkīrtana* devotees, asked me if I was selling any big books at the shopping centers. When I answered that I was selling only magazines and small books, he advised me to try selling big books also. When I asked him how to do it, he replied that I should pray to Śrīla Prabhupāda.
>
> That same night, I did pray to Śrīla Prabhupāda. And the next day something wonderful happened. After getting a copy of *Teachings of Lord Caitanya* from the book room, I went out with the devotees to chant. As usual, during a break I sold some small books. All the while, however, I forgot that I was carrying the TLC. But then, while showing a BTG to one lady,

> she saw the TLC in my bag. Pointing to it, she asked, "What's *that* book?" I showed it to her and she bought it. I thought, "This is magical. Praying to Śrīla Prabhupāda really works!"

Soon Tripurāri was finding ways to sell more and more big books, which meant that he began to regularly attract the attention of the devotee community by his prolific distribution. Word soon spread beyond Los Angeles that Tripurāri was leaving the temple daily and coming back with empty boxes. Tripurāri Swami remembers those days:

> When the unabridged *Bhagavad-gītā As It Is* came out in 1972, we started taking them out and soon got the knack for distributing them. This changed the equation from selling mostly small books and BTGs to selling big books.
>
> Also, when the BBT printed a softbound edition of *Kṛṣṇa Book* packaged in a three-volume boxed set, people found it attractive. It was highly marketable. *Kṛṣṇa Book* sales dramatically increased at that time. The biggest factors were both the beautiful artwork and that George Harrison had funded the printing of the *Kṛṣṇa Book* and had written the foreword for it. This was a huge selling point. We sold thousands of *Kṛṣṇa Books* at concerts and at other events.
>
> The arrival of the new *Śrīmad-Bhāgavatam* volumes, however, was one of the most important events in my life. We had been hearing Śrīla Prabhupāda's lectures on *Śrīmad-Bhāgavatam* for many months. But one night Rāmeśvara pulled me aside and showed me the BBT's newly-released first six volumes of *Śrīmad-Bhāgavatam.* Because the next day was Saturday, a popular day for book distribution, we decided not to show the new books to the devotees until the end of the day, thinking that they would stay home to read them instead of going out.
>
> That day I took thirty of the new *Śrīmad-Bhāgavatam* volumes to the LAX airport and sold them all. It was a big spiritual event for me because I was feeling that "Here is the Deity. *Idaṁ bhāgavataṁ nāma* ..." After they'd purchased a *Bhāgavatam,* I'd tell people, "It's a Deity. Don't take it into the bathroom." They thought I was crazy.

When I came back to the temple that day, the devotees were all sitting around reading the newly released *Śrīmad-Bhāgavatam.* The whole scene was spiritually intoxicating. As I arrived, Rāmeśvara gave me my own personal volumes of the *Śrīmad-Bhāgavatam,* and I went home and performed an *ārati* to them.

New Heights

Tripurāri recalls how the Los Angeles book distribution continued to grow and spread:

> Wanting to fulfill Śrīla Prabhupāda's desire to increase the distribution of his books, Rāmeśvara had begun working with the BBT. He was tuned in to what Śrīla Prabhupāda was saying about printing and distributing books. So, seeing my enthusiasm to read and distribute the books, like a talent scout Rāmeśvara recruited me for bigger things, and my services began to expand.
>
> In 1972, Rāmeśvara and I worked together to start an all-day book distribution party from the Los Angeles temple. We transformed the somewhat disorganized chanting party into a highly structured operation that included the distribution of big books. After this, book distribution increased steadily.
>
> Rāmeśvara and I added another party of householders that would go out all day on Saturdays to do book distribution. Soon, book distribution in New Dvārakā was reaching new heights and we began competing with other ISKCON centers, like San Francisco.
>
> In 1973, Rāmeśvara next sent me outside California to inspire devotees to distribute big books, so I went to New York, where other big distributors, like Buddhimanta and Jadurāṇī, were also going out daily and setting the pace. We had a competition among ourselves there, and I was successful in representing the West Coast.
>
> Gradually, book distribution caught on in other places and I focused on going out every day and also on performing strict *sādhana.* I saw more and more that the key to success was strong *sādhana.*

The BBT Book Distribution Party

With Śrīla Prabhupāda's enthusiastic response to how the book distribution was being organized, and with devotees worldwide now interested in distributing books, Rāmeśvara encouraged Tripurāri to form a team of distributors that would be independent of the temples so they could concentrate solely on perfecting the art of distributing big books. They would also travel to ISKCON centers all over the world to teach the art to others.

Rāmeśvara and Tripurāri inaugurated the BBT Party at ISKCON Chicago, because it was near the nation's largest airport, O'Hare International. Tripurāri lists the early members of the party: Praghoṣa, Sura, Kāśīrāma, Vaiśeṣika, Gaṇapati, Ṛddha, Brahmā, Kavicandra, Pañca-tattva, Kalki, Keśava Bhāratī, and others. A precedent-setting court decision in Los Angeles had made it legal to distribute books in America's airports. Soon thereafter O'Hare Airport became the site of prolific distribution by the BBT team and Chicago's resident devotees. Satsvarūpa Dāsa Goswami writes in *Śrīla Prabhupāda-līlāmṛta* (vol. 2, p. 287): "In 1974 several new parties formed just for distributing books. Tripurāri had been traveling as an emissary from Los Angeles, but now, with Śrīla Prabhupāda's permission, he formed a Bhaktivedanta Book Trust (BBT) *saṅkīrtana* party of some leading book distributors. The BBT distributors stationed themselves in various airports around the country, creating a significant increase in book distribution."

As more men joined the BBT Party and the team began producing big results, Śrīla Prabhupāda wrote to Tripurāri that "book selling is the real preaching." He should, "organize freely" and "take the leadership and do the needful" to increase book distribution. In that letter Śrīla Prabhupāda also referred to Tripurāri as "the incarnation of book distribution," and he prayed "that by Kṛṣṇa's grace you will have all success."[7]

More Than Any Sannyāsī

In that same year, Rāmeśvara wrote to Śrīla Prabhupāda recommending Tripurāri for *sannyāsa*. Śrīla Prabhupāda replied on June 5, 1974:

> You have written to recommend Tripurāri for *sannyāsa*. Tripurāri is however already a *brahmacārī* so in essence there is no difference between *brahmacārī*. I have asked Tripurāri to dedicate his life to distributing my books and he has turned out the most expert of all our sellers. It is certainly miraculous how he is distributing so many big books even to people who are not interested in Vedic literature.... Also, I have decided for the time being not to award *sannyāsa* order. You write that this recommendation is your own idea and that he himself is perfectly happy heading up a traveling party of book distributors. So let him go on as he is doing; Kṛṣṇa is giving him all facility and without question he is doing more than any *sannyāsī* by his personally distributing hundreds of books day after day and inspiring others to follow.

Although *sannyāsīs* in ISKCON were revered and worshiped by all the devotees, Śrīla Prabhupāda's words, "he is doing more than any *sannyāsī* by his personally distributing hundreds of books day after day and inspiring others to follow," were deeply felt by devotees everywhere in the movement. Those words continue to stand today as an expression of Śrīla Prabhupāda's profound gratitude to anyone dedicated to his order to distribute his books.

Vaiṣṇavī Book Distributors

It wasn't only *brahmacārīs* who went out to distribute books; women and married men also went out, and their efforts often equaled or surpassed the *brahmacārīs*'. In fact, on the West Coast, Līlā-śakti Devī Dāsī, Labaṅgalatikā Devī Dāsī, Vṛndāvana Vilāsinī Devī Dāsī, Śaraṇam Devī Dāsī, and Mulāprakriti Devī Dāsī were out-distributing entire temples in North

America. Then there were Gaurī Devī Dāsī, Narataki Devī Dāsī, Jagaddhātrī Devī Dāsī, Mañjuālī Devī Dāsi, Samapriyā Devī Dāsī, Bhaktapriyā Devī Dāsī, Śrīmati Devī Dāsī, and a host of others too numerous to mention. On the East Coast were Jadurāṇī Devī Dāsī, Bhūmi Devī Dāsī, Mahārha Devī Dāsī, Daiviśakti Devī Dāsī, Sunītā Devī Dāsī, and many others.

About the role of women in the art of book distribution, Śrīla Prabhupāda wrote to Karandhara on October 6, 1973: "In Caitanya Mahāprabhu's movement, everyone is a preacher, whether man or woman it doesn't matter. I do not know why Kīrtanānanda Swami is encouraging our women devotees not to go out on *saṅkīrtana* for book distribution. Everyone should go out."

Gaurī Devī Dāsī was one of the women pioneers of book distribution. Distributing Śrīla Prabhupāda's books was her life and soul. Śrīla Prabhupāda recognized Gaurī Dāsī in a letter he wrote to Rūpānuga Dāsa on December 18, 1974: "Your *saṅkīrtana* reports are very encouraging, especially that one girl, Gaurī Dāsī, who has set an all ISKCON women's record of 108 big books. This is very wonderful. Formerly this would have been considered impossible, but now by Kṛṣṇa's grace everything is becoming possible."

Nidrā Devī Dāsī writes about Gaurī, her mentor:

> Gaurī told me that she had a plan to take care of her health so that she could do book distribution until she was sixty-five years old, and after that she would go to Vṛndāvana to hear and chant. The plan included diet, *sādhana,* and so on. Actually, though, she became very ill at forty-five and had to go to Vṛndāvana twenty years early to leave her body.
>
> We all went out to LAX to see her off. On her way to the plane she was in a wheelchair going from person to person distributing books. Her heart was so pure and fixed that the people she approached were deeply touched by her mood.

Nidrā Dāsī was so inspired by Gaurī's dedication to book distribution that she made a vow to continue distributing books throughout her own life. She is still going strong and is known for her steadiness in that service; four decades later she has never missed a day of book distribution.

Śrīla Prabhupāda heartily recognized these empowered women, saying that they were "equally competent" for spreading the *saṅkīrtana* movement. He also insisted that we prove "there is no bar for anyone" who wanted to do preaching work. He had written to Himavatī Devī Dāsī on December 20, 1969:

> So I am especially proud how my householder disciples are preaching Lord Caitanya's Mission. This is a new thing in the history of the *saṅkīrtana* movement. In India all the *ācāryas* and their descendants later on acted only from the man's side. Their wives were at home because that is the system from old times that women are not required to go out. But in *Bhagavad-gītā* we find that women are also equally competent like the men in the matter of Kṛṣṇa Consciousness Movement. Please therefore carry on these missionary activities, and prove it by practical example that there is no bar for anyone in the matter of preaching work for Kṛṣṇa consciousness.

Persistence and Prayer

Encouraged by Śrīla Prabhupāda's generous spirit, many women dedicated their lives to full-time book distribution. Labaṅgalatikā Devī Dāsī joined ISKCON in Los Angeles in 1968, when the temple was located on La Cienega Blvd. An exemplar of determination, she tells how she struggled but became a prolific book distributor through persistence and prayer. She tells about her early days in ISKCON selling BTG:

> My friend Śrīmatī Dāsī told me, "This staying back at the temple is illusion." So we started going out door to door with BTGs. We'd distribute and come home with *lakṣmī,* and Tamal Krishna, our temple president, would give a *whoop* of delight when he'd see what we'd done.

When Śrīla Prabhupāda heard about our going out to distribute BTG, he was very happy and would regularly ask us, "How many magazines did you distribute today?" He would come from his apartment to the nearby La Cienega temple to give *darśana* three evenings a week. At those times he'd also teach us to dance in *kīrtana*. To please him, we'd go out eight hours a day to distribute *Back to Godheads*. For me, each day would start as misery, but after selling *Back to Godhead* all day and bringing the results to Prabhupāda, I'd feel as if I were in the spiritual world, Kṛṣṇaloka.

At first Labaṅgalatikā sold BTG, but later she switched to big books. Here she describes how her sincerity and daily prayer to Kṛṣṇa inspired her distribution:

For me book distribution was a deep meditation. Sometimes I would go out without thinking and I'd get rebuffed. But then I'd start sincerely praying to Kṛṣṇa. But I found that He would only reciprocate when I'd really surrender. If I surrendered to the task at hand, I could talk to people and they'd be open. Otherwise, I'd be on my own and I'd end up crying in a telephone booth. Every day I'd learn good lessons. You had to. It was Kṛṣṇa or the material world. It was a great privilege to even touch Śrīla Prabhupāda's books. I don't know how I managed to find myself in such great association and with Śrīla Prabhupāda's books.

Seeing sincere efforts like this, Śrīla Prabhupāda openly and unreservedly appreciated his disciples, just as his *guru mahārāja* had done. Every day Rāmeśvara would type out the day's book distribution scores in Los Angeles and give them to one of Śrīla Prabhupāda's servants. He would then wait for him to come down from Śrīla Prabhupāda's room and would ask him if Śrīla Prabhupāda had said anything. This went on for weeks. On March 20, 1973, Brahmānanda handed Rāmeśvara back the score sheet. On the back was this handwritten note addressed to the "boys and girls" of Los Angeles:

My dear boys and girls, you are working so hard for broadcasting the glories of Lord Kṛṣṇa's lotus feet and thus my Guru Mahārāja will be so pleased upon you. Certainly my Guru Mahārāja will bestow His blessings thousand times more than me and that is my satisfaction. All Glories to the assembled devotees.

A. C. Bhaktivedanta Swami

N.B. Every one should go with the *saṅkīrtana* party as soon as possible.

Traveling Saṅkīrtana

Another huge lift to book distribution in America was the formation of the Rādhā-Dāmodara Traveling Saṅkīrtana Party (RDTSKP). In 1974, two charismatic *sannyāsīs,* Viṣṇujana Swami and Tamal Krishna Goswami, customized a Greyhound bus, transforming it into a traveling temple, and joined together on a venture across North America to put on festivals and recruit young people to join the Kṛṣṇa consciousness movement. With Śrīla Prabhupāda's encouragement and financial support from his BBT, the two *sannyāsīs* soon expanded their team, adding more buses. With a fleet of "traveling temples," the RDTSKP was soon consistently distributing tens of thousands of Śrīla Prabhupāda's books each month. Tamal Krishna Goswami recalls:

> Śrīla Prabhupāda was reminding me that preaching meant to distribute his books. So I became inspired that our party should distribute so many books that it would equal all of the other book distribution of the rest of ISKCON worldwide. Day and night I was thinking of how to get out more and more books and thus overflood America with transcendental literature. Śrīla Prabhupāda wrote me that this was his real ambition, to turn all of America into Vaiṣṇavas.
>
> Until we formed our Rādhā-Dāmodara party, the method of distributing books had been that an individual would be given either a large, medium, or small book, according to the size of the donation. But Prabhupāda told me that of

> all types of book distribution, it was most important to distribute his large books. So I was always considering how to increase the number of large books. The problem was that people were willing to give small donations, but rarely would they give us large enough contributions for us to feel justified in giving them a large book. Then Kṛṣṇa gave me the idea that by adding together a few small donations from a number of persons, at least one of them could be given a large book while the others could be given a *Back to Godhead* magazine or a small book. By this method we were able to increase the distribution of big books tremendously. Prabhupāda fully approved of this idea. As long as the Book Fund received payment for the books, Śrīla Prabhupāda allowed us to pass them out as quickly as we could, irrespective of the size of the donation. Thus our Rādhā-Dāmodara party was able to distribute as many as fifty thousand big books in a single month.[8]

In a letter to Tamal Krishna Goswami on December 28, 1974, Śrīla Prabhupāda writes about the bus party:

> I was extremely pleased to hear your report from your traveling buses. It sounds as if your program is very, very wonderful and I am very encouraged to hear that such a program is coming along so nicely. I am glad that you have understood the importance of my books, therefore I am stressing it so much. Let everyone take these books. If he simply reads one page then he is getting something substantial, a real eternal benefit. Or if he hands it over to his friend and he reads one page the same result is there. So continue these festivals constantly and make them all Kṛṣṇa conscious. Overflood the whole country by this preaching work. Let the whole United States become Vaiṣṇavas, then everyone else in the whole world will follow. That is my real ambition. Therefore your program is very glorious. This is really preaching. Your intelligence is being properly utilized. In the beginning you took up the distribution of BTGs and you sold the most. Now you have taken up this van program and you will also be successful in the same way. This preaching spirit will make you recognized by Kṛṣṇa. There is so much wonderful potential in USA for this type of program.

> So organize hundreds of such parties. This is fulfilling the mission of Sri Caitanya Mahāprabhu. I am very glad to hear that not only you are maintaining such program but that you want to expand it. Yes, this is our philosophy; *ānandāmbudhi-vardhanam.* It means to expand or to increase. Therefore I strongly encourage you to double your program by getting three more buses if you can do it. There is no difficulty. BBT will help. I have written Haṁsadūta one letter to give you the loan of $30,000. BBT means fifty percent is for printing books and fifty percent for construction of temples. So your buses are all moving temples. Don't worry. There will be no scarcity of money. Go on with your program and increase and increase more and more. In the end of your letter you mention that people are not very much eager to go to Temples but with your program you are bringing the temples to the people. Yes, this is a very important point. You have picked up this idea very nicely, of bringing the temples to the people. In this way you will give everyone the opportunity to step in the direction of back to Godhead, back to home. So you and Viṣṇujana Mahārāja and all of your nice *brahmacārīs* continue strongly with great enthusiasm and determination to spread this Kṛṣṇa consciousness movement all over your country and Lord Caitanya will certainly be pleased with you.

These seeds of desire to distribute Śrīla Prabhupāda's books that were planted in North America would soon be planted and begin to grow in countries around the world, sprouting into a luxuriant forest of bhakti creepers and trees.

CHAPTER SIX

The United Nations of Book Distribution

WHAT WOULD YOU DO if you were alone, had books with spiritual principles that would bring happiness to people all over the world, and a deep desire to share this literature with others? According to the late Apple CEO, Steve Jobs, you would ship. As he said it so famously, "Real artists ship." According to Jobs, it doesn't matter how groundbreaking, stylish, or cool your products are if you never ship them.

Śrīla Prabhupāda understood this principle. He shipped – literally – when he boarded the *Jaladuta* with two hundred sets of his *Śrīmad-Bhāgavatams*. Śrīla Prabhupāda's prime strategy in spreading Kṛṣṇa consciousness – the one he had been handed by his *guru mahārāja* – was to write, publish, and distribute books all over the world in as many languages as possible. He wasn't shy about doing it. In a room conversation in Honolulu on May 7, 1976, Śrīla Prabhupāda told his disciples, "First of all try to push books everywhere, all over the world. They have got so many languages, like Russian ... Black market. Chinese also. Black market. They cannot check."

Similarly, in a letter written from Bombay on November 28, 1970 to Jagadīśa Dāsa, Śrīla Prabhupāda wrote:

> Actually these two books, *KṚṢṆA* book and *Nectar of Devotion,* are revolutionary to your country. Not only your country but all over the world. Nobody has any clear idea of God. In hopelessness they declare that God is dead. So these books will supply clear idea of God, not only that but anyone who will read this *KṚṢṆA* book in two parts, *Nectar of Devotion,* and if possible *Teachings of Lord Caitanya,* I'm sure he cannot go away from becoming a devotee of Kṛṣṇa. So try to push our books, especially *Bhagavad-gītā As It Is,* TLC, *KṚṢṆA,* NOD, backed by a regular supply of our magazines and regular performance of *saṅkīrtana*. Then I'm sure Kṛṣṇa Consciousness Movement will go forward without any hindrance. You have a strong governing body, all determined to push forward this movement and I'm sure of success in the future.

"Profusely Throughout the World"

Once Śrīla Prabhupāda had shipped himself and his *Bhāgavatams* to the US, and after he had established the International Society for Krishna Consciousness, he began to ship his books abroad, first to Germany and London, then to India, South America, and the rest of the world. As he carried out his strategy, a number of his readers were moved by what they were receiving. As proof that his strategy had worked, in July 1977 Dr. Upendraray Jaychandbhai Sandesara, an Indian scholar who had read Śrīla Prabhupāda's books, wrote, "Now that I have gone through many of the volumes of BBT literature, I am of the opinion that this encyclopedic literature containing real gems of Divine Knowledge is just suited for being spread all over the world and in all languages. As such, all educational and religious institutions such as Universities, Colleges, libraries, educational societies, churches, *maths,* temples, and all individuals should have in their stocks of

Śrīla Vyāsadeva, the literary incarnation of Lord Kṛṣṇa, committed the Vedic sound to writing, and then wrote the seminal text of our family business, *Śrīmad-Bhāgavatam,* which delivered the goal of the *Vedas,* pure devotional service to Śrī Kṛṣṇa, the Supreme Personality of Godhead.

books the classics of the Bhaktivedanta Book Trust for the profit of all readers."

Another scholar, Olivier Lacombe, professor of Sanskrit and Indology at Sorbonne University in Paris wrote, "As a successor in direct line from Caitanya, the author of *Bhagavad-gītā As It Is* is entitled, according to Indian custom, to the majestic title of His Divine Grace A. C. Bhaktivedanta Swami Prabhupāda. The great interest that his reading of the *Bhagavad-gītā* holds for us is that it offers us an authorized interpretation according to the principles of the Caitanya tradition."

Although there were almost no trained translators among Śrīla Prabhupāda's disciples, slowly but surely his books were rendered into an assortment of languages. In this chapter, I will touch on the highlights of world book distribution, sometimes even giving you a glimpse into its development after Śrīla Prabhupāda's departure. I have also tried to allow the devotees involved to tell their own stories, wherever possible.

Śrīla Prabhupāda had a deep desire to see his books flood the world. That this flood began even during the short time that Śrīla Prabhupāda was with us is miraculous. Without looking closely into why and how this happened, it might appear that the expansion of book distribution all over the world somehow took place automatically or that it was easy. Neither is true. The growth can be attributed to a series of triumphs achieved by individual devotees who heard about Śrīla Prabhupāda's vision, who worked tirelessly to overcome various hurdles, and who thus helped to make his vision a reality. Śrīla Prabhupāda himself lauded these devotees for sacrificing their lives for distributing his books.

On January 2, 1972 he wrote to Kīrtirāja Dāsa in New York, "I thank you very much for taking so seriously to helping me fulfill the order of Bhaktisiddhānta Sarasvatī to distribute Kṛṣṇa consciousness literature to the whole world masses. What strength our Movement has now got is due in large part to the enthusiasm we have had to distribute our literatures profusely throughout the world." In London on August 22

1973, Śrīla Prabhupāda also gave a lecture in which he said, "I have to thank you. It is all due to you. It is not my credit, but it is your credit that you are helping me in executing the order of my *guru mahārāja*." I've written this chapter to share with you a few of the stories of these intrepid devotees, for their enthusiasm is contagious. I pray that my retelling of these devotees' stories may cause an epidemic of eagerness in my readers to take Śrīla Prabhupāda's books to every nook and corner of the world.

History Repeats

Books were rolling off Dai Nippon's presses in Japan, and Śrīla Prabhupāda shipped these books to North America, India, the UK, and other parts of the world. To support the translation, printing, and distribution of his books in the world marketplace, Śrīla Prabhupāda opened new BBT offices in various countries. It wasn't long before his books were being translated into all sorts of languages. Besides the North American BBT office, Śrīla Prabhupāda also opened offices in Latin America, Southern Europe, and Germany and named new BBT trustees for each of them. Śrīla Prabhupāda named Tamal Krishna Goswami BBT trustee for sales and book distribution, giving him no publishing duties except in China. And although he already had a BBT for English-language books in the US, he established an office for English-language books in the UK.

Just as the devotees had taken up distributing his books in North America on Śrīla Prabhupāda's order, so now devotees took up that order in countries around the world. Everywhere his books were shipped, translated, and distributed by the local devotees, astonishing results followed.

India

Śrīla Prabhupāda's strategy for building the foundation of ISKCON in India was the same as it had been in North

America: to distribute books. In 1973 he underlined the strategy he was already implementing in a letter to Tejīyas Dāsa, temple president of ISKCON New Delhi from 1971 through 1976:

> Without books we will make no progress in India, because practically everything we have done so far in this country has rested on these books. So I am very glad to hear that they are selling nicely in Delhi also. Now try to tax your brain for finding new ways and better ways for distributing our books widely to the intelligent men of Delhi city.

In October of 1970, Śrīla Prabhupāda suspended the usual public *harināma saṅkīrtana* in Bombay; instead of chanting on the streets, he asked his devotees to show his books to the city's respectable businessmen. Giriraj Swami, among the first to take up this task, recalls that Śrīla Prabhupāda instructed him and other devotees to pile up his books on the desks of reputed businessmen. His idea was that when these gentlemen saw the books and heard about the growth of the Kṛṣṇa consciousness movement in the West, they would eagerly become life members. Giriraj Swami recalls Śrīla Prabhupāda introducing the Life Membership program: "Śrīla Prabhupāda said that it was a way to distribute his books. Life members would get a lifetime subscription to BTG, all present and future books, and a free stay in select ISKCON temples."

In response to Śrīla Prabhupāda's suggestion to use his books to make life members, Giriraj and a number of other devotees began approaching businessmen in their offices all over Bombay. They found Śrīla Prabhupāda's method to be effective. Just seeing Śrīla Prabhupāda's books and hearing about the success of ISKCON around the world, the Bombay businessmen were signing up to be life members and taking Śrīla Prabhupāda's books into their offices and homes. Around this time, Gargamuni Swami formed his own team of devotees to travel in vans to various places around India. Gargamuni would approach the proprietors of businesses in their offices while the other team members fanned out to meet the proprietors' employees to show them Śrīla Prabhupāda's books. Satyanārāyaṇa Dāsa, a member of Gargamuni's team, remarks, "Gargamuni's leadership really helped to expand the book distribution. He purchased six Mercedes vans in Europe, guided them overland to India, and sent out men in them in various directions to distribute Śrīla Prabhupāda's books. It was his organizational genius that helped to establish a BBT Library Party in India."

As book distribution in India picked up, Śrīla Prabhupāda pushed to have his books translated into the local languages. First came a magazine in Hindi, and then magazines and books in Bengali. Giriraj Swami remembers:

> In 1971 we saw the first BTG in Bengali. Śrīla Prabhupāda had wanted it translated by someone who would do it for free, because such a person would have a feeling for our cause. I put an ad in the paper searching for the right person, and one man, Mr. Ganguli, came forward to bring out the first of Śrīla Prabhupāda's books in Bengali.

Tejīyas Dāsa, who was the temple president in New Delhi, speaks about book distribution in India during those years:

> I used to have to sell books to maintain our temple in New Delhi and also to help build the Krishna-Balaram temple in Vṛndāvana. I would sell to factories, bookstores, and through life memberships.
>
> I always followed Śrīla Prabhupāda's formula of giving 50% of my collections to the BBT, as he personally told me that this was immensely important to him. Every time I'd meet Śrīla Prabhupāda, he'd ask me, "When you get money, what do you do with it?" I'd say, "I give 50% to the BBT," and he was satisfied. Once I admitted to him that I was only giving 33% of my book profits to the BBT. He had a long conversation with me about it, explaining why it was important that I give 50%. He told me that when he was younger his business

had failed due to lack of capitalization, and that he wanted his BBT fully capitalized so that it would go on printing his books. He also wrote a letter to all the ISKCON temples telling them to give 50% from book distribution to the BBT. This 50% formula was Śrīla Prabhupāda's super core principle of management.

When my service moved from New Delhi to Orissa, the temple in Orissa was deeply in debt to the BBT. To rectify the situation I bought a press and set up a bindery so we could produce an inexpensive *Gītā* in the local language. We also printed *Śrīmad-Bhāgavatam* and other books. As we sold those books, I paid off the debt by following Śrīla Prabhupāda's formula of giving 50% to the BBT. And ISKCON Orissa was soon flush with money.

Jaśomatīnandana Dāsa, the temple president of Ahmedabad, Gujarat, wholeheartedly embraced the distribution of Śrīla Prabhupāda's books. He gives his overview of the progress of book printing and distribution in India:

The Indian BBT, which Śrīla Prabhupāda founded in 1972 in Bombay, was not publishing many of its own books in the 1970s. Rather, the Indian devotees were getting most of their books from the North American BBT. As book distribution through the life member program in India increased, some devotees also started a library party. That party went all over India in the 1970s selling books to professors and librarians on college campuses. Finally, in 1976, Śrīla Prabhupāda noticed the lack of printing at the Indian BBT and said to the BBT trustees, "You got books from America for all these years; now you should print your own." Despite this instruction, the Indian BBT only started its own substantial printing in the early 1980s. At that time the Indian BBT started printing hundreds of thousands of books, which the devotees were distributing with gusto during the December marathons.

In fact, during the early 1980s, the Indian BBT would print and ship as many as half a million copies of *Bhagavad-gītā As It*

Is. The results are clear. During Śrīla Prabhupāda's time there were only five temples in India. Now, after so much book distribution, there are more than one hundred temples in India, with more springing up yearly. Now these new communities are also doing huge amounts of book distribution.

When asked who was behind this increase, Jaśomatīnandana replies, "So much of the credit for this rise goes to Gopal Krishna Mahārāja. He's been inspiring devotees to distribute books in India since the 1970s and still does so wherever he goes."

Gopal Krishna Goswami was one of Śrīla Prabhupāda's first Indian disciples, although he first met Śrīla Prabhupāda in Canada. He learned from being near Śrīla Prabhupāda that whenever the "Saṅkīrtana Newsletter" arrived with his mail, Śrīla Prabhupāda always had his secretary open it before the thirty or forty letters that were awaiting his attention. What's more, he heard Śrīla Prabhupāda persistently speaking about and encouraging his followers to distribute his books.

Gopal Krishna Mahārāja tells of his first attempts to increase book distribution in India and what he learned from those efforts:

> In 1977 I made a deal with India Book House, a popular bookstore in New Delhi, to display Śrīla Prabhupāda's books. After the elaborate display was up for a full month, the owner, Mr. Gupta, informed me that not many books had been sold. When I told Śrīla Prabhupāda about my attempt to sell his books at India Book House, how the display had been nicely done but that there was little result, Śrīla Prabhupāda replied, "My books are sold because of the enthusiasm of my devotees."

And Śrīla Prabhupāda spoke these encouraging words: "In India we can distribute more books than any other place in the world." From these early lessons in the 1970s, Gopal Krishna Goswami went on in the 1980s and beyond to establish thriving devotional communities centered on the distribution of Śrīla Prabhupāda's books. He continues to travel widely throughout the world encouraging devotees to take up book distribution. Although Indian book distribution was slower than in many other parts of the world in the 1970s, from the 1980s to the present day it has flourished like nowhere else. To emphasize how cultivating a mood of book distribution lays the foundation for so many other great projects, I have taken the liberty to take the history of Indian book distribution past 1977 and into the present, whereas in other sections I do not tell the story beyond 1977.

Another devotee who helped build the Indian book distribution team is Bhīmasena Dāsa, an American who had served on the Rādhā-Dāmodara bus party and now was switching places with another American, Jana Pāvana Dāsa, who was in India and wanting to return to the US. Bhīmasena landed in India inspired to create a traveling bus program similar to the Rādhā-Dāmodara party:

> When I first arrived in India in October of 1977, book distribution was scanty. After arriving, I was appointed the *saṅkīrtana* leader in Bombay and thought that maybe I could do in India what the Rādhā-Dāmodara team had done in North America. Śrī Nāthajī Dāsa (then, N. D. Desai) at once donated a bus. Later he gave another one. One of our first big events was in Pandharpur, where we sold over a thousand copies of the newly released Marathi *Bhagavad-gītā As It Is*. We then drove the buses all over Maharashtra, and over time we sold tens of thousands of Marathi *Gītās*. I always wondered what might result from our distributing so many books in Maharashtra. Later, I saw that in that region there were many new devotees. I could see the result for myself.

Jaśomatīnandana Dāsa describes the growth of the Indian bus parties:

> Following Bhīmasena's lead, after some time, both the Māyāpur and Bombay temples, and then other ISKCON

communities, developed traveling bus programs. These traveling buses went to crowded marketplaces, opened the rear doors of their customized temple-buses, and displayed the Deities alongside Śrīla Prabhupāda's books. The distributors then announced over the loudspeakers attached to their buses: "Come and take these books!" People would come in droves to see the Deities and buy books by the thousands. There was a Jagannātha bus in Bombay and a Gaura-Nitāi bus in Māyāpur. Just like the Rādhā-Dāmodara bus parties in North America, the Indian bus parties would cook their own *prasāda* on the buses and distribute it. When devotees joined in those days, in the early 1980s, their main service would be to go out on book distribution.

Mahā-kumbha-melā

Another historical breakthrough for Indian book distribution came in 1977 at the Mahā-kumbha-melā in Allahabad. Bhāgavata Dāsa, who helped Gurudāsa manage the ISKCON camp at the Melā, had signed a contract for what he was told was an ideal place for ISKCON's site, but he and the other devotees were disappointed to find that the ISKCON encampment he had paid for in advance was actually in a remote area under a railroad bridge. Giriraj Swami describes the scene:

> Śrīla Prabhupāda, who always saw how to turn things in our favor, said, "Do massive *harināma* and book distribution throughout the Melā." Despite our being in a remote location, we ended up the hit of the festival. *Easy Journey to Other Planets* in Hindi was selling by the thousands and, after a while, people were approaching the devotees asking for the book, shouting, *Subhan Yātrā*! *Subhan Yātrā*! (*Easy Journey, Easy Journey*!). Gurukṛpa Swami arranged to feed the book distributors and chanters opulent *prasāda* – halavā and fried potatoes – so the devotees stayed enlivened throughout the event.

Thousands of books went out, and people all over the Melā

heard the chanting of the *mahā-mantra*. Śrīla Prabhupāda was very pleased.

This Mahā-kumbha-melā planted the idea among Indian leaders that they could sell a lot of books during big festivals, and the Indian devotees have gone on to push forward book distribution in many ways. They've actualized Śrīla Prabhupāda's statement to Gopal Krishna Goswami, "In India we can distribute more books than any other place in the world."

Japan

In the mid 1970s Gurukṛpa Swami took with him to Japan a team of devotees he called "Nāma Haṭṭa." On the team he included Yaśodānandana Swami and devotees from all over the world, sent by various temples, who would focus on collecting funds for Śrīla Prabhupāda's projects in Māyāpur and Vṛndāvana. The Nāma Haṭṭa party not only gave hundreds of thousands of dollars to help construct ISKCON's new temples in the *dhāmas,* but it distributed thousands of BTGs in Japanese every month throughout Japan.

Bāṇabhaṭṭa Dāsa, one of the biggest collectors on that Nāma Haṭṭa, recalls how he distributed at least two hundred copies of BTG in Japanese every day: "We had green army bags that would hold 1,000 BTGs, and we'd lug the bags around. It was difficult. We'd keep two hundred with us in our side bag and twenty-five in our hands."

Europe Catches Fire

Locanānanda Dāsa, who was stationed at ISKCON France in the early 1970s, describes the beginnings of book distribution there:

> In 1970, we had access to a mimeograph machine, just like the one that the devotees were using in America. The machine was at a cultural hall in Paris called the American Center, where

they held events, including dancing and nightclubbing on Saturday nights. We'd mimeograph papers on that machine and bring them back to my apartment, where we'd assemble them into a simple BTG.

I lived in a studio apartment, which was the first ISKCON temple in Paris. Tamal Krishna and his wife lived there with me. When Tamal and his wife went to L.A., Yogeśvara and his wife moved in. We did *harināma,* but it was hard to get literature; we had to make it ourselves. Later, my father, Dr. Einhorn, gave a donation to print the *Śrī Īśopaniṣad* in French.

When Śrīla Prabhupāda visited Paris, I told him an interpreter for the United Nations had translated his *Kṛṣṇa Book* into French. The man wasn't even a devotee but had read and liked *Kṛṣṇa Book* so much that he had spontaneously translated it. When Śrīla Prabhupāda heard this, tears came to his eyes and he said, "Get it typeset, laid-out, and printed – and then *inundate.*" From that incident I saw for myself how important book distribution was to Śrīla Prabhupāda.

Later I was involved in book distribution in Holland. Devotees translated *On the Way to Kṛṣṇa* and other small books into Dutch. The Dutch devotees were doing really big. We also started doing *saṅkīrtana* in Belgium, where we were getting really big donations. To accommodate both places, we made two editions of BTG, one for Belgium and one for Holland. We sold the fancier ones in Belgium at a higher cost. All together we printed 150,000 BTGs and had no problem selling them. Devotees would go out with two book bags slung over their backs and wouldn't come back until all the books were gone. We had meetings on Sunday so that everyone could learn to distribute books, because Śrīla Prabhupāda had said that everyone should go out on book distribution.

Meanwhile, Hayeśvara Dāsa had been working on translating the *Gītā* into Dutch. When Śrīla Prabhupāda heard about this, he wrote me a letter saying, "Do it nicely – it's very important work." When the book was printed, Hayeśvara went into Śrīla Prabhupāda's room in Māyāpur to show it to him. It was an ecstatic moment. Showing Śrīla Prabhupāda these new publications was always a momentous event.

Between 1971 and 1972, the French devotees went out for six to eight hours a day onto the streets to chant Hare Kṛṣṇa, led by Indradyumna Dāsa and Locanānanda Dāsa. The devotees were out for so many hours each day that they became part of the street scene in Paris. Harivilāsa Dāsa recalls:

> People were amused that they could predict where we'd be every day. Later, when we finally got books, our distributors found it easy to sell them because our chanting was part of the downtown scene and people liked us. They even used to invite us into their shops. We also got into the movies and on the radio.
>
> Some devotees dressed up as Sītā-Rāma and Rādhā-Kṛṣṇa and went door to door to collect donations and to give out the magazines. When the first BBT books arrived in France in 1973, devotees went out everywhere and sold them.
>
> But what really got the book distribution going in Europe was the arrival of Yogeścandra. He made it explode. He came from America and the Rādhā-Dāmodara party and introduced all the techniques for organizing that had started there.

Besides the French devotees learning new techniques for distributing books, a series of new French translations of the books created fresh enthusiasm.

Translating the Absolute Truth

Translating ordinary literature is challenging enough, but when the literature contains terms that don't exist in one's native language, the task becomes more difficult. For example, in Japanese, there is no word for *devotee*. The Japanese translators, therefore, had to invent a term: *kenshinsha*. *Ken* means "offer," *shin* means "body," *aha* means "person," and *ai* means "love." So essentially, a *kenshinsha* is a person who dedicates his or her being to a cause – a devotee. Other languages have their own translation challenges. A phrase like "the Supreme Personality of Godhead," exotic even in English but one we have come to take for granted, has proved difficult to capture in a number of languages. Śrīla Prabhupāda's trademark term "devotional service" has created another translation hurdle.

Still, devotee translators, sometimes in consultation with language professionals and sometimes just among themselves, found workarounds for all the unfamiliar Sanskrit and devotional terms and rendered them into their native languages with the aim of educating their countrymen in the science of bhakti-yoga.

Speaking to a guest in Malaysia on February 26, 1973, Śrīla Prabhupāda urged him to help spread Kṛṣṇa consciousness in his country: "*Bhagavad-gītā* is the science of religion, science of God. So if you take this book seriously and try to spread this knowledge among your countrymen, I think you'll be very much benefited."

In a similar vein, while speaking to devotees in Geneva, Switzerland, on June 1, 1974, Śrīla Prabhupāda tells them, "Try to remain in your position as devotee, and as far as possible teach these rascals who are simply attracted by the glaring material stones and woods, and let them have some knowledge and do benefit to your countrymen, to your society, to your family."

In his 1992 Vyāsa-pūjā offering to Śrīla Prabhupāda, Bhakti Cāru Swami writes, "You instructed me to translate your books into Bengali and personally trained me to do that job. Once when you were in Bombay you even told me, 'Just translate my books and go back to Godhead.'"

Śrīla Prabhupāda encouraged his followers to break the boundaries of language and culture to introduce Kṛṣṇa consciousness. To do this, he frequently gave the example that if a man's house is burning and he needs help, he will somehow or other get his message across to his neighbors, even if he doesn't know their language. Nonetheless, translating philosophical books about Kṛṣṇa is not only a highly technical skill, but it also requires a translator who is devoted to Kṛṣṇa. In his purport to *Śrīmad-Bhāgavatam* 2.4.22, Śrīla Prabhupāda writes, "No mundane scholar can translate or reveal the true import of the Vedic mantras (hymns). They cannot be understood unless one is inspired or initiated by the authorized spiritual master."

At every opportunity, Śrīla Prabhupāda encouraged devotees to print books in every language. Often when he met someone favorable to Kṛṣṇa consciousness and proficient in a language other than English, he would urge that person to translate his books. Śrīla Prabhupāda wanted books in every language possible – Russian, Chinese, Japanese, Swahili, and many others. "I am also very encouraged to hear that Japanese language translations of some of my books will be brought out soon," he wrote in a letter to Sudāmā Dāsa on February 19, 1972, "because without books and magazines, what authority or what basis have we got for preaching?"

Similarly, in another letter Śrīla Prabhupāda notes, "The Chinese-speaking portion of the world is very huge and it requires to infiltrate gradually, especially by distributing our literatures widely in Chinese language."[1]

Later, when Śrīla Prabhupāda heard that a young Chinese man, Yaśomatī-sūta Dāsa, had finished translating three chapters of *Bhagavad-gītā As It Is* into Chinese, he wrote that the devotees should immediately print them as a small book.[2]

In France, Yogeśvara Dāsa and his wife, Jyotirmayī Devī Dāsī, took up the daunting task of translating Śrīla Prabhupāda's books into French. Yogeśvara tells about his involvement with Śrīla Prabhupāda's books after joining ISKCON on December 26, 1969 at Bury Place in London:

> When I first joined, the local ISKCON leaders found out that I had studied literature at the university and put me in charge of the publications office. They asked me to make a magazine. We had a mimeograph machine we'd use to stencil the covers. The first BTG had stories and reprints of lectures – a few pages stapled together. We'd take them out and distribute them.
>
> After being in Bury Place for a year and a half I was asked

to go to France, because I spoke French. I went with my wife, Jyotirmayī Dāsī, and we stayed in Locanānanda's tiny house with a couple dozen other devotees. The shower was in the kitchen, and only a cloth demarcated the men's ashram from the women's ashram.

I already knew that Śrīla Prabhupāda wanted a full-blown BTG in French, so in 1970 my wife and I hitchhiked to Hamburg, Germany, to join Haṁsadūta, because he had the proper equipment with which we could produce it. However, after living in Hamburg for a year, we saw that the devotees there had their attention on German printing, not French books. So my wife and I went off to Brooklyn, New York, to be with the ISKCON Press devotees at Tiffany Place. In that crowded building they were able to give us a small space to live in, near the artists. Because we shared the equipment and machines with the devotees doing English publications, we had to work out a schedule. As it ended up, we did our French publications at night, and the ISKCON Press devotees worked on Śrīla Prabhupāda's books in English during the day. We were able to print a small French booklet, which was a translation of Śrīla Prabhupāda's introduction to the *Bhagavad-gītā As It Is*. After we printed it, I went to show it to Śrīla Prabhupāda in the nearby Brooklyn temple. He was with many *sannyāsīs* when I arrived, but he asked me to come in. I handed him the book. He looked at it carefully and then said, "*Overflood.*"

Soon my wife moved back to France to focus fully on the French translation work, but she first asked Śrīla Prabhupāda if it would be all right for her to live outside the temple to concentrate on her work. Śrīla Prabhupāda approved.

As it turned out, she also had to keep in regular contact with Śrīla Prabhupāda from France because she had many questions about translations. For example, she needed to decide how to translate "soul" into French. The word "soul" happens to have many different meanings in French. Another example is the phrase "The Supreme Personality of Godhead," which doesn't have a parallel in French. Many translators had not considered these challenges and had therefore produced translations that were incomprehensible. The translator's challenge is to not change what Śrīla Prabhupāda said; but when translating, you often can't use Śrīla Prabhupāda exact words, because in many cases they don't exist in the foreign language.

In 1973, Bhagavān came to France and really got the translation and publication going. In his typical style Bhagavān introduced opulent gold embossing and endpapers to the new French translations of Śrīla Prabhupāda's books. When I brought one of these new books to Śrīla Prabhupāda, he looked up at me and asked, "Are you the main man?" I said, "No, Śrīla Prabhupāda, I'm the last man." Everyone in the room laughed, but Śrīla Prabhupāda said, "No, this is Vaiṣṇavism." After looking over the whole book, he simply said, "All right then, what's next?"

Jyotirmayī and others worked on the first French books: *Introduction to Bhagavad-gītā, Śrī Īśopaniṣad, Easy Journey to Other Planets* (in French, called *Antimatière et eternité*), *The Vaiṣṇava Songbook,* and *Bhagavad-gītā As It Is.*

After translating many books in the 1970s, later the BBT asked Jyotirmayī to improve the translations done by earlier, less-experienced translators, a testament to the language finesse required when translating. She worked on several cantos of *Śrīmad-Bhāgavatam, Upadeśāmṛta, Perfect Questions, Perfect Answers, Life Comes from Life, Kṛṣṇa Book,* and *Teachings of Lord Caitanya.* She also made a translator's dictionary of words and phrases that were difficult to translate from English.

Jyotirmayī also improved the French *Vaiṣṇava Songbook* and then worked on the French *Śrī Caitanya-caritāmṛta,* as well as *The Perfection of Yoga* and *Coming Back.* The first three cantos of *Śrīmad-Bhāgavatam, Bhagavad-gītā As It Is,* and *Kṛṣṇa Book* were done early on, and she had to correct them before they went to reprint.

Dynamic Distribution on the Streets of Europe

In 1974, Haṁsadūta, GBC secretary for Germany, announced the release of the *Bhagavad-gītā As It Is* in German. Śrīla

Prabhupāda wrote to him on November 14, 1974: "This further publication of books means that you go further to Kṛṣṇa six steps more. Thank you. Overflood Europe with German books. I think that the German people are the heart of Europe, and your march will be followed by Bhagavān Dāsa in French language."

Maṇidhara Dāsa, a Czech devotee who joined ISKCON in Germany in 1972, remembers the atmosphere at the time:

> I joined on a Monday and was out the door on Tuesday to distribute books. The whole mood of the community was oriented toward going out for book distribution and *harināma.* The only devotee in the temple during the day was the *pūjārī* who stayed back to care for the Deities.
>
> The first day I went out, I sold 250 magazines, and when I came back, everyone at the temple was really nice to me. From this I quickly saw that going out for *saṅkīrtana* was the way to please the devotees. After that I hardly saw a temple because I went out traveling around Europe. We were always traveling and distributing books. We had dozens of devotees rolling across the country in vans, distributing all the time.

Maṇidhara's commitment to book distribution was unshakable, and he soon became one of the most successful distributors in the world. Maṇidhara recalls:

> When I joined, it was considered impossible to distribute big books in Germany. We mostly sold record albums. But then Śrīla Prabhupāda said the record distribution had to stop. When the first edition of *Bhagavad-gītā As It Is* came out in German, and after Śrīla Prabhupāda stopped our distribution of record albums, we began to distribute the *Gītā* in large quantities.

Rohiṇī Sūta Dāsa, a Swiss devotee, soon joined forces with Maṇidhara, and the two became a world-famous book distribution duo. Rohiṇī Sūta remembers:

> Maṇidhara and I were each distributing forty big books a day, but then we discovered that we could sell more than one at a time. So we gradually increased to sixty or seventy books a day each. We would read the scores of the devotees in the United States, who were also selling more and more big books, and then gradually both Maṇidhara and I were able to sometimes sell as many as one hundred books each in a day.

When Śrīla Prabhupāda heard about these two extraordinary book distributors, he wrote them a letter on October 10, 1976:

> My Dear Maṇidhara and Rohiṇī Sūta,
>
> Please accept my blessings. I have received a letter from Jayatīrtha saying that you have distributed in one week 522 and 521 big books respectively. This is very wonderful. I thank you so much. *Ye yathā māṁ prapadyante tāṁs tathāiva bhajamy aham.* Kṛṣṇa becomes more and more pleased by seeing the increment of book distribution. Devotional service is absolute but Kṛṣṇa is especially pleased to see someone preaching His glories.

One year, instead of coming to the annual Māyāpur festival to meet Śrīla Prabhupāda and the international devotees, Rohiṇī Sūta and Maṇidhara stayed in Europe to sell more books. Śrīla Prabhupāda praised their dedication. He even sent a pair of silver *karatālas* to Rohiṇī Sūta with his name engraved on them as a reward for his selling the most big books in the world that year.

Mexico

Meanwhile, in Mexico, Hridayānanda Dāsa Goswami had organized a Spanish office of the BBT. Śrīla Prabhupāda wrote to him from Bombay on December 21, 1974:

> My dear Hridayānanda Mahārāja,
>
> Please accept my blessings. I am in due receipt of your letter dated Nov. 27, 1974 with enclosed Spanish BTG and

have noted the contents very carefully and looked through the new Spanish BTG. This new BTG is done very nicely. The printing is very beautiful and I thank you very much for doing such a nice job. I am very glad to hear you have printed 100,000 copies of this magazine. Now give them to everyone. Also I am very happy to hear the other books will be coming out very soon. If you can finish *Bhagavad-gītā As It Is* in Spanish and show me at the Māyāpur festival that will be very sublime. Please print as many books as possible, this is my real pleasure. By printing these books of our Kṛṣṇa conscious philosophy in so many different languages we can actually inject our movement into the masses of persons all over the world, especially there in the Western countries.

Australia

ISKCON Australia also rose to prominence on the world book distribution scene and by 1974 was competing with ISKCON Los Angeles and the RDTSKP for the top spot. By the fall of 1974, about a dozen Australian and New Zealand devotees were daily selling more than twenty big books each. The centers in Australia, like those in America, more than doubled their book distribution between 1973 and 1974.[3]

Cāru Dāsa, one of the early leaders in Australia, remembers: "In 1973, Madhudviṣa Swami organized a BBT party consisting of elite book distributors around Australia. My wife and I went up the Gold Coast and distributed tons of softbound *Kṛṣṇa Books.* But when Buddhimanta came to Australia, that really got things going. There was no one on the planet who could inspire like Buddhi."

Extreme Enthusiasm

In *The Nectar of Instruction* (3), Śrīla Prabhupāda translates *utsāha* as "enthusiasm." The word *enthusiasm* comes from the Greek *enthous,* "inspired by God." In his purport to text 3, Śrīla Prabhupāda writes:

> Without enthusiasm, one cannot be successful. Even in the material world one has to be very enthusiastic in his particular field of activity in order to become successful. A student, businessman, artist or anyone else who wants success in his line must be enthusiastic. Similarly, one has to be very enthusiastic in devotional service. Enthusiasm means action, but action for whom? The answer is that one should always act for Kṛṣṇa – *kṛṣṇārthe ākhila-ceṣṭā* (*Bhakti-rasāmṛta-sindhu*).

Buddhimanta became an emblem of this enthusiasm for the book distribution movement, inspiring devotees all over the world. Seeing Buddhimanta's extreme enthusiasm and expertise, Rāmeśvara sent him to many communities, New York, London, and Australia among them. Buddhimanta's sincerity was contagious. He became famous for his eagerness, which sometimes seemed to verge on spiritual madness, for distributing Śrīla Prabhupāda's books. Madhudviṣa Dāsa explains Buddhimanta's "madness" upon his arrival in Australia:

> Buddhi was so enthusiastic about distributing books that he used to rip open book boxes with a gleam in his eyes and then place a line of books up his arm. He'd go up and down the city street in a dhoti, with his arm full of books, stopping anyone and everyone to show them the books. Buddhi didn't mention the price of the books. He'd just show them the pictures until they revealed even a little interest, and then he'd say, "By the way, we take a donation to keep the printing presses going."
>
> When Buddhi was packing up his book bags to venture out for the day he would often say, "Were not bringing any books back." And if a fellow devotee would question him, "You're going to sell all these books in one day?" Buddhi, would answer "Yeah! Why not?"

Buddhimanta's teammates remember how he would breathe heavily in anticipation before getting out of the van to distribute books. When the van would finally stop at the destination, he'd literally jump out and get started. He used to say, "The tone for the whole day is set during the first five minutes, so better make them good." When Buddhi's team members asked how long they were supposed to stay out, he'd say, "Until all the books are gone." Buddhimanta's example gives us a good lesson in how even one enthusiastic person can make his or her mark on the world. Śrīla Prabhupāda had told Gopal Krishna Dāsa, "My books are sold because of the enthusiasm of my devotees," and Buddhimanta proved it.

The UK Awakens

Satsvarūpa Dāsa Goswami summarizes the early history of book distribution in the UK:

> When book distribution had been just beginning in America in 1970, no books had been available in England. But within a year, *Kṛṣṇa Book* distribution had begun there, and Śrīla Prabhupāda had written, "All of my disciples in London center are very intelligent, and they should unite around this single task of selling *Kṛṣṇa* book widely throughout Britain." By 1974 the devotees in Britain were valiantly distributing books. During one busy six-day period, they distributed six hundred volumes of *Teachings of Lord Caitanya,* four hundred of *Śrīmad-Bhāgavatam,* and one thousand *Back to Godhead* magazines.[4]

It's uncanny how similar events unfolded to stoke the fire of book distribution around the world. In 1972, a spontaneous outpouring from the devotees in Los Angeles who within days had distributed a record number of books, had boosted expectations of devotees everywhere for their own distribution. Now similar events were being repeated in Europe and the UK. Janānanda Goswami, who was in the UK at the time, gives some of the details of this period:

> It's autumn 1971 – Oxford Street, London – thousands of people going here and there on perhaps the world's busiest shopping street. I stand on the street corner in jeans and a T-shirt, with hair to my waist, nervously holding a pile of *Back*

to Godheads. The daily *harināma saṅkīrtana* is nearby. I am speechless, holding the magazines in the air, hoping someone will stop and take one. Hours pass – three magazines go out for thirty pence each. I was surprised. And I was even more surprised to hear that that was the top score that day. That is what it was like. It seemed next to impossible to sell the literature.

Months later – shaved up – I'm out the door of the temple in the morning, for the first time with big, hardbound *Kṛṣṇa Books,* going door to door. We have to sell them somehow, I'm told. Days would go by, and between us not even one book would be sold. There they would sit in the storeroom, as the temple struggled from day to day to get enough food for the inmates.

We hear it was not long ago that there were devotees in London who did sell books and even get *lakṣmī* for them. But it seemed at this point we had little idea what to do except try and thank Śrīla Prabhupāda and Kṛṣṇa for the opportunity to try. Small books were there for distribution: *Easy Journey, On the Way to Kṛṣṇa, The Perfection of Yoga,* and maybe others like *The Matchless Gift*. It all seemed too foreign to the people and small numbers of books were going out.

Then, in 1972, sometime around spring, the first traveling *saṅkīrtana* party in Europe was formed – a rather motley crew, and not particularly successful in terms of results. It changed the dynamics of the *yātrā*. Prabhaviṣṇu got some money together and secured a vehicle. The spirit for distributing books grew. No particular technique, just enthusiasm, a good spiritual program, and conviction that these books will save the world – we must get them out. Big books, however, still sat dormant.

Around late spring an unexpected arrival of two devotees from Holland, Bidhan Chandra and Sudarśana Prabhus, opened the doors. Bidhan immediately filled up a bag with *Kṛṣṇa Books* and took to the street. We didn't do that sort of thing. How could you sell big books on the street? He came back at the end of the day, ten books *sold* for more than the cost price – unbelievable! I remember my first thoughts: "He must be a *śaktyāveśa avatāra*!"

From then on things changed. The traveling *saṅkīrtana* party spruced up with Prabhaviṣṇu Prabhu taking the reigns, and book distribution became the thing to do. Those doing books were like the special legion – the super squad.

Keśava and Śrīdhara Prabhus came through from the West Coast of the USA on their way to India. They shared stunning news of the book distribution in the US and went out themselves, enlivening the whole temple. We virtually ran out of all literature. On our traveling *saṅkīrtana* party, for many days all we had were leaflets. Then the full-edition softbound Macmillan *Gītās* arrived sometime in mid '72. Our traveling party was streamlined. Dhanañjaya Prabhu, the temple president, bent over backwards to give to whomever he could the strength to do it. The party consisted of Prabhaviṣṇu Prabhu at the helm, a real general and hero of book distribution, Mahāviṣṇu, Vrajendra Kumāra, Devadharma, Tribhaṅgānanda, and myself – a great team.

As we eagerly, enthusiastically, took daily to the streets of towns around the country, book distribution soared. The mood in the temple changed. It was really uplifted – a new level of direction. *Kṛṣṇa Book* trilogies arrived in autumn '72 – the storm was on to blitz the country with *Kṛṣṇa Books*. By later standards it was small. If we could do ten trilogies a day each that was big – and a couple of *Bhagavad-gītās* on the side to those really interested (mostly hippies). In the temple at Bury Place the devotees also became book distribution conscious.

On January 3, 1973, something very special happened, at least for us. A letter arrived from Śrīla Prabhupāda addressed to Prabhaviṣṇu. After that letter, there was not a doubt that book distribution is the thing to do to please Śrīla Prabhupāda, to spread Kṛṣṇa consciousness and to advance spiritually.

> I am very glad to hear from you the wonderful news of traveling party in England. I think the people of that place are becoming more and more inclined for this Kṛṣṇa consciousness movement, they are inviting you to stay at their houses, they are taking books, becoming sometimes devotees – all of these are very encouraging signs to me. If you simply go on in this way, stopping

> in every village and city of England and Scotland, or if there are other places like Ireland, simply stop for some time, distribute books and hold *saṅkīrtana* procession, answer their questions, give some leaflets or small information freely, distribute *prasāda* wherever possible, at least some small thing, and if there is genuine interest being shown, then request the townspeople to arrange some engagements for speaking in their schools, or in someone's home, or a hall, like that. In this way remain always without anxiety for destination or comfortable situations, always relying only on the mercy of Kṛṣṇa for your plan, just go on preaching His message and selling His books, wherever there is interest. We shall not waste time if there is no interest or if the people are unfriendly, there are so many places to go. But I understand from your letter that practically everyone is taking some interest. That means you are presenting the thing in a very nice manner, they can detect that here are some persons who are actually sincere and nice, let me hear them, let me purchase one book. So I can understand that it is not an easy matter to travel extensively over long periods of time without proper food, rest, and sometimes it must be very cold there also, and still, because you are getting so much enjoyment, spiritual enjoyment, from it, it seems like play to you. That is advanced stage of spiritual life, never attained by even the greatest yogis and so-called *jñānīs*. But let any man see our devotees working so hard for Kṛṣṇa, then let anyone say that they are not better than millions of so-called yogis and transcendentalists, that is my challenge!

This and many other letters that began to circulate around the movement were what we needed to cement our conviction and empower us. That was really the incentive in those days, up until the time the Manor was opened in May 1973. Book distribution then slowed down and the traveling party stopped.

Over the next few years it was a struggle. Book distribution dipped until Haṁsadūta Prabhu came along to bail the *yātrā* out of its financial nightmare. Introducing record sales and his hard-line distributors, the focus changed. Few books but lots of *lakṣmī*.

In 1976, when Jayatīrtha Prabhu became the GBC, he synthesized the two. We were out of debt. He kept the record distribution but added books with each record. Amazingly – almost immediately – the books were going out by the thousands. He was so organized, at least by our standards. Huge shipments of books arrived from the US – *The Science of Self Realization,* the new *Kṛṣṇa Book* trilogy, the abridged *Bhagavad-gītā,* and many others.

1976 was the year the UK got on the book distribution map. And in 1977, when Śrīla Prabhupāda's health declined, the UK was challenging the world in books distributed. Thousands of big books were going out each week – combined with the super-effective *bhakta* program headed by Dānavīra Prabhu, the *saṅkīrtana* forces were increasing by the month. At the peak in late '77, we had around seventy full-time distributors, maybe more. Men, women, going to every town and village. The mood was feverish to please Śrīla Prabhupāda and keep him with us forever. It is Śrīla Prabhupāda who is the incentive for all of us. He drew that out more than ever in his declining health. Weekly scores rose – a transcendental competition that carried on every week even after Śrīla Prabhupāda's departure – *samādhi*

Prabhaviṣṇu Dāsa and Ādikartā Dāsa were both engaged in book distribution in the UK during the 1970s. Ādikartā recalls how Yogeścandra Dāsa, who had been a member of the Rādhā-Dāmodara traveling bus party and who knew the art of selling big books, came to the UK and coached him in big book distribution. Prabhaviṣṇu remembers how Keśava, Śrīdhara, and Tripurāri came to the UK at various times to give some inspirational seminars and practical demonstrations on book distribution. It was this spirit of cooperation and sharing of ideas that helped Śrīla Prabhupāda's books be distributed all over the world.

To Russia with Love

In 1971, Śrīla Prabhupāda traveled to the USSR with his disciple, Śyāmasundara. In just five days, Śrīla Prabhupāda not only spoke with Soviet professor G. G. Kotovsky – head of the Indian and South Asian Studies Department of the USSR Academy of Sciences – but also incidentally met a young local man, Anatoly Pinyayev. Later, Śrīla Prabhupāda initiated Anatoly, giving him the name Ananta-śānti Dāsa. This daring devotee became a pioneer of the Hare Kṛṣṇa movement in the USSR and ignited a book distribution revolution that made devotional service to Kṛṣṇa available to tens of thousands of his countrymen.

Author Satyarāja Dāsa details some of the events that unfolded after Śrīla Prabhupāda's visit to Moscow and that led to the Hare Kṛṣṇa movement becoming established in the former Soviet Union:

> Next in 1977 and 1979, the Bhaktivedanta Book Trust received an invitation to the prestigious Moscow International Book Fair, acquainting Muscovites with Prabhupāda's books for the first time. The *New York Times* noted the significance: "[The exhibit] drew curious Russians, the books spread, and Hare Kṛṣṇa was on its way in Russia."[5]

Satyarāja goes on to tell how by the mid 1980s Yuri Andropov was in power. The Hare Kṛṣṇa movement was seen as dangerous under his rule, and the government began harassing the devotees:

> By the mid 1980s Yuri Andropov was in power in the USSR, and he intensified the campaign already underway against the Hare Kṛṣṇa movement. He saw devotees as representing all things religious and was determined to wipe them out. Because of Ananta-śanti's contagious enthusiasm and the staggering results of the book fairs, Semyon Tsvigun, the deputy chief of the KGB under Andropov, said that three main

> threats to the Soviet Union were "pop music, Western culture, and Hare Kṛṣṇa."

ISKCON's leaders in the USSR at the time, Harikeśa Swami and Kīrtirāja Dāsa, as well as Australian child recording artist Śrī Prahlāda, were able to bring international attention to the fact that Hare Kṛṣṇa devotees were being thrown into prisons, labor camps, and psychiatric hospitals. In the same article, Satyarāja writes, the devotees were "suffering vicious mistreatment at the hands of police and political yes-men. Several devotees died in prison, clinging tightly to their faith while being tortured in various ways."

The Soviet government's attempt to stop the Hare Kṛṣṇa movement included a ban on selling Śrīla Prabhupāda's books. Nonetheless, the books had already entered the USSR through book fairs and were circulating at an amazing pace. Devotees living in the Soviet Union would photocopy the books, or sometimes even write them out by hand, and share them with their friends. Meanwhile, devotees outside the country devised ever new ways to smuggle Śrīla Prabhupāda's transcendental books past Soviet border guards, who would arrest anyone trying to bring them into the country. In Sweden, some devotees tossed bags of Śrīla Prabhupāda's books onto Soviet-bound ships as they went under bridges. Other devotees wrapped Śrīla Prabhupāda's books in aluminum foil and hid them in the engines of cars before they crossed the border into the Soviet Union.

Soviet devotees present in the country during that era describe how their countrymen, starving from lack of knowledge about spiritual life, would eagerly buy any of Śrīla Prabhupāda's books that made it through the government security forces.

After the fall of the Communist regime, people were allowed to buy religious literature. So eager were the Russian people for spiritual knowledge that some workers were giving an entire year's salary to purchase a set of Śrīla Prabhupāda's books. In the end, of course, the books outlived the Soviet regime. Now there are tens of thousands of devotees in the former Soviet Union. Book distribution is at an all-time high.

Book Distribution to the World of Academics

As early as 1970 Śrīla Prabhupāda wanted to increase the distribution of books to American universities, and later this distribution would spread to universities all over the world. In a letter to Dinesh Dāsa dated September 25, 1970, he wrote:

> I am especially pleased that you are taking charge in the Boston area of placing my books and literatures in the local school, college libraries and you have already had success with placing all our literatures in the two most important libraries of Harvard University and the Divinity School. When I spoke there sometime back, our Kṛṣṇa consciousness philosophy was very much appreciated, so I think this is an important place for our literatures to be available to the students and faculty. Please go on with this engagement enthusiastically and Kṛṣṇa will give you all success in the venture. You are intelligent and hard working devotee of Kṛṣṇa and Kṛṣṇa will bless you for this very fine service, which you are rendering unto Him.

In mid-April of 1974, Rāmeśvara wrote to Śrīla Prabhupāda the "wonderful news of the traveling library party" that the BBT had just begun. The team was taking orders for full sets of *Śrīmad-Bhāgavatam* and *Śrī Caitanya-caritāmṛta* even before they were published, as standing orders, borrowing the strategy of the world famous Encyclopedia Britannica. The Library Party was putting books in universities like Princeton and Yale and making contacts with big names in the academic world. The party consisted of Mahābuddhi and Ghanaśyāma Dāsa (later, Bhakti Tīrtha Mahārāja). Rāmeśvara not only conceived of the program but also managed and financed it with money from the BBT's mail order department in Los Angeles.

Śrīla Prabhupāda replied to Rāmeśvara on May 9, 1974: "The report of the BBT traveling library party is something new for us and this is also only the beginning. Please give my heartful thanks to the boys, Śrīmān Mahā Buddhi Dāsa Brahmacārī and Śrīmān Ghanaśyāma Dāsa Brahmacārī. These books are specifically meant for the intellectual class of people in your country and I have great hope in the results of this preaching at the Universities."

As Rāmeśvara continued to write to Śrīla Prabhupāda about the Library Party, Śrīla Prabhupāda's secretary, Satsvarūpa Dāsa Goswami, while reading Rāmeśvara's letters to Śrīla Prabhupāda, became its leader with Śrīla Prabhupāda's encouragement. Soon the Library Party picked up other members and spread to Europe, India, Asia, and then all over the world.

As academics around the world received and read Śrīla Prabhupāda's books and gave their favorable reviews, the Kṛṣṇa consciousness movement gained respect in learned circles throughout the world. It was the first time that Gauḍīya Vaiṣṇavism had been spread worldwide, and scholars began to recognize what Śrīla Prabhupāda had done.

On January 15, 1977, Rāmeśvara journeyed by train with Śrīla Prabhupāda and a small party of devotees to the Kumbha-melā. Rāmeśvara shared the same sleeping compartment with Prabhupāda, and while they were traveling Śrīla Prabhupāda asked Rāmeśvara to read recent reviews of his *Gītā* from scholars. He loved to hear the reviews; some of the scholars had prayed that he'd go on writing for the sake of humankind. When Rāmeśvara quoted "The pen is mightier than the sword," Śrīla Prabhupāda replied, "Yes, it is a revolution. That is what I think as I write on and on – a revolution to change the entire course of human history."

As the library party expanded across America into the Communist countries and India, some members of the party were surprised to find that many of the libraries had already purchased the first three-volume set of First Canto *Śrīmad-*

Bhāgavatams from Śrīla Prabhupāda himself. For example, in 1976, Satyanārāyaṇa Dāsa and Vaiyāsaki Dāsa, members of the Asian division of the BBT Library Party, traveled to Kashmir, a state in the Himalayan region of India. They later found out that Śrīla Prabhupāda had gone there himself to sell his *Bhāgavatams*. Satyanārāyaṇa remembers:

> While giving Śrīla Prabhupāda a report about our party's distribution of his books to libraries in India, we told him that we were able to get his books into a Muslim institution in Kashmir called Anant Nagar. To our surprise, this school had taken a full order of *Śrīmad-Bhāgavatams* and had appreciated them very much, even though they were Muslims. When Śrīla Prabhupāda heard this, he was visibly enlivened.
>
> We described the circuitous route that we had taken to reach the school, how we had gone through a tunnel high in the Himalayas at an elevation of four thousand feet. Śrīla Prabhupāda at once corrected us, saying that the tunnel we had gone through was actually at an elevation of fourteen thousand feet, not four thousand. As it turns out, the sign in front of the tunnel had said that it was at an elevation of four thousand meters, but we had read meters as feet. Astonished that Śrīla Prabhupāda knew this detail about the route to this remote part of Kashmir, we asked him how he knew about the tunnel. He then told us that he had been through that tunnel on a mission to sell his *Śrīmad-Bhāgavatam.*
>
> Vaiyāsaki and I had also been to Srinagar, the capital of Kashmir, where we had met a man at the prestigious Oriental Library. This man told us that he had purchased the *Śrīmad-Bhāgavatam* directly from Śrīla Prabhupāda.
>
> Śrīla Prabhupāda's account of the tunnel and of his going to Kashmir not only confirmed the man's story but also solved the greater mystery of how his *Bhāgavatam* had come to that part of the country: Śrīla Prabhupāda had personally gone before us to sell his books.

Satyanārāyaṇa adds, "We marveled at how Śrīla Prabhupāda had traveled alone many years before us to these remote places, and we felt fortunate that he was now engaging us in the same mission. We now saw that Śrīla Prabhupāda was the original book distributor. Actually, he was the original everything."

Postscript of the Explosion

From the time that Śrīla Prabhupāda began to print his books in America in 1968 until 1977, the year he left this world, devotees around the globe, working at a feverish pace, had distributed 55,000,000 books and magazines. The bulk of these were sold in the five-year period beginning in 1973.

At the GBC meetings of 1977, Tamal Krishna Mahārāja read to Śrīla Prabhupāda the breakdown of these 55 million pieces of literature, categorized by language, that had been printed and distributed up until 1977. Here is the transcript of that report just as Tamal Krishna Mahārāja read it to Śrīla Prabhupāda:

English: 43.5 million
Spanish: 3 million
German: 2.25 million
Japanese: 2.25 million
French: 2.75 million
Portuguese (Brazil and Portugal): hundreds of thousands
Dutch: 1 million
Italian: 5 lakhs*
Chinese: 55,000
Korean: 20,000
Yugoslavian: 20,000
Polish: 10,000
Hungarian: 10,000
Czechoslovakian: 10,000
Russian: 5,000
Swahili: 1 lakh

* 1 lakh equals 100,000.

Hindi, Bengali, Telugu, Gujarati, Marathi: many hundreds of thousands

Since 1977 the BBT has continued to publish mass quantities of Śrīla Prabhupāda's books and ship them to ISKCON communities throughout the world. The number of books distributed has recently crossed the half billion mark.

History shows that Śrīla Prabhupāda repeatedly told his inexperienced young disciples to sell his books, and when they did, wonderful, miraculous things happened. Machiavelli once said, "Whoever wishes to foresee the future must consult the past; for human events ever resemble those of preceding times."

I hope that my short summary, including anecdotes from the early history of book distribution, will animate in the reader the same passion for distributing Śrīla Prabhupāda's books that motivated the devotees who walked before us.

Their rush onto the field of service is reminiscent of the way the *gopīs* of Vṛndāvana spontaneously ran out to meet Kṛṣṇa in the forest when they heard His flute-song. It wasn't so different for Śrīla Prabhupāda's disciples, who heard their guru beating the *bṛhat-mṛdaṅga* and, guided by Kṛṣṇa from within, spontaneously ran out to towns, villages, and college campuses to fulfill his desire that people everywhere have a chance to advance in Kṛṣṇa consciousness.

Today many people born well after Śrīla Prabhupāda's disappearance are not only reading his books but also dedicating their lives to distributing them. And as they do, this new generation of book distributors are tasting the same happiness the devotees tasted a few decades ago.

This section of *Our Family Business* concentrates on the beginning of book distribution up to 1977 (and sometimes beyond), when Śrīla Prabhupāda left this world. The history of the book distribution revolution is, of course, much broader than can be contained in these pages. Still, I wanted to give you, the reader, a slice of it in order to illustrate how the fire that ignited the explosion of books going out came from Śrīla Prabhupāda's heart. After all, it was he who immortalized these words: "Whatever progress we have made, it is simply due to distributing these books."[6]

Those who go out to distribute Śrīla Prabhupāda's books today and into the future will discover for themselves how true these words are.

TENETS

Śrī Caitanya Mahāprabhu said:
"I order every man within this universe
to accept this Kṛṣṇa consciousness
movement and distribute it everywhere."

ŚRĪ CAITANYA-CARITĀMṚTA
ĀDI-LĪLĀ 9.36

CHAPTER SEVEN

The Pen Is Mightier Than the Sword

I COMPOSED MY FIRST useful message when I was in first grade and had just learned to write. It was a three-word note to my mother. I had just come back from school, and she was not home from work yet. I wanted to go over to see my friend Lance Bartle at his house, so I picked up a pencil and wrote my mother this note:

I at Lance

When I came home, my mother greeted me like a war hero who had received a medal of honor. For a week she showed off my note to anyone and everyone. In fact, fifty years later, just after she left this world, I found it in one of her drawers.

My mother's reaction to that note was my first exposure to the impact of the written word. Of course, my tiny revelation was nothing new. For centuries humans have esteemed the written word, and books in particular. Thomas Carlyle, the famous nineteenth-century Scottish historian and philosopher, gives this summary of the weightiness of books: "In books lies the soul of the whole past time, the articulate audible voice of the past – all that mankind has done, thought, gained, or been. It is lying as in magic preservation in the pages of books."[1]

Śrīla Prabhupāda assesses the power of his own books in a letter dated March 18, 1969 to his disciple Hṛṣīkeśa Dāsa: "If you kindly read my books carefully then all your spiritual desires will be fulfilled."

The first time I held one of Śrīla Prabhupāda books I instantly felt connected to him. When I read the book, I felt guided. His voice was palpable and articulate. Since then, my dedication to his books has been confirmed and strengthened each time I've shared them with others and seen the effect they have on first-time readers. In this way, throughout my life, my faith in Śrīla Prabhupāda's books has grown stronger. His books contain the sublime vibrations of the spiritual world and thus have the power to transform the material world, one person at a time.

Śrīla Prabhupāda was convinced that the mass distribution of books is an efficient strategy for influencing human society. He also promoted that strategy as the most effective means to deliver Kṛṣṇa conscious knowledge to human civilization. He writes:

> These books and magazines are our most important propaganda weapons to defeat the ignorance of *māyā's* army, and the more we produce such literature and sell them profusely all over the world, the more we shall deliver the world from the suicide course. So your work is the most important preaching work, may Kṛṣṇa bless you more and more. Thank you for helping me in this way.[2]

> My ambition is to spread these books far and wide all over the world so that everyone shall read at least one of our books and that will change his life. If only 1% become devotees, that will change the world.[3]

Now let's examine more closely Śrīla Prabhupāda's strategy to change the world by writing, publishing, and distributing his books. It is a well-known fact that people in every country love books and revere their authors; for this reason alone the mass distribution of books is the perfect plan for instilling Kṛṣṇa consciousness in people's hearts. And as greater numbers of people receive transcendental books written by pure devotees of Kṛṣṇa, the effect on human society will be striking.

The Written Word's Sway on Humanity

To be sure, writing is a gift unique to humanity. Animals can scratch and bite, scream or roar, but they can't write. And humans are singularly equipped not only to write but also to appreciate and glorify each other's writing well done. When people use their wits to compose superb prose, their words bring readers to deeper levels of understanding, and civilized people everywhere applaud such writers' contributions to the world's betterment. The inscription above the entrance to the Brooklyn Public Library is a testament to this truth: "Farther than arrow, higher than the wings, fly poet's song and prophet's word."

History also shows that a few well-chosen words printed and distributed can touch people's hearts, spark them to form movements, and even galvanize them to topple empires. In this regard, the playwright Edward Bulwer-Lytton enshrined these immortal words: "The pen is mightier than the sword."

The writer Michael Wagner, in his essay "What Difference Can a Book Make?" gives a practical example of this mightiness:

> Certainly many books published these days have no other purpose than entertainment, but serious books can fulfill a much more significant role. Indeed, historically, certain books have had dramatic impacts on the thinking of whole societies. Consider, for example, Charles Darwin's book, *The Origin of Species,* published in 1859. The theory of evolution first popularized by this book has dominated the thinking of

> "educated" people around the world for over a hundred years. Hardly anyone reads that book any more, but the movement it helped to spawn continues unabated. It was like a match that started an inferno that is still raging.[4]

Two other examples of authors who have altered the world through their writings are Adam Smith and the co-authors Karl Marx and Friedrich Engels. In 1776 Adam Smith wrote *The Wealth of Nations,* which laid the foundation of modern capitalism and economics. Marx's and Engels's ideas and writings – especially *The Communist Manifesto,* which they completed in 1848 – have had a profound impact on world politics and intellectual thought, an influence felt even today.

Even well-written pamphlets have catalyzed uprisings and popular movements. For example, historians give credit to the pamphlet *Common Sense,* written by the journalist Thomas Paine, for helping spark the 1776 American Revolution. In *Common Sense,* Paine told the colonists to wake up to the fact that they were being unnecessarily subjugated, and called on them to revolt against the British king. *Common Sense* acted as a spark of inspiration for the colonies to seek independence from England.[5] The pamphlet was sold to more than half a million readers in America – at that time about one fifth of the population. The statesman Thomas Jefferson wrote to Paine: "Go on doing with your pen what in other times was done with the sword."

Here is yet another example of the written word's capacity to incite social and political revolution. In Cuba, in 1953, the young and ambitious Fidel Castro – imprisoned after attempting to incite a rebellion – made his own magic using his pen. Behind bars, Castro wrote his speech "History Will Absolve Me," in which he called for the people of Cuba to overthrow the Batista government and bring in democratic elections.

To conceal his writings, he used an ingenious type of ink, lime juice, which on paper is invisible until exposed to the sun. Castro's wife and co-conspirator Mirta, who regularly visited her imprisoned spouse, smuggled out a few pages of the speech with each trip. Eventually twenty thousand copies were printed and distributed clandestinely to the Cuban public. That tiny book had a profound impact on Cuba's populace, and the people later helped Castro rise to power.[6]

In addition to political and social influence, books have also had laid the foundations for the spread of religious movements. Books preserve the authenticity of religious movements by providing a record of and a focal point for their teachings. And they also give adherents a hands-on way to spread those teachings.

An Authentic Record

All major religious and spiritual movements rely on written documents to define and guide their practices. Faithful Christians, Muslims, and Buddhists, for example, are those who obey the Bible, Koran, or who follow the teachings of the Buddhist Sūtras, respectively, and faithful Hindus keep and read the *Bhagavad-gītā*.

In our line of devotion following Śrī Caitanya Mahāprabhu, Śrīla Rūpa Gosvāmī writes, "Devotional service of the Lord that ignores the authorized Vedic literatures like the *Upaniṣads, Purāṇas,* and *Nārada Pañcarātra* is simply an unnecessary disturbance in society."[7] And in the *Bhagavad-gītā* (16.24), Kṛṣṇa Himself says, "One should therefore understand what is duty and what is not duty by the regulations of the scriptures. Knowing such rules and regulations, one should act so that he may gradually be elevated."

The Literary Outspread of Ideas

Books are vessels that carry ideas. The word *idea* is defined as "a thought or suggestion as to a possible course of action."[8] When a person reads a book, the ideas between the covers spill out into his or her mind, just as the seeds broadcast by a gardener find a home in the rich soil where they are strewn. These idea-seeds sprout and soon bear fruit within the reader. The American transcendentalist Ralph Waldo Emerson, who studied the *Gītā,* writes, "Sow a thought and you reap an action; sow an act and you reap a habit; sow a habit and you reap a character; sow a character and you reap a destiny."

Through the same progression, Śrīla Prabhupāda's books yield the fruit of faith in devotional service, faith that inspires the reader to search out the company of devotees who can answer life's questions and teach one how to apply the book's wisdom in one's life.

I would like to tell you about Andrew, a typical example of a sincere soul coming in contact with one of Śrīla Prabhupāda's books and taking to devotional service. I will let Andrew tell his own story:

> I never thought of buying a book. I used to see devotees distributing books near Culver City, but I would avoid them. But one day I saw a devotee girl distributing books and she came over to talk to me. She asked me, "Do you believe in God?" I answered, "Yes." She smiled and continued, "So, if someone told you that they had a book written by God, would you be interested?" "Yes," I replied again. Then she handed me the *Gītā.* But I said, "Well, I'm not really into religion." She said, "But you said you believe in God. Why wouldn't you want to read this book?" She made me promise that I'd keep it and that I'd read it. Then I asked if I should give a donation, and she said, "Yes, ten dollars." That was a lot, and I thought of giving the book back, but instead I gave her the ten dollars. I took that book everywhere because I had paid good money for it.
>
> Later, when my life was in transition, I left that book in storage at my father's house. When I came back to see my father a year later, it was at a time when I felt hopeless about my life, so I went to speak to him. I was amazed to see that the book I had left in storage with him a year earlier was now on his bookshelf, so I pulled it down, thinking I might find solace in it. When I read how Arjuna had thrown down his

> bow in despair, I was expecting Kṛṣṇa to take the Christian approach and to tell him to turn the other cheek. I was surprised, however, when Kṛṣṇa instead told Arjuna to fight. When I came to Kṛṣṇa's words to Arjuna saying, "Get up and fight!" I felt as if He was speaking directly to me.
>
> Those few minutes of reading totally turned my mind to Kṛṣṇa's teachings: "Don't worry about winning or losing or how you appear to others. Your sole duty in life is to perform your duty to God." I wasn't thinking, "Oh, I should now join the Hare Kṛṣṇas." I just went on with my life, but with new insight. For some reason, I had previously shunned the Hare Kṛṣṇas, but now my mind was completely open.

Andrew's story (and there are thousands more like it) justifies the great endeavor it takes to produce transcendental books and distribute them to the masses. Publishing even one transcendental book requires an enormous amount of time and energy on the part of dozens of people, not to mention the needed material resources. However, those who know the power and importance of transcendental books take on this work as a burden of love. A book finally released by the devotees' hard work has a lasting effect on the world.

The Gosvāmīs had a harder time publishing and distributing their books than we do publishing and distributing Śrīla Prabhupāda's books today. Although Johannes Gutenberg invented mechanical book printing around 1440, the technology didn't reach India until just ten years before Śrīla Rūpa Gosvāmī's disappearance. Gutenberg's first major endeavor of printing 180 Bibles started a revolution in publishing. Up to that point, like in India, books had been printed using hand-carved wooden blocks or been laboriously hand-copied by scribes on any number of surfaces, including leaves, wood, shells, or papers created from plant matter or animal skins. Gutenberg's invention of the printing press helped printing make a huge leap forward. Its value wasn't lost on the people of his time. Catholic reformer Martin Luther used the Gutenberg press to print his *Ninety-five Theses,* and in only six weeks copies of his *Theses* could be found throughout Europe, effectively launching his Protestant movement. We know that as the printing press became available in India, our *ācāryas* also used it to standardize and disseminate the teachings of Gauḍīya Vaiṣṇavism.

With each generation, technological developments have revolutionized the book publishing industry. Śrīla Bhaktivinoda Ṭhākura, for one, used these developments to establish a Vaiṣṇava Depository at his home – a library and printing press for publishing canonical devotional texts such as those by the Six Gosvāmīs of Vṛndāvana and their followers, and his own original writings. This endeavor helped restore the purity of Gauḍīya Vaiṣṇava practice in India, but it also made it possible to standardize the presentation of Gauḍīya Vaiṣṇava theology and thought.

Printing may seem like a simple task, but it requires skill, even in the modern age. Even choosing the right paper and inks requires knowledge of the printing process. We know that Śrīla Prabhupāda spent a good deal of his time tracking down good paper in his first publishing efforts to produce his *Back to Godhead* magazine in India. He exhausted much of the money he had saved just to buy that paper, and he also personally transported heavy rolls of it on rickshaws to the printers.

Half a millennium ago when Rūpa Gosvāmī and Sanātana Gosvāmī wrote their books, they used a metal stylus to etch their words onto green palm leaves. The places where they impressed the stylus upon the leaves would turn from green to white. After putting the imprinted leaves in the sun, the green leaves turned beige and the imprinted areas black, displaying the rows of sentences. Lord Caitanya praised Śrīla Rūpa Gosvāmī's handwriting on these palm leaves, saying that his sentences looked like rows of pearls.[9] One can still see original Gosvāmī palm-leaf writings at the Vṛndāvana Research Institute near ISKCON's Krishna-Balaram Mandir.

In Kolkata, India, ISKCON devotees headed by Hari Śauri

Dāsa maintain the Bhaktivedanta Research Centre. There they preserve and catalog thousands of important books that were written or used by previous Vaiṣṇava masters. On a recent tour of the Centre, my wife and I were able to see and touch books written or used by these masters and to feel a deep communion with both the masters and their books.

As I type this page on my laptop computer, using software so sophisticated that I will never use all of its features, millions of people around the world are also downloading digital books from the Internet onto handheld electronic devices and smart phones.

All this goes to prove that humans crave ideas and have readily consumed and distributed them throughout the ages; thus, there is good reason to expect that Śrīla Prabhupāda's campaign to distribute mass quantities of his books will have a far-reaching effect. Here's more evidence that this was Śrīla Prabhupāda's intention:

> Keep distributing as many [books] as possible in huge quantities. This is my pleasure. We must make a large propaganda program for Kṛṣṇa consciousness by distributing these books everywhere, all over the world. Just like the communists they are very expert in distributing their literature, their propaganda. At the present moment they are distributing their literature here in India in nine different languages and it is quite effective. Therefore we must print hundreds and thousands of books and distribute them at the same speed and thus we will have a great effect on the mass population of Europe and America. If we can get the masses in the Western countries like Europe and America to become Kṛṣṇa conscious, then all the rest of the world will follow. That is a fact. So please, I beg you, continue distributing my books in this way and Kṛṣṇa will pour His blessings upon you all. Please keep me informed from time to time of the book sales statistics.[10]

In a letter written on December 28, 1971, Śrīla Prabhupāda addressed Yogeśvara Dāsa, one of his leaders in Europe, where his movement was then lagging behind the US, and gave him this remedy:

> I think now things are not going too well in France and Germany centers. So if somehow or other you can produce profuse books for these places, spend your all time translating, organizing, printing and distributing such books in foreign languages, then I think you will be able to improve the situation there. If there are amply books, everything else will succeed. Practically our Society is built on books.

Śrīla Prabhupāda began his push to bring Vaiṣṇava literature to the world before his arrival in America from India in 1965. And after he arrived, he continued writing. Sitting cross-legged on the floor at a makeshift desk in his simple Bowery apartment, he would tap away on his donated typewriter past midnight until the sun rose. As the people of New York City slept or scrounged for nightlife, he revealed the path back to Godhead through the written word. Typing with two index fingers, he methodically added page after page to the stacks of papers that were his translations and commentaries, manuscripts that would eventually become his celebrated books. Later, he used a dictating machine, speaking his translations and commentaries until his final breath.

In all circumstances, Śrīla Prabhupāda depended on his books to win the day for spreading Kṛṣṇa consciousness and for increasing the internal strength of the devotees who had joined the Kṛṣṇa consciousness movement.

Fire Will Act

In 1976 some radical organizations had began attacking ISKCON in America, claiming that ISKCON was a "brainwashing cult." Śrīla Prabhupāda's response was fiery:

> They are now feeling the weight of this movement. Formerly they thought these people come and go, but now they see we

> are staying. Now we have set fire. It will go on, it cannot be stopped. You can bring big, big fire brigades but the fire will act. The brainwash books are already there. Even if they stop externally, internally it will go on. Our first class campaign is book distribution. Go house to house. The real fighting is now. Kṛṣṇa will give you all protection.[11]

This remark by Śrīla Prabhupāda about "the brainwash books" is, of course, sarcastic and satirical. At the same time, it gives "brainwashing" its true and positive meaning, as if in reply to some critics of his movement: Spiritual progress involves cleaning one's mind and heart of unwanted qualities, such as lust, greed, and anger.

In fact, his emphasis on the importance of his books as maintainers of his Society's internal purity is reminiscent of his own guru's mood. Śrīla Bhaktisiddhānta Sarasvatī Ṭhākura, after establishing his flagship temple in Calcutta, writes in an article of his magazine the *Gauḍīya* (8.639): "Only if herein we protect ourselves from the association of materialists and the tumultuous welter of Kali-yuga will *hari-kathā* be preached from this place. Only by building ideal lives and a mansion of books can the message of *bhagavad-bhakti* remain permanently in this sphere."

Since even ordinary books have had their effect on the world, imagine the profound, lasting effect that *mansions of books* about the Supreme Personality of Godhead will have on human society.

Cut the Knots of Attachment

Unlike common writings that take readers no further than the body and mind, transcendental books take readers to the spiritual plane, freeing them from all anxieties that come from material conceptions. Śrī Kṛṣṇa's timeless wisdom in the *Bhagavad-gītā,* for example, is a kind of "weapon" famous for cutting the mighty knots of illusion, tied by the false ego, that bind a living entity to the material world. Kṛṣṇa tells Arjuna about the beneficial effects of reading such books of knowledge: "Therefore the doubts which have arisen in your heart out of ignorance should be slashed by the weapon of knowledge. Armed with yoga, O Bhārata, stand and fight."[12]

Sūta Gosvāmī says something similar to the sages at Naimiṣāraṇya while speaking *Śrīmad-Bhāgavatam.* He says that transcendental knowledge is like a sword that cuts through the misgivings carried in one's heart and thus ends one's karma and immemorial attachment to the material world: "Thus the knot in the heart is pierced, and all misgivings are cut to pieces. The chain of fruitive actions is terminated when one sees the self as master."[13]

Liberation by Sound

The *Vedas* clearly and repeatedly explain this science of liberation, and the master teachers of devotional service in turn pass that science down to us. Here Śrīla Prabhupāda again elaborates on this science:

> The *Vedānta-sūtra* says that sound is the origin of all objects of material possession and that by sound one can also dissolve this material existence. *Anāvṛttiḥ śabdāt* means "liberation by sound." The entire material manifestation began from sound, and sound can also end material entanglement, if it has a particular potency. The particular sound capable of doing this is the transcendental vibration Hare Kṛṣṇa.[14]

Śrīla Vyāsadeva's *Vedānta-sūtra* also confirms this spiritual science of attaining perfection through reception of transcendental sound carried by scriptures:

- God cannot be known by inference, but only through the scriptures (*śāstra-yonitvāt*).[15]
- Pronouncements of human reasoning can never perfectly

free one from doubt, because there is no finality in human reason. Therefore, the final authority is the scripture (*tarkāpratiṣṭhānāt*).[16]

- The defects of human reasoning do not apply in the case of God (Brahman), because the scriptures so declare it; and the word of God alone is the root from which we learn anything about these transcendental subjects (*śrutes tu śabda-mūlatvāt*).[17]

Kṛṣṇa Dvaipāyana Vyāsadeva, the compiler of the *Vedas,* specifically wrote down these and many other instructions in the form of mantras so they could be distributed to the masses of people in Kali-yuga. In *Śrīmad-Bhāgavatam,* Vyāsadeva's son Śukadeva Gosvāmī points out this ultimate purpose of his father's work: "The material miseries of the living entity, which are superfluous to him, can be directly mitigated by the linking process of devotional service. But the mass of people do not know this, and therefore the learned Vyāsadeva compiled this Vedic literature, which is in relation to the Supreme Truth."[18]

A soul trapped in a material body requires outside help to become free. Only by hearing from a transcendental source can a conditioned soul awaken his dormant spiritual awareness. Kavirāja Gosvāmī mentions this fact in *Śrī Caitanya-caritāmṛta* (*Madhya-līlā* 20.122): "The conditioned soul cannot revive his Kṛṣṇa consciousness by his own effort. But out of causeless mercy, Lord Kṛṣṇa [in His incarnation as Śrī Kṛṣṇa Dvaipāyana Vyāsadeva] compiled the Vedic literature and its supplements, the *Purāṇas.*"

Śrīla Prabhupāda's Books Are Literary Incarnations of God

In fact, scripture enjoins that each volume of the *Vedas* – particularly *Śrīmad-Bhāgavatam* – although appearing in the form of paper and ink, is actually a Deity of Kṛṣṇa that can deliver a conditioned soul from the material world. These

Deities, crafted of sound (rather than of marble or metal), are specifically meant for deep study, practical application, and for distributing to the conditioned souls.

Kṛṣṇa's form is completely spiritual, free from any material defect. Because conditioned souls cannot perceive Kṛṣṇa's spiritual form with their present material senses, the Lord, being all-powerful and compassionate, appears in the material world in His Deity form. The Lord's devotees fashion the Deity according to the direction of the scriptures, using authorized materials mentioned by Kṛṣṇa Himself in His instructions to Śrī Uddhava: "The Deity form of the Lord is said to appear in eight varieties – stone, wood, metal, earth, paint, sand, the mind, or jewels."[19] Just as the form of the Deity (*arcā*) thus crafted is nondifferent from Kṛṣṇa's eternal form, so too, according to scripture, is His *avatāra* in the form of a scriptural book. "This scripture named *Śrīmad-Bhāgavatam* is the literary incarnation of God, and it is compiled by Śrīla Vyāsadeva, the incarnation of God. It is meant for the ultimate good of all people, and it is all-successful, all-blissful, and all-perfect."[20]

The *Padma Purāṇa* elaborates:

> The *Bhāgavatam's* First and Second Cantos are Lord Kṛṣṇa's lotus feet, and the Third and Fourth Cantos are His thighs. The Fifth Canto is His navel, the Sixth Canto is His chest, and the Seventh and Eighth Cantos are His arms. The Ninth Canto is His throat, the Tenth His blooming lotus face, the Eleventh His forehead, and the Twelfth His head. I bow down to that Lord, the ocean of mercy, whose color is like that of a *tamāla* tree and who appears in this world for the welfare of all. I worship Him as the bridge for crossing the unfathomable ocean of material existence. *Śrīmad-Bhāgavatam* has appeared as His very self.

When people intimately connect with these Deities in the form of Śrīla Prabhupāda's transcendental books, they become purified and feel fulfilled and happy. Śrīla Prabhupāda explains

Madhvācārya, the founder-*ācārya* of the Brahma-Madhva-sampradāya in Kali-yuga, engaged in our family business as a writer, and in the process reestablished the authority of Vyāsadeva's pure teachings, which had been distorted by the impersonal speculative philosophy of Śaṅkarācārya. Madhvācārya was authorized by Vyāsadeva, who approved his commentary on the *Bhagavad-gītā.*

why people feel unfulfilled and incomplete: "All forms of incompleteness are due to incomplete knowledge of the Complete Whole."[21]

On the one hand, people who receive complete spiritual knowledge, especially by studying the *Bhagavad-gītā* and *Śrīmad-Bhāgavatam,* become fixed on Kṛṣṇa as their life's goal. They then feel complete and satisfied. On the other hand, those who receive incomplete knowledge, or worse, misinformation and disinformation, feel incomplete and disturbed. Many authors write books that contain vague or misleading descriptions of God: "The Supreme is just a kind of feeling," or "You and I are all the Supreme." Also commonplace today is pseudospiritualists writing books that promote the idea that God is formless or void.

But the *Vedas,* which come from the perfect source, indicate that one can hardly love a feeling or a formless energy in the name of God. Furthermore, if we are all God but have simply forgotten this fact, what is the use of offering prayers? To whom is one praying?

The result, then, of receiving authorized, accurate, and detailed knowledge about Kṛṣṇa, the Supreme Personality of Godhead, and His multifarious spiritual and material energies, is that one develops a relationship with Him. And only by developing a relationship with this Absolute Truth is the taste of real happiness possible. Śrīla Prabhupāda disseminated a straightforward description of Kṛṣṇa as the Supreme Personality of Godhead in his *Bhagavad-gītā As It Is.* In the following *Śrīmad-Bhāgavatam* purport he explains the result:

> The *Bhagavad-gītā* has been well known all over the world for a very long time, especially in the Western world, but because the subject matter was not discussed by devotees, there was no effect. Not a single person in the West became Kṛṣṇa conscious before the Kṛṣṇa consciousness movement was founded. But when the same *Bhagavad-gītā* was presented as it is through the disciplic succession, the effect of spiritual realization was immediately manifested.[22]

In a poetic offering to his spiritual master, Śrīla Prabhupāda writes about the personal revelations he received by hearing the Vedic knowledge from his guru:

> Absolute is sentient*
>   Thou hast proved.
> Impersonal calamity
>   Thou hast moved.
>
> This gives us a life
>   Anew and fresh.
> Worship thy feet
>   Your Divine Grace[23]

Those who distribute books of transcendental knowledge give others a chance to know the Absolute Truth and develop a personal relationship with Him; and the happiness felt by the recipients of such loving service changes the world, one person at a time.

The conclusion is that when fortunate people receive the bhakti scriptures, which describe the beauty, charm, and opulence of the Supreme Personality of Godhead and scientifically explain His unlimited potencies, their doubts, which are like dark clouds, begin to clear. As their hearts are cleared of ignorance, these fortunate souls feel joy, search out the company of devotees, and take to a life of devotional service.

Books Penetrate Society

Owing to their portable nature, books and the ideas they contain become absorbed into societies. What's more, when books are especially inspirational, like Śrīla Prabhupāda's, people tend to pass them around or tell others to read them. In this way books go where people can't go and end up strewn, like seeds, all over the world. As a testament to this truth, devotees

* Here "sentient" means "endowed with senses," that is, a person.

regularly report finding Śrīla Prabhupāda's books in surprising and remote places.

For example, an original set of Śrīla Prabhupāda's First Canto *Śrīmad-Bhāgavatams* somehow or other made its way from India to America and landed in a small library in Boise, Idaho. To lighten her inventory, the local librarian was selling books "by the pound." In the process she unwittingly passed on that great treasure to a fortunate devotee. Another devotee found one of Śrīla Prabhupāda's books at a yard sale in the infamous gambling town Atlantic City, New Jersey, where there had never been an established center to teach or promote Kṛṣṇa consciousness. Thousands of such cases are reported annually.

But Do Books Sell?

Humans have a natural thirst for knowledge, and the greatest concentration of knowledge is available in books. Despite competing technologies like television, therefore, people still gravitate toward books. Andrew Ross, professor of social and cultural analysis at New York University, writes, "The smallest bookstore still contains more ideas of worth than have been presented in the entire history of television."

Nowadays, with the advance of the Internet and electronic publishing markets, there are plenty of ways to read a book. So do print books still sell? Industry experts say that although books are now presented electronically and not just on paper, sales of paperback and hardbound books have not waned: "But the book itself is hanging on and even thriving. More than any major cultural product, it has retained its essential worth."[24]

The print book seems here to stay:

> The digital revolution has left its share of burnt-out carcasses on the side of the information superhighway. Just ask anyone who runs a newspaper or works in the music business. But all of the old media has not succumbed to the Internet's wrath.

> The book business is still alive, and in many ways it's thriving. Sure, many of us have switched to eBooks, which cost less than hardcovers. But we're still handing over ten bucks for what is a huge margin product.[25]

People love their books. In Taipei, Taiwan, a group of entrepreneurs have invented a new way to attract people interested in nightlife: a bookstore that stays open all night.

> It's midnight in the capital of Taiwan. While some people are slowly walking home through the neon-lit streets, or getting ready to hit the club scene, others are on their way to a more unusual nocturnal hangout – a bookstore.
>
> The Eslite store in central Taipei stays open 24 hours and has more night owl visitors than most Western bookstores could dream of during their daytime hours.
>
> Here, young and old sit side by side on small steps or around reading tables, deeply engrossed in literary worlds. Others stand and some sit on the floor, all reading in hushed silence as soft classical music seeps out from the speakers.
>
> "People in Taipei do many things by night," says Wan Hsuan Chang, a teacher who sits on a step in the middle of the store, skimming through the children's classic *When Marnie Was There,* by Joan G. Robinson.
>
> "You can go to the night market, shopping or nightclubbing. I [prefer to] read," she adds, before telling me to keep my voice down. "There are people trying to concentrate on their books here."[26]

Intimate Association

We carry our favorite books with us until they are worn, and they give us all the time we need to drink deep of their lessons, never complaining if we have not taken the time to read them. Just now, over my shoulder, sits my bookshelf, overflowing with all the books I have collected and intend to read. I enjoy and feel inspired being near them, as they embody the best ideas and spiritual philosophy, and I look forward to spending quiet time with them, replenishing my consciousness. Humans actually require very little to be happy. One requirement, however, is access to knowledge, because, according to the *Vedas,* humans are especially designed to assimilate knowledge.

Therefore books are an integral part of human society. They give us privileged and intimate access to higher association. Śrīla Prabhupāda writes in his purport to *Śrīmad-Bhāgavatam* 1.5.11 about how Nārada Muni has appeared within one of the chapters: "We are sure, therefore, that everyone in human society will welcome *Śrīmad-Bhāgavatam,* even though it is now presented with so many faults, for it is recommended by such an authority as Śrī Nārada, who has very kindly appeared in this chapter."

Think about what it's like to sit alone with your favorite book. A book can become your best friend and give you solace even when no one else can. From a book, the author takes the time – again and again – to speak to us personally, even revealing secrets that he shares only with his most intimate friends. Reading a book gives one uninterrupted time with its author. To meet such a person through a book can thus be more rewarding than meeting the author in person. Śrīla Prabhupāda writes, "Whatever I have wanted to say, I have said in my books. If I live, I will say something more. If you want to know me, read my books."[27]

After all, how much can a person tell us during a short personal meeting or even after many such meetings? But when we connect to a truly thoughtful and exalted person through the pages of a book, we get the greatest benefit. Śrīla Prabhupāda commented on this principle in a letter to Bali Mardana Dāsa on September 30, 1972: "So that is the real preaching, selling books. Who can speak better than the books? At least whoever buys, he will look over ... What your lecture will do for three minutes, but if he reads one page his life may be turned."

Writers labor over their work, dedicate much thought to find just the right words, rework and refine passages for precision and power, so that, especially with a writer of Śrīla Prabhupāda's stature, we gain the best form of salutary association – with whom we are granted the privilege of immediate and repeated recourse.

Some Day People Will Come to Understand

People have questioned whether Śrīla Prabhupāda's books are sometimes wasted on those who cannot understand them or who don't read them right away. In a letter to Purañjana Dāsa dated May 4, 1976, Śrīla Prabhupāda answers this doubt by describing how these same people will someday come to understand what valuable knowledge they have received, even if they don't appreciate it when they first purchase a book:

> These books are the life of human society. Others may be disturbed, but they cannot disturb this *Śrīmad-Bhāgavatam*. Let any man come, but here they cannot touch. We are putting these books for deliberation before the topmost thinkers of human society. Therefore, I have to see that in all languages all of our books are published. If we strain, and if he takes one book home, some day people will come to understand what valuable knowledge they have received. It is transcendental literature. Nobody can challenge it. It is done so nicely, without any spot, the spotless *Purāṇa*. Please continue like this to print books in all the languages for the benefit of suffering, misdirected humanity.

Let Kṛṣṇa Do His Magic

Today's well-trained distributors of Śrīla Prabhupāda's books go out of their way to see that the books they distribute are placed in the homes and hands of people who will respect them. In their exchanges with people, these vigilant distributors explain the importance of the books and take time to befriend the recipients. They also collect that contact information of the beneficiaries and try to bring them closer to Kṛṣṇa by staying in touch with them. Devotees who do their best in this way may have faith that, by Kṛṣṇa's arrangement, the books will eventually hit their marks.

However, even as we who distribute books do our best to bring people closer to devotional service by befriending them and staying in touch, we must also let Kṛṣṇa do His magic. In other words, teachers of Kṛṣṇa's message are simply Kṛṣṇa's instruments. They must try their best to convey Kṛṣṇa's message, but in the end no one can make the grand arrangements Kṛṣṇa does to bring souls back into His service.

To illustrate this point, Mitrasena Dāsa tells a remarkable story about how a book he distributed to a cavalier person quickly made its way into the life of a sincere soul.

> You can't make up stuff like this. I met a young man named Hector at Vista Point, the Golden Gate Bridge scenic observation point overlooking the San Francisco Bay and city skyline. Hector had just gotten off a big tour bus when I offered him a book. Our conversation went like this:
>
> **Hector:** So I can give any donation I want and I get to keep this book?
> **Mitrasena:** Yes.
>
> I said this even though I had a feeling he was just trying to "get one over" on a Hare Kṛṣṇa.
> **Hector:** I want you to dedicate the book to me first, before I give my donation. Write it in the book. My name's Hector.
>
> I wrote on the first page of the *Bhāgavatam* Sixth Canto, part one: "To Hector, from Mitra."
>
> Knowing that the book was worth much more, Hector next handed me two dollars and, looking happy to have "pulled a fast one" on a Hare Kṛṣṇa in San Francisco, he walked away with it. I didn't mind, as I was glad to see another book go out and without thinking much more about it, I went on to the next person.
>
> The following morning when I was back at the temple in Berkeley, which is an hour from the Golden Gate Bridge, Cāru Dāsa, our temple president, approached me and asked, "Did you meet someone named Hector yesterday?"

I said, "Uh ... oh, yeah, I think I did."

Cāru continued, "I got an interesting phone call yesterday. A man was walking through Chinatown [another tourist area in San Francisco about half an hour from the Golden Gate Bridge] and saw a book leaning in a windowsill. He picked it up, opened it, and was very surprised to see what was written on the first page: "To Hector, from Mitra." This man called the temple phone number listed in the back of the book right away and said, "My name is Hector. Who is this Mitra, and how did he know I was going to find this book?" The man is very interested in spiritual life, likes the book, and is coming to the temple this morning. Do you want to meet him?"

I met Hector number two only very briefly, and I guess that added to the mystique of his experience. From his point of view, I was on my way out the door to magically place more books for people I hadn't met yet. I didn't express any surprise or try to figure the odds of this Hector finding a book with his name in it. I've only met one more Hector since that day in 1977.

Hector stayed for a couple of hours talking with Cāru and purchased several other books. I wish that I'd kept track of him, as it would have been interesting to hear more of the story from his point of view. In those days we just expected miracles. They had become so common that we didn't get excited or pay much attention to them.

Śrīla Prabhupāda's Pen

During Kārttika a couple of years ago, I was sitting on the steps of Śrīla Prabhupāda's Samādhi Mandir in Vṛndāvana just after *maṅgala-ārati,* chanting *japa* alongside a couple of godbrothers. As we watched thousands of devotees exit the Krishna-Balaram temple with bead bags in their hands, one of my godbrothers remarked in amazement, "Where are they all coming from?" I thought to myself, "From Śrīla Prabhupāda's pen."

Everyone who comes to the Kṛṣṇa consciousness movement has a unique story to tell about his or her relationship with Śrīla Prabhupāda's books. His books induce people to join the Kṛṣṇa consciousness movement and empower them to stay.

Through his pen, Śrīla Prabhupāda planned to reach the whole world with the most exalted ideas passed down to him through the disciplic succession. When distributed, these books bridge political borders and cultural barriers. His books change people's hearts, bring fame to Lord Caitanya's movement, and when distributed in mass quantity will eventually conquer Māyā's empire.

Conquering Empires

In this regard, Śrīla Prabhupāda wrote to a disciple:

> I am so glad to learn that Satyavrata and yourself are trying to get the *Teachings of Lord Caitanya* published. You do not know how pleased I am to hear this news. When one book is published I think I have conquered an empire. So try to publish as many books as possible and that will enhance the beauty and prestige of our Society.[28]

Śrīla Prabhupāda often uses military terms to describe his campaign to spread Kṛṣṇa consciousness. At the top of each of his letters, for example, he specified his location with the word, "camp" – such as "Camp: ISKCON Dallas," or "Camp: Risikesh." These seemingly military expressions show that spreading the Kṛṣṇa consciousness movement is a battle. And in any conflict, the victory goes to the army that is best trained, equipped, and inspired.

Lord Caitanya descended to the material world without the usual weapons that Lord Kṛṣṇa brings (disc, club, and so on) for killing the demons. Caitanya Mahāprabhu instead subdues the demonic spirit of the world's population with His personal beauty and through His associates, who go town to town, door to door, to give people the holy names and the teachings of the *Bhagavad-gītā* and *Śrīmad-Bhāgavatam*.

Śrīla Prabhupāda's books not only display the complete beauty of the Supreme Personality of Godhead but also perfectly deliver Lord Caitanya's and Lord Kṛṣṇa's teachings in a way that conquers the hearts of those who read them. Śrīla Prabhupāda therefore writes:

> There is no doubt about it, to distribute books is our most important activity. The temple is a place not for eating and sleeping, but as a base from which we send out our soldiers to fight with *māyā*. Fight with *māyā* means to drop thousands and millions of books into the laps of the conditioned souls. Just like during wartime the bombs are raining from the sky like anything.[29]

Well aware that the pen is mightier than the sword, Śrīla Prabhupāda brought forth his transcendental books as the primary "weapons" for members of ISKCON to employ in order to win the war against illusion and spread real peace and goodwill.

People everywhere have grown weary of senseless wars and the destruction from bombs, swords, and all kinds of weapons that comes with armed conflicts. We invite activists everywhere to join Lord Caitanya's army for a new kind of war that brings solace rather than suffering to all living entities.

A devotee recently suggested to me that to prepare for ordinary warfare, governments make weapons of mass destruction; Śrīla Prabhupāda, on the other hand, has equipped us with weapons of mass *instruction*.

CHAPTER EIGHT

Book Distribution Is Our Family Business

ON NOVEMBER 15, 1971, Śrīla Prabhupāda wrote to his disciple, Lalita Kumāra Dāsa, "If you simply push on this one activity of distributing my books, your all success will be there."

One activity, all success.

Śrīla Prabhupāda went on to say that he had personally "hatched" this idea – that the mass distribution of his books was his "transcendental plot" to uplift human society. What exactly did he mean by "transcendental plot"? He meant that simply by distributing his books, there would not only be "all success," but book distribution would bring in enough money to finance the expansion of the Kṛṣṇa consciousness movement:

> If you simply push on this one activity of distributing my books, your all success will be there. I have hatched this "transcendental plot" for getting money by selling my books, and if we stick only to this plan, and use our brain for selling books, there will easily be sufficient money.

In the same letter Śrīla Prabhupāda mentions that he has already informed the GBC about his plan to have ISKCON support and expand itself through the sale of his books, and he offers Lalita Kumāra a formula for how to make book distribution work to his temple's advantage; he wanted his disciples to fulfill his "transcendental plot," and he didn't want them to worry about money: "If Kṛṣṇa sees that we are very active to spread information about Him, He is Master of the goddess of fortune, He will give everything."

People everywhere are busy hatching money-making schemes, but how many of these plans are both practical and purely transcendental? In other words, how many schemes easily generate money and at the same time are motivated not by the desire for material profit but only by the desire to do good for others? Finding a plan anywhere in the world with such seemingly contradictory elements is difficult, if not impossible, but Śrīla Prabhupāda's "plot" contains both elements to the full.

How Is Śrīla Prabhupāda's Business Plan Transcendental?

First, Śrīla Prabhupāda's books are by nature transcendental; they are transcriptions of his personal *kīrtana*. Anyone who reads these books contacts a vibration saturated with spiritually uplifting potencies – words vibrated by a pure devotee of Kṛṣṇa. Regarding the special nature of such words, Pṛthu Mahārāja says:

> My dear Lord, You are glorified by the selected verses uttered by great personalities. Such glorification of Your lotus feet is just like saffron particles. When the transcendental vibration from the mouths of great devotees carries the aroma of the saffron dust of Your lotus feet, the forgetful living entity gradually remembers his eternal relationship with You. Devotees thus gradually come to the right conclusion about the

> value of life. My dear Lord, I therefore do not need any other benediction but the opportunity to hear from the mouth of Your pure devotee.[1]

Second, Śrīla Prabhupāda's books contain whatever he wished to say to his disciples and to future generations of searching souls who would come to the path of Kṛṣṇa consciousness in his line. He writes, "Whatever I have to speak, I have spoken in my books. Now you try to understand it and continue your endeavor. Whether I am [physically] present or not present doesn't matter."[2]

The opportunity to have the complete instructions – intact and in one place – of such an accomplished contemporary master of devotional service is rare in this world. As time passes and devotees assimilate and apply the instructions found in these books and then pass them on to others, his gift to humanity will be even more profoundly felt. A compilation of spiritual knowledge like we have in Śrīla Prabhupāda's books gives the clearest guidance possible on the path of spiritual advancement.

Third, Śrīla Prabhupāda's books represent the fulfillment of the sacred order he received from his spiritual master, who told him, "Teach Kṛṣṇa consciousness among the English-speaking public, especially in the Western countries," and, "If you ever get money, print books."[3] So whoever assists Śrīla Prabhupāda in his transcendental plot to distribute his books also helps him satisfy his guru. Spiritually linked to the transcendent luminary Śrīla Bhaktisiddhānta Sarasvatī Ṭhākura, and in turn to the other great masters of bhakti-yoga in his line of disciplic succession, such sincere devotees receive the special grace of all those great souls.

Śrīla Prabhupāda notes this fact in a letter written on April 15, 1973 to disciples distributing his books: "My dear boys and girls, you are working so hard for broadcasting the glories of Lord Kṛṣṇa's lotus feet, and thus my Guru Mahārāja will be so pleased upon you. Certainly my Guru Mahārāja will bestow His blessings thousand times more than me and that is my satisfaction."

Fourth, Śrīla Prabhupāda's books infuse Kṛṣṇa's blessings into the hearts of billions of downtrodden people in the world, a point endorsed by him in many letters, such as this one, written to Hridayānanda Mahārāja on December 21, 1974:

> Please print as many books as possible. This is my real pleasure. By printing these books of our Kṛṣṇa conscious philosophy in so many different languages we can actually inject our movement into the masses of persons all over the world, especially there in the Western countries.

Finally, those who distribute Śrīla Prabhupāda's books bring in funds with which to maintain and expand the Kṛṣṇa consciousness movement, as well as to bestow immense spiritual benefits on those who donate their hard-earned money in exchange for the books. In his purport to *Śrīmad-Bhāgavatam* 5.24.18, Śrīla Prabhupāda confirms this spiritual principle:

> [B]y donating all his possessions to the Supreme Personality of Godhead, [Bali Mahārāja] became a successful devotee and got everything back again with the blessings of the Lord. Similarly, those who give contributions to expand the activities of the Kṛṣṇa consciousness movement and to accomplish its objectives will never be losers; they will get their wealth back with the blessings of Lord Kṛṣṇa.

Śrīla Prabhupāda again asserts this principle in his purport to *Bhagavad-gītā* 12.10. There he writes that one who voluntarily serves the cause of Kṛṣṇa consciousness, which includes helping with the publication of Kṛṣṇa conscious literature, rises "to a higher state of love for God, whereupon one becomes perfect."

The point is that distributing Śrīla Prabhupāda's transcendental books is good for those who distribute them, those who give their money to purchase them, and for all those who invest their time in reading them.

Steven Covey, author of the best-selling *Seven Habits of Highly Successful People,* declares that exceptionally effective people work only for causes that benefit everyone. He calls this philosophy "win-win," "a frame of mind and heart that constantly seeks mutual benefit in all human interactions."

Śrīla Prabhupāda's transcendental plot is a natural win-win venture that results in mutual benefit to the BBT, to ISKCON and its book distributors, and to the recipients of Śrīla Prabhupāda's books, wherever they are sold.

Śrīla Prabhupāda worked tirelessly with single-pointed attention to realize his "transcendental plot," a historical fact verified by his constant writing and speaking about his plan to his disciples. He also displayed his staunch faith in this plot through his personal example: he supported himself by distributing his own books during his first year in America and later nourished infant ISKCON as it grew into healthy childhood from the worldwide sales of his books.

Rough Beginnings

During the late 1960s and into the early 1970s, before there were ample books to distribute, ISKCON centers were typically impoverished, with the temple presidents struggling simply to pay for food and rent. The devotees barely brought in enough money with their BTG sales to keep the temples' doors open.

Book distribution wouldn't fully take hold until 1973. Before that, however, devotees had jobs and donated their salaries. Some, like Gargamuni Dāsa, thought of starting businesses. In 1968, with Śrīla Prabhupāda's blessings, Gargamuni started a business he named Spiritual Sky, hoping that the profits it would generate would make ISKCON financially stable. He recalls:

> I knew that Śrīla Prabhupāda didn't like devotees doing business. He used to say "Business means *māyā*" and that business would eventually lead to fights among devotees. So when I asked him if we could make our own incense and sell it to make money, he had to think about. And when he made the decision to allow us to do it, it was a big change in his usual policy.

Devotees sold Spiritual Sky incense on the streets along with BTG. People were eager to buy the exotic-smelling packs with their alluring picture of Kṛṣṇa on the front. Many devotees sold packs of Spiritual Sky on the street and afterward, as a bonus, gave the buyer a BTG for free. Gargamuni continues:

> What really got the sales of BTG going in a big way was when we started selling packs of Spiritual Sky incense on the streets. We'd offer a pack of incense and a BTG and ask for a donation. People would give a minimum one-dollar donation, and sometimes they'd even give ten dollars. Leading with the packs of incense made distributing the BTGs easier because people were naturally attracted to the incense but not necessarily at first to the BTG. In this way, Spiritual Sky became instrumental to the mass distribution of BTG.

By 1971, in America, ISKCON's finances began to stabilize. But its economic engine really got into gear during the Christmas marathon of 1972 and, in 1973, when devotees discovered how to distribute the more expensive hardbound books. In December 1972, the devotees saw for themselves the incredible power of Śrīla Prabhupāda's transcendental plot. On December 22, 1972, the devotees in Los Angeles stumbled on what has now become the celebrated Prabhupāda marathon. Noting the huge crowds of shoppers and people's more charitable disposition during the Christmas season, each devotee on the Los Angeles *saṅkīrtana* party stayed out much later than usual to try to distribute more books than they had ever distributed before. Most were working alone or in pairs, and didn't realize that the same enthusiasm had spread through each member of their party. As midnight approached, each returned to the temple thinking he or she was surely the last to come home, and each was surprised to find that every devotee had been inspired to stay out late. As the devotees began to gather in the *saṅkīrtana* room, their usual meeting place after a day out, they were amazed to discover that others had only just arrived, and especially that some were still in the city distributing books at such a late hour. When the scores were tallied at the end of the night, it became obvious to them that they could distribute unprecedented numbers of books in the days leading up to Christmas, and they vowed to stay out all day and most of the night through Christmas Eve. That year, the Los Angeles book distribution party distributed a record-breaking 18,000 pieces of literature in just three days.

The news of this momentous event in Los Angeles set a new standard for book distribution all over ISKCON. After that three-day marathon, devotees realized they could distribute books anywhere. With this surge of confidence, book sales turned the steady trickle of income from selling BTGs and incense into a transcendental tsunami.

ISKCON's breakthrough in book distribution is reminiscent of a sensational event from the world of track and field. On May 6, 1954, in Oxford, UK, a student athlete, Roger Bannister, shocked the world by running a mile in under four minutes. No one in track and field history had done it, and many had even claimed that it was impossible for humans to do.

More remarkable than Roger Bannister's running the mile in under four minutes (three minutes fifty-nine and four tenths of a second, to be exact), however, is that his record lasted for only forty-six days. Soon after Bannister broke the four-minute barrier, college runners and even high school runners began to routinely run the mile in under four minutes. Similarly, after the Los Angeles devotees had their book distribution breakthrough, devotees everywhere were soon distributing scores of big books, a feat that had previously seemed impossible. St. Francis of Assisi once said, "Start by doing what is necessary, then what is possible, and suddenly you are doing the impossible."

As the devotees made the transition from doing the necessary to the possible to the impossible, they could see for themselves how Śrīla Prabhupāda's transcendental plot to nourish ISKCON was unfolding. With the surge of book sales in 1972, devotees worked all the more vigorously to open new venues for distributing books, especially at airports, state fairs, and state and national parks. Meanwhile, distributors who were taking out more and more big books had discovered that people eagerly bought books when they saw George Harrison's introduction to *Kṛṣṇa Book* and the books' spectacular display of artwork. With this confluence of favorable circumstances, book distribution soon became ISKCON's primary source of income.

Any enterprise – even a spiritual movement – needs both money and manpower to expand. With the surge of book distribution the stream of devotees joining ISKCON turned into a river. As the flow of new devotees swelled, so did the general enthusiasm in the temples – and greater numbers of books went out into the hands of the public.

As the devotees' desire to distribute his books intensified, Śrīla Prabhupāda was right there to fan the fire. He encouraged devotees to innovate, to become better organized, and to centralize warehousing, accounting, and the training of distributors. In 1970 Śrīla Prabhupāda conceived of a global publishing house, which he called the Bhaktivedanta Book Trust. In 1972 he formalized this Trust in India and North America, and thus made his BBT organizationally and financially independent of ISKCON. Although the BBT was financially independent from ISKCON, it operated for the benefit of ISKCON:

> This trust is created and shall be operated exclusively for the benefit of the INTERNATIONAL SOCIETY FOR KRISHNA CONSCIOUSNESS, incorporated by me ... This

> trust shall exist independently of the International Society for Krishna Consciousness and the Trustees' functions and duties stated herein shall be separate and not dependent on the Governing Body Commission of the International Society for Krishna Consciousness.

The BBT trust agreement goes on to stipulate the exact purpose of the Trust:

> USE OF THE TRUST FUND
>
> The Trustees shall collect all proceeds from the sale of my books, that is One Hundred Percent (100%) of all the proceeds from all of the International Society for Krishna Consciousness Temples and divide these proceeds into two funds, one-half (1/2) for the fund known as the Book Fund, and one-half (1/2) for the fund known as the Building Fund.
>
> The proceeds allocated to the Book Fund shall be used for the following purposes, all in the discretion of the Trustees, in whom I have complete confidence:
>
> > Printing and reprinting of books;
> > Directing and managing all publicity and distribution of my books;
> > Processing all copyrights and legal rights to my books;
> > Allocating funds as they see fit to ISKCON Press and directing the operation of the activities of ISKCON Press in the printing and reprinting of said books.
>
> Those funds allocated to the Building fund shall be applied in the sole discretion of the Trustees in the following manner:
>
> > Purchase of properties for the construction of new temples or renovation of old temples.

And finally, Śrīla Prabhupāda empowers the trustees:

> Without limiting the generality of their powers, for purposes of clarification, I include the following special powers:

> A. To invest any of the principal of the Trust Fund not used for the purposes hereinabove stated;
>
> B. To open bank accounts in the name of the trust for the transaction of business;
>
> C. To pay such administrative expense as may be necessary in the administration of this trust;
>
> D. To appoint a secretary to keep account books and issue a monthly statement to the Trustees.[4]

In the BBT trust agreement, Śrīla Prabhupāda stipulates that the BBT is to operate solely for the benefit of ISKCON. In his final will and testament he named the GBC as the ultimate managing authority of ISKCON. It follows, then, that the BBT trustees and the GBC are obliged to work cooperatively and support one another. To achieve this synergy, it is the GBC's duty to inspire the temple presidents in their zones to increase the distribution of BBT books in their temples, according to Śrīla Prabhupāda's desire; and it is the BBT trustees' duty to produce high-quality books at reasonable prices, provide excellent customer service, and use the BBT's discretionary funds collaboratively to benefit ISKCON through loans and grants to fund the construction of new temples or to renovate old ones.

Thoughtful cooperation in using the BBT's discretionary funds will not only go a long way to fueling ISKCON's global growth but will also encourage leaders at all levels of management to focus their energy on increasing book distribution. Śrīla Prabhupāda personally allocated the BBT's funds while he was physically present; now that he has left us, this responsibility has fallen to the BBT trustees. In practice, the trustees look to the GBC to define financial priorities for ISKCON temple construction and the renovation of old temples, and generally work with the GBC accordingly, allocating those same funds thoughtfully and strategically, cooperatively and transparently, in ways meant to please Śrīla Prabhupāda.

Local ISKCON temples that distribute BBT books realize funds they can use to develop their own projects. Of course, these days temples tend to have a number of revenue streams – capital fundraising, temple gift shops, retreat income, and membership donations – but ISKCON projects can and do still make a good income from the distribution of BBT books.

The BBT Expands

In 1975, Śrīla Prabhupāda wrote to Jaśomatīnandana, one of the Indian BBT trustees, telling him not to worry about making a profit from book sales in India. Instead, he told Jaśomatīnandana to lower the prices and go for massive distribution of the books, assuring him that BBT sales in the West would subsidize any losses experienced by the Indian BBT.

Śrīla Prabhupāda was determined to open at least 108 temples around the world, and wherever there were temples, he wanted a plentiful supply of BBT books. For example, during the 1974 GBC meeting in Māyāpur, Śrīla Prabhupāda called Hridayānanda Dāsa Goswami to his room and asked him to serve as the GBC secretary for Latin America. Hridayānanda Mahārāja understood that this also meant he should get the production and distribution of Spanish and Portuguese books going there.

Hridayānanda Dāsa Goswami recalls that 1974 exchange with Śrīla Prabhupāda:

> When I accepted the service from Śrīla Prabhupāda to develop South America, it was also understood that I would take up the book production of Spanish books. When I arrived in Latin America, there were not many temples and there was practically no book distribution going on at all. The devotees there were instead selling paraphernalia to maintain their operations. I told them we'd have to go out for book distribution. And after we did produce books in Spanish I also had to show them how to sell the books.

> There was no Spanish office of the BBT at the time, so we organized one in a separate house in Cuernavaca, Mexico. Soon after we got organized and the book production and distribution were picking up, the government closed the temple and forced all the foreign devotees to leave. Consequently, we moved the Spanish operations to Los Angeles near the end of 1974.

In Los Angeles, Hridayānanda Mahārāja worked with others to render Śrīla Prabhupāda's books into Spanish. Then he supervised the other aspects of producing Spanish books: buying the paper, binding the books, and finally shipping them to South America. After shipping, he'd fly south to help organize distribution.

Hridayānanda Mahārāja recalls:

> Because of the third-world conditions in South America, we tried to keep the price of the books even lower than usual. To accomplish this, Śrīla Prabhupāda allowed us to adjust some printing standards that he was stricter about in the United States. One example was that he permitted us to print *Śrīmad-Bhāgavatam* in soft cover instead of hard.

By December 1975, the Spanish division of the BBT became the most productive foreign BBT in the world, and the South American devotees became world champions in book distribution.

In that same year, Hridayānanda Mahārāja also deployed Mahāvīra Dāsa to Brazil to open a Portuguese BBT office. Following the usual formula of allotting funds for construction from the printing and distributing of books in Brazil, the devotees were able to build a beautiful new temple. They named it Nova Gokula, and it became yet another vibrant and magnificent ISKCON center.

Meanwhile, the BBT operations Śrīla Prabhupāda had established in Los Angeles continued to thrive. Rāmeśvara remembers:

In order to organize the book distribution, Karandhara and I developed a central warehouse and accounting system for the first time. When we presented this to Śrīla Prabhupāda, he said that it was revolutionary. In effect he said, "You should not hesitate to use your American intelligence, which is Kṛṣṇa's gift to you. Please utilize it to distribute these books."

Śrīla Prabhupāda felt that this warehouse system and central accounting system were going to greatly enhance his book distribution program. The basic system was that we should have a warehouse in Los Angeles and a second in New York. We would have a manager at each warehouse, and we hoped to eventually have five warehouses. There would also be a central accounting office in Los Angeles, and that office would give instructions to the warehouses to release the books in an efficient manner.

ISKCON Jump-started

In centralizing book printing and distribution, Śrīla Prabhupāda meant not only to achieve efficiency in production and distribution but also to make the BBT economically strong enough so that the distribution of its books would help ISKCON boost its expansion. To achieve this end, as stated in the BBT trust agreement, the formula was that the BBT would double the cost of producing the books it sold to its main customer, ISKCON. The BBT's surplus would go for publishing more books and to grants to sponsor construction of new ISKCON temples.

Although the original BBT trust agreement says that BBT funds were for printing books and renovation of buildings or the construction of new temples, Śrīla Prabhupāda also used the BBT's burgeoning surplus to give loans to a number of other projects. True to his plan, and as I mentioned in "The Rest Is History," the rapid increase in BBT books sales, along with the BBT's consequent increasing cash flow, enabled Śrīla Prabhupāda to construct many of the famous ISKCON temples one sees around the world today. The collections from the Nāma Haṭṭa party in Japan, along with BBT book sales in the 1970s, built ISKCON temples in Māyāpur, Vṛndāvana, Bombay, and a number of other places. Many of these projects were huge in scope. For example, the Bombay project included a temple, hotel, restaurant, cultural center, and ashram near plush Juhu Beach. The Krishna-Balaram temple in Vṛndāvana would be an international center for Vaiṣṇavism. Similarly, the Māyāpur project would serve multiple purposes: it would attract people from all over the world and present Lord Caitanya's teachings, with a backdrop of a thriving Vaiṣṇava community.

As the BBT's financial situation improved, Śrīla Prabhupāda could allocate funds more freely. He was now able to fund novel outreach programs such as the Bhaktivedanta Institute (BI), a Kṛṣṇa conscious think tank for research and development of strategies to reach people educated in the sciences. He also gave loans from the BBT to Tamal Krishna Goswami and Viṣṇujana Swami to pay for a fleet of full-sized buses and smaller vans for the Rādhā-Dāmodara Traveling *Saṅkīrtana* Party (Śrīla Prabhupāda considered the buses traveling temples).

The BBT sponsored a Library Party, which sold BBT books exclusively to university libraries and professors. The number of Library Party members grew and eventually went to all parts of the globe, taking orders from academics for all of Śrīla Prabhupāda's books – those already in print and those yet to be printed.

Śrīla Prabhupāda also directed his BBT team to create and print hundreds of thousands of copies of a booklet entitled *The Kṛṣṇa Conscious Movement Is Authorized,* a publicity piece that documented ISKCON's benevolent mission and noble values. Śrīla Prabhupāda directed the BBT to give this booklet to ISKCON temples at no cost, and to mail out 200,000 copies of it to a select list of important persons collected from *Who's Who in America.*

Śrīla Prabhupāda also sanctioned use of BBT funds to pay for attorneys to open new legal avenues for book distribution, and eventually he approved an in-house legal department to further expand markets for the BBT. He also funded and supported the Sanskrit Department, which later expanded into the Sanskrit/Bengali Department.

In addition to the surplus realized by the BBT from wholesaling books to ISKCON temples, the ISKCON temples also realized an income when they sold the books to the public. In this way, ISKCON temples, bookstores, and individuals, made – and still make – a good income from selling BBT books. ISKCON temples in particular used their book and magazine income to purchase, maintain, and expand their local communities and their outreach projects.

Uttamaśloka Dāsa, temple president of ISKCON Chicago in the 1970s, inherited a $20,000 debt when he took over the temple. He remembers, however, how by organizing and concentrating on book distribution, he cleared the debt and soon had a surplus, which he used to take exemplary care of the devotee community. Uttamaśloka explains: "In Chicago we had a monthly overhead of $30,000. I invested more money for high-quality *prasāda* and other amenities than any other temple, because I knew that the devotees going out all day to sell books needed to be taken care of nicely."

The expanding income from the distribution of BBT books was also invested in valuable new ashram space, in opulent Deity worship, and in devotee care. In fact, records indicate that the BBT gave many dozens of loans and grants to help start ISKCON temples and projects all over the world. As ISKCON facilities increased, so did the number of new seekers who had purchased books, liked what they'd read, and moved into the ashrams, attracted by the sublime atmosphere. Soon after joining, many of these new devotees also went out to distribute books, adding momentum to the growth of ISKCON and the BBT.

The BBT's Exclusive Rights

As more devotees distributed books, even more income came in. A growth cycle thus developed from concentrating on book distribution – a growth cycle through which devotees around the world practically realized Śrīla Prabhupāda's words: "If you simply push on this one activity of distributing my books, your all success will be there."

Śrīla Prabhupāda was vigilant about keeping BBT book prices low. He trained his BBT managers to make ever-larger print runs, lowering the unit cost of each book. He had showed the way in the BBT's beginning days by personally negotiating liberal lines of credit with publishers, achieving increasingly lower prices, which encouraged the devotees to distribute books even more rapidly. As they did so, the income for both the BBT and the temples increased.

The principle of stimulating sales through lower unit costs is timeless. Śrīla Prabhupāda taught his BBT managers to continually look for ways to lower book costs without sacrificing quality. Thus Śrīla Prabhupāda established the BBT as the financial root of ISKCON. By watering this root, one gets not only the fruits of Śrīla Prabhupāda's books and a crop of new devotees attracted by the books, but also an uplifting means of engaging thousands of devotees in advanced devotional service to Kṛṣṇa.

Śrīla Prabhupāda not only conceived of this practical formula but also firmly enforced it. Around the time that the California BBT trustees had created a centralized accounting system and warehouse and were shipping BBT books to temples, they noticed that many of the temples weren't paying for the books they had received. In a memo addressed to "All ISKCON Centers" and written by his secretary on his behalf and signed by four GBC men, Śrīla Prabhupāda urged his leaders around the world to pay off any debts they might have to the BBT:

> Śrīla Prabhupāda is concerned that so many temples have got big debts to the BBT, and he wants that the GBC takes a very active interest in seeing that these debts are paid as soon as possible. He is very strong on this point and went so far as to say that temple presidents who do not keep up with their BBT payments must be replaced.

Meanwhile, more BBT offices became necessary in other countries. Śrīla Prabhupāda reiterated his policy that his books were to be printed exclusively through the BBT. If devotees started printing through outside companies, funds would be taken away from the BBT and spoil Śrīla Prabhupāda's transcendental plot.

In the following memo to his disciples, dated March 14, 1974, Śrīla Prabhupāda makes it clear that they must buy their books directly from the BBT and not print them outside in an attempt to save money:

> My dear disciples,
>
> Please accept my blessings. Now that our ISKCON is growing into a huge, worldwide organization, it has come to my attention that sometimes centers are printing my literature, taking collection, and spending, all outside the jurisdiction of the Bhaktivedanta Book Trust. This must not go on.
>
> I specifically formed the BBT to invest in it exclusive rights for the printing of all literature containing my teachings, writings, and lectures. In this way the collections are to be divided fifty percent for printing new books and fifty percent for construction of temples.
>
> The BBT can authorize a center to print, as in the case of foreign translations, with the agreement that when the foreign printing becomes financially solvent they will pay royalties to the BBT. But all printing of ISKCON literature must be by the BBT or under their sanction and approval.
>
> If temples print independently it will be at the cost of the books I am myself printing, and could eventually cause the financial ruin of the BBT, meaning I could not order new books

> from the printer or have sufficient funds for construction of temple projects.
>
> I trust this is now clear and you will all do the needful. If you have any questions in this matter you can write me directly or consult with the GBC representative.

"Our Book Business Is Sufficient"

Śrīla Prabhupāda created, oversaw, and protected the BBT business plan and also personally stated preferences for publishing – approving the artwork and commenting on the number of pages, the book block, and the quality of the paper and binding. He always sought to achieve the best quality at the lowest price.

As all families need a financial support system, Śrīla Prabhupāda devised a way to maintain ISKCON's spiritual family through the business of printing and distributing his transcendental books. Śrīla Prabhupāda's emphasis on book publishing and distribution brings up a legitimate question: "Is the book business the only business Śrīla Prabhupāda sanctioned?" The answer is "no" – but a qualified "no." In a letter to Tamal Krishna Goswami dated August 13, 1974, Śrīla Prabhupāda clarifies his mood toward other businesses:

> Regarding the Society's leaders emphasizing business, you should understand what is the meaning of business. Business means to help the preaching. Preaching needs financial help; otherwise, we have no need for business. So far as I understand our book business is sufficient to support our movement. I do not want the preaching to be at the expense of managing. Manager must also be a preacher otherwise who will want to follow him?

Although Śrīla Prabhupāda sometimes encouraged his followers to conduct various businesses, he emphasized that these should support ISKCON's educational outreach. Furthermore, it was his firm policy that business should never be done at the expense of book publication and sales.

For example, in 1973 a member of the ISKCON community introduced a jewelry business that was supposed to be lucrative. This jewelry business attracted the attention of many devotees at ISKCON Los Angeles and other communities who reasoned that selling jewelry might not only help to bring wealth to individual devotees but also help fund the spreading of Kṛṣṇa consciousness. To calm the fervor over this apparent, get-rich-quick scheme, Śrīla Prabhupāda spoke about it during a morning class in Los Angeles on April 17, 1973:

> Therefore we give different varieties of engagement, Kṛṣṇa consciousness. We should not divert our energy. Now when we are selling book – that is Kṛṣṇa consciousness. We are selling book. But if we think that the selling book may be diverted into selling jewelry, that is not very good idea. That is not very good idea. Then we become again jeweler. *Punar mūṣika bhava:* again become mouse. We should be very much careful. Our Kṛṣṇa consciousness cannot be diverted.

In this lecture and several others, Śrīla Prabhupāda speaks about an earlier part of his own life, during which he conducted business. His spiritual master had instructed him to teach Kṛṣṇa consciousness in the West, and to execute this order Śrīla Prabhupāda worked hard to develop a business that could fund it. In this same lecture Śrīla Prabhupāda explained what happened:

> I have got my practical experience in this connection. Yes. That is Kṛṣṇa's special favor. I do not wish to narrate, but it is a fact. It is a fact. My Guru Mahārāja ordered me when I was twenty-five years old that "You go and preach." But I thought, "First of all, I shall become a rich man, and I shall use that money for preaching work."

> So that's a long history. I got good opportunity for becoming a very rich man in business. And some astrologer told me, "You should have become like the Birlas" [one of the richest families in India]. So there was some chance, very good chance. I was manager in a big chemical factory. I started my own factory. The business was very successful. But everything was dismantled. I was forced to come to this position to carry out my order of my Guru Mahārāja. *Akiñcana-vittāya* [materially impoverished]. When everything was finished, then I took it Kṛṣṇa, that, "You are the only ..." Therefore Kṛṣṇa is *akiñcana-vitta* [the only solace for one who has lost everything materially]. When one becomes finished of all his material opulences.

After his business failed, Śrīla Prabhupāda continued to execute his spiritual master's will. His guru had told him, "If you ever get money, print books," and he did this consistently, whenever he had money, throughout his life. Śrīla Prabhupāda remembers these times:

> So in the face of so many odds and uncertainty, I went there, simply depending on my spiritual master and Kṛṣṇa, with this hope only, that "If there is desire, everything can be done. But otherwise there is no hope. I am going there, hopeless, just to make an experiment. My other godbrothers – they failed. All right, Guru Mahārāja asked me. In the beginning I did not do. Let me do it in this old age." So it became surprisingly success. Business started with forty rupees, and now we have got four crores. Where is that business in the material world that a man started business with forty rupees and he has got four crores within ten years? Not only money but also fame, respect. What do these kings and president or minister get, respect?[5]

Is it any wonder, then, that Śrīla Prabhupāda encouraged his followers to stick to distributing transcendental books and depending on Kṛṣṇa's grace? Śrīla Prabhupāda was wary of devotees becoming entangled in a business that would divert their energy away from book distribution. A devotee named John Milner wrote him about selling candles. Śrīla Prabhupāda replied on April 22, 1971:

> It is so much encouraging to hear how you are introducing this Kṛṣṇa consciousness movement in the schools and colleges there. Especially this is an ideal opportunity for distributing our books also, so you should make all serious endeavor in this connection. These books are so potent that anyone who reads them is sure to become Kṛṣṇa conscious. So it is a very valuable service to distribute our books.
>
> Yes, incense distribution has been very helpful in many centers for maintaining financially, but we are not businessmen. So producing candles for distribution is not at all necessary. We do not want to increase factories. We want to increase Kṛṣṇa consciousness, and this can be done best by distributing our books and preaching. So in that way you can make your program.

Śrīla Prabhupāda's statement "We are not businessmen" may seem puzzling, considering that he made numerous other statements urging his followers to take up the "book business." But in a room conversation in Bombay on December 31, 1976, Śrīla Prabhupāda clarifies:

> This book distribution is the most important task in our Society. Therefore I am giving so much stress and I am working so hard on this. Because this is my life and soul according to the order of my Guru Mahārāja. And by his grace it is to some extent successful. And I took it seriously. I take it seriously still now. That is my life and soul. I never tried in India to construct big temples, or even in your country we didn't. I never tried. But I was selling personally books. That is the history. Sometimes they are criticizing, "What kind of *sannyāsī*? He is doing book business."

How can we understand Śrīla Prabhupāda's apparent ambiguity? On the one hand he encourages the book business, and on the other he warns his followers not to become entangled in business.

Philosophically, this apparent contradiction is easy to resolve. The Vedic mantras say that the Supreme Lord has no legs and hands, but that He can accept whatever is offered to Him (*apāṇi-pādo javano grahītā*). The previous *ācāryas* explain that such statements accept that the Supreme has hands and legs, but they reject the idea that His hands and legs are material.

Similarly, when Śrīla Prabhupāda advises his followers to shun business yet he encourages them to engage in the book business, he is actually showing how selling books about Kṛṣṇa is not a material business. And Śrīla Prabhupāda was consistent in directing his followers to be cautious about doing any business that would distract them from the business of distributing his books.

Another example of this consistent attitude and guidance is found in a story told by Kṛṣṇa Kānta Dāsa, founder of the Golden Avatar recording studio, a studio that produced Kṛṣṇa conscious recordings:

> Around 1974 I recorded Agnideva along with some other devotee musicians and produced the *Gopinātha* album. When Prabhupāda came to L.A., Karandhara invited me into Prabhupāda's room to play the record for him. I was excited. Prabhupāda listened to the record, and when it was over he said, "Yes, that was very nice. What do you plan to do with this record?" We told him that our idea was to try to use it on *saṅkīrtana* – to distribute the record instead of incense.
>
> Prabhupāda thought for a minute. He closed his eyes, bobbed his head, and then said, "Well, that would be okay as long as it doesn't decrease the distribution of my books." Prabhupāda squeezed two of his fingers tightly together and said, "As long as it doesn't decrease my book distribution by this much." I was sitting to the side and understood what he meant right away, but Karandhara said, "What did you say, Prabhupāda?" Again Prabhupāda squeezed two of his fingers

> tightly together as he repeated, "As long as it doesn't decrease my book distribution by even this much." We said, "Oh, yes, oh sure, Śrīla Prabhupāda." After we left the room, Karandhara and I never dared bring up that subject again. Prabhupāda had seen into the future – for later we had trouble when the sale of record albums destroyed the purity of *saṅkīrtana*.

In yet another instance, Śrīla Prabhupāda wrote to Śrī Govinda Dāsa on July 13, 1971 to dissuade him from buying and selling Kṛṣṇa art, advising him instead to stick to distributing books:

> It is much more important that you utilize your valuable time and energy to distribute our magazines and books. That is real propaganda work. And the householders can earn their livelihood by distributing our books also. That is one of the points of our new book distribution program, and you can get more details from Karandhara or Rūpānuga.

Now more than ever before we have the facility to print Śrīla Prabhupāda's books in almost any language and sell them anywhere in the world. We should take advantage of this opportunity and again aim at becoming financially dependent on book distribution.

Giving the Gift

Although the high-tech, rapid production of books is relatively new in human society, sharing knowledge – the aim of book distribution – is not. For countless generations Vaiṣṇavas have been engaged in the family business of distributing knowledge about Kṛṣṇa. The word *sampradāya* literally means "that which is given." The tradition of passing down transcendental knowledge from one generation of spiritual authorities to the next generation of sincere disciples and followers – and through them to the whole human family – has been intact for millennia, both through oral traditions and the printed word.

I recall feeling a profound connection to this tradition as I was distributing Śrīla Prabhupāda's books at the San Francisco airport. I'd just returned from Vṛndāvana, where I'd visited Ter Kadamba, a small forest near Lord Kṛṣṇa's hometown of Nandagrāma. Śrīla Rūpa Gosvāmī wrote many of his famous books about the science of devotional service as he sat beneath a *kadamba* tree at Ter Kadamba. The forest is far enough off the main road that not many people go there, but going there is well worth the bumpy ride. Down the small dirt road, through many thickets, I arrived in a quaint forest next to a tranquil, glassy pond surrounded by bird-filled vines and creepers, and found a place to sit under Śrīla Rūpa Gosvāmī's *kadamba* tree.

A few months after I visited that enchanted forest I found myself back in the San Francisco airport distributing books from my "designated free speech booth," a booth the airport director had allowed ISKCON to use as a base from which to meet passengers and sell them Śrīla Prabhupāda's books. Among the BBT books I kept in stock was *The Nectar of Instruction,* Śrīla Prabhupāda's translation of and commentary on Śrī Rūpa Gosvāmī's *Śrī Upadeśāmṛta.*

That day I met a student from Taiwan and showed him *The Nectar of Instruction*. I told him that a great saint from India had written it, that it contained the formula to achieve complete spiritual perfection, and that I had recently visited the place where he had composed it five hundred years ago.

The young man was interested and happily gave me ten dollars for the book, placed it in his carry-on bag, and soon headed off for his flight, which would take him back to Taiwan for the holidays. As I watched this young student walking away with Rūpa Gosvāmī's book neatly tucked into his luggage, I thought, "Did Rūpa Gosvāmī know there would be airports in the future? Did he foresee that Śrīla Prabhupāda would translate his book into English and print tens of thousands of copies?" Thinking that this airport scenario might please Rūpa Gosvāmī, I felt a sudden and profound communion with him and his tranquil sitting place at Ter Kadamba, even as I worked amid the clamor of a major international airport.

Joining the sales department of Śrīla Prabhupāda's family business has connected me to Śrīla Rūpa Gosvāmī and the rest of our great *ācāryas*. Our family business of distributing transcendental books allows us to serve not only Rūpa Gosvāmī, who descended from Kṛṣṇa's eternal family in Goloka Vṛndāvana, but all the other great souls in our line, as well as Lord Caitanya Himself.

Service to our gurus, according to Śrīla Narottama Dāsa Ṭhākura, is our means of advancement in devotional service. Through such service, Śrī Narottama writes, one gets the transcendental foot dust of the Gosvāmīs of Vṛndāvana.

ei chaya gosāñi yāra, mui tāra dāsa
tāṅ' sabāra pada-reṇu mora pañca-grāsa

I am the servant of the Six Gosvāmīs, and the dust of their lotus feet provides my five kinds of food.[6]

If any devotee, big or small, visits Rūpa Gosvāmī's sitting place at Ter Kadamba and submits to him, "I've distributed one of your books in the West," will Śrī Rūpa not shower his blessings on that devotee? Such are the rewards of working for the family business as it has been handed down to us by Śrīla Prabhupāda.

The Origin of Our Family Business

The Fords and Disneys of America, and the Tatas and Birlas of India, are successful family dynasties. The businesses owned and operated by these families have been around for generations. When it comes to longevity, however, Japan's Hoshi family, which runs the Hoshi Hotels, is the oldest. The Hoshis opened for business in 718 AD, making their business the oldest family-run business in the world. They are fifty generations in!

But is their hospitality business really the oldest? According to Vedic histories, Lord Kṛṣṇa started His family business at the beginning of creation when He poured Vedic wisdom into the heart of Brahmā and empowered him with the knowledge to create a universe, where *jīvas* could rectify their consciousness and return to Him. This was, of course, trillions of years before the Hoshi Hotel opened its doors. Brahmā expanded his family and taught and empowered each of its members to learn what he had been taught and then to pass that Vedic knowledge on, intact, to subsequent generations. Brahmā's son, Nārada, for example, became the mentor of Kṛṣṇa Dvaipāyana Vyāsa, who compiled, edited, and expanded the *Vedas* through his son and many disciples.

Vyāsadeva, eager to broadcast to the people of Kali-yuga the knowledge that would alleviate their miseries, engaged a scribe to write the *Vedas* down. He understood through his mystic vision and scriptural knowledge that the people of Kali-yuga would suffer from a variety of hardships caused by the maleficent influence of Kali, including diminished memory. He knew that in Kali-yuga, in order to remember and follow the *Veda's* sacred teachings, humankind would need them in written form.

The *Veda* was originally a single book, the *Atharva Veda*. To make it easier to teach and learn, Vyāsadeva divided it into four parts – the *Ṛg, Yajur, Sāma,* and *Atharva*. He then gave different disciples different parts of the *Veda* to teach. Some of them divided their parts further to facilitate their students' learning and teaching.

Later, Vyāsa wrote the *Vedānta-sūtras* "with a view to presenting just the cream of Vedic knowledge."[7] He also compiled the *Purāṇas,* Vedic histories that explain the *Vedas*. And he composed a "bridge book" to the *Vedas,* the *Mahābhārata,* which caters to Kali-yuga's less philosophically inclined populace but also contains the *Bhagavad-gītā,* a digestible and succinct summary of Vedic philosophy. The *Gītā,* after taking the reader through a step-by-step process of self-realization, finally reveals the goal of Vedic knowledge, bhakti-yoga, or Kṛṣṇa consciousness, pure love of God.

So from Kṛṣṇa to Brahmā to Nārada to Vyāsadeva to Śrīla Rūpa Gosvāmī sitting at Ter Kadamba and writing his books to Śrīla Bhaktivinoda Ṭhākura with his Vaiṣṇava Depository to Śrīla Bhaktisiddhānta Sarasvatī Ṭhākura and his own use of the *bṛhad-mṛdaṅga* to our Śrīla Prabhupāda writing his Bhaktivedanta purports – all are in the same family business. Visit any BBT office around the world and you will find devotees who share in Vyāsadeva's mood and work ethic, and in Śrīla Prabhupāda's desire that Kṛṣṇa consciousness be made accessible to everyone in every walk of life. In fact, the BBT is translating the *Śrīmad-Bhāgavatam* into so many languages that almost anyone in the world can read it – a feat Śrīla Vyāsadeva would praise, because it fulfills the purpose of his work.

In telling of Vyāsadeva's despondency after his having written down the *Vedas,* the *Śrīmad-Bhāgavatam* describes Vyāsadeva's purpose. When his guru, Nārada Muni, appeared on the scene, Vyāsadeva asked about the reason for his despair. Nārada told him, "You have not actually broadcast the sublime and spotless glories of the Personality of Godhead. That philosophy which does not satisfy the transcendental senses of the Lord is considered worthless. Please, therefore, describe the transcendental pastimes of the Supreme Personality of Godhead Śrī Kṛṣṇa more vividly."

Vyāsa accepted his guru's advice at once. After attaining the perfection of meditation (*samādhi*) and directly seeing Kṛṣṇa, His potencies, and His pastimes, Śrīla Vyāsadeva produced the *Śrīmad-Bhāgavatam,* or *Bhāgavata Purāṇa.* This text is his own commentary on the *Vedānta-sūtra* and is thus the distilled essence of everything he had written before. In it he purely described the Absolute Truth, Śrī Kṛṣṇa, and His activities in vivid detail.

Vyāsadeva taught *Śrīmad-Bhāgavatam* to his liberated son, Śukadeva, and Śukadeva in turn spoke it publicly to Mahārāja Parīkṣit, who was sitting on the bank of the Ganges after having been cursed to die by a *brāhmaṇa* boy. Sūta Gosvāmī, who was present while Śukadeva spoke, later repeated the *Bhāgavatam* to an assembly of learned *brāhmaṇas* and sages in the Naimiṣāraṇya forest. While introducing *Śrīmad-Bhāgavatam* to those sages, Sūta said: "Let me offer my respectful obeisances unto him [Śuka], the spiritual master of all sages, the son of Vyāsadeva, who, out of his great compassion for those gross materialists who struggle to cross over the darkest regions of material existence, spoke this most confidential supplement to the cream of Vedic knowledge, after having personally assimilated it by experience."[8]

Today's distributors of Śrīla Prabhupāda's books, in that same mood of compassion, venture door to door or onto the street, to fairs, rock concerts, and shopping centers – anywhere they can find people in need of spiritual enlightenment – to join in the family business of presenting *Śrīmad-Bhāgavatam* to society. When they do so, they are serving an ancient line of succession of great souls that comes down from Śrī Kṛṣṇa through Brahmā, Nārada, Vyāsadeva, Śrī Caitanya Mahāprabhu and His spiritual descendants, down through His Divine Grace A. C. Bhaktivedanta Swami Prabhupāda and his disciples and their descendants.

All of these personalities are actually spiritual entrepreneurs. Those devotees who today follow Śrīla Prabhupāda's example and exhaustive instructions to expand book publication and distribution will be successful in their entrepreneurship, because they are backed by all of Kṛṣṇa's eternal family members.

Value Added

Everyone loves a success story, especially a true rags-to-riches tale, in which someone starts with no money and no friends, but has a great idea and the determination to create a thriving enterprise. We come from spiritually humble beginnings, but with our family's blessings, we can become spiritual entrepreneurs and make ourselves and others spiritually wealthy beyond anything we could imagine.

I live in Silicon Valley, home of legendary successes like Hewlett-Packard's William Redington Hewlett and David Packard and Apple's Steve Jobs and Steven Wozniak. Both of these legendary success stories feature a couple of bright young people with a fresh idea and a desire to bring it out into the world. Both pairs of entrepreneurs started in dusty garages, but they emerged a few years later with a product that not only became a household name but also earned their inventors billions of dollars.

Success stories like these provide impetus for thousands of would-be entrepreneurs who want to change the world and while doing so net themselves remarkable wealth and fame. Catering to the public's taste for such romantic quests, in November 2010, *Newsweek* ran a story entitled "Amazing Late Bloomers," chronicling thirteen luminaries who attained startling success after the age of sixty. Among these standout achievers was His Divine Grace A.C. Bhaktivedanta Swami Prabhupāda. The article recounts how at the age of sixty-nine "Swami Prabhupāda" came alone to the United States on a freighter. He had no money (he had only seven dollars worth of unspendable rupees in his pocket) and no backers. Within twelve short years he circled the globe fourteen times, developed a worldwide spiritual movement, opened 108 temples, and wrote and published seventy books.

Great Vaiṣṇava *ācāryas* like Śrīla Prabhupāda, whether they start their mission at the dawn of their lives or when they are older, are the premier entrepreneurs. Why? Because they bring to market the most valued product of all: the process for awakening love for Kṛṣṇa, the Supreme Personality of Godhead.

Like conventional entrepreneurs, these *ācāryas* often begin their campaigns in obscurity, sometimes even in isolated garagelike rooms. But instead of designing the gadgets of the future, these compassionate world teachers write books of profound spiritual wisdom; instead of writing complex computer code, they assemble the spiritual formulas found in the *Vedas* into contextualized *sūtras* – mantras that free people from the miseries of birth, death, old age, and disease and transport them back to the spiritual world.

Five thousand years ago, the venerable sage Vyāsadeva sat meditating in a lonely mountain cottage surrounded by berry trees. In his solitude he compiled the epic *Śrīmad-Bhāgavatam,* the hearing of which purifies the hearts of even its most downtrodden readers and quickly brings them to spiritual perfection.

We have already mentioned Śrīla Rūpa Gosvāmī as carrying on Vyāsadeva's spiritual entrepreneurship, but there are also Śrīla Sanātana Gosvāmī and the other Vṛndāvana *gosvāmīs.* These *ācāryas* barely slept, and when they did, it was as mendicants under a different tree each night. But they wrote timeless spiritual instructions on palm leaves, divine poetry and prayers, works so practical yet sublime that they are able to touch the hearts of both refined scholars and simple laborers alike.

The famous Vaiṣṇava teacher and reformer Śrīla Bhaktisiddhānta Sarasvatī Ṭhākura also sat alone for nearly ten years in a jungle hut in Māyāpur, West Bengal. There he completed a vow to chant one billion names of Kṛṣṇa. He emerged from this vow to travel and speak throughout India, establishing a network of sixty-four temples and spiritual communities. He also wrote hundreds of texts.

But the most dramatic example of spiritual entrepreneurialism is on *Newsweek's* list: Śrīla Prabhupāda. Starting from a small, bare, stone-floored room in the rustic village of Vṛndāvana, he actualized what he'd been meditating on since meeting his guru: writing and publishing the books that would enlighten the people of the West (and beyond) using Lord Caitanya's teachings and then showing them how to practice those teachings – something no one before him had done.

Working alone, with barely enough money to clothe himself, he poured out the contents of his devotional heart on a dilapidated typewriter. As mentioned in "Amazing Late Bloomers," Śrīla Prabhupāda's legacy is now world famous.

From his early days at 26 Second Avenue to his phenomenal success at growing an international spiritual organization in twelve short years, Śrīla Prabhupāda's accomplishments are legendary. Establishing the BBT is one of those accomplishments. The BBT helped fund the Matsya Project, which, along with grants from The Smithsonian Institute, saved thousands of translations of Vedic and Gauḍīya Vaiṣṇava scriptures from deteriorating and being lost forever. Matsya's collection of treasured texts was stored on microfilm for future reference in the Vedic Library and Research Center, also funded by the BBT. The thousands of microfilms collected by the Matsya team are now in the care of the Bhaktivedanta Archives. BBT trustees also helped support Yamunā Devī's writing of her award-winning cookbook, *The Art of Indian Vegetarian Cooking.*

Today, decades after Śrīla Prabhupāda's departure, the BBT remains vibrant and committed to publishing Śrīla Prabhupāda's books in as many languages and formats as possible. As Nelson Mandela famously said, "If you talk to a man in a language he understands, he hears with his head; if you talk to him in his language, it goes to his heart." The BBT strives to give people Śrīla Prabhupāda's books in their native tongue as often as possible.

The BBT demands state-of-the-art eco-friendly technologies and materials from its printers. It works to serve the needs of thousands of book distributors worldwide, and as of this writing, publishes in eighty-six languages. Many of these translations are available both in print and as eBooks. In 2015, the BBT completed its translation, editing, and publishing of all of Śrīla Prabhupāda's books in the Russian language.

Besides printing Śrīla Prabhupāda's books, the BBT has also brought out a number of editions of important translations of Gauḍīya Vaiṣṇava texts, such as the *Bṛhad-bhāgavatāmṛta,* the *Tattva Sandarbha, Śrī Kṛṣṇa-līlā-stava,* and the *Laghu-bhāgavatāmṛta.*

The BBT also funds scientific research projects, has held art seminars and international symposiums on book publishing and distribution, taught courses in book production skills, and especially through its full-service website, krishna.com, fostered young talent interested in various aspects of publishing and Internet outreach. The BBT is home to the Bhaktivedanta Archives, whose mission it is to "collect, preserve, protect, and allow dissemination of" Śrīla Prabhupāda's "teachings, images, and life's work." The Archives is constantly updating the media on which Śrīla Prabhupāda's audio is stored and cataloguing and digitizing the literally thousands of photos of Śrīla Prabhupāda and ISKCON's activities that have been collected since 1965. The Archives also offers both an online and offline version of the VedaBase, updating it regularly as more of Śrīla Prabhupāda's letters are discovered or his audio digitally enhanced to fill in what was too hard to hear on tape.

The global BBT has contributed substantially each year to help the construction of the Temple of the Vedic Planetarium (TOVP) in Māyāpur, one of the largest temple construction projects in the world. In fact, the BBT funded land purchases which have facilitated ISKCON's growing communities. It has also funded the printing and free distribution of inspirational books, such as *This Is My Request.*

The BBT has, in the past, given grants for the strategic distribution of Śrīla Prabhupāda's books in third-world countries – one year the BBT shipped 150,000 books to French-speaking Africa so that distributors there could get them out to the people in the cities and villages.

Spiritual entrepreneurs such as Śrīla Prabhupāda and the other *ācāryas* in our line carry a burden: they can see the degree to which people are suffering. They feel the responsibility and especially the compassion to try to relieve that suffering. Their teachings are authorized and empowered by Kṛṣṇa; when their writings go to press and hit the streets, people who read them begin to sing Kṛṣṇa's names and practice devotional service.

In this passage from a prayer Śrīla Prabhupāda wrote to Kṛṣṇa aboard the *Jaladuta,* just before disembarking on American soil, he disclosed to the world that he felt the burden to save people from their suffering:

> How will I make them understand this message of Kṛṣṇa consciousness? I am very unfortunate, unqualified, and the most fallen. Therefore I am seeking Your benediction so that I can convince them, for I am powerless to do so on my own.

As is true of all great spiritual entrepreneurs, Śrīla Prabhupāda had full confidence in the product he was carrying, the transcendental incarnation of the Lord in the form of sound. He confirms this fact as his prayer aboard the *Jaladuta* continues:

> The words of *Śrīmad-Bhāgavatam* are Your incarnation, and if a sober person repeatedly receives them with submissive aural reception, then he will be able to understand Your message.

One last point about Śrīla Prabhupāda's "transcendental plot": the word *plot* comes from the Old French *complot,* "secret project." Śrīla Prabhupāda's project to distribute his books is a kind of secret project, because his books reveal to the world Lord Kṛṣṇa's "most secret of all secrets." What's more, Śrīla Prabhupāda's purports reveal to the world the confidential secrets in his own heart. Śrīla Rūpa Gosvāmī tells us that spiritual disclosure is one of the six loving exchanges between devotees. Śrīla Prabhupāda writes, "If you love somebody, you must give him something, and you must accept something from him. You must disclose your mind to him, and he should disclose his mind to you."[9] So Śrīla Prabhupāda's "plot" to distribute Kṛṣṇa consciousness to suffering humanity, his disclosure of the meaning of Kṛṣṇa's teachings though his own "ecstasies," his Bhaktivedanta purports, and his receiving donations of time and money and devotion in exchange, are expressions of his love for the fallen souls, his spiritual master, and ultimately Śrī Kṛṣṇa Himself. In a letter to Satsvarūpa Mahārāja dated January 5, 1976, Śrīla Prabhupāda discloses his mind to his faithful followers about the family business he left for us to manage:

> Our first business is this book distribution. There is no need of any other business. If this book distribution is managed properly, pushed on with great enthusiasm and determination and at the same time if our men keep spiritually strong, then the whole world will become Kṛṣṇa conscious.

CHAPTER NINE

Literary Kīrtana and the Yuga-dharma

IN THIS CHAPTER I will show how distributing Śrīla Prabhupāda's books is a form of *kīrtana*. Śrīla Prabhupāda called the writing of his books "spoken *kīrtana,*" and said that therefore book distribution is also chanting. So book distribution is literary *kīrtana,* and accordingly forms a vital component of Lord Caitanya's *saṅkīrtana* movement and of the *yuga-dharma*.

The goal of this book is to help preserve Śrīla Prabhupāda's legacy and ensure that his transcendental writings continue to play their essential role in spreading the *saṅkīrtana* movement throughout the world. To help readers who may not be familiar with the meanings and interrelations of the Sanskrit terms I discuss here, I will begin by defining and then connecting them to the authoritative Vedic scriptures.

To distribute the eternal vibration of God's holy names to the public through congregational singing (*saṅkīrtana*) is to produce a love-shower of transcendental bliss. When those same sound vibrations are recorded in writing, bound, and distributed in the form of transcendental books, the reach of that love-shower is greatly expanded. Deliberate sharing of God's names is the *yuga-dharma* for the present Age of Kali, the method prescribed by all bona fide spiritual authorities for making tangible spiritual advancement.

Throughout the *Śrīmad-Bhāgavatam,* Śukadeva Gosvāmī and other saintly pure devotees continuously glorify the process of *saṅkīrtana* with verses like this one, from *Śrīmad-Bhāgavatam* 2.1.11:

> O King, constant chanting of the holy name of the Lord after the ways of the great authorities is the doubtless and fearless way of success for all, including those who are free from all material desires, those who are desirous of all material enjoyment, and also those who are self-satisfied by dint of transcendental knowledge.

Lord Caitanya introduced *saṅkīrtana* as the *yuga-dharma* and asked us to take it up. He also asked us to spread it widely: "Therefore I order every man within this universe to accept this Kṛṣṇa consciousness movement and distribute it everywhere."[1]

Saṅkīrtana cleanses the mirror of the mind, spares one from the terror of death and rebirth by bestowing love of God, instills transcendental knowledge, brings happiness and good fortune, and assures victory and success to all who adopt it. Thus the *yuga-dharma* nourishes those eager to know God and awakens all people to the goal of life and the means to attain it.

The sound of the *mahā-mantra* is unlike any other sound in this material world. It is mysteriously captivating and undeniably alluring, and according to scripture, one who hears it or repeats it but once, even casually or in jest, is blessed with eternal spiritual credit.

Saṅkīrtana Means "In Public"

Keenly aware that *saṅkīrtana* gives instant benediction to all, followers of Śrī Caitanya Mahāprabhu move into the cities and towns and look for opportunities to chant the names of

Rūpa offers *daṇḍavats* as Śrī Caitanya Mahāprabhu reads a verse he composed. Amazed at how well the Gosvāmī understood His mind, Mahāprabhu bestowed His full mercy on Śrī Rūpa, who thus became a key link in the family business through his literary accomplishments.

God in public places where the largest number of people can benefit from it. In America, such a perfect opportunity comes each year on Black Friday, the day after Thanksgiving, when retailers offer huge discounts to kick-start the holiday shopping season. Millions of bargain hunters cram together, queuing up overnight in front of doorways, bearing the cold and wet to be among the first to enter the hallowed halls of retail establishments throughout the country.

Half-starved refugees storming an Oxfam truck for relief supplies could hardly match the crush created by Black Friday shoppers. Just as religious pilgrims relish penance and paradoxically find happiness in the austerity of attending India's overcrowded Kumbha-melā, the largest gathering of human beings on earth, discount shoppers on Black Friday savor the inconvenience and risk – yes, each year shoppers are injured and sometimes even crushed to death in the shopping mayhem – finding solace in reveling with the crowds of fellow loyal shoppers. It's a time the masses can, en masse, prove their faith in material ingenuity, a time to officially marvel at the myriad miraculous combinations and permutations of new gadgets and clothing styles. It's a desperate attempt to stave off boredom and a gnawing sense of low self-esteem, and a perfect distraction from the looming terror of death.

This year, wishing to share the *yuga-dharma* with Black Friday shoppers, our ISKCON Silicon Valley (ISV) congregation of Hare Kṛṣṇa devotees strategically set up a chanting party – thirty-five strong, foreheads decorated with crisp *tilaka,* and equipped with drums and hand cymbals – in downtown San Francisco at the corner of Market and Powell, the busiest shopping district in the city. Working alongside the chanters, a team of book distributors stood ready to engage anyone who looked interested in the chanting.

A river of shoppers surged past our ensemble as we held a steady beat to a simple tune and belted out the Hare Kṛṣṇa *mahā-mantra.* The mantra mingled with the sound of our instruments and echoed from the canyonlike walls of the surrounding skyscrapers. This charmingly distinctive music danced amid the cacophony of sirens, car horns, strains of street music, and millions of chattering voices. From our vantage point we marveled at the varied reactions of passersby as the *mahā-mantra* entered their ears.

"What is this?" the onlookers' eyes inquired. Then suddenly, as if injected with a drug, their faces changed: some smiled, some laughed, some shook their heads in disapproval. Some seemed determined not to succumb to the allure of the sound. Some surrendered their reserve, giving a nod or thumbs up, as if to say, "I get it. I know what you're doing here and it's good." Some bought *Bhagavad-gītās* and carried them away. Whatever the response, no one could avoid being touched by the exotic wave of the *mahā-mantra's* transcendental sound.

The scene made me think of a verse from Śrīla Rūpa Gosvāmī's *Nāmāṣṭaka* (3): "O sun of the holy name, even a dim glimmer of Your splendor swallows the powerful darkness of materialistic life and gives those who are blind to the truth the vision to follow the path of pure devotional service. Who in this world, even if learned and pious, can fully describe Your transcendental glory?"

Near the end of our Black Friday *saṅkīrtana* excursion, a woman from Iran, who was not only visiting the United States for the first time but also encountering her first chanting party, approached me and asked, "Are you singing the names of God?" "Yes we are," I said, and she was visibly pleased. I offered her a copy of *Bhagavad-gītā As It Is,* which she gladly purchased. As she departed, I felt satisfied that her first taste of the public chanting of God's names would be extended and informed by the purchase of one of Śrīla Prabhupāda's books. For this woman, the *kīrtana* would go on.

Giving people this taste is the *yuga-dharma*. What's more, it is the panacea for all suffering souls and is open to everyone in this age. In fact, no work more interesting or valuable than spreading *saṅkīrtana* exists.

From the moment Śrī Caitanya Mahāprabhu appeared in

this world, He promoted *saṅkīrtana*. He chose to appear during a lunar eclipse, traditionally regarded as an inauspicious time, during which people from all sections of Indian society would close their businesses, temples, and homes, seek shelter of a holy river, and loudly chant the names of God to ward off the eclipse's evil influence. During His infancy the Lord would stop crying only when the neighborhood women gathered around Him and chanted Kṛṣṇa's holy names. Throughout His stay in this world He focused on holy books and the holy name. He chanted the holy name in assemblies of devotees and then spilled with them out into the streets to chant with the public. And He taught others to do the same.

Saṅkīrtana Means to Spread the Teachings

In recent times, Śrīla Bhaktisiddhānta Sarasvatī Ṭhākura, following the teachings of Lord Caitanya, promoted *saṅkīrtana* by writing extensively about it as a spiritually advanced practice of bhakti-yoga. In his poem *Duṣṭa-manaḥ,* for example, he praises the power of *saṅkīrtana:* "The transcendental power of congregational chanting automatically awakens remembrance of the Lord and His divine pastimes in relation to one's own eternal spiritual form [*kīrtana-prabhāve, smaraṇa svabhāve*]." In other words, by absorbing oneself in *nāma-saṅkīrtana* one attains the perfection of devotional service.

Although *kīrtana* is often taken to mean "singing or chanting" about God, the literal meanings of *kīrtana* – to glorify, praise, describe, celebrate, or to make mention of[2] – include diverse means of delivering the spiritual messages of Godhead, such as speaking about them or distributing transcendental books about the process of devotional service. Moreover, Mahāprabhu and His followers showed by their example that *saṅkīrtana* also includes going door to door to teach people the process of chanting and performing the other methods of devotional service. In his introduction to *Śrīmad-Bhāgavatam* Śrīla Prabhupāda writes:

> In the course of His preaching work, [Lord Caitanya] used to send daily all His followers, including Śrīla Nityānanda Prabhu and Ṭhākura Haridāsa, two chief whips of His party, from door to door to preach the *Śrīmad-Bhāgavatam* ... As far as preaching work in the *saṅkīrtana* movement was concerned, everyone was expected to do his daily share according to the order of the Lord.

In *Śrī Caitanya-caritāmṛta,* Kṛṣṇadāsa Kavirāja gives more evidence that *saṅkīrtana* means to spread the chanting and the glories of chanting by teaching it to others:

kali-yuge yuga-dharma – nāmera pracāra
tathi lāgi' pīta-varṇa caitanyāvatāra

> The religious practice for the Age of Kali [*yuga-dharma*] is to broadcast the glories of the holy name. Only for this purpose has the Lord, in a yellow color, descended as Lord Caitanya.[3]

Here Kṛṣṇadāsa Kavirāja Gosvāmī describes the *yuga-dharma* as *nāmera pracāra*. In other words, *saṅkīrtana* means not only congregationally chanting God's names but also spreading the process to others. Śrīla Prabhupāda, in his word-for-word translation of this verse, defines the word *pracāra* as "propagate." In the full translation of the verse he renders it "broadcast."

To propagate means to spread or promote. Broadcast – a word that comes from the mid-eighteenth century – means, literally, "sow by scattering," as in broadly casting seeds. Later, in the twentieth century, the word broadcast became associated with radio and television, as these technologies enabled people to transmit information and images widely through the ether and across continents.

Throughout his writings Śrīla Prabhupāda consistently renders *pracāra* as "preaching"[4] or "spreading the *saṅkīrtana* movement."[5] In this way, he points to the broad meaning of the present *yuga-dharma* as not only to sing and glorify the names of the Lord congregationally but also to widely spread both the *saṅkīrtana* process and the Lord's teachings for the benefit of all living entities.

Saṅkīrtana and the Written Word

The Sanskrit word *saṅkīrtana* combines the prefix *sam-* with *kīrtana* ("to glorify," or "to describe"). The prefix *sam-* means "with, together with, along with," so that *saṅkīrtana* indicates that speaking or singing about Kṛṣṇa and His glories is conducted as a group activity. Thus Śrīla Prabhupāda typically translates *saṅkīrtana* as "congregational chanting," or "congregational glorification of the Lord." Accordingly, when *kīrtana* is performed within a temple by a group of singers, that is *saṅkīrtana,* and when that chanting is taken outside, into public spaces, it is *even more so*. The scope, the inclusivity, of *saṅkīrtana* expands. The idea of expansion and intensification – qualitative and quantitative – is included within the meaning of *saṅkīrtana,* for the prefix *sam-* not only expresses union but also thoroughness, intensity, or completeness.

Group singing is one specific realization of *saṅkīrtana;* another is *kṛṣṇa-kathā,* conversation concerned with topics about Kṛṣṇa among interested parties. In fact, it was in this form of *saṅkīrtana* that *Śrīmad-Bhāgavatam* first became manifest. The *Bhāgavatam* relates the story of its own origin, which took place just after the disappearance of Lord Kṛṣṇa and just prior to the onset of Kali-yuga. Before *Śrīmad-Bhāgavatam* became a book, it became manifest as the spoken word, as speech uttered and heard by advanced devotees. It appeared first from the mouth of Śrīla Śukadeva Gosvāmī, who related *kṛṣṇa-kathā* to Mahārāja Parīkṣit and an attendant audience of great sages. It made its second appearance when one member of that audience, Sūta Gosvāmī, later repeated that conversation just as he had heard it to a group of sages assembled at Naimiṣāraṇya. The sages had gathered at the sacred place in order to perform a chain of ritual sacrifices that would counteract the malefic effects of Kali-yuga, "which deteriorates all the good qualities of a human being." The sages opted instead to listen to Sūta's *kṛṣṇa-kathā,* in which he repeated what he had heard earlier from Śukadeva Gosvāmī. In this way, *Śrīmad-Bhāgavatam* itself exemplifies what it will explicitly declare further on in the work to be the *yuga-dharma,* the specific way of salvation, for this Kali-yuga: *saṅkīrtana.*

Sūta Gosvāmī could exactly repeat the words of Śukadeva because he had what to us would be an astounding power of memory. However, *Śrīmad-Bhāgavatam* informs us that one of the deleterious effects of Kali-yuga on humans will be the atrophy of the power of memory. Because of this, the whole vast corpus of Vedic literature, including *Śrīmad-Bhāgavatam* itself, was edited and put down in writing by Śukadeva's own father, the sage Kṛṣṇa Dvaipāyana Vyāsa.

So today, because of our Kali-yuga infirmities, *Śrīmad-Bhāgavatam,* the *Bhagavad-gītā,* and other spiritual writings are now shared and distributed not through oral transmission by sages blessed with perfect memory, as with Śuka to Sūta to the Naimiṣāraṇya sages, but in the form of books. In this way, book distribution is "literary *saṅkīrtana,*" and, by Kṛṣṇa's mercy, it is the way we can continue the book distribution tradition begun by Śukadeva Gosvāmī and Sūta Gosvāmī.

Distributing Books Is also Saṅkīrtana

Distributing the writings of Vyāsadeva, then, is also regarded as *kīrtana,* or chanting Kṛṣṇa's glories, and when such literary *kīrtana* in the form of book distribution is done cooperatively to spread Lord Caitanya's movement, it is *saṅkīrtana.* Śrīla Prabhupāda writes:

> Regarding *saṅkīrtana* and book distribution, both should go on, but book distribution is more important. It is *bṛhat-kīrtana.* In Tokyo airport one boy had come up to me asking if he could speak with me. I said yes, and then he asked me,

> "Swamiji, where do you get all that knowledge in your books?" Of course it is Kṛṣṇa's knowledge, not mine. But the effect is there. So for wider *kīrtana,* book distribution is better.[6]

Therefore devotees who with humble hearts distribute Śrīla Prabhupāda's books perform the *yuga-dharma* for this Age of Kali perfectly. And the previous authorities in bhakti, including Śrīla Bhaktisiddhānta Sarasvatī Ṭhākura and Śrīla Jīva Gosvāmī – who sent his disciples out to distribute the books of the Six Gosvāmīs of Vṛndāvana – have all emphasized writing, publishing, and distributing literature as an especially effective means of more widely spreading Lord Caitanya's *saṅkīrtana* movement.

Thus Śrīla Prabhupāda's use of the words *broadcast* and *spread* to describe *saṅkīrtana* and the *yuga-dharma* – not to mention his persistent drive to write, publish, and distribute his books – clearly follows the mood and methods of the previous great teachers of devotional service.

Bhaktivinoda Ṭhākura, for example, sent his book *Śrī Caitanya Mahāprabhu: His Life and Precepts* from India to Europe and North America. Following Bhaktivinoda Ṭhākura, Śrīla Bhaktisiddhānta emphasized book distribution by calling it the *bṛhat-mṛdaṅga,* or the "greater *mṛdaṅga.*" The *mṛdaṅga* is a drum traditionally used to accompany group *kīrtana.* Śrīla Bhaktisiddhānta placed on his Society's logo an image of a printing press next to a *mṛdaṅga.* Under the logo were the words "*Rāga-mārga,*" to point out that the *saṅkīrtana* of printing and distributing transcendental books is elevated devotional practice. In fact, most Vaiṣṇava authorities in the line of Caitanya Mahāprabhu have made literary contributions and promoted the written word as the primary way to preserve and broaden the pure teachings of devotional service. As already mentioned, thousands of years ago, the literary incarnation of God, Śrīla Vyāsadeva, first wrote down the *Vedas* and charged his disciples and followers with the duty of spreading the teachings widely in human society.

So when it comes to broadcasting the eternal name and fame of the Supreme Personality of Godhead, Śrī Kṛṣṇa, those who distribute Śrīla Prabhupāda's books are performing literary *kīrtana* to expand the *yuga-dharma*. They do this by broadcasting spiritual seeds in the form of the knowledge contained in transcendental literature, seeds that germinate and grow into luxuriant bhakti creepers as people all over the world are induced to chant the Hare Kṛṣṇa *mahā-mantra* in ecstasy.

Those who distribute transcendental literature not only perform *kīrtana* locally but also expand its influence in the long term as the books travel throughout the world and stay around for hundreds of years. It is in this sense that the authorities in bhakti-yoga call book distribution the *bṛhat-kīrtana,* the "big" *kīrtana.*

In November 1974, when Śrīla Prabhupāda was informed that a disciple had distributed one of his books to the son and daughter of the President of the United States, he wrote to Rāmeśvara Dāsa: "This is another example of how the book distribution is better than the street *saṅkīrtana* alone. Now the books are in the President's house; but by your chanting you could never approach the President's house."

In a letter written a month earlier to Rūpānuga Dāsa, Śrīla Prabhupāda explicitly instructs his disciple that his books are transcriptions of his *kīrtana,* and that distributing them disseminates that *kīrtana:*

> Regarding *saṅkīrtana* and book distribution, book distribution is also chanting. Anyone who reads the books – that is also chanting and hearing. Why distinguish between chanting and book distribution? These books I have recorded and chanted and they are transcribed. It is spoken *kīrtana.* So book distribution is also chanting. These are not ordinary books. It is recorded chanting. Anyone who reads, he is hearing.

And clearly indicating that distributing his books pleases Kṛṣṇa and His devotees, Śrīla Prabhupāda told the devotees: "I'd especially request my disciples who are cooperating with me that try to publish books as many as possible and distribute throughout the whole world. That will satisfy Śrī Caitanya Mahāprabhu as well as Bhaktisiddhānta Sarasvatī Ṭhākura."[7]

In both his writing and his public talks, Śrīla Prabhupāda stresses the importance of distributing his transcendental books as a limb of the *yuga-dharma*. A stirring example of this occurs on June 20, 1975. Śrīla Prabhupāda had just arrived at his Western world headquarters in Los Angeles. After being greeted by a temple room packed with enthusiastic disciples, he began his talk: "Our speaking is the same, *harer nāma harer nāma harer nāmaiva kevalam*. We have no new discovery. We don't manufacture. This is our process. We simply follow the predecessor's instruction. That's all." Śrīla Prabhupāda then listed some of the masters who had preceded him and said that executing their instruction with one's heart and soul is "our success." He then went on to tell of his *guru mahārāja's* fondness for books. He said that the last order he had heard directly from Śrīla Bhaktisiddhānta's mouth was "If you ever get money, print books."

"Where Is Book?"

During that short speech in the Los Angeles temple room, Śrīla Prabhupāda's disciples strained their eyes and ears to pick up clues from their spiritual master about how they could best serve him. Fulfilling their desire, Śrīla Prabhupāda next expanded on his opening phase, "This is our process ... We simply follow.":

> Therefore I am stressing on this point: "Where is book? Where is book? Where is book?" So kindly help me. This is my request. Print as many books in as many languages and distribute throughout the whole world. Then Kṛṣṇa consciousness movement will automatically increase.

Conspicuously, Śrīla Prabhupāda began his short talk with the *Bṛhat-nāradīya Purāṇa* verse quoted above, which repeats three times for emphasis that chanting the holy names of God is the most important sacrifice in the Kali-yuga (*harer nāma harer nāma harer nāma*). Then Śrīla Prabhupāda asked, "Where is book? Where is book? Where is book?" thus making his request not only pointed but also parallel to the famous *Bṛhat-nāradīya Purāṇa* verse about chanting the holy name. He concluded, "Print as many books in as many languages and distribute throughout the whole world."

Śrīla Prabhupāda's purports, public speeches, conversations, and private letters make clear his wish that his followers vigorously promote *saṅkīrtana,* including both the public chanting of the holy names and the distributing of his books. He also says that it would be best if the two were to go on simultaneously, because the chanting would increase the book sales:

> Regarding your question is it all right to assign the entire *saṅkīrtana* party for distributing books so that no one will be free for street chanting? Of course we should not understand the meaning of *saṅkīrtana* very narrowly, that only chanting and dancing and playing instruments, no, *saṅkīrtana* means to glorify the Lord in a congregational manner. So if many devotees are going out daily on the streets and public places for distributing our literature, that is also *saṅkīrtana,* even if there is no one chanting. Hearing and chanting are essential processes for *saṅkīrtana.* So if someone is hearing us singing on the street, or if he is purchasing one book and if he reads sincerely, these two activities are the same. So if there is any occasion of necessity, if there are not very many men available or if there is prohibition by the municipal authorities, something like that, we may assign everyone for distributing our literatures, there is no loss for that. But it is always better if there are also some devotees chanting loudly on the street. If there is even one man to two men or a small party who are chanting Hare Kṛṣṇa, that will increase also the book sales. So if there are sufficient men, and if we have got sanction by the authorities, it is always better to have at least a small party chanting along with as many distributors of books as possible.[8]

As Śrīla Prabhupāda's followers increasingly understood his fondness for book distribution and the urgency he felt for increasing it, they came up with ways to do just that. One such follower named Śrutadeva Dāsa began a weekly circular entitled "The Saṅkīrtana Newsletter," through which he reported the numbers of Śrīla Prabhupāda's books devotees were distributing around the world. Śrutadeva recalls:

> The BBT newsletter reported money sent to the BBT, so I decided to do a weekly newsletter to report the number of books that were being distributed. At first I reported only weekend book scores. Distributors could pick their two best days out of Friday, Saturday, and Sunday and send them in for me to report. Later, I included scores from the whole weekend; and sometime after that, the whole week.

At the printing of the nineteenth issue, Śrutadeva asked Śrīla Prabhupāda's secretary, Rūpānuga Swami, for permission to send the newsletter to Śrīla Prabhupāda for his perusal. Rūpānuga Mahārāja agreed, and Śrutadeva sent his newsletter. Śrīla Prabhupāda replied:

> I am in due receipt of your letter dated August 15th, along with the Saṅkīrtana Newsletter Number 19, and I thank you very much for it. You can continue sending me these newsletters as you publish them weekly. It is this *saṅkīrtana* which is the life and soul of our movement. *Saṅkīrtana* and book distribution should go on together side by side. I am always glad when these activities are increasing, and my pleasure is always increasing.[9]

Nearly five weeks later, Śrīla Prabhupāda wrote another letter to Śrutadeva:

> These statistics are very nice. I like very much to receive the report of my book sales. I think it also gives encouragement to the devotees who distribute the books. Here at Māyāpur, my Guru Mahārāja was printing one paper. It was selling

for only a few *paisa*. Sometimes whenever one *brahmacārī* would go to Navadvīpa and sell even a few copies, I would see my Guru Mahārāja become very much pleased. Even if the *brahmacārī* was not a very important member, my Guru Mahārāja would become very, very pleased with him. He personally instructed me that books are more important than big temples. At Rādhā-kuṇḍa, he told me that since constructing the big marble temple at Bagh Bazaar, there have been so many difficulties. Our men are envious over who will live in which room. I think it would be better to take off all the marbles and sell them and print books. He told me this personally. So I am always emphasizing book distribution. It is the better *kīrtana*. It is better than chanting. Of course chanting should not stop, but book distribution is the best *kīrtana*.[10]

"The Sales Figures Give Me Life"

From the early days of ISKCON, Śrīla Prabhupāda had sent his devotees out worldwide to chant together in public. Surely, then, we might expect a circular named "The Saṅkīrtana Newsletter" to report the numbers of devotees chanting in the streets. But instead the newsletter kept track exclusively of the numbers of books that were being distributed. Śrīla Prabhupāda's enthusiasm for reading "The Saṅkīrtana Newsletter" is legendary. He writes:

> Regarding sales figures, please endeavor in this way. The sales figures – this is the only solace in my life. When I hear that my books are selling so nicely, I become energetic like a young man.[11]

His eagerness to read "The Saṅkīrtana Newsletter" went on until his final days. Toṭagopīnātha Dāsa recalls the train ride to Kumbha-melā in 1977. Although Śrīla Prabhupāda was very ill and lying down, Rādhāballabha Dāsa showed him the latest issue of "The Saṅkīrtana Newsletter." Śrīla Prabhupāda sat up, pointed to Toṭagopīnātha's name, and said "This is what gives me life – when I see my disciples distributing my books like this."[12]

Later in 1977, when Śrīla Prabhupāda was confined to bed and preparing to leave this world, Tamal Krishna Goswami remembers:

> This evening Gopal Krishna arrived with new books. When Prabhupāda found out, he raised his eyebrows very high and emphatically ordered, "Bring them!" Prabhupāda was quite satisfied and had Bhakti Cāru read in Hindi from one of them. Later, he listened to "The Saṅkīrtana Newsletter" no. 47 with great interest. He really appreciated the work of listing all statistics, and he was very enlivened to hear that nearly 40,000 big books had been distributed. He said, "If book distribution increases, I will never die. I will be living for centuries.[13]

All this affirmation, combined with his emphatic promotion of "The Saṅkīrtana Newsletter," which described book sales, makes it clear that for Śrīla Prabhupāda, book distribution and *saṅkīrtana* were synonymous – and that Śrīla Prabhupāda considered distributing his books not only *saṅkīrtana* but the "big *saṅkīrtana*."

Our Real Business

As "The Saṅkīrtana Newsletter" became an integral part of life in ISKCON, devotees throughout the world were thrilled to know that Śrīla Prabhupāda was reading the reports of how they were increasing sales of his books. The more Śrīla Prabhupāda heard about such increases, the more he asked the devotees to increase their sales. He emphasized that book printing and distribution is "our real business" and that those who were reading and distributing his books would "enter into the spiritual world to live with Kṛṣṇa eternally."

> I am in due receipt of your weekly *saṅkīrtana* newsletters. I am always happy to hear of increasing book sales. These reports

> are very encouraging to me. Our real business is to print and distribute books. By doing this business, you are all becoming recognized by Kṛṣṇa. Please try to continue working so nicely for Kṛṣṇa, following the rules and regulations, chanting sixteen rounds, and studying my books and you will finish your business in this material world in this life and enter into the spiritual world to live with Kṛṣṇa eternally.[14]

Big Saṅkīrtana

Śrīla Prabhupāda came to teach and spread the *yuga-dharma.* While doing so, he did more than push the chanting of the holy names; he consistently stressed that distributing his books be considered in the same category: "Preach as much as possible. By *saṅkīrtana,* big *saṅkīrtana.* Big *saṅkīrtana* is book distribution and small *saṅkīrtana* is with *mṛdaṅga.* Big *saṅkīrtana* is going on all over the world, small *saṅkīrtana* locally."[15]

The Bookstore

In summary, by distributing books and other publications, the members of ISKCON achieve the main purposes for which Śrīla Prabhupāda formed ISKCON. Acting on this principle, Śrīla Prabhupāda always included the distribution of his books as a vital aspect of any program and insisted that devotees include a display of his books whenever he spoke or led the public in chanting the holy names.

For example, according to Balavanta Dāsa, whenever Śrīla Prabhupāda gave an open lecture or performed *kīrtana* in public, he asked that his devotees set up a table displaying his books so that people could buy them after the program. Śrīla Prabhupāda referred to this mandatory display as the bookstore.

Evidence for this is found in a dialogue that took place in 1971 after Śrīla Prabhupāda's lecture at the Atlanta airport in the Eastern Airlines VIP Lounge. Directly after addressing a public gathering that included airline officials, Śrīla Prabhupāda said, "This is not sentimental chanting, but it is based on the soundest philosophy, Vedic literatures. We have got so many books, and you can buy them in our bookstore. Where is the bookstore?"

According to Balavanta, after Śrīla Prabhupāda asked this question there was a long pause. Balavanta recalls:

> The devotees had remembered fruits, flowers, a special chair for Śrīla Prabhupāda to sit on, the *prasāda* feast, invitations to the Indians – but they had forgotten Prabhupāda's books.
>
> Prabhupāda continued to wait for an answer to his question, until finally the senior disciple present, Janamejaya Dāsa, replied, "Prabhupāda, we usually have a bookstore."
>
> Śrīla Prabhupāda's only comment, "Hmm," was followed by another long silence. Finally, he looked out at the audience and broke the silence, "Any questions?"

One thing is made clear by this exchange: experts in promoting *saṅkīrtana* – especially those acquainted with the mood and methods of ISKCON's founder-*ācārya* and keen to follow them – need to understand His Divine Grace's strong desire that his books be highly visible and always readily available at all ISKCON events. In that way, for Śrīla Prabhupāda's pleasure, people moved by hearing about Kṛṣṇa or chanting His holy names can take home a book that explains the process of bhakti and teaches them how to practice it themselves: they can be blessed by the "great *kīrtana*."

Chanting Goes with Books

Saṅkīrtana organizers also know that when the congregational singing of the holy names goes on alongside the distribution of transcendental literature, increased book sales follow and the chanters and distributors inspire one another. Book distributors stay enlivened and feel protected by hearing the sound of the holy names. They also find that the hearts of bystanders become pacified and more favorable to buying Śrīla Prabhupāda's books because they have become imperceptibly liberated by the holy names. At the same time, the members of the chanting party sing with more gusto when they see how people are enthusiastically buying Prabhupāda's books. Inspired by one another, chanters and distributors often switch places to relish the varieties of spiritual feelings from services that are simultaneously one and different.

A *kīrtana* accompanied by *mṛdaṅgas* and *karatālas* is exotic enough to capture people's minds and cause their hearts to dance, even as they try to restrain themselves from joining in. This is because the vibration of the offenseless chanting of the Hare Kṛṣṇa mantra by devotees is a manifestation of Kṛṣṇa's flute-song. In *Śrī Caitanya-caritāmṛta* (*Madhya-līlā* 21.144), Kṛṣṇadāsa Kavirāja says that the sound of Kṛṣṇa's flute "is just like a bird that creates a nest within the ears of the *gopīs* and always remains prominent there, not allowing any other sound to enter their ears." In his purport to this verse Śrīla Prabhupāda adds, "This vibration of Kṛṣṇa's flute is represented by the Hare Kṛṣṇa *mahā-mantra*."

Therefore, expert *saṅkīrtana* devotees always try to combine public chanting of the *mahā-mantra* with the liberal distribution of Śrīla Prabhupāda's books so that those touched by hearing the congregational singing can also carry with them a book of written *kīrtana* containing the instructions they need to begin the process of devotional service at home. Śrīla Prabhupāda writes: "Hearing from the text of *Śrīmad-Bhāgavatam* is considered the most important process of hearing. *Śrīmad-Bhāgavatam* is full of transcendental chanting of the holy name, and therefore the chanting and hearing of *Śrīmad-Bhāgavatam* are transcendentally full of mellows."[16]

Best of all is when people walk away with the holy name still vibrating in their heart and one of Śrīla Prabhupāda's books tucked under their arm. Such persons have surely achieved Lord Caitanya's embrace.

Vyāsadeva's Influence

Thousands of years before Śrīla Prabhupāda had a chance to promote literary *kīrtana* as a means to spread Kṛṣṇa consciousness, Nārada Muni exalted the *Śrīmad-Bhāgavatam* as the means to change the hearts of the masses because of its being packed full of the blissful names of the unlimited Lord (*nāmāny anantasya*).[17] Of course, Nārada's disciple Śrīla Vyāsadeva, taking up Nārada Muni's mood, famously put the *Śrīmad-Bhāgavatam* into writing. Now, thousands of years later, anyone who reads or hears Vyāsa's writings – *Śrīmad-Bhāgavatam,* but also the *Bhagavad-gītā* and his other texts – is touched by Kṛṣṇa's names and instructions, and in parts of the world where they were never widely distributed before.

A wonderful example of this phenomenon is Śrīla Prabhupāda's disciple Dāru Brahma Dāsī, who tells how she received a book in a shopping mall before she became a devotee and by its influence decided to dedicate her life to Kṛṣṇa.

One day in 1971, twenty-one-year-old Dāru Brahma went to the Eastridge shopping mall in San Jose, California, "looking to buy something pretty." Seemingly from out of nowhere a devotee distributing books in the mall approached her, handed her a *Śrīmad-Bhāgavatam* Second Canto, part one, and encouraged her to take it home and read it.

Being spiritually minded, Dāru Brahma appreciated the devotee's message and character. She gave him a twenty-dollar donation for the book, a large contribution considering that it was a substantial portion of her weekly spending allowance. The devotee also asked her to repeat the *mahā-mantra,* which she did.

Dāru Brahma remembers that after bringing the book home she looked it over but was unable to fully appreciate it. She recalls: "The book seemed special to me, and it was constantly attracting me. I couldn't walk into the room without glancing at it where it sat in my apartment; but it took some time before I could actually understand what was inside the book."

One evening, however, as she sat in front her fireplace to read the book, it made complete sense to her. She was especially drawn to the chapter entitled "The Lord in the Heart." The idea that God is the supreme person captivated her. "After that, I would fall asleep reading my book, and I would keep it by my head while sleeping. It was my introduction to Kṛṣṇa consciousness and my lifeline to Kṛṣṇa. It drew me in."

At work, one of her colleagues tried to convince her that God is formless and that our ultimate goal is to merge with God. But based on what she had read in *Śrīmad-Bhāgavatam,* she was equipped to defeat her colleague's arguments and to establish that God is a person, that He has names and a form, and that the goal is to serve Him with love. "Slowly Kṛṣṇa introduced me to other means of association, and this made me understand how personal Kṛṣṇa is and how He was giving me so much of His mercy."

In due course, Dāru Brahma was initiated by Śrīla Prabhupāda into the lifetime practice of chanting the holy names. She and her husband, Puṣṭa Kṛṣṇa Dāsa, also a disciple of Śrīla Prabhupāda, have lived their lives in Kṛṣṇa consciousness, raising their children in devotional service and distributing *Śrīmad-Bhāgavatam* and the holy names to others. Dāru Brahma says: "I still own that book I purchased in the Eastridge Mall that day, and I am eternally grateful to the devotee who sold it to me. I understand that this book is my Deity."

While speaking to devotees around the world I have heard hundreds of similar stories about people who, after purchasing Śrīla Prabhupāda's books, reawakened their relationship with Kṛṣṇa and His devotees and began chanting Hare Kṛṣṇa. Ask around and you'll hear such stories wherever you go.

The Connoisseur of Written Scriptures

Book distribution has been going on for a long time. The father of the *saṅkīrtana* movement, Śrī Caitanya Mahāprabhu, the supreme connoisseur of written scriptures, relished personally distributing *Śrī Brahma-saṁhitā* and *Śrī Kṛṣṇa-karṇāmṛta* to His confidential associates. *Śrī Caitanya-caritāmṛta* (*Madhya-līlā* 1.120) records one of these immortal pastimes: "Śrī Caitanya Mahāprabhu also found two other books, namely, the *Brahma-saṁhitā* and *Kṛṣṇa-karṇāmṛta.* Knowing these books to be excellent, He took them to present to His devotees."

Śrīla Prabhupāda explains in his purport to this verse:

> In the olden days there were no presses, and all the important scriptures were handwritten and kept in large temples. Caitanya Mahāprabhu found the *Brahma-saṁhitā* and *Kṛṣṇa-karṇāmṛta* in handwritten texts, and knowing them to be very authoritative, He took them with Him to present to His devotees. Of course, He obtained the permission of the temple commander. Now both the *Brahma-saṁhitā* and *Kṛṣṇa-karṇāmṛta* are available in print for the world to relish.

Kṛṣṇadāsa Kavirāja also recounts how when Lord Caitanya toured South India, He personally obtained and carried an original page from the *Kūrma Purāṇa* to Rāmadāsa Vipra in order to alleviate that *brāhmaṇa's* anxiety about Sītādevī being kidnapped by Rāvaṇa.[18]

Passing on these works to his associates was so important to Mahāprabhu that He had them copied by hand – a painstaking method in an age before printing presses. Today, by Mahāprabhu's arrangement, technological advances have made these same books and many others readily available to everyone in a variety of languages.

When one receives and reads these sacred writings to oneself, the *kīrtana* resonates in one's mind and heart and the seeds of bhakti are planted and watered. For instance, while distributing books in San Francisco, our devotees met a young man named Terrence, a visitor from the East Coast who was staying at a local San Francisco hotel. After checking into his hotel room he had looked in the drawer and discovered a copy of *Bhagavad-gītā As It Is,* placed there by our MotelGita team. When he met us on the street he was excited to buy all of Śrīla

Prabhupāda's other books. After I spoke with him for a while, I asked him to write a short testimonial to inspire others. Here is what he wrote: "I got my first *Gītā* in a hotel room, and ever since I read the first verse my life has been ever increasingly in Kṛṣṇa consciousness. Life is a journey back to Kṛṣṇa. Peace."

Here is an excerpt from *Viraha-aṣṭaka* (8.2–3), written by Śrīla Prabhupāda to his spiritual master in a mood of deep separation before coming to America to propagate the *saṅ-kīrtana* movement. He highlights the redemption of the brothers Jagāi and Mādhāi, considered to be the most degraded persons of their time:

> Just as the Lord delivered Jagāi and Mādhāi
> Out of His own causeless mercy,
> You explained to everyone that this same method
> Of preaching work has to go on.
>
> The world has now filled up
> With many Jagāis and Mādhāis to deliver.
> Everyone is anxiously looking down the road
> Waiting for Caitanya-Nitāi to come to their rescue.

Dear readers, let us not keep these souls waiting. Let us pick up drums, *karatālas,* and Śrīla Prabhupada's books and go out to meet them today. Let us give them the medicine of the holy names and Kṛṣṇa's teachings and thus perfectly and completely execute the *yuga-dharma.*

CHAPTER TEN

Heavy Lifting

HOW DO YOU THINK you'd feel after carrying and distributing three tons of Śrīla Prabhupāda's books in one day? Tired but blissful, right?

I write this having just returned to my home in Burlingame, California, from the annual Jagannātha Ratha-yātrā festival in Los Angeles. While devotees and guests eagerly pulled the three huge carts on procession, our team of young, enthusiastic devotees worked hard to distribute 20,000 books, weighing all together three tons.

First, the team packed into individual bags sets of three books – *Śrī Īśopaniṣad, The Higher Taste,* and *The Nectar of Instruction* – along with a Jagannātha sticker, a pamphlet explaining the meaning of Ratha-yātrā, a *prasāda* lollipop, and an invitation card to the local temple. It took fifty devotees eight hours to complete the task.

Next, the team put these individual bags into the larger carry bags the devotees would use to distribute the sets to people along the parade route. After a couple of devotees rented a van and a bunch of California-style rickshaws, the whole team then loaded the carry bags into the van and transported them to the Ratha-yātrā site. There they loaded them onto the rickshaws that would follow the parade. The loading and unloading of these heavy bags of books required many hands working together.

During the procession, several dozen distributors fanned out into the crowd of onlookers, greeting them with smiles and waves as they distributed the book packs. I saw rows of people clutching the colorful books, some absorbed in reading them. I saw book packs peeking out from purses, backpacks, and baby strollers. Seeing the results of their labor, the distributors smiled and chanted Kṛṣṇa's names with great pleasure.

When the books were all distributed, one of the team leaders observed that all the team members who had participated were blissful but also physically exhausted from the day's work. In America it is said that when someone does some substantial work, he or she did the "heavy lifting."

The book distribution team at this Ratha-yātrā definitely did some heavy lifting. And my account doesn't even touch on the work that others did to make the books available: the writing, editing, prepress, shipping, and so on. To produce and distribute even *one* of Śrīla Prabhupāda's books requires heavy lifting. But because all this heavy lifting is for Kṛṣṇa, the minds and senses of all those involved are purified and fixed on Him. Śrīla Prabhupāda writes in his purport to *Śrīmad-Bhāgavatam* 10.2.37:

> The word *kriyāsu,* meaning "by manual labor" or "by work," is important in this verse. One should engage in practical service to the Lord. In our Kṛṣṇa consciousness movement, all our activities are concentrated upon distributing Kṛṣṇa literature. This is very important. One may approach any person and induce him to read Kṛṣṇa literature so that in the future he also may become a devotee. Such activities are recommended

in this verse. *Kriyāsu yas tvac-caraṇāravindayoḥ*. Such activities will always remind the devotees of the Lord's lotus feet. By fully concentrating on distributing books for Kṛṣṇa, one is fully absorbed in Kṛṣṇa. This is *samādhi*.

Here Śrīla Prabhupāda is stressing the importance of doing "manual labor" for Kṛṣṇa. The word *manual* comes from the Latin root *manus* ("hands"). In other words, manual labor is work done with one's hands and other senses.

Even Kṛṣṇa's most celebrated devotees find pleasure in doing manual labor for the Lord. Mādhavendra Purī, for example, in order to fulfill the orders of his Deity Śrī Gopāla, traveled thousands of miles to beg for sandalwood, then carried it home with his own hands. Śrīla Kṛṣṇadāsa Kavirāja Gosvāmī writes:

> Without considering his personal comforts, Mādhavendra Purī carried one *maund* [about eighty-two pounds] of sandalwood and twenty *tolās* [about eight ounces] of camphor to smear over the body of Gopāla. This transcendental pleasure was sufficient for him ... Although Mādhavendra Purī did not have a farthing with him, he was not afraid to pass by the toll officers. His only enjoyment was in carrying the load of sandalwood to Vṛndāvana for Gopala ... With great trouble and after much labor, Mādhavendra Purī brought the load of sandalwood to Remuṇā. However, he was still very pleased; he discounted all the difficulties.[1]

Śrī Caitanya Mahāprabhu also worked hard with His hands to cleanse the Guṇḍicā temple with His devotees. Kṛṣṇadāsa Kavirāja Gosvāmī states that it appeared as though "Śrī Caitanya Mahāprabhu were cleansing and washing with a hundred hands. He approached every devotee just to teach him how to work."[2]

In *Śrī Caitanya-bhāgavata,* Vṛndāvana Dāsa Ṭhākura writes about how Mādhāi built a bathing *ghāṭa* with his hands on the order of Lord Nityānanda:

> When Mādhāi then expressed to Nityānanda his desire to become free from the offense of causing trouble to numerous living entities, Śrīmān Nityānanda Prabhu instructed Mādhāi to build a bathing *ghāṭa* on the bank of the Ganges and to offer respectful obeisances to those who came to bathe in the Ganges. Following the order of Nityānanda, Mādhāi built and then daily cleansed the bathing *ghāṭa* while chanting the names of Kṛṣṇa with tears in his eyes. He would offer obeisances to those who came there. Upon seeing this behavior of Mādhāi, people were astonished. Seeing Jagāi and Mādhāi's drastic change of heart, even those who previously blasphemed and ridiculed Mahāprabhu due to not understanding His position now also realized Mahāprabhu's unlimited mercy and glories. Due to the performance of severe austerities, Mādhāi became renowned as a *brahmacārī.*[3]

The bathing *ghāṭa* built by Mādhāi by his own hard labor still stands on the banks of the Gaṅgā, an enduring monument to his service and surrender. Śrīla Rūpa Gosvāmī specifically states in his *Bhakti-rasāmṛta-sindhu* that devotional practice is to be done "by manual labor."[4] Anyone who works hard to expand Lord Caitanya's mission, then, perfectly emulates these great souls by dint of his or her scripturally authorized service.

The word Śrīla Rūpa Gosvāmī uses to define the practice of bhakti-yoga is *anuśīlanam.* Contained within *anuśīlanam* are the verbs *śīl* ("to work" or "to contemplate") and *anu* ("to follow"). In other words, the practice of devotional service includes both contemplation of Kṛṣṇa and physical services done for Kṛṣṇa that follow the mood and method of previous authorities.[5]

The Gosvāmīs Rūpa and Sanātana Worked Hard

Commenting on Śrī Rūpa's definition of *sādhana-bhakti,* both Viśvanātha Cakravartī Ṭhākura and Jīva Gosvāmī confirm that one should not only mentally serve the Lord – as in meditation on Him – but also physically serve Him, just as Rūpa Gosvāmī and his brother Sanātana Gosvāmī did while they lived in Vṛndāvana.[6] Rūpa and Sanātana are both eternal associates of the Lord and have their spiritual forms in Goloka, but while living in earthly Vṛndāvana they performed practical services for Mahāprabhu, and the results of their work clearly show that they worked hard.

Śrīla Prabhupāda uses the term "exegetical endeavors" to describe one aspect of the practical service of Śrīla Rūpa and Śrīla Sanātana:[7] the two brothers, along with other *gosvāmīs* in Vṛndāvana, produced hundreds of handwritten books that would eventually establish Lord Caitanya's teachings all over the world. They also excavated holy places and oversaw the building of temples. And as mentioned in the *Bhakti-ratnākara,* even after Rūpa and Sanātana left this world, their exalted nephew Śrī Jīva Gosvāmī not only wrote extensively but also engaged his disciples – especially Narottama, Śrīnivāsa, and Śyāmānanda – in the hands-on work of copying and distributing the books written by the Six Gosvāmīs of Vṛndāvana in particular.

In *Śrī Caitanya-caritāmṛta, Madhya-līlā* 19.132, Śrīla Prabhupāda specifically requests his followers to focus on book writing, printing, and distribution, and by so doing, to follow in the footsteps of Rūpa Gosvāmī: "According to Bhaktisiddhānta Sarasvatī Ṭhākura, distributing literature is like playing on a great *mṛdaṅga.* Consequently we always request members of the International Society for Krishna Consciousness to publish as many books as possible and distribute them widely throughout the world. By thus following in the footsteps of Śrīla Rūpa Gosvāmī, one can become a *rūpānuga* devotee."

Śrīla Prabhupāda's dedication to his books is storied. For as long as he was with us he incessantly urged his disciples to produce and distribute them. Assisted by his editorial staff, he dictated his final purports right up to his last days, even when his body was wholly emaciated, a spiritual feat clear for all to see – a feat possible only for those in the most exalted state of Kṛṣṇa consciousness. We also celebrate the humility he showed by never claiming any personal credit for having performed such superhuman deeds in order to execute his guru's order. And that humility was also shown throughout the years of his mission as he repeatedly professed that his followers were achieving transcendental states of consciousness through their own hard work of publishing and distributing his books, in spite of living in the commotion of big cities and far from places where meditation would have come easier.

After the devotees of ISKCON Los Angeles had completed a challenging six-day marathon to distribute a large number of his books, Śrīla Prabhupāda wrote them this letter, addressed to Rāmeśvara Dāsa and dated January 12, 1976:

> The book distribution in Los Angeles during the six-day period is transcendental *samādhi*. They are working in trance, not on the material platform. No common man can work so hard. It is not possible. Working without sleep means no death. Sleeping is dead condition – *jīv jāgo, jīv jāgo, gauracānda bole, kota nidrā jāo māyā-pīśācīra kole.* Your book distribution is really intoxication.

In the *Gītā* (3.15), Lord Kṛṣṇa reveals why such work induces spiritual intoxication. He says that "the all-pervading Transcendence is eternally situated in acts of sacrifice" and that "having tasted the nectar of the results of sacrifices, they advance toward the supreme eternal atmosphere."[8] In other words, such scripturally authorized work puts one directly in touch with Kṛṣṇa, who delights the senses of such a servitor.

Carry Firewood

Scripture clearly supports the idea that employing one's physical senses in practical service to Kṛṣṇa and the spiritual master is foundational to one's spiritual advancement. The *Muṇḍaka Upaniṣad* (1.2.12), for example, says that a disciple must "carry firewood in his hand [*samit-pāṇiḥ*] for his guru to use in sacrifice."

Why firewood? In past ages a spiritual master would daily prepare and light a sacrificial fire as the means of worshiping God, and his disciples would assist him by collecting wood for that fire. Such a manual task performed to serve the guru not only fostered humility, opening the disciple's heart and mind to the guru's teachings, but also invoked the spiritual master's blessings. Kṛṣṇa also recommends in the *Gītā* (4.34) that one approach a guru with a submissive spirit, render him service, and inquire from him.

Śrīla Prabhupāda explains the importance of submission:

> [The Supersoul's] existence can be realized by one who has the single qualification of submissiveness and who thereby becomes a surrendered soul. The development of submissiveness is the cause of proportionate spiritual realization, by which one can ultimately meet the Supreme Lord in person, as a man meets another man face to face.[9]

Submissive service to one's spiritual master expressed through practical work is so important that Lord Kṛṣṇa Himself set the example by personally gathering and carrying firewood to please His spiritual master, Sāndīpani Muni. Lord Kṛṣṇa reminisces with His friend, Sudāmā:

> O *brāhmaṇa,* do you remember what happened to us while we were living with our spiritual master? Once our guru's wife sent us to fetch firewood, and after we entered the vast forest, O twice-born one, an unseasonal storm arose, with fierce wind and rain and harsh thunder. Then, as the sun set, the forest was covered by darkness in every direction, and with all the flooding we could not distinguish high land from low. Constantly besieged by the powerful wind and rain, we lost our way amidst the flooding waters. We simply held each other's hands and, in great distress, wandered aimlessly about the forest. Our guru, Sāndīpani, understanding our predicament,

> set out after sunrise to search for us, his disciples, and found us in distress. [Sāndīpani said:] "O my children, you have suffered so much for my sake! The body is most dear to every living creature, but you are so dedicated to me that you completely disregarded your own comfort. This indeed is the duty of all true disciples: to repay the debt to their spiritual master by offering him, with pure hearts, their wealth and even their very lives. You boys are the best of the twice born, and I am satisfied with you. May all your desires be fulfilled, and may the Vedic mantras you have learned never lose their meaning for you, in this world or the next."[10]

Just as the firewood Kṛṣṇa submissively carried for his spiritual master came from trees, the paper from which transcendental books are made today also comes from trees. Just as firewood is carried by hand, so too are transcendental literatures. I've watched our local devotees tote heavy boxes of *Śrīmad-Bhāgavatam* or *Śrī Caitanya-caritāmṛta* up and down staircases while going door to door to distribute them. I've also seen devotees spend days preparing, transporting, and displaying varieties of Śrīla Prabhupāda's books at big events and fairs, and then spend hours a day selling them. Clearly, those who work in these ways to distribute Śrīla Prabhupāda's books fulfill the wood-carrying spirit recommended in the *Muṇḍaka Upaniṣad.* Is it any wonder, then, that Śrīla Prabhupāda so much stressed distributing his books?

Sacred Fire

According to *Śrīmad-Bhāgavatam* (12.3.52), the blessed fire sacrifice that was the recommended process for worshiping the Supreme Personality of Godhead in previous ages is completed in the present age by performing *saṅkīrtana:*

> Whatever result was obtained in Satya-yuga by meditating on Viṣṇu, in Tretā-yuga by performing sacrifices, and in Dvāpara-

> yuga by serving the Lord's lotus feet can be obtained in Kali-yuga simply by chanting the Hare Kṛṣṇa *mahā-mantra.*

Following in the spirit of this verse, Śrīla Prabhupāda glorifies the preeminence of *saṅkīrtana:*

> Recently, when we established a large Kṛṣṇa-Balarāma temple in Vṛndāvana, we were obliged to have Vedic ceremonies enacted by *brāhmaṇas* because the inhabitants of Vṛndāvana, especially the *smārta-brāhmaṇas,* would not accept Europeans and Americans as bona fide *brāhmaṇas.* Thus we had to engage *brāhmaṇas* to perform costly *yajñas.* In spite of these *yajñas,* the members of our Society performed *saṅkīrtana* loudly with *mṛdaṅgas,* and I considered the *saṅkīrtana* more important than the Vedic ritualistic ceremonies.[11]

Just as in Tretā-yuga a qualified Vedic priest lit the daily sacrificial fire by mantra, in Kali-yuga distributors of transcendental literatures ignite the sacred fire of knowledge in the hearts of their recipients. The words these distributors speak to motivate people to purchase and read these books are just as potent and authorized as were the Vedic mantras uttered by *brāhmaṇas* in Tretā-yuga as they spooned oblations of ghee into the sacrificial fire. In the *Gītā* (15.15), Kṛṣṇa says that the ultimate purpose of the *Vedas* is to bring people to full knowledge of Him, the Supreme Personality of Godhead: "By all the *Vedas,* I am to be known."

Trust the Hand

Regarding the great sacrifice of distributing his books, Śrīla Prabhupāda remarks:

> Somehow or other, if the book goes in one's hand, he'll be benefited. At least he'll see, "I have taken so much price – let me see what is there." If he reads one *śloka,* his life will become

> successful. If he reads one *śloka,* one word! This is such a nice thing. Therefore we are stressing so much, please distribute book, distribute book, distribute book![12]

When I teach devotees how to distribute books, I tell them to trust the hand – that is, be sure to place the book in the prospective reader's hand. Let the person get a physical feel for the book. Often prospects think they don't want the book, but as I extend it, their hand overrules their head and they accept it. The hand's nature is to grasp things first and ask questions later. When unwilling persons' hands grasp a transcendental book, they are benefited. Furthermore, as they continue to hold the book they often become attached to it and decide they want it after all.

Recently, a man I met was in the process of saying "I'm not interested" just as I was handing him a *Bhagavad-gītā As It Is.* But although his tongue said "no," his hand still accepted the book. Then, after hearing how the *Gītā* had been studied and revered by the likes of Thoreau, Emerson, and Gandhi, and how it is taught in mainstream universities, he changed his mind and bought the book.

Transferring transcendental books from one's hand to another's hand is a practical form of sacrifice that benefits both the distributors and the potential readers. The books are tangible, pleasing to the eye and mind, and can be carried from place to place. A distributor uses all his or her senses while showing a book to someone, and the book connects that soul to Kṛṣṇa directly.

In his purport to *Śrīmad-Bhāgavatam* 7.13.25, Śrīla Prabhupāda writes:

> Material life is called *pavarga* because here we are subject to five different states of suffering, represented by the letters *pa, pha, ba, bha,* and *ma. Pa* means *pariśrama,* very hard labor. *Pha* means *phena,* or foam from the mouth. For example, sometimes we see a horse foaming at the mouth with heavy labor.

> *Ba* means *byarthatā,* disappointment. In spite of so much hard labor, at the end we find disappointment. *Bha* means *bhaya,* or fear. In material life, one is always in the blazing fire of fear, since no one knows what will happen next. Finally, *ma* means *mṛtyu,* or death. When one attempts to nullify these five different statuses of life – *pa, pha, ba, bha,* and *ma* – one achieves *apavarga,* or liberation from the punishment of material existence.*

The five different states of material suffering are overcome by serving Kṛṣṇa with one's physical senses and mind. Those who read Śrīla Prabhupāda's books and then labor honestly to distribute them will never know the disappointment or fear that result from ordinary karmic work. What's more, because of their hard labor these devotional workers will go back to Godhead.

Śrīla Prabhupāda concludes:

> Many fanatic spiritual movements have come and gone, but without the flawless philosophy of Kṛṣṇa, they cannot stand. Therefore I want especially that my books and literature should be distributed profusely. This is our substance, real philosophical information, not some weak sentiments. So try for this, to give all men this Kṛṣna philosophy, and many real devotees will come with us back to Home, back to Godhead.[13]

* Here Śrīla Prabhupāda is presenting a clever and instructive play on words. The Sanskrit word *apavarga* is actually formed by the addition of the prefix *apa-* to the word *varga*, and means "liberation" or "emancipation." However, here he ingeniously divides *apavarga* in another way, as *a-pa-varga,* where prefix *a-* indicates negation and the compound *pa-varga* is the standard, familiar grammatical term denoting the group (*varga*) of consonants in the Sanskrit alphabet that begins with *pa*. This set, the *pa-varga,* contains the five labial consonants, and Śrīla Prabhupāda sounds them out in their alphabetical order: *pa, pha, ba, bha, ma*. Each consonant begins (and signifies) a word which denotes one of the conditions of bondage or material suffering, and *a-pavarga* is then the negation of them.

CHAPTER ELEVEN

Faith in God and Strength of Mind

NĀRADA MUNI RECOUNTS in *Śrīmad-Bhāgavatam* how as a little boy he tolerated life's adversities and then fearlessly wandered through God's creation, depending fully on the Lord's grace. Śrīla Prabhupāda comments: "It is the duty of a mendicant (*parivrājakācārya*) to experience all varieties of God's creation by traveling alone through all forests, hills, towns, villages, etc., to gain faith in God and strength of mind, as well as to enlighten the inhabitants with the message of God."[1]

Book distributors do just that. They go forth fearlessly through all "varieties of God's creation" to introduce people to Kṛṣṇa consciousness. As they do, they see Kṛṣṇa's energies at work. Śrīla Prabhupāda talked about his impressions of his own fearless traveling, done in order to teach Kṛṣṇa consciousness: "So far my experience is concerned, everywhere I go, people are the same. It is by artificial, I mean to say, they have been designated as communist and this and that ... As soon as we speak of Kṛṣṇa consciousness, they respond immediately. That is my experience."[2]

In the *Bhagavad-gītā* (4.35) Kṛṣṇa speaks of this core realization – the equal vision that brings about genuine affection for other souls: "Having obtained real knowledge from a self-realized soul, you will never fall again into such illusion, for by this knowledge you will see that all living beings are but part of the Supreme, or, in other words, that they are Mine."

As book distributors move about their local cities and towns or travel beyond them, meeting people from different cultures and backgrounds, political and religious persuasions, social and economic standings, each with a different outlook on life, they gain their own equal vision: in essence, all people have similar needs and desires, and this can be seen by watching all the ways in which they respond to Kṛṣṇa consciousness.

What's more, by taking risks and facing adversities in their service, book distributors realize something else of value too: that the principles they read about in scripture are true. Thus they develop "faith in God and strength of mind." Because of these benefits derived from distributing Śrīla Prabhupāda's books, devotees everywhere consider book distribution to be high *sādhana*.

But There Are Risks ...

About the risks involved in teaching Kṛṣṇa consciousness Śrīla Prabhupāda writes:

> A devotee situated in Kṛṣṇa consciousness knows that only devotional service to Kṛṣṇa can relieve a person from all the problems of life. He has personal experience of this, and therefore he wants to introduce this system, Kṛṣṇa consciousness, into human society. There are many examples in history of devotees of the Lord who risked their lives for the spreading of God consciousness. The favorite example is Lord Jesus Christ. He was crucified by the nondevotees but he sacrificed his life for spreading God consciousness.... Similarly, in India also there are many examples, such as Ṭhākura Haridāsa and Prahlāda Mahārāja. Why such risk? Because they wanted to spread Kṛṣṇa consciousness, and it is difficult.[3]

It is out of compassion for others' sufferings and a desire to please Caitanya Mahāprabhu that devotees are willing to face the risks of spreading Kṛṣṇa consciousness; this is because they know the Supreme Lord's purpose. Again, Śrīla Prabhupāda writes:

> Men who are ignorant cannot appreciate activities in Kṛṣṇa consciousness, and therefore Lord Kṛṣṇa advises us not to disturb them and simply waste valuable time. But the devotees of the Lord are more kind than the Lord because they understand the purpose of the Lord. Consequently they undertake all kinds of risks, even to the point of approaching ignorant men to try to engage them in the acts of Kṛṣṇa consciousness, which are absolutely necessary for the human being.[4]

Facing Adversity for Kṛṣṇa Makes One Strong

Those who risk distributing Śrīla Prabhupāda's books are regularly exposed to public scrutiny, even harassment. Think of adversity on book distribution as being a stress test. In the medical world, a stress test is used to tell the doctor how well your heart is performing, particularly whether sufficient blood is flowing into the heart. Meeting the public and accepting both physical risks and risks to the ego can show us how well we are developing qualities like tolerance and compassion. Whenever we may find ourselves losing our poise, disturbed by unfriendly speech, seized by anger, or even offending the people we are trying to help, we are in fact seeing the sign – the big red flashing warning light – of our deficiencies in *sādhana* and *sevā,* because the feedback we get is proportionate and immediate. This creates an ideal environment for self-examination in which one may develop an acute sense of responsibility for one's actions. Faithful devotees, thus sensitized, refine themselves by studying *śāstra* and taking guidance from advanced devotees polished by years of sincere practice and realization.

Guided by these conduits of Kṛṣṇa's mercy, one learns to take whatever difficulties one faces as arrangements by

Kṛṣṇa for one's purification. As Prahlāda Mahārāja tells his classmates, "The Lord is pleased only if one has unflinching, unalloyed devotion to Him. Without sincere devotional service, everything is simply a show."[5] Book distributors have daily opportunities to learn tolerance and to show Kṛṣṇa that their faith in His instructions and their devotion to Him are unflinching.

"Street Smarts"

By going out into the public to distribute Śrīla Prabhupāda's books, devotees meet and interact with people, learn to befriend them even when those people do not agree with them, and try to touch their hearts. When distributors meet people holding opposing ideas, they learn to skillfully answer questions and counteract people's objections to receiving a book about Kṛṣṇa consciousness. This gives devotees a kind of transcendental "street smarts," a mix of knowledge and commonsense wisdom that allows them to relate affectionately with all kinds of people even as they quick-wittedly defend the Kṛṣṇa conscious philosophy. Distributors become independently thoughtful as they grow in their service, and increasingly competent to deal with the practical complexities of life. In a letter to Karandhara dated December 22, 1972, Śrīla Prabhupāda includes the development of these qualities as one of the objectives of the Kṛṣṇa consciousness movement: "Kṛṣṇa consciousness movement is for training men to be independently thoughtful and competent in all types of departments of knowledge and action."

Distributing Books Helps Overcome the Mind

As I distribute books, my mind often dictates which among the possible prospects would or would not be interested in receiving one. But if I approach everyone equally, without listening to my mind's appraisal, I often find that my mind has misjudged.

One day, while distributing books door to door in Southern California, I encountered a Gujarati couple. My mind announced that these were pious Hindus who would surely take a book. But they showed not even the slightest interest in what I presented and cut our conversation short.

When I knocked on the next door I found four Muslim students from Saudi Arabia sharing an apartment. When they opened their door my mind said, "Oops, wrong door!" But I showed them a *Bhagavad-gītā* anyway. They invited me in, sat me down, and asked me to tell them all about it. Each of the students purchased a *Gītā* and expressed appreciation for the work I was doing, and they even waved goodbye from their doorway as I left.

While distributing books in Santa Cruz, California, I once watched Akrūranātha Dāsa become friends with a homeless man. My mind told me the man was an unlikely candidate for devotional service, but he gradually purchased and read the entire *Śrīmad-Bhāgavatam* and *Śrī Caitanya-caritāmṛta,* paying the full price in installments. The man was so interested in Śrīla Prabhupāda's books that he arranged with a local homeless shelter to keep them in a locker there. Then he pulled out one book at a time and sat in the nearby park to read it.

What do distributors learn from experiences like these? That they can't judge people by their bodies or their circumstances. Gradually, distributors gain the ability to see beyond a person's external trappings and to become aware of and then tune in to each person's internal quality. Opportunities to exercise this yogic vision occur regularly in the lives of those who go out to meet people and introduce them to Śrīla Prabhupāda's books.

The bhakti scriptures say that those who have learned to distinguish between devotees, the innocent (those who are ignorant of God), and nondevotees (those who are envious of God) have advanced beyond the neophyte stage. They are *madhyama,* or "middle," devotees.

In *Śrīmad-Bhāgavatam,* Havi Yogendra tells Mahārāja Nimi about this distinction between levels of faith and knowledge in a devotee. He says that the neophyte (*kaniṣṭha*) devotees, in the lowest stage of devotional service, see God only in the temple, church, or mosque. Neophytes do not know how or why to respect God's devotees or appreciate and benefit other living beings. The more advanced, mid-level devotees see Kṛṣṇa not only in the temple but also in the hearts of others. They know, therefore, how to honor devotees, in whose heart Kṛṣṇa has manifested, as well as how to respect all living beings as parts of Kṛṣṇa and do good for them.

Because the ability to distinguish between the innocent and the nondevotee envious of God is a skill necessary for book distribution, devotees who distribute Śrīla Prabhupāda's books find themselves spurred on to step up from their *kaniṣṭha* faith and knowledge to a higher platform, where they acquire the almost instinctive ability to honor each person they meet in an appropriate manner. For example, on meeting an envious person, expert book distributors know how to avoid conflict by graciously excusing themselves and even by expressing their gratitude to such nondevotees for having met them; in this way, the devotees kindly help forestall such persons from committing any further offenses.

The Blessing of Tolerance

In *Śrīmad-Bhāgavatam* (4.11.13), Svāyambhuva Manu tells Dhruva Mahārāja, "The Lord is very satisfied with His devotee when the devotee greets other people with tolerance, mercy, friendship, and equality." It takes purification and practice to develop a tolerant disposition. As Kṛṣṇa recounts the story of the Avantī *brāhmaṇa,* He admits to Uddhava that the insults of uninformed or even belligerent people are almost impossible to bear. The Avantī *brāhmaṇa* lost his home, fortune, and family, finally accepting the renounced order of life, but when he left his home to pursue a life of devotion to the Supreme Lord, people harassed him wherever he went: "They would criticize and insult him, saying, 'This man is just a hypocrite and a cheat. He makes a business of religion simply because he lost all his wealth and his family threw him out.'"[6]

But fixed on his higher goal of spiritual realization, the Avantī *brāhmaṇa* explains: "These people are not the cause of my happiness and distress. Neither are the demigods, my own body, the planets, my past work, or time. Rather, it is the mind alone that causes happiness and distress and perpetuates the rotation of material life."[7]

Book distributors are inspired to learn tolerance by hearing of the stalwart personal associates of the Lord, such as Nityānanda Prabhu, Advaita Ācārya, and Haridāsa Ṭhākura, who also had to endure insults and were even physically harmed as they went door to door to preach Lord Caitanya's message. Such inevitable adversities become extremely valuable when one handles them by depending on Kṛṣṇa the way the Avantī *brāhmaṇa* or Lord Caitanya and His associates did. Kṛṣṇa says:

> A saintly person should never let others frighten or disturb him and, similarly, should never frighten or disturb other people. He should tolerate the insults of others and should never himself belittle anyone. He should never create hostility with anyone for the sake of the material body, for he would thus be no better than an animal.[8]

In the *Bhagavad-gītā* (5.23), Kṛṣṇa also tells Arjuna that a person who is able to control his senses and check the force of desire and anger before leaving this present body lives happily in this world.

Śrīla Prabhupāda was well aware of what his devotees were going through as they reached out to the public. He rarely inserted parenthetical comments into his word-for-word translations of *Śrīmad-Bhāgavatam* verses, but in *Bhāgavatam* 5.5.2, in his gloss of *vimanyavaḥ,* "without anger," he adds that "one must distribute Kṛṣṇa consciousness to persons who are hostile without becoming angry at them."

Controlling Anger

In 1975, while distributing books in New York City's LaGuardia airport, I received a lesson in controlling anger. It happened one day when I became annoyed with a man of Indian origin who was deliberately rude when I offered him a *Bhagavad-gītā As It Is.* Forgetting Lord Caitanya's edict that I should be more tolerant than a tree, with a tinge of disdain in my voice I asked, "Would your parents approve of the way you're acting?"

The man was insulted by my snide remark. He became furious and ran off in the direction of the police station to lodge a complaint. When the police came, I spent a lot of time explaining and apologizing. Not only did I waste a lot of time, I felt embarrassed that I had become irritated. I had selfishly upset someone's mind and given him a bad impression of a devotee. I meditated on the incident for weeks and resolved to be on guard against anger in the future. My unrelenting, inescapable conclusion was, "Becoming angry isn't worth it."

Subsequent decades of book distribution have implanted this realization in me: When I speak to someone with anger or envy in my heart – or with *any* selfishly impelled emotion – the other person's response and my counter-response almost always produce a dramatic inflation of negative emotions. The outcome is never favorable. It doesn't take much to get things started; even a drop of anger or envy leaking into an exchange can set off a reaction that disturbs one's own consciousness for a long time, not to mention the disturbance it causes others. This realization, gained through multiple lessons while on book distribution, has also inspired me to practice tolerance in all other aspects of my life as well. For good reason, both Lord Kṛṣṇa and Lord Caitanya repeatedly stress the importance of tolerance, or forbearance – of remaining undisturbed when there is every reason to become disturbed and of remaining respectful even to the disrespectful.

Spiritual Blood

Śrīla Bhaktisiddhānta Sarasvatī Ṭhākura explains that when devotees deal with opposition while teaching Kṛṣṇa consciousness, their "spiritual body (*cit-śarīra*) is nourished by spiritual blood (*cid-rakta*)." Śrī Sarasvatī Ṭhākura goes on to say that devotees who continue to speak about Kṛṣṇa in spite of being misunderstood, neglected, or opposed become infused with this spiritual blood.[9]

So those who go out to distribute Śrīla Prabhupāda's books receive regular infusions of spiritual blood because they inevitably become variously misunderstood, neglected, and opposed as they encounter all sorts of people conditioned by the modes of nature. By practicing tolerance in the face of these challenges, one gets spiritual realization and advances to higher stages of devotional service.

In summary, controlling the senses is not easy; therefore the scriptures contain an abundance of instructions on how to train the senses. Especially blessed, then, are those who have ample opportunity to practice being undisturbed in the face of provocation. The field of book distribution is an ideal testing ground in which one can practice humility and tolerance in the face of all kinds of disturbing elements: drunken people, angry people, people who ignore you, street noise, and on and on. To be effective a book distributor must develop skills to defuse anger, to be detached, and to give proper respect to people under all circumstances. For a distributor, the world is a giant workshop for sensitivity training.

Special Mercy

In the *Śrīmad-Bhāgavatam* (10.14.8), Lord Brahmā speaks of a devotee who practices tolerance in the face of suffering and adversity by accepting and enduring such difficulty with the recognition that Kṛṣṇa is mercifully sending it just to purify His servant of all traces of the enjoying spirit. Such a faithful devotee, Brahmā says, thereby attains the right to go back to Godhead.

The purport to this verse cites the original *Bhāgavatam* commentator Śrīla Śrīdhara Svāmī, who elaborates on how the Lord purifies the heart of a sincere devotee:

> Lord Kṛṣṇa explains in the *Bhagavad-gītā* that a devotee who fully surrenders unto Him is no longer liable to suffer the reactions of his previous karma. However, because in his mind a devotee may still maintain the remnants of his previous sinful mentality, the Lord removes the last vestiges of the enjoying spirit by giving His devotee punishments that may sometimes resemble sinful reactions. The purpose of the entire creation of God is to rectify the living entity's tendency to enjoy without the Lord, and therefore the particular punishment given for a sinful activity is specifically designed to curtail the mentality that produced the activity. Although a devotee has surrendered to the Lord's devotional service, until he is completely perfect in Kṛṣṇa consciousness he may maintain a slight inclination to enjoy the false happiness of this world. The Lord therefore creates a particular situation to eradicate this remaining enjoying spirit. This unhappiness suffered by a sincere devotee is not technically a karmic reaction; it is rather the Lord's special mercy for inducing His devotee to completely let go of the material world and return home, back to Godhead.

Five hundred years ago in Navadvīpa, Bengal, even Lord Caitanya and His followers faced adversity as they inaugurated the Lord's *saṅkīrtana* movement. In fact, as soon as Mahāprabhu took the congregational chanting out of Śrīvāsa Ṭhākura's home for the first time and onto the streets, someone called the police. Constables came, broke the *mṛdaṅgas,* and ordered the devotees to stop chanting. In the same way, since Śrīla Prabhupāda launched ISKCON in 1966, his chanting and book distribution parties have been harassed by members of the public.

In the 1970s most of ISKCON's book distributors were in their teens or early twenties. On seeing them selling books on city streets or in airports, people frequently heckled them, calling out things like "Get a job!" Of course, no devotee seeks out such encounters. Śrīla Prabhupāda taught us to go out of our way to be perfect gentlemen and gentlewomen while presenting Kṛṣṇa consciousness. Still, harsh encounters come our way and devotees who are willing to meet them learn to tolerate them as Kṛṣṇa's mercy and deal with them appropriately.

Labaṅgalatikā Devī Dāsī tells of an ordeal she feels purified her as she distributed books at the Los Angeles airport in the early 1970s:

> We were working undercover because the airports had not yet been legalized for book distribution. So, sometimes I would be arrested and taken off to the police station. Every time I got arrested, I felt like I had been caught by the Yamadūtas. One day, the police caught me distributing, arrested me, and chained me to the bench in the police station, and all the while they heaped insults on me. During the ordeal, I unexpectedly had an overwhelming realization. Instead of going to hell as I deserved for all my past sins, Kṛṣṇa was now releasing me from them by giving me a token of what I actually deserved. The realization came to me so clearly, and the purification was so profound, that I suddenly felt my mind become lucid and enthusiastic. Those early days were very austere, but we got so much mercy poured on us.

Devotees who isolate themselves, on the other hand, who move only among those who tend to see things the same way they do, miss opportunities to cultivate forbearance, deepen their faith, and have their hearts melted by awakening compassion. Such untested faith remains weak, buried in shallow soil like the undeveloped roots of a sapling. Regular practice of forbearance expands and strengthens one's faith to the point that one can see that whatever happens is Kṛṣṇa's arrangement, or grace. With this vision comes the broadmindedness that enables the book distributor to accommodate the various needs, interests, and concerns of a wide range of people.

Meditation

In *aṣṭāṅga-yoga,* or the eightfold path, a yogi is considered to have achieved the topmost level of yoga when his or her mind is fully absorbed in Kṛṣṇa (*samādhi*). This stage may take decades or even lifetimes of practice to attain. But here Śrīla Prabhupāda says that the act of distributing his books in a mood of love naturally fixes the mind on Kṛṣṇa:

> Meditation will automatically be there. If you do, if you sacrifice your life for serving Kṛṣṇa, you'll always remember Kṛṣṇa. You'll always remember Kṛṣṇa. Just like you are taking so much trouble, going place to place to give one book to somebody. Why? Because you love Kṛṣṇa and you are thinking if this gentleman takes one book, never mind, small or big, he'll read at least one page about Kṛṣṇa. So you are thinking of Kṛṣṇa. That is meditation.[10]

Seeing how people everywhere are suffering, and personally realizing how the practice of devotional service alleviates one's own suffering, devotees develop empathy and a desire to do good for others. This is the hallmark of an advanced devotee. As Lord Kṛṣṇa says in the *Gītā* (6.32), "He is a perfect yogi who, by comparison to his own self, sees the true equality of all beings, in both their happiness and their distress, O Arjuna!"

In his purport to this verse, Śrīla Prabhupāda writes that "One who is Kṛṣṇa conscious is a perfect yogi; he is aware of everyone's happiness and distress by dint of his own personal experience."

In the *Bhakti-rasāmṛta-sindhu,* Śrīla Rūpa Gosvāmī writes

that the purpose of *sādhana-bhakti* is to soften the heart, because a hard-hearted person can neither understand Kṛṣṇa nor feel compassion for those who are suffering without Him. He advises devotees to avoid artificial hardships that torture the body and the useless strain of trying to capture God by the limited strength of one's own intellect. Both of these efforts harden the heart because they are based on selfish interests and entail militant confrontation with the mind and senses.

In contrast, devotional service is soft and sweet. The devotee knows that the underlying source of all human suffering is a broken relationship with Kṛṣṇa. Each and every soul in this world longs for Kṛṣṇa, and no substitute will satisfy that yearning. And Kṛṣṇa Himself craves reunion with every one of his alienated spiritual particles. The faithful devotee wants more than anything to bring the two together so that all are thereby fully satisfied.

In this endeavor, even the God-sent adversities inherent in book distribution *sevā* appear sweet to a devotee, because when engaged in the selfless act of giving Śrīla Prabhupāda's books to others, the distributors remember that they are working only to please Kṛṣṇa, a thought that naturally makes their hearts soft and open to Kṛṣṇa's grace and correction. A devotee thinks, "I live to be corrected." By that correction, my service improves so that I can better satisfy the desires of Kṛṣṇa and of all *jīva* souls.

Don't Be Liberated Alone

In his prayers to Lord Nṛsiṁha, Prahlāda Mahārāja says that out of compassion advanced devotees prefer to stay in big towns and villages where they can teach Kṛṣṇa consciousness to the innocent populace rather than live in secluded places in the mode of goodness, or even in transcendental holy places.

> O best of the great personalities, I am not at all afraid of material existence, for wherever I stay I am fully absorbed

in thoughts of Your glories and activities. My concern is only for the fools and rascals who are making elaborate plans for material happiness and maintaining their families, societies, and countries. I am simply concerned with love for them.

My dear Lord Nṛsiṁhadeva, I see that there are many saintly persons indeed, but they are interested only in their own deliverance. Not caring for the big cities and towns, they go to the Himalayas or the forest to meditate with vows of silence [*mauna-vrata*]. They are not interested in delivering others. As for me, however, I do not wish to be liberated alone, leaving aside all these poor fools and rascals. I know that without Kṛṣṇa consciousness, without taking shelter of Your lotus feet, one cannot be happy. Therefore I wish to bring them back to shelter at Your lotus feet.[11]

Teaching Kṛṣṇa consciousness is so important and exalted that Śrīla Prabhupāda also notes that a Kṛṣṇa conscious teacher does not even depend on living in a holy place.

Unless one is very advanced in spiritual life, it is recommended that he live in such holy places and execute devotional service there. But an advanced devotee like Nārada Muni who is engaged in preaching work can serve the Supreme Lord anywhere.[12]

It does not matter whether one lives in a holy place like Vṛndāvana, Navadvīpa, or Jagannātha Purī or in the midst of European cities, where the materialistic way of life is very prominent. If a devotee follows the instructions of Śrī Caitanya Mahāprabhu, he lives in the company of the Lord. Wherever he lives, he converts that place into Vṛndāvana and Navadvīpa. This means that materialism cannot touch him. This is the secret of success for one advancing in Kṛṣṇa consciousness.[13]

Don't Stop

On the strength of these statements alone, devotees can feel confident that they can reach maturity in devotional service by hearing, chanting, and going out into society to invite people to read transcendental literature, to chant Hare Kṛṣṇa, and to eat *kṛṣṇa-prasāda*. What is the need, then, to retire from distributing Śrīla Prabhupāda's transcendental books when one can attain perfection by doing it until the end of one's life?

Śrīla Prabhupāda was an exemplar of this principle. He set off on his great preaching venture past the age of retirement, and after twelve active, adventurous years, the last thing he stopped – except for his breath – was dictating his commentary on *Śrīmad-Bhāgavatam*. This is the quality of a truly great soul's heart; melting with compassion for suffering humanity, it pours out loving service for as long as it beats.

CHAPTER TWELVE

Confidential Service

IT WAS INK-DARK one Sunday at 4 A.M. a number of years ago when I slipped out of my apartment on Charnock Ave. in Los Angeles, California. I was walking to *maṅgala-ārati.* Three blocks from the temple I turned onto Watseka Ave., and a group of revelers in a white SUV slowed down to check me out. As I looked up, my gaze caught one of theirs and we both shrugged, as if to say, "What are *you* doing up at this time in the morning?" Freshly bathed, having just applied *tilaka,* I felt invigorated. I was starting my day. The merrymakers, on the other hand, were rumpled, blurry-eyed, and on their way home from the L.A. bar scene, winding up what looked like a long Saturday night.

In a few minutes I would enter the effulgent atmosphere of Śrī Śrī Rukmiṇī-Dvārakādhīśa's temple and sing and dance in ecstasy with Their devotees. The carousers, like millions of other Los Angelinos, however, would be falling into bed, probably sleeping past noon, and waking up to the sound of afternoon television.

This encounter brought to mind Kṛṣṇa's words in the *Gītā* (2.69): "What is night for all beings is the time of awakening for the self-controlled; and the time of awakening for all beings is night for the introspective sage." Thankfully, Śrīla Prabhupāda and his transcendental books had introduced me to Lord Caitanya's teachings and the process of pure devotional service, and I was awake and living on the light side of the night.

This is the beauty of Lord Caitanya's movement: Although Kali-yuga is infamous for obscuring the light of dharma, the confidential devotees of Mahāprabhu are never bewildered. Rather, they celebrate the arrival of this dark age because it heralds the appearance of the golden *avatāra,* Lord Caitanya, by whose merciful light even the downtrodden can take to the process of pure devotional service to Lord Kṛṣṇa, the king of Vṛndāvana. Prabodhānanda Sarasvatī writes:

> I pray that the splendid moonlight of Lord Caitanyacandra, which dispels the darkness in the hearts of the entire world, which stirs tidal waves in the nectar ocean of pure love of Kṛṣṇa, and which instills coolness in a universe burning day and night in the threefold miseries of material existence, may shine in our hearts.[1]

In this chapter I list the reasons why those who distribute Śrīla Prabhupāda's transcendental books stand in the light and shine that light into the dark for the benefit of others. This act constitutes confidential service to Lord Caitanya Mahāprabhu, a service that brings satisfaction to the self and takes one back to the topmost planet in the spiritual world, Goloka Vṛndāvana. Śrīla Prabhupāda confirms the liberated status of those who spread the *saṅkīrtana* movement in his purport to *Śrī Caitanya-caritāmṛta, Madhya-līlā* 11.89: "One should not think that because Śrī Caitanya Mahāprabhu was personally present five hundred years ago, only His associates were liberated. Rather, Śrīla Narottama dāsa Ṭhākura says that anyone is a *nitya-siddha* if he acts on behalf of Śrī Caitanya Mahāprabhu by spreading the glories of the holy name of the Lord. We should respect those devotees preaching the glories of the Lord as *nitya-siddha* and should not consider them conditioned."

This Is Service

The word *confidential* comes from the Latin for "trusted." The following verse – an excerpt from a conversation between Lord Caitanya and His intimate associate Haridāsa Ṭhākura – and Śrīla Prabhupāda's purport to it elaborate on how a person becomes a deeply trusted servant of Lord Caitanya by reaching out to save fallen souls.

> My dear Lord, do not be in anxiety. Do not be unhappy to see the condition of the *yavanas** in material existence.
>
> Purport: These words of Haridāsa Ṭhākura are just befitting a devotee who has dedicated his life and soul to the service of the Lord. When the Lord is unhappy because of the condition of the fallen souls, the devotee consoles Him, saying, "My dear Lord, do not be in anxiety." This is service. Everyone should adopt the cause of Śrī Caitanya Mahāprabhu to try to relieve Him from the anxiety He feels. This is actually service to the Lord. One who tries to relieve Śrī Caitanya Mahāprabhu's anxiety for the fallen souls is certainly a most dear and confidential devotee of the Lord. [2]

So Śrī Caitanya Mahāprabhu's devotees serve Him best by spreading the *saṅkīrtana* movement in order to uplift the poor conditioned souls who have fallen into the material world. Śrīla Prabhupāda writes:

* See the purport to *Caitanya-caritāmṛta, Antya-līlā* 3.50, where Śrīla Prabhupāda states that "the word *yavana* does not refer only to a particular class of men." Rather, the word refers to "anyone who is against the behavior of the Vedic principles."

> As a good son of the father behaves in a friendly way with all his other brothers, so also the devotee of the Lord, being a good son of the supreme father, Lord Kṛṣṇa, sees all other living beings in relation with the supreme father. He tries to bring back the upstart sons of the father to a saner stage and to get them to accept the supreme fatherhood of God.[3]

Why is this considered intimate service? Because it relieves the anxiety the Lord feels seeing the conditioned souls suffering in material existence.

In *Śrīmad-Bhāgavatam* 4.11.14, Svāyambhuva Manu confirms in a statement to Dhruva Mahārāja the power of satisfying the Lord: "One who actually satisfies the Supreme Personality of Godhead during one's lifetime becomes liberated from the gross and subtle material conditions. Thus being freed from all material modes of nature, he achieves unlimited spiritual bliss."

Become an Intimate Friend

Kṛṣṇa reciprocates with the sincere service of His devotee, and an intimate friendship blossoms between the two. In his purport to *Bhagavad-gītā* 9.29, Śrīla Prabhupāda explains how this friendship develops:

> One may question here that if Kṛṣṇa is equal to everyone and no one is His special friend, then why does He take a special interest in the devotees who are always engaged in His transcendental service? But this is not discrimination; it is natural. Any man in this material world may be very charitably disposed, yet he has a special interest in his own children. The Lord claims that every living entity – in whatever form – is His son, and so He provides everyone with a generous supply of the necessities of life. He is just like a cloud which pours rain all over, regardless of whether it falls on rock or land or water. But for His devotees, He gives specific attention. Such devotees are mentioned here: they are always in Kṛṣṇa consciousness, and therefore they are always transcendentally

> situated in Kṛṣṇa. The very phrase "Kṛṣṇa consciousness" suggests that those who are in such consciousness are living transcendentalists, situated in Him. The Lord says here distinctly, *mayi te:* "They are in Me." Naturally, as a result, the Lord is also in them. This is reciprocal. This also explains the words *ye yathā māṁ prapadyante tāṁs tathaiva bhajāmy aham:* "Whoever surrenders unto Me, proportionately I take care of him." This transcendental reciprocation exists because both the Lord and the devotee are conscious.

In *The Nectar of Devotion* (p. 96) Śrīla Prabhupāda describes two ways in which a devotee becomes an intimate friend of the Lord: "The first is to act as the confidential servant of the Lord, and the other is to act as the well-wisher of the Lord."

Śrīla Prabhupāda goes on to say that a devotee shows the first kind of friendship by systematically following the rules and regulations of devotional service with faith that in doing so he or she will reach the platform of transcendental life. And in that same section Śrīla Prabhupāda describes the second kind of friendship:

> The second display of devotional friendship – becoming a well-wisher of the Supreme Personality of Godhead – is attained by those who teach Kṛṣṇa's confidential message of devotional service to others.

The act of distributing Śrīla Prabhupāda's books brings Kṛṣṇa's message to others, an act that Kṛṣṇa says in the *Gītā* is the most pleasing to Him. In the purport to *Śrīmad-Bhāgavatam* 9.4.64, Śrīla Prabhupāda again explains how one who spreads the *saṅkīrtana* movement becomes a confidential servant of the Lord:

> The Supreme Personality of Godhead is self-sufficient, but to enjoy His transcendental bliss He requires the cooperation of His devotees. In Vṛndāvana, for example, although Lord Kṛṣṇa is full in Himself, He wants the cooperation of His devotees like the cowherd boys and the *gopīs* to increase His

> transcendental bliss. Such pure devotees, who can increase the pleasure potency of the Supreme Personality of Godhead, are certainly most dear to Him. Not only does the Supreme Personality of Godhead enjoy the company of His devotees, but because He is unlimited He wants to increase His devotees unlimitedly. Thus, He descends to the material world to induce the nondevotees and rebellious living entities to return home, back to Godhead. He requests them to surrender unto Him because, unlimited as He is, He wants to increase His devotees unlimitedly. The Kṛṣṇa consciousness movement is an attempt to increase the number of pure devotees of the Supreme Lord more and more. It is certain that a devotee who helps in this endeavor to satisfy the Supreme Personality of Godhead becomes indirectly a controller of the Supreme Lord. Although the Supreme Lord is full in six opulences, He does not feel transcendental bliss without His devotees. An example that may be cited in this regard is that if a very rich man does not have sons in a family he does not feel happiness. Indeed, sometimes a rich man adopts a son to complete his happiness. The science of transcendental bliss is known to the pure devotee. Therefore the pure devotee is always engaged in increasing the transcendental happiness of the Lord.

By engaging in the confidential service of book distribution, the distributors attract Kṛṣṇa's grace and are constantly enlivened by His friendly reciprocation.

Transcendental Anxiety

Of course, distributing books is not without its challenges, and challenges produce anxiety in the mind and heart of the devotee. I have seen many a *saṅkīrtana* leader lose sleep from worrying about how to meet goals he or she has set for book distribution.

Just as businesspersons become absorbed in developing plans to increase productivity and deal with the daily anxiety of reversals and problems, so do book distributors. This anxiety, purified of selfish motives, deepens one's intimate relationship with the Lord.

The *Bhakti-ratnākara* describes the angst Śrīnivāsa, Narottama, and Śyāmānanda felt after they discovered that the Gosvāmīs' precious books they had been entrusted to distribute in Bengal had been stolen. But the transcendental anxiety from the mishap empowered them to understand what steps to take in order to retrieve their sacred treasure.

Śrīla Prabhupāda confirms this truth in a room conversation dated April 26, 1976:

> **Guru-kṛpā:** So some people say that when I go on *saṅkīrtana* to sell books, I become in too much anxiety if I'm not doing well. So I'd rather not do it.
> **Prabhupāda:** No, that is Kṛṣṇa-anxiety. He does not know. Let him know that that is Kṛṣṇa-anxiety. Yaśodā, Mother Yaśodā, became mother of Kṛṣṇa so that she would always remain in anxiety for Kṛṣṇa, whether Kṛṣṇa is safe. That is mother's anxiety. Therefore she became mother. How to become in Kṛṣṇa-anxiety. This philosophy nobody knows.

Whatever a devotee's service, the greater the personal responsibility he or she feels to advance the *saṅkīrtana* movement, the deeper the transcendental anxiety he or she develops. Devotees who know this secret voluntarily tie themselves to Mahāprabhu's lotus feet with the ropes of transcendental anxiety.

Transcendental Maneuvers

The devotees who have tied themselves most tightly to the Lord's lotus feet with the ropes of "Kṛṣṇa-anxiety" live in the spiritual world. In *Śrī Rādhikā-stava* of the *Stava-mālā,* Śrīla Rūpa Gosvāmī explains the confidential nature of their service. There he says that Śrīmatī Rādhārāṇī, Kṛṣṇa's dearest and most perfect devotee, is always anxious to make arrangements to bring others closer to Kṛṣṇa. She is heavily laden with mercy (*karuṇa-bharite*) and is restless to distribute that mercy everywhere.

In *Teachings of Lord Caitanya,* Śrīla Prabhupāda reveals Śrīmatī Rādhārāṇī's tenderhearted selflessness:

> Although the associates of Rādhārāṇī do not expect any personal attention from Kṛṣṇa, Rādhārāṇī is so pleased with them that She arranges individual meetings between Kṛṣṇa and the damsels of Vraja. Indeed, Rādhārāṇī tries to unite Her associates with Kṛṣṇa by many transcendental maneuvers, and She takes more pleasure in these meetings than in Her own meetings with Him. When Kṛṣṇa sees that both Rādhārāṇī and Her associates are pleased by His association, He becomes more satisfied.[4]

Śrīla Kṛṣṇadāsa Kavirāja Gosvāmī states that in Kali-yuga, Rādhā and Kṛṣṇa, although eternally two personalities, appear as one (*eka-ātmānau*). In that radiant golden form of Lord Caitanya, Kṛṣṇa takes on the mood of Śrīmatī Rādhārāṇī and gives the highest spiritual favors to everyone in a way that no other incarnation has ever done before.[5]

The Navadvīpa-Vṛndāvana Link

In his commentary on *Śrī Brahma-saṁhitā* 5.5, Śrīla Bhaktisiddhānta Sarasvatī elucidates the relationship between the servants of Lord Caitanya and those of Rādhā and Kṛṣṇa and reveals that the forms of Lord Caitanya and His intimate associates are, like those of Rādhā and Kṛṣṇa, eternal in the spiritual realm:

> The pure devotees following the devotees of Vraja and those following the pure devotees in Navadvīpa are located in the realm of Kṛṣṇa and Gaura respectively. The identical devotees of Vraja and Navadvīpa simultaneously attain to the pleasures of service in the realm of Kṛṣṇa and Gaura.

Śrī Caitanya Mahāprabhu instructed the two brothers Śrīla Rūpa Gosvāmī and Śrīla Sanātana Gosvāmī to write books with references from the Vedic literature. Thus He empowered them to establish the philosophical basis of His *saṅkīrtana* movement. In this way their books brought the family business into the modern era.

Śrīla Prabhupāda showed this relationship between Lord Kṛṣṇa's and Lord Caitanya's pastimes graphically by commissioning one of his artists to paint the first illustration for his *Śrī Caitanya-caritāmṛta*. The work depicts Lord Caitanya and His associates dancing in *saṅkīrtana* on the bottom half of the canvas, and Lord Kṛṣṇa and the *gopīs* in the *rāsa* dance on the top half. When Lord Caitanya comes to the material world, His associates from the spiritual world come with Him to taste and distribute the fruits of pure love for Kṛṣṇa to the world.

> The internal devotees or potencies are all eternal associates in the pastimes of the Lord. Only with them does the Lord advent to propound the *saṅkīrtana* movement, only with them does the Lord taste the mellow of conjugal love, and only with them does He distribute this love of God to people in general.[6]

The recipients of these fruits who taste them and distribute them not only become confidential servants of Lord Caitanya; they also come to understand the mystery of the most esoteric personal form of Godhead, Rādhā and Kṛṣṇa.

Mood of the Gopīs

Now let's hear how Śrīla Prabhupāda practically applies this esoteric principle to those engaged in distributing his transcendental books. In 1974 at ISKCON Los Angeles (New Dvārakā), Rāmeśvara Dāsa, the appointed *saṅkīrtana* leader, had gleaned from Śrīla Prabhupāda's teachings that those who distribute Śrīla Prabhupāda's books are directly participating in Lord Caitanya's pastimes and in doing so following in the footsteps of Kṛṣṇa's most intimate servants in the spiritual world. Here Rāmeśvara gives an inkling of the mood in 1974:

> I began to see that the *saṅkīrtana* devotees were in direct contact with the storehouse of love of Godhead that Lord

> Caitanya had broken open five hundred years before, and that Śrīla Prabhupāda had brought that same storehouse to the earth again. The *saṅkīrtana* devotees were connected to Śrīla Prabhupāda and also, therefore, to the divine pleasure energy of Caitanya Mahāprabhu through this service. It was flowing through His Divine Grace, filling the world with ecstasy and transcendental knowledge.

In his lectures at the New Dvārakā temple, Rāmeśvara repeatedly referred to the service of book distribution as a tasteful arrangement for souls to be joined in loving service to Kṛṣṇa, a service that follows the mood of the *gopīs* of Vṛndāvana. Rāmeśvara recalls that his classes about *saṅkīrtana* were going out to all the temples to enliven the book distributors but that some devotees doubted his conclusions.

Indeed, a number of devotees wondered if Rāmeśvara's conclusions were accurate. To clarify the matter, Nandulal Devī Dāsī wrote to Śrīla Prabhupāda on May 23, 1974:

> I have heard Rāmeśvara Prabhu in Los Angeles say that when we are performing *saṅkīrtana* we are engaged in the *līlā* of Lord Caitanya. Lord Caitanya is the union of Rādhā and Kṛṣṇa, and he explained that just as Rādhārāṇī is even more anxious to arrange for the other *gopīs* to meet with Kṛṣṇa than She is for Herself to meet Kṛṣṇa, and that the other *gopīs* are also always trying to think of ways in which to arrange meetings between Rādhā and Kṛṣṇa, so when the devotees are going out and trying to engage the suffering conditioned souls, actually what we are doing is trying to arrange for some of Her lost souls to meet with Kṛṣṇa once again, and that this is the *līlā* of Lord Caitanya. Is this the proper understanding of *saṅkīrtana*?

Śrīla Prabhupāda replied on June 9, 1974: "The explanation given by Rāmeśvara that *saṅkīrtana* is Lord Caitanya's *līlā,* which he compares to the *gopīs* trying to engage in Kṛṣṇa's service, is the correct understanding."

That this esoteric service is available even to newcomers

is thus a great opportunity. Anyone who takes up the service of distributing Śrīla Prabhupāda's transcendental books in a humble mood is at once linked to such confidential devotional service: "The *saṅkīrtana* devotees are very, very dear to Kṛṣṇa. Because you are doing the fieldwork of book distribution, Kṛṣṇa has immediately recognized them as true servants."[7]

Go On Hearing

Even if the effects of service to Lord Caitanya's *saṅkīrtana* movement sound fantastical, the author of *Śrī Caitanya-caritāmṛta,* Śrīla Kṛṣṇadāsa Kavirāja, writes that one should go on hearing Lord Caitanya's pastimes until one can appreciate and realize how wonderful they actually are.

> If one does not understand in the beginning but continues to hear again and again, the wonderful effects of Lord Caitanya's pastimes will bring love for Kṛṣṇa. Gradually one will come to understand the loving affairs between Kṛṣṇa and the *gopīs* and other associates of Vṛndāvana. Everyone is advised to continue to hear over and over again in order to greatly benefit.[8]

In his famous song *Śrī Nāma-kīrtan* (2), Bhaktivinoda Ṭhākura certifies unequivocally that Lord Caitanya's mercy takes one back to Godhead: "Oh! If one receives the mercy of Lord Gaura, he will see Rādhā and Kṛṣṇa in Vṛndāvana at the end of his life [*ese vṛndāvana rādhe śyāma pabe darśana. Gaura kṛpa hale he!*]."

Service to Lord Caitanya Leads One to Vṛndāvana

Narottama Dāsa Ṭhākura, in his song *Savaraṇa-śrī-gaura-mahimā,* compares Lord Caitanya's *saṅkīrtana* movement to an ocean of nectar. Śrīla Prabhupāda, in his purport to this song, says that this ocean is always dancing with the waves of the transcendental activities of Lord Caitanya and His associates. As one tastes and distributes the fruits of the *saṅkīrtana* movement, one enters the ocean of Lord Caitanya's activities. By diving deep into that ocean, one comes to the service of Śrī Śrī Rādhā and Kṛṣṇa in Vṛndāvana.

Śrīla Prabhupāda comments further: "If one knows the secret and says, 'Let me dive deep into the ocean of the transcendental loving movement introduced by Lord Caitanya,' he immediately becomes one of the confidential devotees of Rādhā and Kṛṣṇa.[9]

In the *Navadvīpa-dhāma-māhātmya* (pp. 49–50), Śrīla Bhaktivinoda Ṭhākura also writes about how by worshiping Gaurāṅga one will attain service to Rādhā and Kṛṣṇa in Vṛndāvana:

> Now, with Kṛṣṇa there are five relationships: *śānta, dāsya, sakhya, vātsalya,* and *mādhurya.* By first worshiping Gaurāṅga in the mood of *śānta* and *dāsya,* the devotee attains Kṛṣṇa's service in the other *rasas.* According to his relationship with the Lord, the devotee's eternally perfect mood spontaneously manifests in the course of his devotional service.
>
> Whoever makes a distinction between Gaurāṅga and Kṛṣṇa is contemptible and will never attain a relationship with Kṛṣṇa. But, in the association of devotees, one who possesses the qualities beginning with humility will first worship Gaurāṅga in *dāsya,* or servitude, relationship. This *dāsya-rasa* is the highest mood in the worship of Gaurāṅga. It is in that mood that the devotees call Śrī Gaurāṅga Mahāprabhu.
>
> When the worship of Gaurāṅga in *dāsya-rasa* reaches full maturity in the heart of the living entity, *mādhurya-rasa* naturally develops in his heart. At that time one's worship of Gaurahari qualifies him to worship Rādhā and Kṛṣṇa in Vṛndāvana. Gaurāṅga then drowns the devotee in the nectar of Rādhā and Kṛṣṇa's eternal pastimes, which the devotee enters as he attains Vṛndāvana.
>
> The materialist, who is blind to spiritual life, cannot see the deep relationship between Navadvīpa and Vraja, which

are simultaneously one and different. Know for certain that this same relationship exists between Gaura and Kṛṣṇa, who are also simultaneously one and different.

Finally, Śrīla Prabhodānanda Sarasvatī confirms this principle in *Śrī Caitanya-candrāmṛta* (88):

yathā yathā gaura-padāravinde
vindeta bhaktim kṛta-pūnya-rāsiḥ
tathā tathotsarpati hṛdy akāsmad
rādhā-padāmbhoja-sudhambu-rāsiḥ

For one who sticks firmly to the service of the lotus feet of Lord Gaura, automatically the ocean of nectar from the lotus feet of Śrīmati Rādhārāṇī floods his heart.

Spiritual Currency

In conclusion, one who serves Śrī Caitanya Mahāprabhu's *saṅkīrtana* movement by distributing Śrīla Prabhupāda's transcendental books gains the spiritual currency to attain the higher stages of devotional service. In his purport to *Śrī Caitanya-caritāmṛta, Ādi-līlā* 7.17, Śrīla Prabhupāda elaborates:

> By attachment to the devotional service of Lord Caitanya Mahāprabhu, one immediately comes to the ecstatic position. When he develops his love for Nityānanda Prabhu he is freed from all attachment to the material world, and at that time he becomes eligible to understand the Lord's pastimes in Vṛndāvana. In that condition, when one develops his love for the Six Gosvāmīs, he can understand the conjugal love between Rādhā and Kṛṣṇa. These are the different stages of a pure devotee's promotion to conjugal love in the service of Rādhā and Kṛṣṇa in an intimate relationship with Śrī Caitanya Mahāprabhu.

In the *Gītā,* Lord Kṛṣṇa teaches Arjuna what He calls "confidential knowledge," and shows him His *most confidential* two-armed form. In *Śrīmad-Bhāgavatam,* Śukadeva Gosvāmī reveals confidential talks between Kṛṣṇa and Uddhava, Vidura and Maitreya, and many others. The bhakti scriptures tell us, then, about the path of confidential service to Kṛṣṇa – specifically mentioning that the path passes through service to confidential devotees and to the confidential places where Kṛṣṇa and His devotees have their pastimes.

A Guarantee

Nonetheless, Kṛṣṇadāsa Kavirāja Gosvāmī declares that although very few could understand or take up these confidential practices during Kṛṣṇa's appearance five thousand years ago, Kṛṣṇa Himself returned in Kali-yuga as Lord Caitanya to show by His own example how anyone and everyone can gain entry into confidential service by joining the *saṅkīrtana* movement. One who does so, he writes, is refreshed:

> O my merciful Lord Caitanya, may the nectarean Ganges waters of Your transcendental activities flow on the surface of my desertlike tongue. Beautifying these waters are the lotus flowers of singing, dancing, and loud chanting of Kṛṣṇa's holy name, which are the pleasure abodes of unalloyed devotees. These devotees are compared to swans, ducks, and bees. The river's flowing produces a melodious sound that gladdens their ears.[10]

Śrīla Prabhupāda has kindly showed the people of the world how to become recognized by Kṛṣṇa and attain His confidential service by spreading Lord Caitanya's *saṅkīrtana* movement. And for those who like guarantees, here's one from Śrīla Prabhupāda that you can take to the bank:

> You go on with book distribution. They will be benefited, and distributors also will be benefited. Kṛṣṇa says, *ya imaṁ paramaṁ guhyaṁ mad-bhakteṣv abhidhāsyati* and *na ca tasmān*

manuṣyeṣu kaścin me priya-kṛttamaḥ. If you want to become quickly recognized by Kṛṣṇa, then make propaganda this Kṛṣṇa consciousness movement. And once recognized by Kṛṣṇa, then your going back to home, back to Godhead is guaranteed.*

* Morning walk, July 5, 1975, Chicago. On this walk Śrīla Prabhupāda is quoting *Bhagavad-gītā* 18.68: "For one who explains this supreme secret to the devotees, pure devotional service is guaranteed, and at the end he will come back to Me."

AXIOMS

Śrī Caitanya Mahāprabhu said:
"When a person receives the seed of devotional service, he should take care of it by becoming a gardener and sowing the seed in his heart. If he waters the seed gradually by the process of *śravaṇa* and *kīrtana* [hearing and chanting], the seed will begin to sprout."

ŚRĪ CAITANYA-CARITĀMṚTA
MADHYA-LĪLĀ 19.152

CHAPTER THIRTEEN

Your Sādhana Must Be Strong

AS A CONCLUSION to my seminars, I ask my audience what they are taking home with them – what practical principles have they heard that they can "put in their pockets" and apply in their daily lives. The next five chapters are based on what my audiences have told me are the most useful tools for them. I call them The Four Laws of Book Distribution, and they are:

- Your *Sādhana* Must Be Strong
- Get Books!
- The More You Show, The More You Sell
- You Must Organize

After reading about these laws, I encourage you to apply them as soon as possible, for by doing so, you will see for yourself how each one fits into the definition of a "law": "A statement of fact, deduced from observation, to the effect that a particular natural or scientific phenomenon always occurs if certain conditions are present." In other words, when you apply these laws, you'll get the expected results.

*

The main thing is to keep the main thing the main thing.[1]

The following letters from Śrīla Prabhupāda make clear to his disciples what is *the main thing* for those who wish to practice and teach devotional service:

> The main thing is that you must set nice example for the others by following very rigidly the regulative principles, such as chanting sixteen rounds on the beads, reading the books, getting up to attend *maṅgala-ārātrika,* etc. In this way everyone shall be encouraged.[2]

And on the very same day, he wrote to another disciple:

> It is so very nice to hear how the book distribution is going on. This is our main business, distributing these books all over the world and thus turning the minds of the fallen souls towards Kṛṣṇa.

In his purport to *Bhagavad-gītā* (6.24), Śrīla Prabhupāda comments:

> The yoga practitioner should be determined and should patiently prosecute the practice without deviation. One should be sure of success at the end and pursue this course with great perseverance, not becoming discouraged if there is any delay in the attainment of success. Success is sure for the rigid practitioner.

In the Kṛṣṇa consciousness movement, then, *the main thing* should be to rigidly practice devotional service and share the nectar of advancing in spiritual life with others.

Śrīla Rūpa Gosvāmī elaborates on this principle in *The Nectar of Instruction* (8):

> The essence of all advice is that one should utilize one's full time – twenty-four hours a day – in nicely chanting and remembering the Lord's divine name, transcendental form, qualities, and eternal pastimes, thereby gradually engaging one's tongue and mind. In this way one should reside in Vraja [Goloka Vṛndāvana-dhāma] and serve Kṛṣṇa under the guidance of devotees. One should follow in the footsteps of the Lord's beloved devotees, who are deeply attached to His devotional service.

In summary, the *essence of all advice,* or *the main thing,* is to organize one's life around a strict, serious, and sincere practice of devotional service with the aim of becoming sufficiently strong spiritually to turn conditioned souls toward loving service to Śrī Kṛṣṇa, especially by distributing transcendental knowledge through Śrīla Prabhupāda's books.

Devotees derive unlimited benefits from adhering to the rigid practice of devotional service: (1) By developing all good qualities, they become attractive; (2) They develop a taste for all things related to Kṛṣṇa and for sharing that taste with others; (3) They develop a deep affinity for hearing and studying scripture; (4) They develop transcendental vision. All these qualities make for highly effective distributors of Śrīla Prabhupāda's transcendental books. In short, the distributors become empowered – invested with spiritual power.

Devotees Who Practice Strong Sādhana Are Attractive

People appreciate and respond to kindness, thoughtfulness, and integrity. Among the many other attractive divine qualities described by Lord Kṛṣṇa in the *Gītā* (16.1–3) are fearlessness, self-control, truthfulness, modesty, nonviolence, freedom from anger, aversion to faultfinding, and compassion for all living entities. *Śrīmad-Bhāgavatam* (5.18.12) says that such qualities naturally arise in those who practice devotional service: "All the demigods and their exalted qualities, such as religion, knowledge, and renunciation, become manifest in the body of one who has developed unalloyed devotion for the Supreme Personality of Godhead, Vāsudeva."

Living entities are sensitive and are deeply impressed when they meet a devotee who is truly generous owing to his or her practice of devotional service. More than anything else, devotees' noticeable good qualities are what cause the people they meet to accept a transcendental book, to read it, and later to look for more of the same kind of company.

Generally, people who read the books vividly remember the first devotee they met who exemplified the principles in the book. All the bhakti scriptures say that by associating with both the book and the person dedicated to devotional service – the book *Bhāgavata* and the person *bhāgavata* – one can come to the perfect stage of life.

In the *Bhagavad-gītā* (5.7), Lord Kṛṣṇa says that devotees who dedicate their lives to practicing devotional service not only remain free from entanglement but also become attractive: "One who works in devotion, who is a pure soul, and who controls his mind and senses is dear to everyone, and everyone is dear to him. Though always working, such a man is never entangled."

What's more, in the *Gītā* (12.16), Lord Kṛṣṇa says that He especially appreciates devotees who are pure, unmotivated, and strictly engaged in devotional service: "My devotee who is not dependent on the ordinary course of activities, who is pure, expert, without cares, free from all pains, and not striving for some result, is very dear to Me."

Just as a diamond's beauty is crafted by pressure and heat brought to bear over time, the devotees' beautiful characteristics are formed by the intensity of their long-standing personal practice of devotional service. As lumps of common carbonate turn into brilliant, precious diamonds over years underground, so devotees' hearts shine with good qualities as the devotees strictly practice devotional service, even when behind closed doors.

For example, devotees who spend the early morning hours chanting the Hare Kṛṣṇa mantra with full attention come to perceive the Lord's presence in His sacred name. Such regular contact with the Supreme Personality of Godhead fills the practitioner with knowledge and detachment. A devotee dedicated to the daily practice of devotional service also tastes inner happiness, gains a healthy sense of aloofness from worldly distractions, and develops the jewel-like qualities of tolerance or forbearance. Tolerance cannot be faked, and it is of inestimable value.

> These are the symptoms of one who chants the Hare Kṛṣṇa *mahā-mantra*. Although he is very exalted, he thinks himself lower than the grass on the ground, and like a tree, he tolerates everything in two ways. When a tree is cut down, it does not protest, and even when drying up, it does not ask anyone for water. The tree delivers its fruits, flowers, and whatever else it possesses to anyone and everyone. It tolerates scorching heat and torrents of rain, yet it still gives shelter to others. Although a Vaiṣṇava is the most exalted person, he is prideless and gives all respect to everyone, knowing everyone to be the resting place of Kṛṣṇa. If one chants the holy name of Lord Kṛṣṇa in this manner, he will certainly awaken his dormant love for Kṛṣṇa's lotus feet.[3]

All these good results come simultaneously to the strict, serious, and sincere practitioner of devotional service, just as satisfaction, nourishment, and eradication of hunger come naturally to a person who eats a healthy, delicious meal.[4] Since these spiritual qualities shine forth from such devotees, those devotees are naturally attractive. People rarely see true satisfaction and detachment lighting up others' countenances, but when people see these qualities lighting up the countenances of devotees, they become attracted to the devotees.

Strict practice means to push on even during dark days, days in which one's practice seems harder then usual in the midst of distraction or crises, or even when one's mind says that there's no point in continuing. Through such painstaking daily practice a devotee becomes increasingly more capable and fit to share devotional service with others.

Śrīnivāsa Ācārya in his poem *Ṣaḍ-gosvāmy-aṣṭaka* (1) gives testimony to the attractive nature of strong devotees when he tells how the Six Gosvāmīs of Vṛndāvana, as a result of their purity and their exemplary, strict practice of devotional service became dear to the ruffians as well as the gentle.

There's no doubt, then, that those who strictly practice devotional service become attractive. People who see these effulgent devotees, even if but for a moment, are often inspired to inquire about Kṛṣṇa consciousness immediately, or even to take up the practice of devotional service.

Here is an example of such a case shown through an email written by a woman named Ammora. She had never been to an ISKCON temple nor had she personally met any devotees, but she was spontaneously attracted simply by the aura they radiated. She found herself longing to come closer to them and know more about them.

Driving home from work, Ammora was stopped at a traffic light adjacent to the ISKCON temple in Denver, Colorado. The temple is situated on a busy one-way thoroughfare. When her vehicle came to a halt, Ammora found herself next to a group of local devotees engaged in an ecstatic *kīrtana* outside the temple. (They were the temple's reception party for a delegation of visiting Vaiṣṇavas from Māyāpur, who happened to be carrying Lord Nityānanda's shoes.)

Upon reaching her home, Ammora immediately found ISKCON Denver's email address on Google and sent this message:

> Hello to whomever receives this message. I hope you are having a great day.

> I was driving home on Wednesday evening around 6:45 P.M. and as I typically do, I drove past your temple. But tonight everyone was outside singing, moving in and out of a circle together. When I got stopped at the traffic light right next to all of you, I couldn't contain my smile. In fact, it brought tears to my eyes. A monk saw me and smiled back. I felt this immediate overwhelming sense of joy and peace from the energy! I almost pulled the car over and joined in, but I truly had no idea what was occurring.
>
> I would love to learn about this: what it meant, what everyone was doing. I would love to participate.
>
> I looked you up on Google and found that your restaurant, Govinda's, next door to your temple, is entirely vegetarian. I've been vegetarian since birth – 32 years and counting!
>
> I hope to hear from you soon and to learn more.
>
> Thank you for taking the time to read my note.

In *Śrīmad-Bhāgavatam* (1.2.7), Sūta Gosvāmī explains how devotees attain these self-effulgent qualities that attracted Ammora: "By rendering devotional service unto the Personality of Godhead, Śrī Kṛṣṇa, one immediately acquires causeless knowledge and detachment from the world."

Endowed with transcendental knowledge, a practitioner sees all living beings as spirit souls – what to speak of human beings who naturally have the potential to accept a transcendental book – and thus respects and feels affection for them. And armed with detachment, the strict follower of devotional practices remains equipoised even in the face of rejection or provocation.

One summer day when I was in Hawaii distributing Śrīla Prabhupāda's books, I directly witnessed the dual influence of knowledge and detachment that had come from my practice of devotional service and the grace of the devotees at ISKCON Hawaii, who had allowed me to stay with them for one week.

During my stay at the Honolulu temple, I would go out every day to distribute books along Kalakawa Avenue. One day, I happened to approach a newlywed couple from Kansas

City, Missouri. After I greeted them, showed them the first volume of *Śrīmad-Bhāgavatam's* First Canto, and gave them a brief summary of the book, they abruptly handed it back. They told me that they were born-again Christians, that they only read the Bible, and that they only give donations to their church. Despite this rebuff I didn't feel even slightly disturbed. Here's why.

All week long in Hawaii I had been hearing and chanting with my friend and traveling companion, Satyadeva Prabhu, as well as the devotees at ISKCON Honolulu's beautiful temple. Every day, we had the luxury of rising together early in the morning to attend *maṅgala-ārati,* to sit and chant sixteen very focused rounds in the temple room, to hear a discourse on *Śrīmad-Bhāgavatam,* to perform *kīrtana,* to dance before Śrīla Prabhupāda's form and the Deities of the Pañca-tattva, and to honor *kṛṣṇa-prasāda.*

By this intense practice, I felt happy, equipoised, and enthusiastic. Consequently, when the newlyweds summarily rejected me, I neither expressed nor felt disappointment or annoyance. On the contrary, as a result of my strict practice of devotional service at the temple, I was able to feel and express nothing but goodwill toward them. Warmly, I voiced my appreciation for them, saying, "I completely understand your position. In fact, I am indebted to you for taking your valuable time to talk with me. I feel truly honored to have met you." I uttered these words as they rose directly from my heart. I later found out that those words had had a strong effect on the newlyweds. Anyone who practices strong *sādhana,* starting with focused chanting of *japa,* receives such empowerment. Śrī Caitanya Mahāprabhu affirms in His famous *Śikṣāṣṭaka* that the Supreme Lord has kindly invested all of His spiritual potencies in His holy name (*nija-sarva-śaktis tatrārpitā*). And Śrīla Prabhupāda writes that by chanting the Lord's holy name, "one can derive all the stipulated energy synchronized from all sources."[5] Therefore, devotees who take the time each day to chant Hare Kṛṣṇa with rapt attention purify their hearts and automatically develop good qualities such as tolerance and goodwill toward others, qualities that attract people's minds and hearts.

Having parted ways with the newlyweds, I happily continued distributing Śrīla Prabhupāda's books. Thirty minutes later, as I was showing a college student a *Bhagavad-gītā As It Is,* I noticed that the newlywed couple was standing nearby, watching me. When I finished speaking to the student, the newlyweds approached me to give a five-dollar donation. As they handed it to me they apologized for being dismissive earlier. They said that they had changed their minds about not giving a donation, that they felt I was sincerely trying to do something good to help the world, and that they wanted to help me. I thanked them and accepted their donation, but I also offered them the same book they had earlier rejected. I explained that it was my rule never to accept a donation without giving something in return. They hesitated for a moment, but then smiled and accepted the book. We spoke for a while and then parted as friends.

Needless to say, I was delighted to see the change in this newlywed couple. What's more, this encounter left me with two indelible impressions. First, people are sensitive; that is, they can perceive the motive of another person, just as the newlyweds sensed mine. Living entities are called sentient precisely because they have the ability to feel and perceive. Even animals are known for their capacity to sense goodwill in their caretakers or aggression in their abusers; how much more, then, must human beings be able to perceive such things.

The second impression I was left with was that the quality and effectiveness of my speech directly corresponds to the quality of my devotional practice. The warm words I had spoken in response to the newlywed couple's annoyance were manifestations of a descending grace that had come to me owing to my chanting of Kṛṣṇa's holy name and the friendship I had enjoyed with the devotees of the Honolulu temple.

Book distributors who faithfully take the prescribed

spiritual medicine of strong daily *sādhana* become naturally endowed with appealing and invaluable assets such as knowledge, detachment, and goodwill – assets that empower their service. What's more, since their practice of devotional service affords them an overflow of taste, they have plenty to share with others.

Share the Overflow

The devotees' desire to share Kṛṣṇa consciousness expands in direct proportion to the taste they themselves have received from their practice of devotional service. And the more they attend to the details of their practice, the more their taste for devotional service grows. In this regard, Śrīla Rūpa Gosvāmī writes:

> I do not know how much nectar the two syllables "Kṛṣ-ṇa" have produced. When the holy name of Kṛṣṇa is chanted, it appears to dance within the mouth. We then desire many, many mouths. When that name enters the holes of the ears, we desire many millions of ears. And when the holy name dances in the courtyard of the heart, it conquers the activities of the mind, and therefore all the senses become inert.[6]

This verse shows how a devotee's taste dramatically expands and overflows. Poets and thinkers everywhere note that it's natural for people to share what they love.

The Roman dramatist and philosopher Seneca declares, "There is no delight in owning anything unshared." And the English novelist Charlotte Bronte writes, "Happiness unshared can scarcely be called happiness; it has no taste."

One may think that it must take a long time to develop a taste for devotional practice, but Rūpa Gosvāmī says that even beginners get benefits such as freedom from distress, all-auspiciousness, and transcendental pleasure. What's more, even a small taste for these devotional benefits is so potent that on savoring them devotees have more than enough to share.

It makes perfect sense, then, that devotees who have developed an affinity for reading the *Bhagavad-gītā, Śrīmad-Bhāgavatam,* and other bhakti scriptures would be eager to share them.

Sādhakas Appreciate Scripture

Thus to read daily from Vaiṣṇava scriptures such as *Bhagavad-gītā As It Is* and *Śrīmad-Bhāgavatam* is an essential part of strong *sādhana.* In stark contrast, devotees who neglect to read these foundations of spiritual knowledge soon become blind to the glories of these works and think, "Why should I bother people by distributing these books?"

Śrīla Prabhupāda's own affinity for the bhakti scriptures was obvious, and he repeatedly exhorted his followers, especially those who were distributing his books, that they must themselves read his books daily. Particularly for book distributors, it is important to read from the scriptures every day, for such reading clarifies one's intelligence and gives one the transcendental vision to see the suffering of others and therefore the importance of distributing transcendental literature to relieve them of their suffering. Śrīla Prabhupāda clarifies this point: "Reading the books will purify the intelligence. A purified heart and mind means Kṛṣṇa consciousness."[7]

Strong Sādhana Gives Transcendental Vision

In the *Gītā* (18.20), Kṛṣṇa describes how a person in the mode of goodness perceives the world: "That knowledge by which one undivided spiritual nature is seen in all living entities, though they are divided into innumerable forms, you should understand to be in the mode of goodness."

The Lord also points out (*Gītā* 4.35) that this spiritual vision not only securely anchors a devotee's position in spiritual life, preventing him or her from falling down, but also tests whether the devotee has truly assimilated transcendental knowledge from the spiritual master: "Having obtained real knowledge from a self-realized soul, you will never fall again into such illusion, for by this knowledge you will see that all living beings are but part of the Supreme, or, in other words, that they are Mine."

By seeing all living beings as belonging to Kṛṣṇa one naturally develops affection for them. The effects of such transcendental vision are attested to by *Śrī Īśopaniṣad* (6): "He who sees systematically everything in relation to the Supreme Lord, who sees all living entities as His parts and parcels, and who sees the Supreme Lord within everything never hates anything or any being."

And we find in Śrīla Prabhupāda's purport to *Śrīmad-Bhāgavatam* 2.7.47:

> The Supreme Lord is the Supreme Soul of everything, and therefore in the supreme conception affection is realized. The conception of affection is due to the relationship of soul to soul. A father is affectionate to his son because there is some relationship of nearness between the son and the father. But that sort of affection in the material world is full of inebriety. When the Personality of Godhead is met, the fullness of affection becomes manifested because of the reality of the affectionate relationship. He is not the object of affection by material tinges of body and mind, but He is the full, naked, uncontaminated object of affection for all living entities because He is the Supersoul, or Paramātmā, within everyone's heart. In the liberated state of affairs, the full-fledged affection for the Lord is awakened.

In *Śrīmad-Bhāgavatam* 7.7.21, Śrī Prahlāda Mahārāja gives an analogy that further elucidates how one achieves this rarefied vision:

> An expert geologist can understand where there is gold and by various processes can extract it from the gold ore. Similarly, a spiritually advanced person can understand how the spiritual particle exists within the body, and thus by cultivating

> spiritual knowledge he can attain perfection in spiritual life. However, as one who is not expert cannot understand where there is gold, a foolish person who has not cultivated spiritual knowledge cannot understand how the spirit exists within the body.

In summary, the assimilation of spiritual knowledge and detachment through performing the primary devotional practices, beginning with hearing and chanting, endows a devotee with the ability to see how both the Supreme Spirit and the subordinate spirit soul exist within all material bodies.

For emphasis, Lord Kṛṣṇa repeatedly makes this point in the *Gītā:*

> The humble sages, by virtue of true knowledge, see with equal vision a learned and gentle *brāhmaṇa,* a cow, an elephant, a dog, and a dog-eater [outcaste].[8]

> A true yogi observes Me in all beings and also sees every being in Me. Indeed, the self-realized person sees Me, the same Supreme Lord, everywhere.[9]

> One who sees the Supersoul accompanying the individual soul in all bodies, and who understands that neither the soul nor the Supersoul within the destructible body is ever destroyed, actually sees.[10]

All Vaiṣṇava authorities concur, therefore, that one who strictly practices devotional service develops the understanding that the body and soul of the living entity are different. One with this understanding becomes highly effective in distributing Śrīla Prabhupāda's books.

The conclusion is that to distribute books effectively one must read them and follow what they teach. Rooted firmly in daily *sādhana,* a devotee not only remains enthusiastic to distribute transcendental knowledge but also becomes spiritually empowered to do so. As far as spreading Kṛṣṇa consciousness goes, nothing can replace such devotees in the world.

Such spiritual maturity must be earned by practice – lots of it! The author of *Śrī Caitanya-caritāmṛta* (*Madhya-līlā* 25.278) confirms these truths:

> Men become strong and stout by eating sufficient grains, but the devotee who simply eats ordinary grains but does not taste the transcendental pastimes of Lord Caitanya Mahāprabhu and Kṛṣṇa gradually becomes weak and falls down from the transcendental position. However, if one drinks but a drop of the nectar of Kṛṣṇa's pastimes, his body and mind begin to bloom, and he begins to laugh, sing, and dance.

And finally, Śrīla Prabhupāda's profoundly clear purport to this verse teaches us how to apply this essential spiritual principal in our daily lives today as Kṛṣṇa conscious devotees.

> All the devotees connected with the Kṛṣṇa consciousness movement must read all the books that have been translated (the *Caitanya-caritāmṛta, Śrīmad-Bhāgavatam, Bhagavad-gītā,* and others); otherwise, after some time, they will simply eat, sleep, and fall down from their position. Thus they will miss the opportunity to attain an eternal, blissful life of transcendental pleasure.

CHAPTER FOURTEEN

What Is Strong Sādhana?

MY *MṚDAṄGA* TEACHER Akiñcana Kṛṣṇa Dāsa recently blessed me with this gem of wisdom about the magic of practice: "Start slow and be precise. By slow and accurate practice you will eventually play fast and correctly. But if you play too fast in the beginning, with flawed technique, you will never come to play fast and well."

Śrīla Prabhupāda was an advocate of methodical practice. He liked to say, "Drops a day wear the stone away." Once, pointing to a shelf of the books to the prolific writings he had produced in such a short time, he said to his servant Śrutakīrti Dāsa, "I have done all this a little at a time."

One of the best things about being human is that we can get better at something with practice. In fact, with knowledge and practice, we can set a new course in life. If I don't like something about myself now, I can learn new ways of being, practice them, and eventually transform myself. For example, if I want to become equipoised, I can practice not reacting to the things that people do that usually cause me distress. Or, if

I don't like my occupation, I can enroll in school, study diligently, and learn a new profession. Śrīla Prabhupāda notes this ability in people: "So nobody is born *brāhmaṇa,* or intelligent class of men, but by cultivation of knowledge, by practice, by good association, one can come to the higher standard of life."[1]

So what is this thing called practice? It is the acquiring of proficiency at an activity or state of being by repeatedly going over it. Practice means repetition – most often, the dogged, persistent repetition that's required for mastery. When you see someone especially proficient at a task, you can be sure that he or she has practiced it well. Aristotle writes, "For the things we have to learn before we can do them, we learn by doing them."

Thus good guidance, willpower, and regular practice – even if in the beginning the amount is small but regular – comprise the formula for improving the quality of one's life. Now that's exciting! But most encouraging is that by the incremental practice of devotional service one can cheat death by becoming a great soul and going back to Godhead.

Scripture gives abundant detail on how to practice devotional service. With the help of scripture and the guidance of the bona fide spiritual master, one can achieve pure love for Śrī Kṛṣṇa. Lord Kṛṣṇa instructs Brahmā in *Śrī Brahma-saṁhitā* (5.59): "The highest devotion is attained in slow degrees by the method of constant endeavor for self-realization with the help of scriptural evidence, theistic conduct, and perseverance in practice."

This highest devotion, pure love of God, brings the practitioner unconditional happiness and good fortune. And according to Śrī Caitanya Mahāprabhu, it is the ultimate goal of life.

The boy saint Śrī Prahlāda gives us nine general categories of devotional practice that one can perform to attain these treasures:

> (1) Hearing about Kṛṣṇa; (2) chanting of Kṛṣṇa's transcendental holy names, forms, qualities, paraphernalia, and pastimes;

> (3) remembering Kṛṣṇa; (4) serving the lotus feet of Kṛṣṇa; (5) offering Kṛṣṇa respectful worship with sixteen types of paraphernalia; (6) offering prayers to Kṛṣṇa; (7) becoming Kṛṣṇa's servant; (8) considering Kṛṣṇa one's best friend; and (9) surrendering everything unto the Lord, in other words, serving Him with the body, mind, and words.

Śrī Prahlāda goes on to accept these nine processes as pure devotional service. And he concludes that one who has dedicated his life to the service of Kṛṣṇa through these nine methods is the most learned person, or one who has acquired complete knowledge.[2]

Back to Basics

Śrī Prahlāda, one of the twelve most respected authorities in Vedic literature, has defined these nine basic categories of practice as the framework on which to build our devotional lives. Additionally, the bhakti scriptures and bhakti masters explain the hierarchy of these practices in terms of degree of importance as one advances through the various stages of Kṛṣṇa consciousness.

For example, Śrīla Bhaktisiddhānta Sarasvatī writes that the most important bhakti practice, especially in the beginning, is to hear about Kṛṣṇa: "In the neophyte stage one should always engage in hearing *kṛṣṇa-kathā*. This is called *śravaṇa-daśā,* the stage of hearing."[3]

Śrīla Bhaktisiddhānta Sarasvatī goes on to say that one enters successively higher stages of devotional service through the doorway of one's initial attachment for hearing about Kṛṣṇa. Furthermore, although the scriptures contain mountains of rules and regulations – do's and don'ts – the *Padma Purāṇa* distills the myriad commands and proscriptions into a list of two: "Kṛṣṇa is the origin of Lord Viṣṇu. He should always be remembered and never forgotten at any time. All the rules and prohibitions mentioned in the scripture should be the servants of these two principles."[4]

Thus the short list of devotional practices reads: (1) Always remember Kṛṣṇa; and (2) Never forget Kṛṣṇa.

Various followers of Lord Caitanya have also presented condensed lists of devotional practices. For example, Lord Caitanya gives his disciple Śrīla Sanātana Gosvāmī a condensed list of only five items, saying that out of sixty-four distinct limbs (*aṅgas*) of devotional practice, these five are the best:

> (1) Association with devotees; (2) Chanting the holy names of the Lord; (3) Hearing *Śrīmad-Bhāgavatam;* (4) Residing in a holy place like Mathurā or in a temple; and (5) Worshiping the Deity.[5]

In response to a question asked by Sārvabhauma Bhaṭṭācārya, Caitanya Mahāprabhu further boils down His list of five most important items to a single practice: "Then the Bhaṭṭācārya asked Caitanya Mahāprabhu, 'Which item is most important in the execution of devotional service?' The Lord replied that the most important item was the chanting of the holy name of the Lord."[6]

Similarly, Śrīnātha Cakravartī Ṭhākura, in his commentary on *Śrīmad-Bhāgavatam* called *Caitanya-mātā-mañjuṣā*, gives what he considers the essence of Mahāprabhu's devotional practices as follows:

> (1) The Supreme Personality of Godhead, the son of Nanda Mahārāja, is to be worshiped along with His transcendental abode Vṛndāvana; (2) The most pleasing form of worshiping the Lord is that which was performed by the *gopīs* of Vṛndāvana; (3) *Śrīmad-Bhāgavatam* is the spotless authority on everything; and, (4) Pure love of God is the ultimate goal of life for all men.

An analysis of the intricacies of these various lists of the essential practices and characteristics of devotional service and how to apply them as we advance is beyond the scope of this book. I list them here simply to highlight the importance of the basics and to inspire devotees in their practice and serious study of the science of pure devotion as Śrīla Prabhupāda laid it out in his books.

Devotees who learn and steadfastly apply these basics without fail will rise to the highest levels of perfection in devotional service. Or, as Śrīla Prabhupāda puts it, "Success is sure for the rigid practitioner."[7]

This principle applies to all areas of practice, even in the material sphere. Celebrated martial arts master Bruce Lee, for example, attests to the powerful results of repeatedly practicing the basics of his discipline in this famous saying: "I fear not the man who has practiced ten thousand kicks once, but I fear the man who has practiced one kick ten thousand times."

Considering that in the present age most people have short lives and must contend with many distractions, these scriptural digests are not only useful but vital. Even amid the unavoidable interruptions and disturbances in the whirlwind of a modern life's duties, one may thrive in spiritual life by suitably applying oneself to the basic devotional practices. Extolling the astounding spiritual potency of the five core practices of Kṛṣṇa conscious, Lord Caitanya told Sanātana Gosvāmī: "The power of these five principles is very wonderful and difficult to understand. Even without faith in them, a person who is offenseless can awaken his dormant love of Kṛṣṇa simply by being a little connected with them."[8]

And regarding the acme of all the processes taught by Mahāprabhu – chanting the holy names of the Supreme Personality of Godhead – *Śrīmad-Bhāgavatam* (11.5.36) declares: "Those who are actually advanced in knowledge are able to appreciate the essential value of this Age of Kali. Such enlightened persons worship Kali-yuga because in this fallen age all perfection of life can easily be achieved by the performance of *saṅkīrtana*."

The founder-*ācārya* of ISKCON, Śrīla Prabhupāda, prescribed the following basics for his followers: chant at least sixteen rounds of the Hare Kṛṣṇa *mahā-mantra* on beads every day and avoid the four pillars of sinful life – meat eating, illicit sex, intoxication, and gambling. Beyond this, the daily ISKCON temple schedule he put in place comprises Mahāprabhu's five most essential practices of devotional service: chanting the holy name, worshiping the Deity, living in a holy place, associating with devotees, and hearing *Śrīmad-Bhāgavatam.*

Even those who don't live in or near a temple can easily integrate these five items of devotional service into their daily schedules at home. Śrīla Prabhupāda has given us all the support, instructions, and paraphernalia we need to do so.

In short, the devotional practices recommended by Caitanya Mahāprabhu are so potent and easy to perform that wherever and in whatever condition we live, and in any stage of life, we can keep our bhakti *sādhana* strong.

Of course, the topmost agent of Lord Caitanya's teachings, Śrī Rūpa Gosvāmī, does say that the essence of all advice is that we should organize our lives such that we remain engaged in devotional service twenty-four hours a day. In fact, many verses of the bhakti scriptures say that one's practice should be performed continuously (*satatam,* or *nityam*).

Śrīla Viśvanātha Cakravartī Ṭhākura, however, encourages beginners by advising them that the nonstop practice of bhakti can be taken to mean regular, or at least every day. He goes on to say that continuous practice and remembrance of Kṛṣṇa is impractical for beginners and that taking such scriptural directives literally can cause neophyte practitioners, who cannot possibly follow such literal interpretations, to lose faith in the rules of bhakti. He concludes that for them "*satatam* means 'every day' not 'every moment'"[9]

Now that we have heard about the power of following the basic practices of devotional service, I will list five important characteristics of strong *sādhana* and elaborate the ways we can cultivate them. Strong *sādhana* has five basic characteristics: It is performed with the proper attitude, it is regular, it is attentive, it is goal-oriented, and it is best carried out according to one's capacity.

Strong Sādhana Means Proper Attitude

Whatever one does and wherever one goes, one's attitude is important. It is said that "Your attitude determines your altitude in life." And some say, even more forcefully, "Attitude is everything." Attitude is the way we think and feel about something, an outlook that determines the way we act. Śrīla Prabhupāda writes about the importance of attitude in practicing devotional service: "Advancement in Kṛṣṇa consciousness depends on the attitude of the follower."[10]

What is the ideal attitude for a practitioner eager to advance in devotional service? Śrīla Prabhupāda uses three adjectives to define it: strict, serious, sincere.

To be strict means to be rigorous with oneself in following one's chosen method of practice. Śrīla Raghunātha Dāsa Gosvāmī, for example, was so strict in his daily routine that *Śrī Caitanya-caritāmṛta* (*Antya-līlā* 6.309) compares his devotional practices to "lines on a stone."

To be serious means that during one's practice one is thoughtful and attentive to the details. It also means that one does not back down from doing the needful to attain one's goal, even in the face of temptation, distraction, or calamity.

In *Śrīmad-Bhāgavatam* (4.12.8), Dhruva Mahārāja is described as thoughtful and intelligent because when asked by the lord of wealth Kuvera to accept a reward for his austerities, Dhruva declined and in turn asked only for unflinching faith in and remembrance of the Supreme Personality of Godhead.

The word *sincere* comes from the Latin *sincerus,* meaning "clean, pure, free from pretense or deceit; proceeding from genuine feelings." To be sincere in one's practice of devotional service means to accept and follow Kṛṣṇa's directives without envy or ulterior motive. Śrīla Prabhupāda describes the attitude of the sincere devotee in his purport to *Bhagavad-gītā* 3.7:

> Instead of becoming a pseudotranscendentalist for the sake of wanton living and sense enjoyment, it is far better to remain

> in one's own business and execute the purpose of life, which is to get free from material bondage and enter into the kingdom of God.... A sincere person who follows this method is far better situated than the false pretender who adopts show-bottle spiritualism to cheat the innocent public. A sincere sweeper in the street is far better than the charlatan meditator who meditates only for the sake of making a living.

Śrīla Prabhupāda does not use all three terms – strict, serious, and sincere – together in a thread as I am doing; rather, he invokes them individually. However, taking advantage of the opportunity offered by the alliteration of these three key words, I can string them together, like nicely matched gemstones on a thread (*sūtra*). They do go beautifully well together. (Stringing them together like this also employs the helpful technique of summary.) The concise mantra- or *sūtra*-like union of these deeply meaningful terms makes the string convenient to keep on the tongue and bear in the mind. "Strict, serious, sincere": this *sūtra* provides a constant reminder and prompts us to realize its meaning in our lives.

To be strict, serious, and sincere may seem daunting at first, because these traits demand moral courage and elevated character. In fact, being strict, serious, and sincere in one's *sādhana* often brings one into conflict with the currently prevailing familial, social, or business values, and, of course, with one's own material desires and false ego. For instance, I sometimes hear from devotees who work in corporations that their fellow workers chide them for not coming to the bar or to see the latest film. To keep on the path of transcendence, one has to relinquish easy pleasures and forgo facile popularity, facing the risk of being misunderstood, unappreciated, or even ostracized. A hero is one who confronts and overcomes all kinds of adversity to achieve an illustrious goal. Kṛṣṇa consciousness is the highest goal of all, and the best kind of hero, then, is the person who remains steadfast on the path and controls his or her senses for the sake of satisfying Kṛṣṇa.

Śrīla Prabhupāda writes about the heroism of those who carefully practice devotional service:

> Every living entity is a hero in two ways. When he is a victim of the illusory energy, he works as a great hero in the material world, as a great leader, politician, businessman, industrialist, etc., and his heroic activities contribute to the material advancement of civilization. One can also become a hero by being master of the senses, a *gosvāmī.* Material activities are false heroic activities, whereas restraining the senses from material engagement is great heroism.[11]

The following prayer by a heroic devotee is a sample of the mentality of such devotees:

> O my Lord, there is no limit to the unwanted orders of lusty desires. Although I have rendered these desires so much service, they have not shown any mercy to me. I have not been ashamed to serve them, nor have I even desired to give them up. O my Lord, O head of the Yadu dynasty, recently, however, my intelligence has been awakened, and now I am giving them up. Due to transcendental intelligence, I now refuse to obey the unwanted orders of these desires, and I now come to You to surrender myself at Your fearless lotus feet. Kindly engage me in Your personal service and save me.[12]

Spiritual heroes are those who have decided to follow the instructions of the bona fide spiritual masters and the instructions of Kṛṣṇa in the *Bhagavad-gītā,* even if as yet unable to fully execute them. In this regard, Śrīla Prabhupāda writes:

> But an ordinary man with firm faith in the eternal injunctions of the Lord, even though unable to execute such orders, becomes liberated from the bondage of the law of karma. In the beginning of Kṛṣṇa consciousness, one may not fully discharge the injunctions of the Lord, but because one is not resentful of this principle and works sincerely without consideration of defeat and hopelessness, he will surely be promoted to the stage of pure Kṛṣṇa consciousness.[13]

More on Attitude: One Should Feel Helpless

With an attitude of helplessness, a devotee cries out with feeling to Kṛṣṇa: "O Kṛṣṇa! I am weak and powerless. Please help me!" Śrīla Prabhupāda tells us how only those who develop this disposition are able to call out to the Lord with ardent feelings:

> A helpless man can feelingly utter the holy name of the Lord, whereas a man who utters the same holy name in great material satisfaction cannot be so sincere. A materially puffed up person may utter the holy name of the Lord occasionally, but he is incapable of uttering the name in quality.[14]

Śrīla Bhaktivinoda Ṭhākura displays this attitude in *Śaraṇāgati* (song 3, verse 6): "I am utterly helpless. Without Your mercy, everything is lost. Please give me the shelter of Your lotus feet."

As the *Jaladuta* approached the American coast, Śrīla Prabhupāda wrote in his diary, "Although my Guru Mahārāja ordered me to accomplish this mission, I am not worthy or fit to do it. I am very fallen and insignificant. Therefore, O Lord, now I am begging for Your mercy so that I may become worthy, for You are the wisest and most experienced of all."

In such a humble and helpless state of mind, one can sincerely pray to Kṛṣṇa and His devotees for help. With this attitude, which is pleasing to Kṛṣṇa, a tiny, powerless living entity becomes a real hero. The unlimitedly powerful Lord Kṛṣṇa exalts such a sincere soul, empowering him to perform more and more devotional service.

Heroic devotees therefore declare themselves helpless but, taking full shelter of Kṛṣṇa and the practice of devotional service, accomplish amazing feats.

The Strong Sādhaka Is Vigilant

Another important trait that leads to powerful *sādhana* is vigilance. To be vigilant means to keep careful watch for possible danger. As the adage (often attributed to Thomas Jefferson) proclaims, "Eternal vigilance is the price of liberty."

This statement tallies with those Kṛṣṇa makes in the *Bhagavad-gītā,* where He repeatedly says that real freedom is freedom from the oppressing dictates of the senses, and that with that freedom we should choose to serve Him rather than *māyā*. Such unimpeded freedom to practice devotional service depends on our vigilance; we must control the mind and senses. In *Bhagavad-gītā* 2.64, Kṛṣṇa explains how the freedom to obtain the Lord's mercy derives from following regulative principles: "But a person free from all attachment and aversion and able to control his senses through regulative principles of freedom can obtain the complete mercy of the Lord."

Practically speaking, to merit such freedom, and especially to preserve it, one must be careful. In summary, maintaining a healthy fear of *māyā* is actually a regulative principle for those engaged in strong *sādhana*. In his purport to the *Bhāgavatam* 7.6.5, Śrīla Prabhupāda comments on this caution:

> A sane man, therefore, is always fearful of falling from his position. This is a regulative principle. One should not fall from his exalted position. The highest goal of life can be achieved as long as one's body is stout and strong. We should therefore live in such a way that we keep ourselves always healthy and strong in mind and intelligence so that we can distinguish the goal of life from a life full of problems. A thoughtful man must act in this way, learning to distinguish right from wrong, and thus attain the goal of life.

We see this same cautious attitude reflected in the thoughts of even the most advanced devotees. Prahlāda, for example, says to Lord Nṛsiṁhadeva in *Śrīmad-Bhāgavatam* 7.9.16:

> O most powerful, insurmountable Lord, who are kind to the fallen souls, I have been put into the association of demons as a result of my activities, and therefore I am very much afraid of my condition of life within this material world. When will

> that moment come when You will call me to the shelter of Your lotus feet, which are the ultimate goal for liberation from conditional life?

It is important for those advancing in spiritual life to recognize how this healthy fear of *māyā* is an intrinsic component of humility. In *Bṛhad-bhāgavatāmṛta* (2.5.222, commentary), Nārada Muni explains to Gopa-kumāra that utter humility is the essential prerequisite for attaining pure love for Kṛṣṇa. In that same section Sanātana Gosvāmī comments that a healthy fear of *māyā* is one of the qualities of such humility:

> Someone might say that the quality of thinking oneself very fallen may also be seen in persons who are simply lazy or those who abandon auspicious work or indulge in sinful acts. Therefore Nārada specifies that one who actually has *dainya* [utter humility] is endowed with all good qualities; for instance, such a person observes positive and negative regulations, he is free of false ego, and he has a healthy fear of material life.

In contrast, those who join the Kṛṣṇa consciousness movement but whose practice of devotional service over time becomes casual may unwittingly drift away from the path, only to be captured again by Kṛṣṇa's illusory energy. Śrīla Prabhupāda confirms this truth:

> The nature's illusory methods are two kinds: one is covering energy, and another is throwing energy. Nature is acting upon us in two ways. Just like somebody may think, "Here is a nice movement, Kṛṣṇa conscious movement. Let me take part in this." And nature dictates, "Why shall you go there? Don't go there. Better enjoy like this." This throwing energy throws him from the path. And another is covering energy. Covering energy means a person or a living entity may remain in the most abominable condition, still, he thinks he's happy.[15]

Benjamin Franklin, who organized Philadelphia's first firefighting company, coined the useful precept "An ounce of prevention is worth a pound of cure." Again, Śrīla Prabhupāda sums up this regulative principle: "A sane man, therefore, is always fearful of falling from his position. This is a regulative principle. One should not fall from his exalted position."[16]

In this way, caution is the creed of the strict, serious, and sincere practitioner of devotional service. Such an advanced devotee remains modest, thinking, "I am not liberated; nor am I entitled to honor."

This humility or freedom from false pride within the *sādhaka* also fosters vigilance, an awareness that Māyā can attack at any time and from any direction. Māyā is so expert, in fact, that she makes a proposition just suited to each victim, working in subtle ways to exploit that person's weakest point. For most, that weakest point, and the door through which Māyā finds her way in, is false pride. The moment one thinks "I'm more advanced than others" or "Because I am liberated I may slacken my practice of bhakti," one opens the door for Māyā to enter one's life.

Why is pride so pernicious in spiritual life? Pride breeds the enjoying spirit, which in turn brings laxity. And laxity convinces one to give up the fortifying daily practice of devotional service, or worse, to offend other living entities, or worse still, to offend devotees of the Lord.

To justify one's laxity one develops a sense of entitlement. With this attitude of entitlement one thinks, "I've done so much in the past, I deserve special treatment; I can cut corners in my practice; I can treat others harshly or with disdain." Living with these insidious cousins of entitlement attracts Māyā to stay permanently in one's mind and heart, and one's devotional life is stifled.

Spiritual advancement is not cheap. Freedom, therefore, is for the vigilant, a point Kṛṣṇa confirms in the *Bhagavad-gītā* (5.7): "One who works in devotion, who is a pure soul, and who controls his mind and senses is dear to everyone, and everyone is dear to him. Though always working, such a man is never entangled."

Strong Sādhana Is Regularly Performed

Regular practice over time fosters purity, and reliable practice over time evokes faith, both of which are pleasing to Kṛṣṇa. Śrīla Prabhupāda writes, "Kṛṣṇa is pleased to award benediction upon the aspiring devotee engaged in His service with patience, determination, and regularity."[17]

Regular and reliable practice is also a cornerstone of strong *sādhana*. The Sanskrit word *vrata* ("vow") is related to the reliability of serious devotees. At the time of initiation, therefore, a devotee makes promises to, or takes vows before, the spiritual master and Kṛṣṇa. Persons who always fulfill their promises, who always do what they say they will do, are deemed "reliable." One who remains reliable over time invokes faith and confidence in others.

Kṛṣṇa explains the principle of making a determined vow (*dṛḍha-vratāḥ*) in the *Bhagavad-gītā* (7.28): "Persons who have acted piously in previous lives and in this life and whose sinful actions are completely eradicated are freed from the dualities of delusion, and they engage themselves in My service with determination."

We frequently hear the words *nityam* and *satatam* used in scripture to describe the nature of devotional service. These words are usually translated as "eternal" and "always," respectively. In the context of practice, however, these words generally mean consistent, constant, or regular. Devotional practice that is *nityam* or *satatam* is either continuous nonstop practice or practice done daily or at regular intervals. For example, a daily morning session of chanting the Hare Kṛṣṇa mantra on beads at the same time for the same duration acts as a powerful tonic that builds spiritual strength.

The world-famous concert violinist Jascha Heifetz says about the importance of regular practice, "If I don't practice for one day, I know it. If I don't practice for two days, my critics know it. If I don't practice for three days, everyone knows it."

One of the secrets of strong *sādhana,* therefore, is to somehow or other show up every day for your practice without fail.

The Power of Showing Up

Economists refer to money as "dollar votes," because people spend their money on what they value most. Every dollar spent, they say, is a vote for what a customer values most. Similarly, showing up for one's daily *sādhana* is a devotee's deliberate vote for Kṛṣṇa over illusion. Those who vote by showing up, therefore, need not say much. And since in any relationship consistency and reliability nurture faith, our consistency in showing up for our daily practice builds Kṛṣṇa's faith in us and ours in Him.

Strong Sādhana Is Attentive

As one's faith in Kṛṣṇa grows, so too does one's *intention* to serve Him by practicing devotional service. The words "intention" and "attention" both derive from the same Latin word *intentio,* which means "to stretch toward."

Persons with a strong intention to practice devotional service will naturally fix their attention on it. In other words, one's clear intention leads to one's fixed attention, which is another mark of strong *sādhana.* Bhakti scriptures say not only that our attention is our most valuable asset but also that a progressive human being must study well the science of how to invest his or her attention in order to receive the highest return. The great masters of devotional service therefore consider inattentiveness the eleventh offense against the holy names, because from inattentive chanting the other ten offenses spring.

As conscious living entities, we can choose where to place our attention at every moment. And those who choose to fix their attention on one or more of the nine practices of Kṛṣṇa consciousness – daily, and over time – are demonstrating their chastity to Kṛṣṇa. Śrīla Prabhupāda explains chastity in his purport to *Śrīmad-Bhāgavatam* 3.6.36: "One should not become unchaste by stopping the activities of pure consciousness. If the activities of pure consciousness are stopped, certainly the conscious living force will be otherwise engaged because unless engaged the consciousness has no standing. Consciousness cannot be silent, even for a moment."

Where we choose to place our attention, then, determines the quality and direction of our lives. The choice to give one's attention to a particular topic, object, or task is an investment. In other words, when a person "pays attention," he or she is acquiring an asset.

The bhakti scriptures suggest, therefore, that to attain the perfection of life we acquire the assets of purposefully and repeatedly turning our attention to the sound of Kṛṣṇa's holy name, form, and pastimes. *Śrīmad-Bhāgavatam* (1.2.14) says that because human life is exceedingly rare and precariously temporary, one should give one-pointed attention to this pursuit: "Therefore, with one-pointed attention, one should constantly hear about, glorify, remember, and worship the Personality of Godhead, who is the protector of the devotees."

Bhakti-yogis, having received this insider information from guru and *śāstra* about how and where to get the best return on their most important investment, pay exclusive attention to topics about Kṛṣṇa. They also meditate on Kṛṣṇa's forms and at the same time do their work to please Him. As Kṛṣṇa Himself advises Arjuna in *Bhagavad-gītā* 8.7: "Therefore, Arjuna, you should always think of Me in the form of Kṛṣṇa and at the same time carry out your prescribed duty of fighting. With your activities dedicated to Me and your mind and intelligence fixed on Me, you will attain Me without doubt."

When we absorb the mind in worldly affairs, we spend our time absorbed in worrying about and scheming over future events. When things don't go our way, or haven't in the past, we spend our time lamenting. With all this – and more – going on, we may find it difficult to pay strict attention to our practices, especially in the initial stages of devotional service. But Kṛṣṇa reminds Arjuna in the *Bhagavad-gītā* (6.35) that it is possible to train the mind to become attentive and amenable to devotional service "by suitable practice and by detachment."

Kṛṣṇa also gives Arjuna practical guidance how to go about training the mind: "From wherever the mind wanders due to its flickering and unsteady nature, one must certainly withdraw it and bring it back under the control of the Self." (*Bhagavad-gītā* 6.26)

One friend, the father of two energetic boys, once told me that he had to wake each day earlier than his boys and make a clear plan to engage them throughout the morning. "Otherwise," he said, "they run wild, making it practically impossible to settle them down for the rest of the morning." The mind is just like an unruly child. It needs a strong authority figure, a resolute intelligence, and a plan to keep it engaged in positive and productive ways.

To control the mind, then, one must similarly have a plan to engage it in devotional service. For instance, one may make a plan and suitable arrangements the night before to hear and chant with attention during the morning hours. Before going to bed one can neatly arrange one's sitting place, *japa* beads, and the books one intends to read the following morning. With one's devotional articles set up the night before, one's attention naturally goes to them as soon as one wakes up, increasing the impetus to perform one's practice.

Strict practitioners also turn off electronic devices and inform friends, family members, and associates that they are not to be disturbed during their attentive bhakti practices. One who wakes up in the morning with such a solid plan sets the stage for the attentive practice of devotional service.

The time one sets aside for devotional practice belongs to Kṛṣṇa and the spiritual master. With this in mind one cultivates feelings of intimacy in relationship with one's guru and Kṛṣṇa, further inspiring one to be regular and reliable in devotional service.

Śrīla Prabhupāda once remarked that some *sādhus* who live by the Ganges go elsewhere to take their bath due to becoming overly familiar with Mother Gaṅgā and thus taking her for granted. Over time it is easy to take our devotional service so much for granted that we become inattentive while doing it. And even though devotional practices are full of bliss, when our mind goes elsewhere during our practice we do not taste the bliss.

Here Śrīla Prabhupāda tells of the importance of attentive hearing:

> When you hear about Kṛṣṇa, that is also Kṛṣṇa. Actually, when you are reading *Kṛṣṇa Book,* Kṛṣṇa is fighting with demons, that is also His pastime. So Kṛṣṇa is present. So you should be very attentive and worship this hearing. Unless we come to this point, there is lack of realization what is Kṛṣṇa.[18]

And here is another example of Śrīla Prabhupāda's many comments on regular, attentive chanting:

> As you chant, try to hear each word very carefully and always complete your sixteen rounds. Regular and attentive chanting, along with following the four regulative principles, will keep one pure. Simply by following these principles and chanting Hare Kṛṣṇa one can make his life successful and perfect.[19]

Such regular and attentive practice arises especially when one keeps a clear goal in mind.

Sādhana Should Be Goal-oriented

In the *Bhagavad-gītā* (2.66, purport), Śrīla Prabhupāda writes, "Disturbance is due to want of an ultimate goal." Humans are meant for accumulating transcendental assets (*daivī-sampāt*). This they can accomplish by hearing about Kṛṣṇa and rendering service to Kṛṣṇa's pure devotees, as mentioned in two of *Śrīmad-Bhāgavatam's* most celebrated verses (1.2.16–17):

The Six Gosvāmīs of Vṛndāvana pictured here – Rūpa Gosvāmī, Sanātana Gosvāmī, Jīva Gosvāmī, Raghunātha dāsa Gosvāmī, Raghunātha Bhaṭṭa Gosvāmī, and Gopāla Bhaṭṭa Gosvāmī – together carried on the family business on the order of Śrī Caitanya Mahāprabhu by compiling a veritable library of transcendental books, thus establishing the canon of Gauḍīya Vaiṣṇavism.

> O twice-born sages, by serving those devotees who are completely freed from all vice, great service is done. By such service, one gains affinity for hearing the messages of Vāsudeva.
>
> Śrī Kṛṣṇa, the Personality of Godhead, who is the Paramātmā [Supersoul] in everyone's heart and the benefactor of the truthful devotee, cleanses desire for material enjoyment from the heart of the devotee who has developed the urge to hear His messages, which are in themselves virtuous when properly heard and chanted.

By performing attentive devotional service we deposit spiritual credits that accumulate in a transcendental bank account within our hearts. When the balance becomes great enough we can purchase the most valuable of fixed assets: transcendental loving service to Kṛṣṇa in the company of His eternal associates in the kingdom of God.

The *Bṛhan-nāradīya Purāṇa* (4.33) confirms that this process works: "The awakening of bhakti takes place when one associates with the Lord's pure devotees. Such association with pure devotees is attained only by the accumulation of transcendental pious activities performed over many lifetimes."

One who accumulates sufficient spiritual wealth, therefore, becomes qualified for higher levels of devotional service. In fact, the bhakti scriptures say that just as a capitalist hoards gold, a devotee, enlivened by the prospect of advancing in spiritual life, stockpiles sacred knowledge and mantras in the association of like-minded devotees. This truth is confirmed by a verse in Śrīla Rūpa Gosvāmī's *Padyāvalī* (30): "O Lord, just as a miser continually collects, counts, and remembers his money, in the same way let us continually collect, count, and remember Your holy names."

In the material sense, greed is considered to be a low-grade quality. But when one's greed is applied to advancing in devotional service, it becomes a high-grade desire because it is perfectly utilized in divine service. Indeed, Rūpa Gosvāmī says that one must have greed for pure devotional service in order to obtain it: "Pure devotional service in Kṛṣṇa consciousness cannot be had even by pious activity in hundreds and thousands of lives. It can be attained only by paying one price – that is, intense greed to obtain it. If it is available somewhere, one must purchase it without delay."[20]

With these spiritual perspectives in mind, we can easily understand why the great teachers of bhakti say that goal-oriented practice of devotional service is vital. Śrīla Prabhupāda stresses "numerical strength," or carefully counting and maintaining one's daily vow to chant a set number of Kṛṣṇa's names.

Similarly, Śrīla Prabhupāda encourages his followers to set daily reading goals. For example, he writes the following about reading a chapter of the *Bhagavad-gītā* every day:

> I thank you so much for having nicely appreciated the *Bhagavad-gītā As It Is*. This book should be read by all of my students at least one chapter per day, and in *kīrtana* class it should be discussed *śloka* after *śloka*. Practically, we have tried to explain in this book all of the basic principles of Kṛṣṇa consciousness. If you can simply cram *Bhagavad-gītā,* then you will surely become a very good preacher.[21]

When I learned about Śrīla Prabhupāda's guideline to read a chapter of *Bhagavad-gītā* a day, I started doing it myself. Later, I formed the Chapter-A-Day Club (CHAD) so that I could share this treasure with other devotees interested in following Śrīla Prabhupāda's teaching.

CHAD is now a worldwide circle of devotees who have vowed to chant at least one chapter from *Bhagavad-gītā As It Is* every day. To be a card-carrying member, one must chant all the verses of at least one entire chapter of the *Gītā,* either the Sanskrit *ślokas,* the English translations, or both.*

We advertise the following list of benefits for joining CHAD:

* For those who choose to chant only the Sanskrit *ślokas,* the BBT has published them as a small book, just suitable for this purpose.

1. Knowing that others are doing it with you, you'll feel greater impetus to chant the *Gītā* every day.

2. By reciting and hearing the divine conversation between Kṛṣṇa and Arjuna, you'll gain superior strength and knowledge in devotional service.

3. You'll be cleared of offenses you've committed while worshiping the Deity.

4. Because "Repetition is the mother of learning," you'll automatically learn multiple *Bhagavad-gītā* verses through reciting a chapter a day.

5. You'll gain skill in citing important *ślokas* from *Bhagavad-gītā* as evidence when you teach Kṛṣṇa consciousness.

6. Because Kṛṣṇa reveals Himself to those who daily chant the *Bhagavad-gītā,* you'll awaken a sweet relationship with Him.

To count and keep track of one's daily practice of devotional service follows the mood and method of the great predecessor teachers of devotional service. The Six Gosvāmīs of Vṛndāvana are especially known for their daily, scheduled practices. In fact, Śrīnivāsa Ācārya, a contemporary of the Six Gosvāmīs who witnessed their exemplary devotional practices, writes that they chanted the holy names of the Lord and bowed down in a "scheduled measurement."[22]

Haridāsa Ṭhākura, an eternal associate of Śrī Caitanya Mahāprabhu, is also celebrated for maintaining a strict vow – his was to chant three hundred thousand names of Kṛṣṇa daily. The Hare Kṛṣṇa *mahā-mantra* consists of sixteen names, and one round consists of 108 mantras. To chant three hundred thousand names, therefore, the Ṭhākura would daily complete 192 rounds. He would not do anything else in his day until he had honored his vow.

Of course, one cannot imitate devotees like Haridāsa Ṭhākura, who are liberated, perfected beings, and Śrīla Prabhupāda was critical of devotees who tried to do so in order to avoid the practical services required to spread the Kṛṣṇa consciousness movement. Still, strong *sādhana* means to set numerical goals for one's various devotional practices – according to one's capacity – and to monitor one's progress toward reaching those goals. For instance, all initiated devotees in ISKCON carefully chant at least sixteen rounds of *japa* on beads every day without fail. And some devotees log the number of pages of scripture they read each day. Others track their daily waking times and the days they attend the morning program in the temple, and so on.

Organizing one's life around spiritual goals is very productive. For example, those who read a set number of pages of *Śrīmad-Bhāgavatam* every day soon find that such regular reading gives them a noticeable spiritual boost.

In the course of modern daily life, the complexities generated by unlimited options and argumentative attitudes often press us to make difficult decisions. A devotee who daily reads Śrīla Prabhupāda's purports, however, develops a clear intelligence and fortifies himself against bad choices.

In my own devotional life, I had long admired devotees who were able to regularly read through the entire *Śrīmad-Bhāgavatam* every year. I noticed that these devotees were making advancement and were also becoming expert at presenting the Kṛṣṇa conscious philosophy. Looking at all the volumes of *Śrīmad-Bhāgavatam* together, however, my mind would sometimes tell me, "You could never finish all of these books in a year with all that you have going on in your life." One day, however, I read in a book by Brian Tracy the following simple suggestion. It changed my mind.

> Psychologically, you will find it easier to do a single, small piece of a large project than to start on the whole job. Often, once you have started and completed a single part of the job, you will feel like doing just one more "slice." Soon, you will find yourself working through the whole job one part at a time, and before you know it, the job will be completed.[23]

After reading this, I thought of a way that I might read the whole *Śrīmad-Bhāgavatam* in a year by dividing it into small slices. My friend Śrīvāsa Paṇḍita helped me by going through the *Bhāgavatam* and calculating the total number of pages: 15,119. By dividing that number by 365, I computed the number of pages I would have to read daily to finish the *Śrīmad-Bhāgavatam* in one year – forty-one. Then all I had to do was decide to take a part of my day to read those forty-one pages.

With the overall goal now divided into small, daily slices, my mind suddenly changed its tune. Instead of being intimidated, it asked, "When can I start?"

On a roll, Śrīvāsa and I next calculated the number of pages in *all* of Śrīla Prabhupāda's books and ascribed to each the number of pages one would have to read per day to complete each book within various periods of time. For example, the *Bhagavad-gītā* has 868 pages, so one can read it in a month by reading just twenty-nine pages a day, and so on.

With all this information, we made a handy chart. And one day, while brainstorming with my friend Keśava Bhāratī Dāsa Goswami, we jointly came up with what we felt was the perfect name for this chart: Be a Sage, Page by Page.

Truly, by setting challenging goals, and by segmenting into reasonable slices the activity needed to achieve those goals, one can easily reach them. Such goal-oriented practice sets one's life on a new, positive course. In fact, not only is planning and implementing devotional service fun and natural, but it results in strong *sādhana*. And by keeping such strong *sādhana,* one can become a true sage within one's lifetime.

Practice by Personal Capacity and Taste

Enthusiastic devotees naturally ask how to advance in devotional service. The invariable answer is that one must dutifully practice devotional service according to one's present capacity. For example, in the *Gītā* (3.35) Kṛṣṇa recommends that one adhere to the level of devotional practice one can honestly perform: "It is far better to discharge one's prescribed duties, even though faultily, than another's duties perfectly. Destruction in the course of performing one's own duty is better than engaging in another's duties, for to follow another's path is dangerous."

And in *Śrīmad-Bhāgavatam* (11.21.2), Kṛṣṇa tells Uddhava: "Steadiness in one's own position is declared to be actual piety, whereas deviation from one's position is considered impiety. In this way the two are definitely ascertained."

Śrīla Bhaktivinoda Ṭhākura, in *Śrī Caitanya Śikṣāmṛta* (p. 5), gives the following points about how to grow in spiritual life:

> One should have constancy in setting one's steps firmly in whatever stage of life one is now placed. Secondly, advancement from one's present position is like climbing a ladder: when one's foot is securely placed on one rung of the ladder, one must determinedly move to the next higher rung, giving up the lower. Giving up the present rung and moving to the next higher rung should be done simultaneously. If it is done in a hurry, however, there is chance of a fall. And, if one's progression is delayed, the result will be distant.... Therefore, considering hurry and delay both as obstacles, one has to rise up the ladder.

In other words, neither imitation of higher standards of devotional practice nor delaying one's practice while claiming that one is permanently unqualified will help one advance in devotional service.

In fact, scripture says that imitative practice is merely a disturbance to the devotional community. But a simple devotee who accepts his or her level of qualification and acts accordingly, unafraid to take the next step upward, is perfectly situated in spiritual life.

Śrī Caitanya Mahāprabhu also speaks about a serious devotee's progressive, incremental advancement in devotional service when He invokes the words *krame krame,* "step by step," in this verse: "One whose faith is soft and pliable is called a neophyte, but by gradually following the process [*krame krame*], he will rise to the platform of a first-class devotee."[24]

In Śrīla Prabhupāda's explanation of this verse, he says: "Everyone begins his devotional life from the neophyte stage, but if one properly finishes chanting the prescribed number of rounds of *hari-nāma,* he is elevated step by step to the highest platform, *uttama-adhikārī.*"

This sincere and balanced approach to devotional service will attract the mercy of the Vaiṣṇavas, who will bless the devotee to make further advancement.

With guidance from guru, scripture, and advanced devotees, one should fix a regular amount of practice into one's daily schedule and stick to it even if at first the quantity seems minuscule. Even a little devotional practice, especially of hearing transcendental sound, will gradually expand to fill one's life. Adding a small amount of yogurt to even a large pot of milk will transform the entire pot to yogurt overnight, especially when the milk is kept in the right environment. Those who add even a small amount of hearing and chanting to their schedules will soon find all aspects of their lives becoming spiritualized, especially when they keep themselves in contact with a devotional environment. Kṛṣṇa helps those who sincerely do their best.

In summary, proper attitude, regularity, attentiveness, goal setting, and acting according to one's present capacity are the elements of strong *sādhana.* Following these principles and practicing the basics of devotional service prescribed by the great authorities, a devotee will grow as strong as the Himalayas.

Start the Regulation Habit

Just as we develop bad habits by gradually slipping into them, we can develop good habits by voluntarily accepting discipline. Here's a recipe for developing good habits: Decide which good devotional habits you want to start and write them down. Cultivate them each day until they become a natural part of your life. Śrīla Prabhupāda calls this technique "getting practiced automatically."

Human beings can make voluntary life changes. One who does so based on the order of the spiritual master, scripture, and elevated devotees will taste strong, uncommon confidence, clear knowledge, and happiness.

> One should therefore understand what is duty and what is not duty by the regulations of the scriptures. Knowing such rules and regulations, one should act so that he may gradually be elevated.[25]

CHAPTER FIFTEEN

Get Books!

YOU CAN'T DISTRIBUTE books you don't have!

At first glance, this principle – this law of book distribution – may appear simplistic, perhaps even an insult to the intelligence. Isn't it obvious that you can't distribute books you don't have? So you have to get books, and that's why this principle follows as the second law of book distribution. You can't distribute books you don't have. And this law applies to everyone in all circumstances. If you're thinking about distributing books, get some! If you live in a house, if you live in a trailer, if you live in a temple, if you live in a dorm, it doesn't matter. If you want to distribute books, you must get books.

Don't let the simple wording of this law mislead you into not taking it seriously. In truth, if you go out of your way to get books and simply intend to distribute them one day, you'll naturally start to think of ways to do it as soon as you have them. And even if you forget you have a stock of books, Lord Caitanya will remind you in amazing ways to pass them on to others.

Success = Preparation + Opportunity

Bobby Unser, the celebrated race driver, coined the phrase "Success is where preparation and opportunity meet." To have Śrīla Prabhupāda's books in your physical possession, then, means to be prepared to distribute them. Opportunities to pass them on will seem to come to you like magic, but such openings are actually the divine arrangement of Lord Caitanya. In summary, when you have books to give, you're surely on the verge of distributing them.

Here's an example of this second law in action, told by Ajita Dāsa:

> After attending a powerful seminar on book distribution at the ISKCON Chicago temple and hearing about the four laws of book distribution, my best friend and business partner Yaśodānandana Dāsa and I decided to implement the second law – Get Books – in a practical way by always carrying a box of Śrīla Prabhupāda's books in our car. Soon after starting this discipline we had an experience that convinced us of this law's effectiveness.
>
> It happened one day when Yaśodānandana and I were invited to a home program hosted by a wealthy gentleman. Our host had invited a few devotees from our local ISKCON temple along with a group of his friends. We came in our own car and met the devotees at the program. At our host's request the devotees performed *kīrtana.* After the chanting, he spontaneously asked us if he could sponsor *Bhagavad-gītās* for all his friends who had come to the program.
>
> None of the devotees who had come in the temple's van had anticipated such a request. Thus they had come to the program without bringing any books. When Yaśodānandana and I heard our host's request, we at once remembered the box of books we had put in our car as standard equipment. Luckily the car was parked just outside the house, so we ran out, brought in our box of books, and presented it to our host. We had fifteen copies of *Bhagavad-gītā As It Is,* five copies of *Kṛṣṇa, the Supreme Personality of Godhead,* and twenty small

books. To our surprise, our host, noticeably pleased, at once wrote us a check for one thousand dollars.

He then asked us to distribute the books to all his friends, so Yaśodānandana and I spent the rest of the evening at a book table in the living room, glorifying Śrīla Prabhupāda's books and inspiring the guests to take them home and read them. By the end of the evening, all the books were gone. The next day we brought the check for a thousand dollars to the temple. What's more, two of the guests we had met that night later attended the Chicago Ratha-yātrā with their families.

This is only one instance of many distribution opportunities we've had since we started following the second law of book distribution – Get Books!

Avoid Violence

If a devotee misses a chance to distribute a book to an eligible soul, he or she should feel pain. A kindhearted devotee who has forgotten to have a transcendental book on hand, on meeting a receptive person will think, "Oh, I am so cruel for not being prepared!"

And such a missed opportunity should be painful because it is a form of violence. Why? Śrīla Prabhupāda gives the answer in this purport:

> People in general are trapped by ignorance in the material concept of life, and they perpetually suffer material pains. So unless one elevates people to spiritual knowledge, one is practicing violence. One should try his best to distribute real knowledge to the people, so that they may become enlightened and leave this material entanglement. That is nonviolence.[1]

During an epidemic, doctors who have access to the medicine that will cure the disease are morally and ethically responsible to distribute it and administer it to the sick. If they neglect to do so, they are violators of the Hippocratic oath, which states in part, "I will for the benefit of the sick apply all measures which are required ... I will prevent disease whenever I can."

In the same way, devotees, who are doctors of the soul, who know that distributing transcendental knowledge is the panacea to alleviate people's suffering, and who are aware of the unparalleled spiritual potency of Śrīla Prabhupāda's books, must keep them on hand and distribute them.

Books to Go

Putting a transcendental book in your pocket, handbag, or baby stroller before going out into the world can transform an ordinary excursion into a transcendental adventure. It's not difficult. It just takes a conscious effort.

Here's an example of how bringing a book along can turn a commonplace saunter around the block into a life-changing event. One summer, I was asked to give a book distribution seminar at the Brooklyn ISKCON temple. During the seminar I told the audience about the second law of book distribution, Get Books! I said that devotees should always carry at least one of Śrīla Prabhupāda's books with them when going out into the world. If they did, Lord Caitanya would arrange for them to meet someone ready to receive a book.

During our noon break from the seminar I decided to take a walk around the block, and Mitrasena Dāsa, my godbrother and friend, agreed to join me. We walked down the several flights of stairs from the seminar room and exited the temple through the front door, which locked behind us. Suddenly I remembered that I was breaking the law: I didn't have a book with me. Our break time was short, but I didn't want to be a hypocrite. As I was about to run back up the three flights of stairs to get a book, Mitrasena told me he had one. Luckily, he had followed the second law. Pulling a *Śrī Īśopaniṣad* from his coat pocket he smiled and said, "We're good to go!"

Vincent Gets a Book

As it turned out, Lord Caitanya did have a plan for that book and we were to be His instruments. We walked a half block south from the ISKCON temple, turned right on Nevins Avenue, and made another right turn onto State Street. Just as we rounded the corner, we came upon a construction worker taking a break from his demolition work inside a brownstone a hundred yards away. He was stocky, he wore dusty blue overalls on top of a smudged white T-shirt, and his hefty work boots were well-worn. I made him out to be in his mid-thirties. As he relaxed, leaning his left elbow against the side of an enormous white dump truck, he looked like he was trying to figure out what he was seeing: two large American men with shaven heads wearing dhotis and *tilaka*. His probing eyes latched onto the two of us, and as we drew near, the man, whose name turned out to be Vincent, squinted his eyes, slightly tilted his head, and suddenly blurted out in a loud voice, "What are you, Buddha?"

His question could have been a taunt. Although it wouldn't have been the first time I had heard one from a New Yorker, Vincent's eyes looked sincere to me. But how does one reply to a person who asks, "What are you, Buddha?" I didn't have a glib comeback, so I replied, "Not exactly." The instant I answered him I thought of the *Īśopaniṣad* in Mitrasena's pocket. Mitrasena knew what I was thinking and, as if choreographed, he took the book out, handed it to me, and I handed the book over to Vincent.

Lord Caitanya had set the scene, using Mitrasena and me as instruments to give spiritual knowledge to Vincent. And all we had done to deserve this privilege was to ready ourselves by following the second law of book distribution: Get Books!

Vincent listened attentively as Mitrasena and I explained the nature of the book we had handed him. And when he asked if it was a religion, I suggested that he let me read him a sample of what's in the book. He could then decide for himself if it was religion or not.

I took the *Śrī Īśopaniṣad* out of Vincent's hand and read him the English translation of mantra 6: "One who sees everything in relation to the Supreme Lord and who sees the Supreme Lord within everything never hates anything or any being."

This was June 2002, just nine months after terror attacks had collapsed the World Trade Center's twin towers in Manhattan on September 11, 2001. People around the world, especially New Yorkers, were rattled and tense. Around this time, as I distributed books in New York, I found that people in general were wary of sectarian religious sentiments. They felt that they had been attacked due to hatred grown from intolerance, the offspring of dogmatic and sectarian religious institutions.

But when Vincent heard mantra 6 he was noticeably pleased. His face brightened. He took the book back and flipped through it, looking at the pictures.

After we had answered several of Vincent's questions, I told him he could keep the book, and if he gave a donation in return, he would earn spiritual credit to go deeper into the book's philosophy. Vincent nodded in agreement and enthusiastically climbed into the cab of his dump truck, rummaged through a cluttered glove box, climbed back down, and gave us sixteen dollars for the book.

We pointed out that our temple was just around the corner, invited him to stop in, and parted ways.

As Mitrasena and I continued our walk we talked about how amazing it was that Lord Caitanya had so quickly reciprocated with us for bringing along a book. The setup couldn't have been clearer: Vincent was thirsty and the Lord had used Mitrasena and me to pour the spiritual beverage of transcendental knowledge into his open heart.

In the *Bhagavad-gītā* (13.26) Kṛṣṇa says: "Again there are those who, although not conversant in spiritual knowledge, begin to worship the Supreme Person upon hearing about

Him from others. Because of their tendency to hear from authorities, they also transcend the path of birth and death."

Lord Caitanya also tells Sanātana Gosvāmī:

> Wandering and wandering throughout the universe, [a living entity] may by chance get the association of a devotee physician, whose instructions and hymns make the witch of the external energy flee. The conditioned soul thus gets into touch with devotional service to Lord Kṛṣṇa, and in this way he can approach nearer and nearer to the Lord.[2]

Kṛṣṇa used us to deliver the book to Vincent. Kṛṣṇa knew that Vincent was waiting there for us. Kṛṣṇa knows everything. "The Supreme Lord is situated in everyone's heart, O Arjuna, and is directing the wanderings of all living entities, who are seated as on a machine, made of the material energy."[3]

Arguably, our bringing that *Śrī Īśopaniṣad* had changed the course of one soul's journey through the universe.

Back at the seminar in the temple only twenty minutes later, Mitrasena and I shared our experience with the rest of the devotees at the seminar. They were impressed, and all vowed to get books and have them at hand.

A Rare Privilege

It is a rare privilege to have all of Śrīla Prabhupāda's books not only for reading ourselves but also for distributing to others. Śrīla Prabhupāda invested much of his energy into writing and publishing his books. Many of us have heard the phrase "Books are the basis." Naturally, anyone who invests in Śrīla Prabhupāda's books and carefully keeps those invaluable gems begins to dream of ways to distribute them.

Get books, stack them in front of your television or refrigerator, and distribute them all before you turn on the daily news or have your next meal!

CHAPTER SIXTEEN

The More You Show, The More You Sell

AS SOON AS A SIGN GOES UP showing a product for sale, someone somewhere comes to check it out. Why? Because he or she saw it. In the *Bhagavad-gītā* (2.62), Kṛṣṇa explains how living beings become attached to things: "While contemplating the objects of the senses, a person develops attachment for them."

Therefore, the third law of book distribution – The More You Show, The More You Sell – is based on an eternal principle. All advertisers know that when they make their products or services visible, people will begin to contemplate them. Contemplation means to think about a possible course of action or to seriously consider something. While contemplating a product or service, some people become attached and think, "There may be something in this for me." From that thought comes the next: "How can I get this thing?" In this way products are sold.

Pour Out the Happiness

A good example of this is found in the soft drink industry. A recent Coca-Cola ad shows a stream of Coca-Cola cascading in slow motion from Coke's new larger-sized bottle into several frosty glasses, along with the caption: "Pour out the happiness." Most people know that a soft drink won't actually bring them happiness; but amazingly, just because the sugary drink is put before them in an appealing ad, they still accept it as a possible means to happiness.

The same principle applies when you show Śrīla Prabhupāda's transcendental books. People will take a look, and some will be attracted and buy them. The difference is that Śrīla Prabhupāda's books really do pour out happiness. Unfortunately, people regularly buy an uncountable number of things that cannot bring them fulfillment. Compassionate devotees therefore show people Śrīla Prabhupāda's transcendental books, which can actually satisfy their souls.

The Best Book Distributors

The well-known BBT artist Puṣkara Dāsa once lamented to Śrīla Prabhupāda that he was too busy to go out and sell his books because he was always absorbed in painting pictures for them. Śrīla Prabhupāda eased Puṣkara's mind by saying, "The artists are the best book distributors." In a letter to Jadurāṇī dated July 11, 1970, Śrīla Prabhupāda spoke about the art's appeal in selling his books: "People become attracted with these unusual transcendental pictures at first, so even without reading the book they become inclined to purchase it."

While it's a fact that the paintings in Śrīla Prabhupāda's books catch people's attention, those people must see the artwork to become attracted. That is, a picture may be worth a thousand words, but if no one sees it, how will the picture's value be realized? Therefore this law of book distribution: The More You Show, The More You Sell.

Aside from the remarkable paintings, Śrīla Prabhupāda's books are extraordinary in every respect due to their being the literary incarnation of Kṛṣṇa.[1] Devotees who simply increase the ways in which they display Śrīla Prabhupāda's transcendental books will increase without fail the number of books they distribute.

Display the Books

Books need to find their readers. If their authors hadn't wanted others to read what they'd written, they wouldn't have undergone the labor to publish their works in the first place. Śrīla Prabhupāda certainly wanted his books displayed. He said so hundreds of times. One meaning of the word *display* is "a prominent exhibition of something in a place where it can be easily seen." Here are two of many examples in which Śrīla Prabhupāda requests his disciples to display his books:

> I think so many men will be glad to receive our books, so please utilize this opportunity. Simply it requires determination and imagination. Maybe you can get the Indian Ambassador and his wife to hold a meeting at which many important men can be invited. If he and his wife are favorably impressed, certainly they can hold a nice meeting one evening. At that meeting you can speak and explain what our movement is and show slides and movies. Make a book table and display all of our books. Never mind if they also like to read from Ramakrishna. If you give them our KṚṢṆA book to read, very soon all other tastes will go away."[2]

> Please report to me fortnightly, and correspond with your other GBC men as well. I request that you always display and distribute my books wherever possible.[3]

The statements Śrīla Prabhupāda makes about displaying his books contain three basic elements: To display his books with (a) determination, (b) imagination, and (c) wherever possible. Let me clarify.

Determination Pays

When it comes to being determined to display Śrīla Prabhupāda books, I think of my friend, Vijaya Dāsa. Many years ago, at the Los Angeles Ratha-yātrā at Venice Beach, I had the privilege of working with Vijaya side by side at the booth where we display Śrīla Prabhupāda's books. At Ratha-yātrā festivals we typically sell many small books like *Easy Journey to Other Planets,* along with some hardbound ones like *Bhagavad-gītā As It Is.* During this festival, however, Vijaya was determined to sell full sets of *Śrīmad-Bhāgavatam.*

While we worked, I noticed that whenever people told him that they already had a copy of *Bhagavad-gītā As It Is,* Vijaya would draw their attention to the full set of *Śrīmad-Bhāgavatams* he had set up behind us at the back of the booth. Repeatedly, he'd say to these people, "Oh, you have the *Gītā*? Then you need the full set of *Śrīmad-Bhāgavatam*!" As he said this he would make a sweeping gesture with his hand to draw the potential buyer's eyes to the line up of books behind him. After seeing him do this dozens of times with no result, I began to think Vijaya's routine to be more an exercise in devotion than an effective means to sell sets of *Śrīmad-Bhāgavatam.*

I was wrong. A while later, after having been absorbed in selling individual books, I again turned my attention to the booth and was startled to see that the set of *Bhāgavatams* was gone. I turned to Vijaya and asked, "What happened?" He chuckled and replied, "I sold it!" The moral of the story? Be determined to show Śrīla Prabhupāda's books. Someone will always come along to buy them.

Innovative Displays

Śrīla Prabhupāda's second recommendation about displaying his books is that one should be innovative. If ever there was an innovation, here it is: In San Jose, California, Haṁsapriyā Devī Dāsī made a special backpack for her dog Yogi to carry

Śrīla Prabhupāda's books. Because Yogi was an attractive dog, people would come over to pet her. Seeing Yogi's unusual cargo they would naturally ask Haṁsapriyā about the books her dog was carrying. Haṁsapriyā would then take the opportunity to hand the inquirer a book and explain it. When people came to know that a dog named Yogi was carrying books on yoga, they couldn't resist buying one. In this way, lots of Śrīla Prabhupāda's books were sold from Yogi's backpack during her lifetime. We even added an accounting of the books distributed from Yogi's backpack to our local distribution newsletter under Yogi's name.

The third recommendation Śrīla Prabhupāda gave us was to display his books "wherever possible." There are many ways to show his books, but until we think deeply about it, we may miss some ideal or even obvious places. In the mountains of West Virginia, ISKCON New Vrindavan maintains Śrīla Prabhupāda's Palace of Gold as well as a beautiful Rādhā-Kṛṣṇa temple. Even though these landmarks are in a remote area, tour buses full of curious sightseers regularly come to New Vrindavan to see them.

One day, a devotee resident of New Vrindavan, Kamalāvatī Devī Dāsī, found an empty niche for displaying Śrīla Prabhupāda's books and filled it. Kamalāvatī tells her story:

> After going to the workshop on book distribution at the Festival of Inspiration in New Vrindavan, where I live, I became very inspired to take up a more imaginative approach to distributing Śrīla Prabhupāda's books. We have so many guests visiting New Vrindavan every week, and yet many walk away without even one of Śrīla Prabhupāda's books. Lord Kṛṣṇa made this point very clear to me.
>
> One day I was talking to a guest who was a minister from Texas. He saw the huge poster on our temple room wall near Śrīla Prabhupāda's *vyāsāsana*. The poster portrayed Lord Kṛṣṇa manifesting His universal form to Arjuna with the header "*Bhagavad-gītā As It Is.*" After seeing the poster, the minister said, "I would like a *Bhagavad-gītā*."

I was embarrassed and at a loss for words when I realized there was not one *Bhagavad-gītā* in the temple to distribute to this gentleman! Just then I remembered the adage that we'd memorized during the book distribution seminar, the third law of book distribution: "The more you show, the more you sell." I suddenly realized that it was up to me to transform our temple into a place from which to distribute books.

The next day, I set up a book table under that *Bhagavad-gītā* poster. I already had a supply of *Gītās* and small books at home. I dragged them out and attractively displayed them on the table. Next, I purchased sheets of bright-yellow round, removable stickers. Any office supply store has these. I then used my home computer to print a suggested donation on each sticker. For instance, "$10 donation. Thank You!" I labeled each book according to its cost by placing the price sticker on the front of the book.

Next I also printed small, rectangular stickers that read: "For more books and information: www.krishna.com." Finally I created the following simple sign, framed it, and placed it on the table:

> Dear Honored Guest,
>
> These books, written by His Divine Grace, A. C. Bhaktivedanta Swami Prabhupada, are a treasure house of spiritual knowledge. When you read the *Bhagavad-gita As It Is,* Lord Krishna will impart to you the most secret wisdom, knowing which you shall be relieved of the miseries of material existence. Please feel free to take some books home with you.
>
> In the envelopes we've provided, please enclose your donation to pay for the printing costs. Then kindly put your book donation envelope into the large box up front at the main altar. Thank you very much. Hare Krishna!

On the dozens of envelopes I placed on the book table, I wrote: "Book Donation. Please place in box." The results? The system worked! A week after setting up the table, I came back and saw that the books were almost all gone and the

> envelopes full of money were placed in the donation box. Upon counting, I found that people had been honest, always leaving enough money to cover the printing, and in many envelopes, more.

Over the next year, Kamalāvatī refined the look, efficiency, and size of the table. She displayed the books on professional racks and affixed a large metal donation box to the table. She also dramatically improved the signage. Soon, her book table was selling thousands of dollars of books each month, and today that magic book table even sells full sets of *Śrīmad-Bhāgavatam* and *Śrī Caitanya-caritāmṛta*. All this was due to one person's innovative display of Śrīla Prabhupāda's books in a place they had not been visible before.

I've had times, while getting ready to show Śrīla Prabhupāda's books, when people came to buy them even before the books were fully visible. One example comes to mind. I was in Santa Cruz, California, having gone there to distribute books for a couple of hours on a busy sidewalk. Just after I arrived I set down my box of books and used a key to break through the clear tape that sealed it.

As the box opened with a pop and the box's cardboard flaps swung slightly open, the colorful books peeked out. This caught the attention of a curious passerby, who came to see what I had in my box. Noting his interest, I took out a book, handed it to him, and briefly explained what it was about. He accepted the book and happily gave me fifteen dollars and his email address. With hardly any effort I had sold a book and made a new friend just because I was following the third law of book distribution – The More You Show, The More You Sell.

Showing Śrīla Prabhupāda's books on the Internet is also a good way to display them, even if one lives in a remote location. Many devotees are distributing in this way. In Brazil, devotees are finding innovative ways to display Śrīla Prabhupāda's books – for example, by placing small books in vending machines. In America, Europe, and India devotees are displaying books in Smart Boxes – boxes placed in stores, restaurants, and boutiques, from which people can take a book and leave a donation on the honor system.

Looking for Love

Sellers everywhere are using the same law, but they are vending products and services that cannot satisfy people's souls. Thus humankind's search for ultimate happiness and love perpetually lets them down.

It's natural to the soul to seek happiness and love. Even America's founding fathers included in the Declaration of Independence the pursuit of happiness as a fundamental right of all citizens. Be that as it may, the United States – or anywhere else in the material world – is the wrong place to look for lasting love or happiness. In the *Gītā* (8.6) Lord Kṛṣṇa gives this sweeping pronouncement about the miserable nature of the material world: "From the highest planet in the material world down to the lowest, all are places of misery wherein repeated birth and death take place. But one who attains to My abode, O son of Kuntī, never takes birth again."

Still, the bhakti scriptures are not promoting fatalism. Rather, they encourage people to never give up their search for everlasting happiness and eternal love. In fact, they inform us that a human being's search for the highest happiness is the main duty of human life. But the *śāstra* also says that to attain such love and happiness, one must search in the right place.

That's where we can help by offering people Śrīla Prabhupāda's transcendental books in as many ways as possible. Truly, it is the business of Kṛṣṇa's devotees to show people the bhakti scriptures. If those of us who have inherited Śrīla Prabhupāda's legacy don't show his books to the world, who will?

When someone sees, becomes attached to, and buys a transcendental book from a devotee, that person's auspicious life begins. But that auspicious beginning can only take place if we do our part and show the books. Offering this boon to the people of the world is not at all difficult. It simply requires that one follow the third law of book distribution: The More You Show, The More You Sell.

Every good businessperson knows that if you don't trumpet your product you'll soon go out of business. That's why in business circles there's a common saying: "A business with no sign is a sign of no business." By now you're already following the second law – Get Books! Now, take the next step and experiment with making those books visible. Watch what happens. You'll be amazed.

CHAPTER SEVENTEEN

You Must Organize

BEFORE WE HEAR about why and how we must organize, let's listen in on a monologue that reveals what it means to be disorganized.

"You want to go out and distribute books? You need books? Sure, I'll get you some. Follow me.... Yeah, I know, it's not exactly a book room – for now, we're just using this closet next to the boiler here in the basement to store Śrīla Prabhupāda's books. Anyway, *we* call it a book room. Oops, it's locked. Wait here while I get the key. Come to think of it, the only person who has the key is out of town. Oh, and I just remembered – I heard a rumor the other day that he might not be coming back. Anyway, we'll be lucky if there are books inside. We were supposed to pick some up at the BBT warehouse a few months ago, but the temple van's engine froze, so the temple president postponed the trip. Apparently no one had changed the oil for a couple of years. And ... well ... to be honest, we couldn't afford to buy books this year anyway."

Such nattering won't go away until we've employed the fourth law of book distribution: You Must Organize.

I have statistics to prove that those who organize sell far more of Śrīla Prabhupāda's books than those who don't. It's not even a close race. After organizing themselves, communities that were distributing only a few hundred of Śrīla Prabhupāda's books a year, or even none at all, have been able to dramatically increase the numbers of books they sell per month by the thousands or even tens of thousands. And I've seen over the years that organized communities not only increase the quantity of books they distribute but also improve the quality of their distribution. In stark contrast, those who fail to organize themselves never increase or improve.

Moreover, those who don't set goals and then measure their results – two foundational principles of organization – cannot know whether they are increasing or decreasing; nor can they taste the exhilaration of striving to achieve a specific goal.

In fact, a disorganized life is not only tedious but also unproductive. I state this stark truth with firm conviction because I've seen the fourth law of book distribution repeatedly transform less productive teams into invigorated high-achieving ones almost overnight.

I have also measured these quantum leaps in results. For example, after intently organizing themselves, the devotees at ISKCON Toronto went from distributing 10,000 books in 2009 to more than 35,000 in 2010. ISKCON Laguna Beach increased from distributing just 400 books in 2011 to more than 15,000 in 2012. And between 2010 and 2012, ISKCON of Washington, D.C. increased from 5,000 books to 50,000. New Delhi, Philadelphia, Baltimore, Chicago, Budapest, Kaunas, London, as well as centers in Brazil, Australia, New Zealand, and many more communities worldwide have also increased dramatically by applying the fourth law of book distribution: You Must Organize. Numbers don't lie. Hard statistics show that the efforts of both individuals and teams that organize themselves pay off handsomely.

Of course, the most dramatic transformation I've had the privilege to witness – as a community applied the magic of organizing themselves – has been in ISKCON of Silicon Valley (Team ISV). I've watched Team ISV grow over the last decade from a few eager but green book distributors into a thriving, well-oiled team with dozens and then hundreds of highly trained distributors.

Ten years ago, Team ISV was distributing only a few dozen of Śrīla Prabhupāda's books per month, but by organizing themselves, the results improved, month by month, until the team was able to distribute thousands and now tens of thousands of books per month. We expect that the results will continue to grow both quantitatively and qualitatively, because this is Lord Caitanya's *saṅkīrtana* movement, which expands the blissful ocean of transcendental life (*ānandāmbudhi-vardhanam*).

Someone may question, "But aren't these examples simply a result of lucky breaks?" Certainly not. Progress in book distribution is based on organization, not luck. In fact, every community that has embraced the fourth law of book distribution has also seen similar proportionate, astounding increases in its results.

But, someone else may argue, "I don't have the time to organize. I'm too busy. My work is too urgent to stop. I have too many emergencies to deal with." In reply to these busy people – and who isn't busy these days? – expert organizers tell the following story: A wise passerby saw a boy struggling to cut a tree with a dull ax and advised the boy to take a break from chopping to sharpen his ax. The boy looked at the wise man with disdain and replied, "Can't you see I'm in a hurry? I don't have time to stop even for a moment."

From the same vein of wisdom, the respected management expert, Brian Tracy, writes: "Every minute you spend planning can save you five to ten minutes in execution."[1]

Śrīla Prabhupāda, our exemplar of how to organize, spent years planning his campaign to spread Kṛṣṇa consciousness throughout the world. In fact, the first sixty-nine years of his life appear to have been an investment in planning that prepared him to spread the Kṛṣṇa consciousness movement at an unprecedented pace worldwide in just twelve years. Śrīla Prabhupāda's management mantra: "Organize to increase."

Here's what he told a young Jayapatāka Dāsa about organizing to increase the results of *saṅkīrtana:* "Please organize your sales there to increase at a steady rate. *Saṅkīrtana* is the tried and proven method of propagating all aspects of our Kṛṣṇa consciousness movement."

In fact, every successful enterprise starts with sound organizing. Here are seven basic organizational principles that will help make your book distribution program a success and your life more productive on all levels.

1. Brainstorm
2. Define your mission
3. Set goals
4. Plan
5. Execute
6. Create efficient systems
7. Get the right tools

Brainstorm

Humans are walking idea factories. Brainstorming puts these invaluable factories into full production mode. And even if you don't have any people to work with yet, you can begin brainstorming alone. Sit in a quiet place with a blank sheet of paper and a pen and write down your ideas. Start by writing a relevant question about book distribution on the top of your page. Then write down every thought that comes into your mind about how you can start to distribute books or improve the way you are doing it now.

If you do have people to work with, you have the most valuable asset of any organization. Some Japanese companies brainstorm by regularly polling their employees, especially the ones doing the manual labor. They do this because their workers see things about the company – its products and the ways they are manufactured and sold – that the managers may not see.

Other companies, such as Proctor & Gamble, brainstorm by inviting their customers to write or call in with their ideas for improving the company's products. They print the company's phone number and email address on every product, along with a request for the consumers to give ideas on how they can improve their goods and services.

Brainstorming is the best and quickest way to unearth valuable ideas and discover creative solutions to persistent problems. It is not only useful but fun, because it brings people together, reveals their hidden talents and ingenuity, and cultivates working relationships that help groups of people form teams.

To brainstorm with a group of people, first call them to a comfortable, peaceful environment. To start the session, ask a question, such as "How can we increase and improve book distribution?" Write the question at the top of a whiteboard (or project it on a screen) so that it is plainly visible to everyone. Then invite and encourage all the participants to contrib ute their ideas while someone writes them on the board. At this stage, don't stop to analyze the ideas; just list as many as you can.

Once you have your list, work with your group to prioritize the ideas and identify the top seven to ten by numbering them. This list of top ideas will be the primary seeds from which you will start to grow your team of book distributors. Victor Hugo writes about the importance of ideas: "An idea whose time has come is a force. It changes the world. It alters reality. It's unstoppable! There is nothing so powerful as an idea whose time has come."

ISKCON's communities are chockablock with skilled, imaginative people. Leaders who know how to tap this rich vein of talent and insight by inviting these bright people to share their ideas through brainstorming will never lack ideas on how to improve or develop.

Śrīla Prabhupāda advocates brainstorming in a 1973 letter to Tejīyas Dāsa, temple president of ISKCON Delhi: "Now try to tax your brain for finding new ways and better ways for distributing our books widely to the intelligent men of Delhi."

Indeed, brainstorming is the most efficient way to tax our own brain and the brains of those around us. And the tax extracted from these brainstorming sessions is lucrative to say the least. For example, in a brainstorming session at a temple presidents' meeting in Dallas, I worked with a group of leaders to brainstorm how to work with an idea I had to make a book-vending machine. In a single session our group was able to develop this innovative idea to the point at which it would soon become what we now call the Smart Box. Smart Boxes have spread all over the world and distribute thousands of books each year, especially in North America.

Practically everyone has good ideas. The problem is that most people offer their ideas randomly or at inopportune moments. For example, with a great idea in mind, a person might walk up to a manager hurrying to an engagement and say, "Excuse me, I have an idea I want to tell you about." Ideas offered erratically in this way often don't get gathered, planted, and cultivated; rather, because they are not carefully recorded, considered, or followed up, they remain on the ethereal plane and are never practically pursued.

But when a leader convenes a brainstorming session, not only do the team members feel empowered to give their best ideas but the organizers are also in a better position to capture the ideas and make concrete plans to implement them. What's more, a kind of synergy exists among the group members in a brainstorming session that gives results greater than the sum of the individual ideas themselves.

In the process of brainstorming, the group can effectively

consider and list all the aspects of the project that are most important to them. These main points then become the basis from which the team can craft its mission statement. A team that has a clear understanding of its mission is blessed. Patañjali, author of the *Yoga-sūtras,* agrees with this conclusion:

> When you are inspired by some great purpose, some extraordinary project, all your thoughts break their bonds: Your mind transcends limitations, your consciousness expands in every direction, and you find yourself in a new, great, and wonderful world. Dormant forces, faculties and talents become alive, and you discover yourself to be a greater person by far than you ever dreamed yourself to be.

Mission Statement

Start with a statement of your main purpose. This will enable you to guide and inspire your team to simplify and clarify your team's purpose and come up with a mission statement. For example, Amazon's simple mission is "To be earth's most customer-centric company; to build a place where people can come to find and discover anything they might want to buy online." The Nature Conservancy, a nonprofit organization, expresses its mission in this statement: "To leave a sustainable world for future generations."

In short, a mission statement is an action-oriented outline of how your team can fulfill its potential. Śrīla Prabhupāda expresses his mission through the seven purposes of ISKCON. He frequently stresses the special role the printing and distribution of his books will play in fulfilling his purposes:

> My special mission is to complete the *Śrīmad-Bhāgavatam* in sixty volumes, so the most important thing on the part of the International Society is to organize the sales propaganda of all the books that you are publishing. If there is less sales propaganda, then the outlet of the books will be bottlenecked, and smooth printing work will stop. You have not only to print, but you have to sell them.[2]

> I want that each and every one of my centers should be fully stocked with all of my books.[3]

> I want that every respectable person has a full set of *Bhāgavatam* and *Caitanya-caritāmṛta* in his home.[4]

Many such directives state the essential action Śrīla Prabhupāda wanted done to guide in perpetuity the organizations he created – ISKCON and the BBT – in order to fulfill his mission: "Organize and sell books."

In my service as both a manager and a book distributor, I have seen that when an ISKCON community's mission revolves around Śrīla Prabhupāda's directive to "organize and sell books," multiple benefits accrue to the entire community. In fact, Śrīla Prabhupāda wrote about how good management follows enlightened outreach in a letter to Satsvarūpa Dāsa on November 21, 1971: "Yes, preaching is more important than managing. Just because you are preaching nicely and distributing so much *prasāda,* the management will follow like a shadow and Kṛṣṇa will send you no end of help."

Human beings are always on the move and want to be part of an organization or community that's going somewhere. In ISKCON, when that "somewhere" includes increasing the distribution of Śrīla Prabhupāda's books, every one in the group is lifted to a higher conception of life, because distributing books is a purely transcendental activity that directly pleases our founder-*ācārya* and Lord Caitanya.

Once your mission statement is in place, you need to regularly communicate it to your community and team members, because a collective awareness of the mission "affects their identity and determines their degree of cohesiveness."[5] Stephen Covey, the famed management guru, comments in this regard that having a mission statement helps to overcome "the baggage of the past, or even the accumulated noise of the present."[6]

What's more, when you have your clear mission on paper, you will also have a basis from which to make sound decisions.

When you're not sure how to proceed or what to accept or reject, reviewing your mission statement will give you clarity about how to continue on the right path to accomplish your goals.

In his last days, the disciples in the room with Śrīla Prabhupāda heard him make a statement that beautifully sums up his mission: "Just go on discussing *Śrīmad-Bhāgavatam* among yourselves and everything will remain clear." He also enshrined this idea in one of the last purports he dictated: "Thus the more we read *Śrīmad-Bhāgavatam,* the more its knowledge becomes clear. Each and every verse is transcendental."[7]

Thus Śrīla Prabhupāda taught us how to get fresh energy in order to improve and increase by always reiterating the mission enshrined in his books. To read and distribute his books, then, is the essence of his mission.

Indeed, the effectiveness in conveying your organization's mission will determine how well your team unites and operates. Rick Warren, the founder of the highly successful Saddleback Baptist Church in Orange County, California, writes:

> One of your most important roles as a pastor is as vision caster. Sharing the vision of your church can't be a one-time event. The Bible says, "If people can't see what God is doing, they stumble all over themselves" (Proverbs 29:18, MSG).
>
> As the leader, God has called you to help your congregation see what God is doing in your midst.
>
> That's why you must continually put the vision of your church before your congregation – at least every 26 days. That's the *Nehemiah Principle.*
>
> In Nehemiah's story of rebuilding the wall around Jerusalem, halfway through the project people got discouraged and wanted to give up. Like many churches, they lost their sense of purpose and, as a result, became overwhelmed with fatigue, frustration, and fear. Nehemiah rallied the people back to work by reorganizing the project and recasting the vision. He reminded them of the importance of their work and reassured them that God would help them fulfill His purpose (Neh. 4:6–15).
>
> Although the wall took only 52 days to complete, the

> people became discouraged at the halfway point: just 26 days into the project! Nehemiah had to renew their vision.
>
> You've got to do that, too. It's amazing how quickly human beings – and churches – lose their sense of purpose and vision. Vision casting is not a task you do once and then forget about. You must *continually clarify* and *communicate* the vision of your church. This is the number one responsibility of leadership.[8]

Imagine what might happen if you were to randomly interview some of the people in your community or on your team about your mission? What would they tell you? Do the core members of your team and community know their team's mission? Do *you* know your team's mission?

If you don't, you should. Take time to define and write it down. Once you do, you'll feel new life and so will your team. With your mission statement in hand, you can read and reread it and thus not only encourage your team members but also attract new people to join your team.

The investment guru and legendary organizer Charles Schwab writes, "We are all salesmen every day of our lives. We are selling our ideas, our plans, our enthusiasms to those with whom we come in contact." Therefore, make the clarity of your mission the foundation of your organization and then sell it to others.

For if you don't have a clear mission, why would anyone else want to join you? Furthermore, even if you have a beautifully crafted mission statement, if you don't tell people about it, what use does it have?

Again, with this purpose in mind for his movement, Śrīla Prabhupāda consistently stressed the reading, discussing, and distributing of his books as the essence of our spiritual lives and the means for uplifting ourselves along with the rest of the world.

> Anyone, however, who tries sincerely to present *Bhagavad-gītā* as it is will advance in devotional activities and reach the pure

> devotional state of life. As a result of such pure devotion, he is sure to go back home, back to Godhead.[9]

French Renaissance author Michel de Montaigne writes about clarifying one's mission: "No wind favors he who has no destined port." Lewis Carroll in *Through the Looking Glass*, illustrates the same point in a dialogue:

> Alice: Which way should I go?
> Cat: That depends on where you are going.
> Alice: I don't know where I'm going!
> Cat: Then it doesn't matter which way you go.

Again, Rick Warren attributes his church's success to its clear mission: "I cannot overemphasize the importance of defining your church's purposes. It is not merely a target that you aim for; it is your congregation's reason for being."[10]

One's mission is also considered to be vital in the business world. For example, Guy Kawasaki, a venture capitalist and the original marketer of Apple products, in his book *Art of the Start,* lists the top three steps for starting a corporation: Make meaning; Make mantra; Get going. Here's how he defines these steps:

1. *Make meaning:* find a cause that inspires you and that makes the world a better place.
2. *Make mantra:* craft a pithy description of the spirit and purpose of your venture. For example: Nike: "Authentic athletic performance." Disney: "Fun family entertainment." IBM: "Think."
3. *Get going:* Don't wait until everything is perfect. Instead, move ahead with your project as soon as you've defined the meaning of your project and have created a mantra that embodies its spirit and purpose.[11]

Kawasaki prefers a mantra to a formal lengthy mission statement because a mantra is easy to understand and to propagate whereas a long mission statement tends to bog down the team.

Team ISV's mission statement: To serve all living beings by widely distributing the holy names, transcendental literature, and *kṛṣṇa-prasāda*.

Team ISV's mantra: Always Better Service.

Frame or Be Framed

Those who have not clearly defined their mission are sure to be dragged off course. That's why Kawasaki, like Rick Warren, recommends that leaders frame their organization or product by clearly and regularly relating why their organization exists. Inevitably, even those in the same organization will have conflicting ideas about what's important and why the organization was established. Therefore Kawasaki advises that leaders, "frame or be framed" – that is, unless you clearly define and display your mission, just as you would frame a picture and hang it in a prominent place, others will put up their own pictures of the way they think your organization should look and bifurcate and confuse your mission.

Not only does Śrīla Prabhupāda clearly frame his mission in The Seven Purposes of ISKCON, but he constantly reminds his followers of those purposes. For example, in a letter to Satsvarūpa Dāsa about *saṅkīrtana,* dated June 21, 1971, he frames his mission for outreach:

> *Saṅkīrtana* party and distribution of our magazines and books is our real program. Other things are secondary. So during the summer time you should utilize this program of *saṅkīrtana* and book distribution vigorously. Attention diverted to incense business is not a very good sign. We should give all our energy for distributing BTG.

Here Śrīla Prabhupāda has prioritized: books and magazines are the real program; other things are secondary. This is framing the mission. Those with a clear mission and a burning desire to fulfill it can do so by setting appropriate goals.

Setting Goals

The human mind chases a goal the way a heat-seeking missile pursues a jet engine. It's natural, then, that after making your mission clear, your mind will look for ways to achieve it. This leads us to the next fundamental phase of organizing: goal setting.

Regarding goal setting – which is a means to push ourselves to do better than we are doing now – the poet T. S. Eliot writes, "Only those who will risk going too far can possibly find out how far one can go."

For balance, you must set both quantitative and qualitative goals. For instance, one might set a goal to distribute a certain number of books within a given time period. The moment you set your mind on such a numerical goal, your mind will work, even as you sleep, to reach it.

But one must also make goals to improve the quality of one's presentation of Śrīla Prabhupāda's books. For example, I've seen devotees at ISV set goals to learn how to present a book in Mandarin, Vietnamese, Spanish, Farsi, or other languages. By setting qualitative goals, your team members not only become well-rounded but stay interested, because setting qualitative goals stimulates the imagination and intelligence.

To be effective, goals must be specific, measurable, achievable, and time-bound. There is power in setting deadlines on your goals – for example, things you will achieve within a week or a month or a year or in five years. Each deadline is effective in its own way.

The Magic of Setting Goals

Setting a goal is like flipping a light switch. When you flip on a light switch, electricity flows through the bulb and radiates light. Similarly, when you set a goal, your mind and intelligence at once consider how to reach it: creative energies stream through the subtle body, carrying images of practical steps one can take to reach your goal.

ISKCON leaders dedicated to distributing Śrīla Prabhupāda's books do not hesitate to flip this switch by making goals to distribute more books and to improve in the quality of how they are distributing them. In contrast, some managers may find themselves reluctant to set goals for distributing Śrīla Prabhupāda's books. Such leaders might find it helpful to examine their hearts to find the reasons they're not willing to make such a commitment.

In working with devotees, I've noticed that those willing and eager to set goals for distributing books make dramatic and rapid improvements. But those who are hesitant to set goals find it difficult to move forward. How can they move forward? They have nowhere to go.

In any case, progress begins at the most basic level: faith in one's cause. One's ability to set goals is determined by this faith. Kṛṣṇa Himself tells Brahmā, "Realization will correspond to the nature of one's faith."[12] Śrīla Bhaktisiddhānta Sarasvatī, in his commentary to this verse, writes: "The more transparent the faith, the greater the degree of realization." Śrīla Prabhupāda makes repeated statements such as this: "Our preaching work will be measured by the quantity of books we distribute, so continue ever-increasingly."[13] Faithful devotees take such statements to heart and regularly set goals to increase the numbers of books they distribute.

The Written Plan

Setting a goal starts one on a journey, and savvy travelers who embark on long journeys always take along a map. The map that guides us to reach our goals is our written plan. As a testament to the value of a written plan, Thomas Boone Pickens, an American business magnate and financier, states, "A fool with a plan can outsmart a genius with no plan any day."

Planning means to decide what you need to do to reach your goal and then to *write it down*. An early secretary of Śrīla Prabhupāda's in India, Tejīyas Dāsa, told me that Śrīla Prabhupāda insisted that his secretaries write everything down. Tejīyas recalls: "Śrīla Prabhupāda once called for me at 3:00 A.M., and when I came he asked me where my pen and paper was."

It is common knowledge that Śrīla Prabhupāda often said that in Kali-yuga, to forget means to forget to write it down. In different ways, other people say the same thing about the benefits of writing things down:

- What gets written gets done.
- What gets written gets improved.
- What gets measured gets managed.

The point is that one must commit one's plan to writing; otherwise, one's goals will remain in the mind – rarely to be realized. Writing down what needs to be done is so simple that people often forget to do it. Simple, but it takes effort. When I see that people are habituated to writing things down, knowing how important it is, I at once think, "These people are not only serious, they're organized."

All creations start from the subtle world of thought and then manifest themselves in progressively more solid forms. The act of transferring your plans from your mind to paper makes them more tangible and commanding. A person with a list of action items in hand moves from the realm of daydreams to that of doing.

For example, you might write the following simple plan: "I'll organize a brainstorming session in my community to develop ideas about starting a team of book distributors." Next, you might break down this plan into small, doable parts:

- Set a date
- Decide on the venue for the meeting
- Make a list of possible participants
- Send email invitations to possible participants.

And so on ...

Experts at organizing agree that one should work from a list. For example, Brian Tracy writes: "Always work from a list. When something new comes up, add it to the list before you do it. You can increase your productivity and output by 25 percent or more from the first day you begin working consistently from a list." Śrīla Prabhupāda's room in Vṛndāvana contains museum cases. In one of them is a small booklet containing Śrīla Prabhupāda's goals and a to-do list written in his own hand.

Following this practice of writing down the details of your plan on paper or in electronic form and ticking off the to-do's as you accomplish them will keep you moving forward toward your goals. You'll be efficient and make progress like never before – by carrying out your plan.

Carry Out Your Plan

The famous military leader George S. Patton used to say: "A good plan executed today is better than a perfect plan executed next week."

That's the spirit of Kawasaki's third step to starting a business: *get going*. This advice is important in all works of creation; that is, don't wait until your vision, mission, goals, and plans are perfect. All of these can be adjusted later, as needed.

Śrīla Prabhupāda spoke about Lord Caitanya's penchant for action on a morning walk on December 5, 1973:

> Caitanya Mahāprabhu is God Himself. He comes down to preach, to become *sannyāsī,* and to take so much trouble all over India and everywhere, and giving instruction and

> sending men, "Go, go, go, go" ... Why He's coming? He doesn't require. No. For the benefit of others, we must follow the footsteps of Caitanya Mahāprabhu.

Following in the footsteps of Mahāprabhu means one should "go, go, go, go." Go, go, go, go means to carry out the mission. You should start carrying out your plan as soon as possible with the aim to improve as you go. Moving in this way, making incremental improvements, anyone can build a book distribution juggernaut.

Incremental Improvements

Good organizers draw on this mantra: "Everything and everyone counts." Even the tiniest of improvements is important, because each improvement compounds – after the fashion of bank interest – and each person's contribution counts.

Good managers therefore have a "bias for action."[14] They begin working on their plan at once and constantly try to spot places needing improvement. They know that each tiny incremental improvement starts a chain reaction of enhancements.

In sports, business, management, and any other discipline, one "wins in the margin." The famous photo finish in track and field or horseracing reveals that the victor often wins "by a nose." In finance those who intelligently negotiate even slightly higher interest rates over time end up with compounded gains significantly greater than those who settle for a lower rate of return.

Don't fail to do all that you can in the moment, even if you can't do everything you want to do. Even the smallest improvement keeps one moving in the right direction and over time has dramatic effects. What's more, organizers who look for and make incremental improvements find ways to systematize them. Creating systems therefore, is another aspect of astute organizing.

Create Systems

A system is a set of connected things or parts forming a complex whole. The successful fresh-juice franchise Jamba Juice uses systems well. At Jamba you can see for yourself what a good system looks like. As you walk in to a Jamba shop, the first thing you see is a menu of juices above the service counter. After you've chosen your juice, a person behind the counter takes both your order and your payment. The worker enters your order into a computer, and the order is relayed to a clearly visible computer screen, in front of which attendants are standing by to make the blend of juice you ordered. The workers add the fruits and other ingredients using measuring cups and spoons. Every ingredient and tool is lined up in sequence so that the workers don't have to backtrack, guess, or waste any movements. As a result, the customer's juice comes out quickly and perfectly mixed and presented.

Such systems take time to design and institute, but once they're in place, the operation hums. When organizers neglect such details, however, the operation has ragged edges that lead to annoying and costly mistakes – and to lost customers. I once attended a Monthly Saṅkīrtana Festival at which the team members were held back from their outing for more than an hour because the organizers had failed to plan the transportation in advance.

At ISV, a devotee on our book distribution team found that by using WhatsApp, an instant messaging application for smart phones, he could better keep in touch with his team members while out distributing books. Afterward, he brought up his innovation on a conference call. WhatsApp soon became a standard system for ISV's teams. WhatsApp had been available for months, but it took a team member to systematize its use in our organization. Now that it's a system, it has considerably increased the efficiency of our teams' communications.

Each new system that your team creates saves everyone

both time and money. These economies soon begin to show up in the overall results. As you build systems, you'll also need to invest in tools to maintain them.

Get the Right and Best Tools

The most important mantras about getting tools for your project are:

Get the right tools for the job.
Get the best tools available that money can buy.

For example, book distributors need a way to carry their books. At ISV, after much research we found that the *JanSport Driver 8,* a backpack with wheels, was the best tool for carrying books. This backpack is more expensive than most others, but because it does the best job for the distributors, we invested in it anyway. It also comes with a lifetime warranty. By investing in these backpacks for all the distributors, we've saved them a lot of bodily wear and tear from lugging books on their shoulders. And by spending more in the beginning, we not only got more out of the product but also saved money in the end.

There are myriad tools, including software needed to track and stay in touch with people, good shoes, and proper hats to protect the distributors from the sun.

Employ the Principles

By employing these seven principles of organization for distributing Śrīla Prabhupāda's books, you will dramatically increase your results:

1. Brainstorm
2. Define your mission
3. Set goals

4. Plan
5. Execute
6. Create efficient systems
7. Get the right tools

A while back, when I visited ISKCON Alachua, Florida, to conduct a book distribution seminar, I witnessed how important organizing is for increasing the distribution of Śrīla Prabhupāda's books.

Caitanya Dāsī, an Alachua local, volunteered to help me put on the seminar, which would include taking a large group of devotees out to distribute books. She worked tirelessly before my arrival to reach the manager of one of Alachua's biggest grocery stores and secure a permit so we could distribute books from a display table near the front door – something that had never been done before. When she finally reached the manager, he asked her to fill out paperwork and submit samples of the books we would be selling. It took weeks, but she finally obtained the needed paperwork, filled it out, and sent it back to the manager, along with the required samples of Śrīla Prabhupāda's books. She repeated this process at other venues.

After all that hard work, she finally secured several venues. Next, she gathered all the paraphernalia that the seminar's participants would need to make nice displays during their outings: tables with professional bookracks, baskets for carrying the *prasāda,* drinking water to keep the distributors hydrated while in the hot sun, and so forth.

Caitanya Dāsī then made posters advertising the event, repeatedly made announcements to the Alachua community, signed up those eager to participate, placed their names on a chart, and assigned each devotee a time for distributing books.

In fact, her work of organizing, assisted by dozens of devotees behind the scenes, showed up in the results. In one day at each of the venues she had secured, team members peacefully distributed hundreds of Śrīla Prabhupāda's books and large quantities of *prasāda*. Because the distributors had permits and were authorized, they felt comfortable taking time to meet and get to know shoppers from the local area, some of whom later came to visit their local ISKCON community.

And even more important was that Caitanya Dāsī learned much about the process of getting permits, setting up book displays, and so on. For future events she would therefore be able to systematize the process to save even more valuable time and money. Indeed, the kind of work she did is foundationally important to the expansion of book distribution and the Kṛṣṇa consciousness movement. Śrīla Prabhupāda encouraged his devotees to invest their time and energy in such organizational work to expand the distribution of his books. He even invested money from the BBT to help with such organizing.

A devotional community is a center where devotees come together to glorify Kṛṣṇa and enact the six loving exchanges. From that base we are meant to go out and invite other people to join us. Śrīla Prabhupāda set up his temples to act as such bases, but for them to do so they too must be organized. A well-organized temple attracts increasing numbers of people to come and taste the sublime atmosphere. In fact, organization done locally is later implemented globally. It is therefore said, "Think globally, work locally."

Embrace this fourth law of book distribution and see for yourself how through organizing you can grow from a one-person operation to a thriving team of distributors who cover the earth with Śrīla Prabhupāda's transcendental books.

Organizing is a discipline that requires constant effort. But the more time and effort one spends organizing, the less time and effort one wastes. And the less time and effort one wastes, the more time one has to hear and chant about Kṛṣṇa and to bring others into His loving network.

CHAPTER EIGHTEEN

Mood and Method

PEOPLE HAVE PLACES to go and things to do, and most of them are in a hurry. Due to their advanced intelligence, they also have perspectives unique to themselves. So when devotees go out into the public to distribute transcendental books and the holy names, they must be prepared for the great challenge of leaving everyone they meet with a good impression.

In the *Gītā* (12.13–14) Lord Kṛṣṇa describes the mood of a real devotee:

> One who is not envious but is a kind friend to all living entities, who does not think himself a proprietor and is free from false ego, who is equal in both happiness and distress, who is tolerant, always satisfied, self-controlled, and engaged in devotional service with determination, his mind and intelligence fixed on Me – such a devotee of Mine is very dear to Me. He for whom no one is put into difficulty and who is not disturbed by anyone, who is equipoised in happiness and distress, fear and anxiety, is very dear to Me.

Everything devotees say and do to bring people closer to Kṛṣṇa matters. People notice not only what devotees say but also how they say it. People notice how devotees behave, whether we are aware of it or not. When devotees go out as ambassadors of goodwill, with the intention to befriend people, to give them priceless gifts, and to benefit their souls, people feel it.

Our Prime Objective

Therefore, at all our seminars on distributing books I stress that our prime objective is to leave everyone we meet with a good impression. Our credo goes like this: "People will remember and tell others about the experience they had with me. Therefore, I must always do my best to leave each person I meet with a good impression."

Even when people scorn us, we should tolerate that scorn and give affectionate respect in return. This is a preacher's *sādhana*. Never losing poise, we stand up for our philosophy and our devotees without malice and with integrity.

Śrīla Prabhupāda writes:

> Similarly, all preachers will have to meet opponents, but they should not make them more inimical. They are already enemies, and if we talk with them harshly or impolitely their enmity will merely increase. We should therefore follow in the footsteps of Lord Caitanya Mahāprabhu as far as possible and try to convince the opposition by quoting from the *śāstras* and presenting the conclusion of the *ācāryas.* It is in this way that we should try to defeat all the enemies of the Lord.[1]

And what better way could there be to clarify śāstric conclusions than to present people with Śrīla Prabhupāda's books? Those who distribute his books must always remember that the service they have accepted is a great honor, a privilege. Not everyone has the good fortune to distribute Śrīla Prabhupāda's books. Those who have the privilege should approach their service in the proper mood.

The word *mood* is defined as "the atmosphere or pervading tone of something; inducing or suggestive of a particular feeling or state of mind." The proper mood can be taught – we can learn it.

In the beginning days of ISV I spoke to a group of young devotees going out on book distribution for the first time on their own after four weeks of instruction. Before they left, I asked them, "So, what is your primary goal?"

"To distribute books!" someone replied.

"No," I said, "that's your secondary goal. Your primary goal is to leave every person you meet with a good impression. Whether the person takes a book or doesn't take a book, whether the person is a local or a visitor, whether the person is friendly or inimical, you must do your best to leave that person with a good impression. Leave everybody with a gift, whether it be a book, some *prasāda,* the holy name, or simply a smile. For those who are antagonistic, your gift may simply be a cheerful 'Thanks anyway' or 'It was a pleasure meeting you.' Please go out in this mood and leave every single person with the feeling that you are a *sādhu,* a person with spiritual values. This is the goal."

When the team returned from their day's work, their leader wrote: "We made a good impression on many people: the shopkeepers, the police, and everyone else we met. We distributed *prasāda* to all the local workers, and they were happy. And by the way, we also distributed all of our books."

Besides building a good image of the Kṛṣṇa consciousness movement, one person at a time, the practice of leaving people with a good impression also keeps our distributors thinking in terms of our movement's long-term interests. Leaving people with a good impression requires that a distributor check his or her false ego in the interest of the greater mission.

Here are some of the mantras we promote at ISV to remind

ourselves to stay in the proper mood while going out on book distribution:

- Teaching Kṛṣṇa consciousness means giving.
- I am in the business of serving.
- I distribute books for self-purification.
- I save one soul at a time, beginning with myself.
- I treat people with respect.
- I express gratitude and thanks to the people I meet, live with, and associate with.
- I am Kṛṣṇa's instrument.
- Every person is special, and I remind them that they are.
- I make friends with as many people as possible.
- I am a team player.

Methods

Regarding how to present his books, Śrīla Prabhupāda wrote to Govinda Dāsa on December 25, 1972: "There is sufficient merit in our books that if you simply describe them sincerely to anyone, they will buy." Śrīla Prabhupāda personally distributed his own books and magazines throughout India before coming to America. In New Delhi, for example, he sold his *Back to Godhead* at tea stalls and hand-delivered copies to donors around the city. And while doing all this, he contemplated what to say in order to persuade people to accept his literature. He also heard and dealt with many of the objections that book distributors deal with today. For example, in one of those early BTG articles, Śrīla Prabhupāda writes: "When we approach some gentleman and request him to become a reader of 'Back to Godhead,' sometimes we are replied with the words 'NO TIME.'"

In another BTG article from the same period, he writes: "Sometime we meet gentlemen of up-to-date taste and try to make them interested in the matter of 'Back to Godhead'...

they say very frankly that they have not only no interest in such theistic subject but also they condemn the attempt to bring back people in general to the path of 'Back to Godhead.'"

During Śrīla Prabhupāda's first year in America, he continued to sell his books at every opportunity. As his disciples took up the distribution of his books, it was natural for him to want to hear what they were telling people and how people were responding.

Tripurāri Swami remembers:

> On morning walks Śrīla Prabhupāda used to ask me, "So, Tripurāri Mahārāja, what are they saying?" That was his standard kind of question to me, because he knew I was always in the field preaching to people, distributing literature, and so forth. He knew that I would need arguments to counteract the people's objections to taking the books, and he was curious what their arguments were. Each time Prabhupāda asked me I would give one or two of their arguments, and Prabhupāda would defeat them in an enlightening way.

One of the most successful American book distributors was Mulāprakriti Devī Dāsī. She recounts a conversation she had with Śrīla Prabhupāda one day in Los Angeles when he asked her what she and other distributors were telling people about his books: "We say to people, 'You look like a spiritual person. This is a book from ancient India on spiritual knowledge.'"

Śrīla Prabhupāda took out a First Canto *Śrīmad-Bhāgavatam,* turned to a verse, and slowly read it aloud: "This *Bhāgavata Purāṇa* is as brilliant as the sun, and it has arisen just after the departure of Lord Kṛṣṇa to His own abode.... Persons who have lost their vision due to the dense darkness of ignorance in this Age of Kali shall get light from this *Purāṇa.*"[2]

He then turned to Mulāprakriti and said, "If you just tell people this one verse, it is so wonderful. How could they resist? The *Śrīmad-Bhāgavatam* will sell itself."

Kūrma Dāsa, author of *The Great Transcendental Adventure,* gives another example of a phrase that Śrīla Prabhupāda personally suggested, this time to a disciple in Australia: "These books will help you to solve all the problems and miseries of life and save you from so much suffering."[3]

After hearing Śrīla Prabhupāda advise that we present his books on their own merit and even suggest a verse from the *Śrīmad-Bhāgavatam* with which to explain the books, many distributors in those days took up this practice.

Here's how I took it up: I would greet people, hand them one of Śrīla Prabhupāda's books, and recite the verse Prabhupāda had suggested to Mulāprakriti. I also memorized other verses from *Śrīmad-Bhāgavatam* and regularly recited them while presenting his books. Here's one that people really seem to like to hear:

> Completely rejecting all religious activities which are materially motivated, this *Bhāgavata Purāṇa* propounds the highest truth, which is understandable by those devotees who are fully pure in heart. The highest truth is reality distinguished from illusion for the welfare of all. Such truth uproots the threefold miseries. This beautiful *Bhāgavatam,* compiled by the great sage Vyāsadeva [in his maturity], is sufficient in itself for God realization. What is the need of any other scripture? As soon as one attentively and submissively hears the message of *Bhāgavatam,* by this culture of knowledge the Supreme Lord is established within his heart.[4]

Sometimes when I'm distributing Śrīla Prabhupāda's books I meet people who express an aversion to "organized religion." I respond by saying, "Perfect! This book completely rejects all religious activities that are materially motivated." I then recite the rest of the verse. Most of the time, this satisfies their objection and they accept the book.

This verse says so much and provides a complete introduction to any one of Śrīla Prabhupāda's books. If you are showing a book other than the *Bhāgavatam,* you can substitute the name of the book you are showing and use the same verse, and it will still be relevant.

In the nineteenth century, Śrīla Bhaktivinoda Ṭhākura single-handedly reestablished the authenticity of Lord Caitanya's *saṅkīrtana* movement, reviving our family business by establishing a printing press and then writing and publishing more than one hundred books on the science of Kṛṣṇa consciousness. One book, *Lord Caitanya: His Life and Precepts,* he sent to libraries in the West, proving that the *saṅkīrtana* movement was meant to go international.

I've noticed over the years that many people listen carefully to such scriptural presentations, ask questions about what you've said, and then gladly take a book. Meanwhile, both hearer and presenter get to listen to the pure vibration of *Śrīmad-Bhāgavatam.*

Śukadeva Gosvāmī says, "The Ganges, emanating from the toe of Lord Viṣṇu, purifies the three worlds, the upper, middle, and lower planetary systems. Similarly, when one asks questions about the pastimes and characteristics of Lord Vāsudeva, Kṛṣṇa, three varieties of men are purified: the speaker or preacher, he who inquires, and the people in general who listen."[5]

The best way to learn to distribute Śrīla Prabhupāda's books, then, is to read and hear from them attentively each day and then present what one has heard and realized. Anyone who follows this method will be successful and blissful wherever he or she goes.

This process is not mechanical. The enthusiasm to go out and distribute the books, as well as the inspiration to find the right words to say to people spring from a devotee's deep appreciation of what's in the books and the taste one has acquired for reading them and following the principles they contain.

As devotees pore over Śrīla Prabhupāda's books, hearing and reading from them with care, they find compelling phrases and fashion them into *sūtras* – concise, eloquent statements that convey principles – and use these *sūtras* as persuasive tools to induce people to buy the books. As they sift through Śrīla Prabhupāda's books and lectures, looking for these phrases, they resemble miners panning for gold nuggets in a mountain stream.

This is how Saṅkīrtana-yajña Dāsa, for example, explains the *Bhagavad-gītā* in a nutshell to college students: "This is about a guy who hated his job, and he was so stressed out that he wanted to quit. After hearing this book he became peaceful, he loved his job, and did it with even greater skill than before. What changed? He didn't change his job, he didn't change his clothes; he changed his heart. Read this book. It will bring you new insight and energy."

Here's another example. Recently, on a hot day, I overheard a distributor saying this while distributing a book: "These books are ice-cold refreshment for the soul. They quench one's thirst for higher consciousness." Such presentations remind me of a verse from *Śrī Caitanya-caritāmṛta:* "Essential truth spoken concisely is true eloquence."[6]

One aspect of distributing books that gives prospective distributors pause is the need to ask for a donation for the book. As I will explain in some detail in "The Penny Principle," asking for a donation in return for a transcendental book brings immense benefits to the donor. Śrīla Prabhupāda summarizes the principle behind this statement: "Our policy is that his money, which would have been used for purchasing cigarettes, liquor, sex literature, meat, will give him the opportunity to gradually become purified.... If we can take some money and give some literature, that is a good service."[7]

Here is the best advice I can give about asking for donations. First, keep in mind that those who give something get great benefit and are much more likely to value the book. Second, clearly explain why you are asking. For example, after showing a book, here is what I say to request a donation:

> We don't sell these books like they do in stores. Instead we accept a donation. We don't need the money. We ask because it's an ancient tradition to give something in return for spiritual knowledge. Giving connects you to the previous teachers who have painstakingly passed down this wisdom over many generations, and their blessings allow the donor to enter deeply into the subject matter.

People often ask what their donation will be used for. I tell them that it goes toward the cost of producing and printing the book and our work to make the world a better place. I also like to read them this part of Śrīla Prabhupāda's mission statement: "To systematically propagate spiritual knowledge to society at large, and to educate all people in the techniques of spiritual life in order to check the imbalance of values in life and to achieve real unity and peace in the world."

I recommend that distributors keep this mission statement on a printed card, because most people like it very much when they hear it. You can then give them a little bonus by gifting them the card.

After selling a book I ask the recipients if they believe in the power of prayer. If they say, "Yes," I say, "Great, I'll teach you a prayer that is meant to wake up pure love for God in your heart." If they say, "No," I say, "Great, I'll teach you a mantra." Next, I hand them a card with the *mahā-mantra* on it and ask them to repeat after me. I then recite the *mahā-mantra* and have them follow, two names at a time:

Hare Kṛṣṇa Hare Kṛṣṇa
Kṛṣṇa Kṛṣṇa Hare Hare
Hare Rāma Hare Rāma
Rāma Rāma Hare Hare

After they repeat the *mahā-mantra* I give them *kṛṣṇa-prasāda* and thank them for their valuable time. I also ask them if they are interested in staying connected or finding out more about bhakti-yoga. If they are, I take down their name and contact information so that we can stay in touch with them.

Meeting People Who Don't Speak Your Language

Kṛṣṇa speaks Sanskrit and *sauraseni,* the language of the residents of Vraja and Mathurā, but He also speaks the languages of the animals and all the human languages in the universe. We can't imitate Kṛṣṇa, of course, but *saṅkīrtana* devotees can learn at least some words in the languages of the people they are likely to meet. The world is becoming smaller by the day, so we are more likely to meet people traveling internationally wherever we go. Simply knowing how to say things like "hello" and "thank you" in people's native tongues makes a strong impression on them and opens their hearts. Knowing a few key words in different languages and, if possible, carrying Śrīla Prabhupāda's books translated into those languages, are all you need for success.

It's also helpful to use the smartphone app "Google Translate" to help you say what you'd like to say to people of different nationalities. And it's a good idea to ask a favorable person who speaks a language you're likely to encounter to write out a message on a card so that you can show it to those who speak that language.

Distributing eBooks

Distributors often meet people who prefer eBooks to print books. Now many mass distribution titles are being published as print/eBook combos. On the back cover of books the BBT prints a note alerting readers that the book contains a redemption code for a free download of the same title in eBook format. All readers have to do is go to bbtmedia.com, enter their redemption code, and within seconds they have their eBook formatted to work on the device of their choice. For those who want only the eBook, the distributor can tell them to buy the print book, use their code, and pass the printed book onto a friend.

Sending interested people to a website featuring Śrīla Prabhupāda's books extends the book distributor's reach. Instead of being limited by the choice of books the distributor is carrying, a book buyer can see all that the BBT has to offer.

The Smart Box

In this chapter I could write about many more methods for distributing Śrīla Prabhupāda's books, methods such as the Smart Table, corporate *saṅkīrtana,* traveling *saṅkīrtana,* and many more. There are as many ways to present Śrīla Prabhupāda's books as there are people who distribute them, but in this section I wish to discuss only the Smart Box.

The Smart Box is a vending system for selling Śrīla Prabhupāda's books. Devotees have had great success with Smart Boxes in a number of countries. Ask permission to place a small display of books, along with a locked box attached to the display, where people can leave donations. Ask stores, boutiques, restaurants, and wherever it seems there is a lot of foot traffic. The Smart Box is placed in a visible location with a sign inviting people to take a book (all marked with price stickers) and to place their donation in the box. The sign can also include a short message about the benefits of reading books of spiritual knowledge. It's an honor system that works anywhere. All that's needed is a good location and a volunteer to regularly pick up the donations and replenish the book supply.

I invite you to visit ourfamilybusiness.info and let us know how you distribute Śrīla Prabhupāda's books. Come share and learn.

Śrīla Kṛṣṇadāsa Kavirāja Gosvāmī writes, "I am a very insignificant living being, like a small red-beaked bird. Just as such a bird drinks the water of the sea to quench its thirst, so I have touched only a drop of the ocean of Śrī Caitanya Mahāprabhu's pastimes. From this example, you may all understand how expansive are the pastimes of Śrī Caitanya Mahāprabhu."[8]

As an aspiring servant of that red-beaked bird, I've given only a small sample in this chapter from the ocean of possible methods for distributing Śrīla Prabhupāda's books. But listing them all is not necessary, because Śrīla Prabhupāda told us that our main method for distributing books is sincerity and a willingness to read the books ourselves, and to sell them on their own merit. These are things you can do in your own way, wherever you may be.

CHAPTER NINETEEN

Distributing Books Door to Door

A DOOR IS AN ENTRYWAY to somewhere. In the *Gītā* Lord Kṛṣṇa says that our bodies are like cities and our senses doors to the outside world, and each of us can choose what we let in or out through those doors.

The homes in which humans live have doors, too, and whatever those people let in through their doors guides their destiny. People who open their doors to devotees distributing Śrīla Prabhupāda's books get a rare opportunity to let in the spiritual world.

Unless people are given an opportunity to open their senses to the beauty of Kṛṣṇa, whatever they see, hear, taste, smell, or feel – all of which is made of the same inert elements of earth, water, fire, air, and ether, in myriad combinations and permutations – will simply perpetuate their confusion about who they are and what will make them happy.

When Lord Caitanya's devotees pass by long lines of doors in neighborhoods filled with houses and apartments, they feel an urge to approach those doors and meet the people behind them, and to leave those people with something that will bring them true good fortune.

In fact, door-to-door *saṅkīrtana* is a Vaiṣṇava tradition. Lord Caitanya used to send out all His followers daily door to door to preach *Śrīmad-Bhāgavatam*. More recently, Śrīla Bhaktivinoda Ṭhākura went door to door to spread Kṛṣṇa consciousness: "Śrīla Bhaktivinoda retired from his government position and personally went door to door in Calcutta to raise funds for the construction of a temple memorializing Lord Caitanya's birthplace."[1]

The efforts of devotees who go door to door today are particularly fruitful because they can not only meet people and tell them about Kṛṣṇa, they can leave them with Śrīla Prabhupāda's transcendental literatures. These books will often stay in people's homes for generations, bringing good fortune to the family members and their guests.

Devotees sometimes describe Śrīla Prabhupāda's transcendental books as spiritual time bombs. Whenever I remember this I envision my door-to-door distribution as a military exercise. Just as soldiers in the First World War crawled up to enemy bunkers and tossed in hand grenades, so book distributors make their way to people and "toss" Śrīla Prabhupāda's books into their hands. After I successfully get a book into someone's home, sometimes scenes of war movies I watched as a child come to mind. The brave infantryman stealthily approaches a fortified bunker and, after tossing in a hand grenade, covers his head as the grenade explodes and fire and smoke pour from the obliterated bunker. I imagine Śrīla Prabhupāda's books suffusing people's homes with spiritual energy and obliterating their anxieties and miseries forever.

Here's a behind-the-scenes look at what happens when devotees distribute Śrīla Prabhupāda's books door to door. In Italy, a book distributor sold a *Kṛṣṇa Book* to a housewife. The woman was pious, but she had no idea what the book was about. Still, she appreciated that the devotee selling it was religious and therefore gave him a donation and accepted the book. Even though she wasn't interested in reading the book, she had a son whose birthday was coming up, so she gift-wrapped the *Kṛṣṇa Book* and gave it to him as a present.

Her son was incredulous when he saw the unusual book. To him, *Kṛṣṇa Book,* with its picture of Rādhā and Kṛṣṇa on the front cover and an Indian guru on the back seemed so incongruous. He had not asked for such a gift; nor was he interested in it. Still, out of respect for his mother he accepted the book and kept it in his room.

A year later, out of curiosity he lifted *Kṛṣṇa Book* off his shelf and looked at the pictures. They piqued his interest. Gradually, he developed the habit of occasionally looking at the paintings. Next he started reading small sections from the book, gradually but with some interest. He explains what happened next: "Miraculously, after I began reading *Kṛṣṇa Book,* I met the devotees while I was in town one day. It's a long story, but one thing led to another and I ended up joining ISKCON as a full-time devotee. Now my service is distributing books."

That young man has since been initiated as Citta-hārī Dāsa, "Servant of the Lord in the heart." What a befitting name for one whose path back to Godhead was so obviously lit up by the Supersoul, who from within the heart sent a devotee to Citta-hārī's door and prompted his mother to give him *Kṛṣṇa Book* as a gift.

At first this story might sound extraordinary, but hundreds of distributors will tell you that it's just the kind of thing that happens when Śrīla Prabhupāda's books enter people's homes.

Citta-hārī's story also points to another reason that door-to-door book distribution is so effective: the books are well placed. The BBT prints millions of books annually, and devotees try to distribute them in places where people are most likely to read them. When we distribute books in public places, however, it may take them longer to reach their readers. That's not the case when one distributes books door to door.

There's no question, therefore, that door-to-door book distribution is a boon. That may be why Śrīla Prabhupāda advocates in literally hundreds of places throughout his purports, lectures, and letters that members of the Kṛṣṇa consciousness movement go door to door to give people transcendental knowledge. For example:

> A devotee travels all over the country, from door to door, preaching, "Be Kṛṣṇa conscious. Be a devotee of Lord Kṛṣṇa. Don't spoil your life in simply fulfilling your animal propensities. Human life is meant for self-realization, or Kṛṣṇa consciousness."[2]

> The preachers of Kṛṣṇa consciousness go from door to door to inform people how they can be relieved from the miserable conditions of material life.[3]

> Every member of the Kṛṣṇa consciousness movement is interested in going door to door to try to convince people about the teachings of *Bhagavad-gītā As It Is,* the teachings of Lord Caitanya. That is the purpose of the Hare Kṛṣṇa movement.[4]

> Our ... Kṛṣṇa consciousness movement is simply to make propaganda from door to door, that "Please chant Hare Kṛṣṇa mantra." That's all.[5]

Before coming to America, Śrīla Prabhupāda personally went door to door to sell his *Back to Godhead* magazine and to engage people in Lord Caitanya's *saṅkīrtana* movement. Those who go door to door to distribute Śrīla Prabhupāda's books not only follow in his and the other great *ācāryas'* footsteps but get to taste the sweetness of meeting people in their own homes and introducing them to Kṛṣṇa consciousness. There are millions of doors to knock on all over the world, and behind each of them someone is sitting, waiting for someone to bring them something that can relieve them from the painful boredom of material existence.

Advantages of Going Door to Door

Here are a few features that make door-to-door book distribution especially advantageous.

PEOPLE FEEL SAFE AT HOME

At home people feel safe because they're in their own environment surrounded by their own things. When one knocks on a door, therefore, the residents are generally relaxed and able to concentrate on what you are presenting to them. What's more, at home, a person can make a preemptive decision not to talk to the distributor simply by not opening the door. This saves time and energy for both the distributor and the resident. Also, if residents are not interested in what the distributor is presenting after they have opened the door, they can simply say so and shut the door. But once people open their doors, they usually take the time to listen, and they sometimes invite the distributor in.

IN FAIR OR FOUL WEATHER

Door-to-door book distribution can be done even in bad weather. When the weather is bad, people are more likely to be home.

IT'S EASIER TO ESTABLISH RELATIONSHIPS WITH FAVORABLE PEOPLE

One of the best things about distributing books door to door is that when you meet favorable people you automatically know where they live. It's then easier to establish and maintain relationships. For instance, you might visit them again, bring them *prasāda* and more books, or come back to personally invite them to events, such as local home or temple programs.

WE'RE CALLED TO PRAY

Behind each door is something unknown. So going door to door leaves you dependent and called to pray. Since the success of each encounter depends on Kṛṣṇa's grace, distributors may take each door they approach as an opportunity to pray for Lord Caitanya's help. I have noticed that in the moments between my knocking on a door and the door opening my heart speeds up slightly in anticipation. I have also found this juncture to be an excellent time to ask Lord Caitanya to allow me to act as His instrument and do something nice for whomever opens the door.

Think about the number of prayers you might offer Lord Caitanya when approaching countless doors.

Tips for Going Door to Door

BE PREPARED

Be prepared with a variety of books, including foreign-language books and full sets of *Śrīmad-Bhāgavatam* and *Śrī Caitanya-caritāmṛta,* because you are sure to meet a wide variety of people.

CARRY FREEBIES

Carry fliers that include basic concepts about the soul, yoga, meditation, the chanting process, and so on. The fliers should also contain your local temple's or group's contact information, including directions for reaching it, a program schedule, and so on. It's also nice to have a flyer you can leave at the doorstep, whether the residents take books or not, or when they're not at home or don't open the door.

CHOOSE THE RIGHT NEIGHBORHOOD

Visiting apartments is usually better than going to houses,

because apartments are close together in a single building, making it easier to contact more people in a shorter period of time.

We've also found that there tend to be differences in the responses we get based on the socioeconomics of various areas. We've found, for example, that upscale neighborhoods tend to be more insular, their residents less inclined to unannounced visitors.

Śrīla Prabhupāda writes about this phenomenon in the tenth chapter of *Kṛṣṇa Book:*

> A poor man is seldom puffed up with false pride, and he may be freed from all kinds of infatuation. He may remain satisfied by whatever he gets for his maintenance by the grace of the Lord.... Another advantage of poverty is that a saintly person can easily enter a poor man's house, and thus the poor man can take advantage of the saintly person's association. A very opulent man does not allow anyone to enter his house; therefore, the saintly person cannot enter. According to the Vedic system, a saintly person takes the position of a mendicant so that on the plea of begging something from the householder, he can enter any house. The householder, who has usually forgotten everything about spiritual advancement because he is busy maintaining family affairs, can be benefited by the association of a saintly person. There is a great chance for the poor man to become liberated through association with a saint. Of what use are persons who are puffed up with material opulence and prestige if they are bereft of the association of saintly persons and devotees of the Supreme Personality of Godhead?

Śrīla Prabhupāda was not one to discriminate between classes of people, however. In fact, he often said that rich people need Kṛṣṇa too – in some ways even more so than the poor or middle class. So my suggestion about which neighborhoods are best for distribution is just a general rule of thumb, and you'll have to see what's best for your region and taste. In Toronto, for example, the ISKCON temple is in one of the wealthiest neighborhoods in the city. Some years ago, one of

ISKCON Toronto's leaders went door to door in that neighborhood to visit these wealthiest of Canadian citizens in their mansions. The devotee felt a strong sense of compassion, and wanted these materially fortunate people to also have the opportunity to hear about Lord Caitanya. So there are no hard and fast rules when it comes to the class of people one should approach.

ALWAYS GO OUT WITH OTHERS

It's always better to go door to door in the association of other distributors. It's safer and more fun to go at least in pairs. We've also noticed that people are more inclined to open their doors when they see, for instance, a husband and wife with their children outside their doors.

DRESS FOR SUCCESS

Dress nicely. Over the years, studies have consistently shown that people notice and judge you by how you are dressed. An article in *Psychology Today* makes the case for dressing well: "Our clothes make a huge difference to what people think about us – and without us knowing or in ways we couldn't even imagine. People make their assessments in the first few seconds of seeing another [person]."[6]

When you go out, it's best to wear what you're comfortable in – whether that's Vaiṣṇava dress or neat and clean secular clothing. If you're comfortable in what you're wearing, you'll be comfortable meeting people.

APPROACHING A DOOR

As I approach someone's door, I think of the people inside as long-lost friends whom I'm coming to meet again. I hold this feeling in my heart until the residents open their doors, then let the feeling out and greet the residents with the warmth I would have for such loved ones. I also remember that I'm speaking to spiritual beings who are dear to Kṛṣṇa and with whom I share an eternal kinship.

KNOCK, KNOCK

There's an old saying that friends knock and strangers ring the doorbell, so I usually knock. After knocking, if the door has a peephole I keep my eyes glued to it, because when the peephole changes from light to dark I know a person has come to look through it. The moment I see this, I smile and wave to let the person know I'm friendly.

If no one responds the first time I knock, I knock again to give the residents a second chance. If I hear a loud television or music blaring inside, I don't hesitate to knock loudly.

Sometimes, before opening their doors, residents will ask from inside, "Who is it?" I am straightforward in my reply, something like, "We're from the local ISKCON temple and we're showing books on yoga and meditation all over the neighborhood." Or, "We're showing books on yoga."

Many times the person will shout back through the door, "No thank you." If this happens, it's usually best to thank them and move on to another door. But when people actually open the door, greet them and hand them a business card that shows the name and address of your temple, center, or group.

KEEPING TRACK

Keep a record of all the areas you visit with notes about people's responses and any other information that will be useful in the future. A contact logbook will help you notice and keep track of patterns in your door-to-door book distribution. Important to list are "took book," "no answer," "rejected," "not interested," etc.

When you meet people interested in knowing more about Kṛṣṇa consciousness, ask them for their name, phone number, and email address and record them in your log. When asking for personal information, you can say something like, "If you'd like to receive information, about events on yoga and meditation or events at our temple/center, we can add you to our mailing list. Would you like to give us your contact information?"

It's also helpful to note people's interest level on a scale from 1–10, with 1 meaning slight interest and 10 meaning they're ready to start practicing Kṛṣṇa consciousness.

Any other information you can record about the people's backgrounds, situations, and so on goes a long way when you contact them a second time. It's also important to write down what books they bought and how much they donated.

Keep an accurate inventory of books before and after you go out to distribute each time. This will tell you how many of each book you sold that day. Be sure to report your book scores to your local *saṅkīrtana* leader or directly to the "Saṅkīrtana Newsletter." Keep meticulous accounts of whatever donations you collect.

A FEW TIPS

Don't present books to minors. If a child opens the door, ask the child if his or her parents are home and ask to speak with them. And don't knock on the same door twice. When people don't open their doors or they express disinterest, keep track of which apartment or house they live in and carefully avoid approaching the door a second time.

WHAT TO BRING

- Books (in hand).
- Book bag or wheeled cart (to carry extra books).
- *Prasāda* (optional) to give as gifts.
- Fliers.
- Personalized business cards.
- Response sheet (or small notebook that fits in your pocket).

- Book score sheet (to keep track of inventory before and after distribution).
- Contact logbook.
- Pen.

How many people live in your city, town, or village? Whatever the population, you can be sure that the people in your area live behind closed doors. Why not make a plan to visit all of them and to make friends by giving them Śrīla Prabhupāda's books, the *mahā-mantra,* and *kṛṣṇa-prasāda*?

CHAPTER TWENTY

Selling Sets of Śrīla Prabhupāda's Books

O nectar from the ocean of all scriptures, singular fruit of all the *Vedas,* rich mine of the precious gems of all conclusive truths, You are the only giver of light to all the worlds.

O life air of all the Supreme Lord's devotees, O master, *Śrīmad-Bhāgavatam*! You are the sun risen in the darkness of Kali. You are the exact image of Śrī Kṛṣṇa.

I bow down to You, who are supremely blissful to read. Your every syllable pours down a flood of *prema.* You can always be served by everyone. You are Śrī Kṛṣṇa Himself.

My only friend, my constant companion, my spiritual master, my great wealth! My savior, my good fortune, my source of ecstasy, I bow down to You.

O bestower of saintliness to the unsaintly, O exalter of the most fallen, please never leave me. Always appear in my heart and my voice with pure love.

THESE ARE ŚRĪLA SANĀTANA GOSVĀMĪ'S profound words of praise for *Śrīmad-Bhāgavatam,* recorded in *Śrī Kṛṣṇa-līlā-stava* (412–16), after he heard of those glories from Śrī Kṛṣṇa Caitanya Mahāprabhu. Is it any wonder, then, that when a family or household agrees to accept a full set of *Śrīmad-Bhāgavatams* into their home you can be sure you've made an impact on their life? You perceive it directly, and so do the recipients of the books.

Recently we met a man who bought a *Śrīmad-Bhāgavatam* set and placed it in his home. After reading from it in small installments for some time, he stopped eating meat, began chanting Hare Kṛṣṇa on beads, and started strictly following the process of devotional service.

We regularly see transformations like this after people agree to place a set of *Bhāgavatams* in their homes. One of the main reasons is that by agreeing to keep this array of books about pure devotional service, people somehow naturally begin to identify themselves as devotees of Kṛṣṇa. Here's one reason why.

Making Space

People have limited space in their homes for all their belongings. In fact, most people, at least in America, have accumulated so many things that they end up having to keep many of their things in outside self-storage facilities.

When asked to buy a *Śrīmad-Bhāgavatam* set, many people reply, "But where will I put it?" I scan their bookshelves to see where a set of books might go. Inevitably I notice that most people's shelves are crammed with things that have no inherent spiritual value – novels, games, hairbrushes – all kinds of things. Psychologists have noted how people identify with their own possessions, incorporating them into their self-image, so that their things become themselves.[1] Most people can without much trouble find space for a large flat-screen television, but when asked to make room for a set of spiritual books they often find themselves at a loss. So when they decide to receive these effulgent books, they are bringing in something categorically different from the jumble of their material acquisitions, and so they must make a conscientious choice to remove other things – in effect, to replace matter with spirit.

Therefore, when people buy sets of Śrīla Prabhupāda's books and place them in their homes, whether they know it or not they're making a personal statement: "I have faith in these books. They are part of my life."

I have found, therefore, that people are far less concerned about the price of the books than they are about what displaying the books in their homes says about them – to themselves and others. In some ways, it's daunting to keep literary deities in the home. People can sense that keeping them will mean changing their lives in some tangible way. Change, as we all know, can be scary.

And this is just to the point! Taking up Kṛṣṇa consciousness means literally moving some things out of your life in order to make room for Kṛṣṇa. The conclusion is that when people decide to take a set of *Śrīmad-Bhāgavatams,* it's a life-changing decision.

The Nuclear Option

Book distributors accustomed to distributing full sets of *Śrīmad-Bhāgavatam* and *Śrī Caitanya-caritāmṛta* consider them to be the biggest weapons in the war against *māyā*. Continuing with our metaphor of munitions: periodicals, small books, or even hardbacks like the *Bhagavad-gītā As It Is* may be compared to (spiritual) bullets and mortar shells, respectively; but full sets of *Śrīmad-Bhāgavatam* and *Śrī Caitanya-caritāmṛta* are the nuclear warheads in the arsenal.

As we begin to realize the potential of selling full sets of books, we may combine *Śrīmad-Bhāgavatam* with *Śrī Caitanya-caritāmṛta* and go on to add all the other books published by the BBT to make the fullest set: *The Nectar of Devotion, Bhagavad-gītā As It Is, The Science of Self-Realization,* and the others.

At ISV we combine *all* the books and present the set as a package called "The Perfectly Complete Śrīla Prabhupāda Library." We even include a bookcase, photos of the disciplic succession and the Pañca-tattva, and a year's subscription to BTG. We find that many people are very happy to have everything in one place and readily buy this package.

The idea of combining books in packages is sound business practice. Some years ago I read a book by Tom Hopkins entitled *How to Master the Art of Selling.* There he advises that you bundle products together rather than sell them one at a time. His mantra: "Always sell in bunches, like bananas."

Veteran book distributors Maṇidhara and Rohiṇī Sūta told me that selling Śrīla Prabhupāda's book "in bunches" revolutionized their bookselling in Europe as far back as the mid 1970s.

Standard Practice

When people buy a set of *Śrīmad-Bhāgavatam* or *Śrī Caitanya-caritāmṛta* (or both), or even all of Śrīla Prabhupāda's books at one time, they become noticeably more active in their practice of Kṛṣṇa consciousness – and much more so if they regularly read them.

Nowadays, many people come to the Kṛṣṇa consciousness movement and want to know what they can do to be more connected with Kṛṣṇa and how they can adopt the values of the Kṛṣṇa conscious way of life. ISKCON leaders and teachers can help such sincere people by encouraging them to purchase and keep a full set of Śrīla Prabhupāda's books in their homes and, of course, to read those books regularly. Making this a prevailing practice will help people convert their homes into temples and their lives into those of practicing devotees.

This step is not only practical but aligned with Śrīla Prabhupāda's values and mission. In a lecture given on January 24,

1977, he said, "I want that every respectable person has a full set of *Bhāgavatam* and *Caitanya-caritāmṛta* in his home." What's more, in a letter to Hṛṣīkeśa Dāsa dated March 18, 1969, he mentions the great benefit one gets from reading these books: "If you kindly read my books carefully then all your spiritual desires will be fulfilled."

In addition to people's homes, Śrīla Prabhupāda often mentioned libraries as needing full sets of his books. Libraries of all varieties – public, university, hospital, prison, and so on – in the tens of thousands are waiting and will remain incomplete until graced by a set of Śrīla Prabhupāda's extraordinary books.

A Śrīmad-Bhāgavatam Presentation

What follows is a talk I gave at an ISKCON Sunday program in Dallas, Texas, to present *Śrīmad-Bhāgavatam*. A full set of *Śrīmad-Bhāgavatams* stood next to me on display as I spoke. Just after the talk, we sold six sets.

Before us tonight is a set of *Śrīmad-Bhāgavatam* volumes. And it took no ordinary journey to arrive here. These books were brought to America and the rest of the world by our founder-*ācārya* Śrīla Prabhupāda, who came to America with no money or connections when he was sixty-nine years old. His only cargo was his three-volume First Canto of *Śrīmad-Bhāgavatam,* newly published in India.

Today it's easy to take books for granted because the world has high-speed printing presses by which millions of copies of magazines, newspapers, and books can be printed in one day. The population receives these publications casually because they are so easy to get; and after the day is done, all those publications become obsolete and discarded – vaporized along with the day's news.

However, although the *Śrīmad-Bhāgavatam* appears before us in the form of paper and ink, make no mistake: it is not a normal creation. It is not a book from this world, as are the other publications I just mentioned. The *Śrīmad-Bhāgavatam* (1.5.11) itself proclaims:

tad-vāg-visargo janatāgha-viplavo
yasmin prati-ślokam abaddhavaty api
nāmāny anantasya yaśo 'ṅkitāni yat
śṛṇvanti gāyanti gṛṇanti sādhavaḥ

"On the other hand, that literature which is full with descriptions of the transcendental glories of the name, fame, form, and pastimes of the unlimited Supreme Lord is a transcendental creation meant to bring about a revolution in the impious life of a misdirected civilization. Such transcendental literatures, even though irregularly composed, are heard, sung, and accepted by purified men who are thoroughly honest."

This means that the *Śrīmad-Bhāgavatam* comes from the spiritual world, which is far beyond the world of birth and death that we now inhabit. What's more, *Śrīmad-Bhāgavatam* is directly the incarnation of Lord Kṛṣṇa, who has kindly appeared in this literary form in the age of Kali-yuga to give us His association, to light our path back to Godhead. *Śrīmad-Bhāgavatam* (1.3.43) states:

kṛṣṇe sva-dhāmopagate
dharma-jñānādibhiḥ saha
kalau naṣṭa-dṛśām eṣa
purāṇārko 'dhunoditaḥ

"This *Bhāgavata Purāṇa* is as brilliant as the sun, and it has arisen just after the departure of Lord Kṛṣṇa to His own abode, accompanied by religion, knowledge, etc. Persons who have lost their vision due to the dense darkness of ignorance in the age of Kali shall get light from this *Purāṇa*."

When Kṛṣṇa departed for His own abode five thousand years ago, He left this *Śrīmad-Bhāgavatam* to give light to everyone in this age. This is the light in this age; this is Kṛṣṇa. He has made His appearance, in the form of *Śrīmad-Bhāgavatam.* Again from *Śrīmad-Bhāgavatam* (1.3.40):

idaṁ bhāgavataṁ nāma
purāṇaṁ brahma-sammitam
uttama-śloka-caritaṁ
cakāra bhagavān ṛṣiḥ
niḥśreyasāya lokasya
dhanyaṁ svasty-ayanaṁ mahat

"This scripture named *Śrīmad-Bhāgavatam* is the literary incarnation of God, and it is compiled by Śrīla Vyāsadeva, the incarnation of God. It is meant for the ultimate good of all people, and it is all-successful, all-blissful, and all-perfect."

The *Kūrma Purāṇa* also confirms that *Śrīmad-Bhāgavatam,* which has eighteen thousand verses, is the divine incarnation of the Lord. The *Kūrma Purāṇa* goes on to say that anyone who makes a gift of *Śrīmad-Bhāgavatam* on a full-moon day receives the benediction of going back home, back to Godhead.

Śrī Caitanya Mahāprabhu considered *Śrīmad-Bhāgavatam* to be the ultimate authority on everything. Therefore Vaiṣṇavas, especially the followers of Lord Caitanya, keep *Śrīmad-Bhāgavatam* in their homes, worship it, and also share it with others.

In the *Bhagavad-gītā,* Lord Kṛṣṇa reminds us that as soon as we are born in this world, we begin ticking off the days until our inevitable death. He also reminds us that during this limited time period, we have a duty to perform. And what is that specific duty? The *Vedānta-sūtra* says*, athāto brahma-jijñāsā:* You must ask ceaselessly about the Absolute Truth. And the *Śrīmad-Bhāgavatam* similarly says that a human being's only duty is to inquire about self-realization at all times, in all places, and in all circumstances.

But scripture also says that without outside help, without divine intervention, our search for higher knowledge will be futile. Śrī Caitanya Mahāprabhu therefore tells Sanātana Gosvāmī:

māyā-mugdha jīvera nāhi svataḥ kṛṣṇa-jñāna
jīvere kṛpāya kailā kṛṣṇa veda-purāṇa

"The conditioned soul cannot revive his Kṛṣṇa consciousness by his own effort. But out of causeless mercy, Lord Kṛṣṇa compiled the Vedic literature and its supplements, the *Purāṇas,* especially *Śrīmad-Bhāgavatam,* the reading of which frees one from illusion."[2]

Because our lives are uncertain in this temporary world, people sometimes consult astrologers to find out how long they will live, whether they will get some money, whether they will be happy, and so on. Everyone wants to know these things.... Because we are controlled by the three modes of material nature, our future is mapped out along with our birth. It's written on our palms and it's in our stars. Really, people get exactly what they deserve – no more and no less. Everything comes according to one's past karma.

We're also living in the Devīdhāma, where Devī grabs hold of us and pokes us with her trident.[3] Each point on her trident represents one of the threefold miseries that is built into this world: miseries from one's mind and body; from other living beings; and from the *devas* who control the natural world and who bring us heat, cold, earthquakes, and so on.

Someone may think, "Maybe if I get one billion dollars I can buy my freedom from Devī." But no! She has ten arms. So, even if we free ourselves from one arm, she has nine more with which to grab us. How, then, will it be possible for us to get free?

Kṛṣṇa tells us in the *Bhagavad-gītā* (7.14):

daivī hy eṣā guṇa-mayī
mama māyā duratyayā
mām eva ye prapadyante
māyām etāṁ taranti te

"The material nature is Mine and is therefore impossible to overcome. But if you surrender to Me, I will free you from Māyā."

This is *śāstra*. And an intelligent person will hear this and think, "Yes, I will surrender to Kṛṣṇa."

So, when we look at our astrological chart, we see how the planets, which are ruled by the *devas,* have their effect on us. Each planet is known as *graha,* "that which grasps." They grasp us and move us in various ways. This is beyond our control.

However, the great *ācāryas* tell us that the most munificent planet, Goloka Vṛndāvana, has now appeared in this world in the form of *Śrīmad-Bhāgavatam*. It also grabs us. But this planet grabs us and takes us away from the miseries of the material world, back to Godhead.

Therefore, when we accept the *Śrīmad-Bhāgavatam* and take it into our home, the Goloka Vṛndāvana planet becomes prominent in our life. This powerful spiritual planet then obscures the influence of all the material planets. This is no exaggeration.

Everyone is looking for happiness. And everyone wants to avoid distress as far as possible. Everyone wants some good fortune. Am I correct about this? But where does the good fortune come from? And how do we find happiness and avoid distress?

Well, we can definitely rule out saying that it comes from working harder. Because lots of people work hard, sometimes even keeping two or three jobs, and they still do not get any happiness; nor do they avoid distress. According to *śāstra,* one can taste real happiness only by contacting Kṛṣṇa, by being in close proximity to Kṛṣṇa.

Because *Śrīmad-Bhāgavatam* is directly Kṛṣṇa Himself, our founder-*ācārya* A. C. Bhaktivedanta Swami Prabhupāda brought *Śrīmad-Bhāgavatam* to America. He brought nothing else. His only cargo was trunks full of *Śrīmad-Bhāgavatam*. He knew that there is no greater wealth on this planet, and that there is no wealthier family than the family that keeps the *Śrīmad-Bhāgavatam* in their home.

It is for this reason that Śrīla Prabhupāda dedicated his entire life and very breath to write and speak the *Śrīmad-Bhāgavatam* and to see to it that it was printed in quantity. So our mission, which is one and the same with the mission of our spiritual master, is to present *Śrīmad-Bhāgavatam* to you for your greatest benefit.

I'm here to beg you to please take *Śrīmad-Bhāgavatam* tonight and put it in your home. Just putting it there will change everything. Your home will become a holy *tīrtha* that the demigods in the heavenly planets will glance on and worship. This is the benefit of keeping *Śrīmad-Bhāgavatam* in your home.

I've come here to Texas all the way from California just for this.

Please take a set of *Śrīmad-Bhāgavatams* tonight and the local devotees will give you a free one-year subscription to *Back to Godhead* magazine. Also – and this is the best part – the devotees will bring the *Śrīmad-Bhāgavatam* set to your home and perform an installation ceremony for this most sacred literature when they place it there.

This means you just have to find one place in your home for the books, invite the devotees in, and they will come there, perform some *kīrtana* and a special *pūjā* to *Śrīmad-Bhāgavatam* in order to inaugurate the appearance of the Supreme Personality of Godhead in your home. If you like, you can invite your friends so that they can also take part in the ceremony. We'll also have *prasāda* for all.

In *Śrī Caitanya-caritāmṛta* (*Madhya-līlā* 25.270, 277), Kṛṣṇadāsa Kavirāja Gosvāmī explains the benefits of hearing the pastimes of both Lord Caitanya and Lord Kṛṣṇa together. When we hear them both, we not only understand the highest spiritual truth – we taste ambrosia.

> By understanding the pastimes of Śrī Caitanya Mahāprabhu, one can understand the truth about Kṛṣṇa. By understanding

> Kṛṣṇa, one can understand the limit of all knowledge described in various revealed scriptures.
>
> The pastimes of Śrī Caitanya Mahāprabhu are full of nectar, and the pastimes of Lord Kṛṣṇa are like camphor. When one mixes these, they taste very sweet. By the mercy of the pure devotees, whoever tastes them can understand the depths of that sweetness.

Wherever and whenever you decide to display sets of Śrīla Prabhupāda's books, you can start by following the third law of book distribution: "The more you show, the more you sell." When you make the sets visible, you will sell them. The more visible you make them, the more readily you will sell them. And this can easily be done just by talking about the historical and spiritual significance of *Śrīmad-Bhāgavatam* and *Śrī Caitanya-caritāmṛta.*

An Outline for How to Introduce Śrīmad-Bhāgavatam

Here is an outline of ideas developed by Team ISV for introducing *Śrīmad-Bhāgavatam* to prospective buyers and educating them in some basics that may make the set more attractive.

1. GENERAL TOPICS FOR INTRODUCING ŚRĪMAD-BHĀGAVATAM

- The reason Śrīla Vedavyāsa composed the *Śrīmad-Bhāgavatam.*
- Why and how the *Vedas* were divided.
- Why Nārada instructed Śrīla Vyāsadeva.
- The significance of Mahārāja Parīkṣit being cursed by a *brāhmaṇa* boy.

2. ŚRĪMAD-BHĀGAVATAM IS *NOT* THE BHAGAVAD-GĪTĀ

Most people have never heard of *Śrīmad-Bhāgavatam,* but

they have heard of the *Bhagavad-gītā,* so when we offer them *Śrīmad-Bhāgavatam* they think we are speaking about the *Bhagavad-gītā.* It's necessary, therefore, to thoroughly explain the difference. The *Bhagavad-gītā* is a conversation between Kṛṣṇa and Arjuna, whereas *Śrīmad-Bhāgavatam* contains not only Kṛṣṇa's direct instructions but details about the Lord's pastimes, histories of various pure devotees, and comprehensive spiritual instructions.

The *Bhagavad-gītā* is the undergraduate study, *Śrīmad-Bhāgavatam* is the graduate study, and *Śrī Caitanya-caritāmṛta* is the postgraduate study of the Absolute Truth, Śrī Kṛṣṇa, the Supreme Personality of Godhead.

3. ŚRĪMAD-BHĀGAVATAM IS THE ESSENCE OF ALL VEDIC SCRIPTURES

Śrīmad-Bhāgavatam is the ripened fruit of the vast tree of the Vedic literature. Presently, we do not have access to or the capacity to study the vast, variegated branches of Vedic knowledge. Śrīla Vyāsadeva has therefore given us *Śrīmad-Bhāgavatam,* through which we can assimilate the *Vedas* by taking their essence.

4. ŚRĪMAD-BHĀGAVATAM IS IN THE FORM OF STORIES

The stories in the *Bhāgavatam* explain even the complex philosophy of the *Bhagavad-gītā* in simple and relatable ways. For example, the poignant story of King Citraketu summarily clarifies the difference between the body and the soul (*ātmā*). Such stories are appreciated even by children, yet these stories deliver highly philosophical points.

5. ŚRĪMAD-BHĀGAVATAM IS AUTHENTIC

Śrīmad-Bhāgavatam is the last work of Śrīla Vyāsadeva, the compiler of all Vedic literature. As such, it is his most mature realization of Vedic knowledge. It was written under the guidance of his spiritual master, Nārada Muni, who is widely regarded as the topmost teacher of the Vedic literature. The translator and commentator of the BBT edition of *Śrīmad-Bhāgavatam* is His Divine Grace A.C. Bhaktivedanta Swami Prabhupāda, who comes in an unbroken line of authorities coming directly from the original author, Vyāsadeva. Śrīla Prabhupāda is accepted and revered by scholars worldwide for the depth of his scholarship and his fidelity to the original text and the previous authorities and commentators.

6. ŚRĪMAD-BHĀGAVATAM IS PREDICTIVE

Śrīmad-Bhāgavatam predicted the appearance of Lord Buddha thousands of years before His appearance. The Twelfth Canto, written five thousand years ago, contains an uncannily accurate description of the characteristics of modern times.

7. ŚRĪMAD-BHĀGAVATAM IS SCIENTIFIC

Although *Śrīmad-Bhāgavatam* was written thousands of years ago it contains concepts that are consistent with modern scientific research. For example, the Third Canto describes what is referred to in modern terms as embryology. Time is calculated according to how long it takes the sun to pass over various objects, from the smallest (the atom) to the largest material form. Historical events can be confirmed by the position of the planets.

The original creation of the various elements, how they transform from subtle to gross, what their original functions and characteristics are, and many other fascinating facts can be confirmed by what we see in the visible universe.

Śrīmad-Bhāgavatam goes beyond the range of our current material science by presenting a complete and coherent science of self- and God realization that is systematic, doable, and full of conclusions the practitioner can confirm. Thus subjects like God, soul, and spirit are not merely matters of faith or belief but matters of direct experience – of knowledge. Anyone who masters the requisite knowledge and training can verify these truths by direct perception.

8. ŚRĪMAD-BHĀGAVATAM IS IMPORTANT FOR CHILDREN

From hearing and reading the *Śrīmad-Bhāgavatam,* children gain a spiritual education that helps them make the right moral and spiritual decisions when faced with tough choices. Parents who may not be interested in reading *Śrīmad-Bhāgavatam* themselves are often happy to take a set for their kids. You can suggest to parents that they read *Śrīmad-Bhāgavatam* to their children at bedtime instead of other storybooks that have little or no spiritual value. What's more, because the English in *Śrīmad-Bhāgavatam* is rich, children who hear from it cultivate good language skills.

9. ŚRĪMAD-BHĀGAVATAM IS A SPIRITUAL ASSET

People leave behind estates, large sums of money, cars, and other material assets. However, the best asset to leave behind for our children as well as the generations to come is *Śrīmad-Bhāgavatam.* Even if we don't read it entirely in our lifetime, our children and others may benefit from reading it.

10. ŚRĪMAD-BHĀGAVATAM SETS MUST NOT BE BROKEN

Many people ask if they can take one book in the set. We respond by saying that *Śrīmad-Bhāgavatam* is a deity of the Supreme Personality of Godhead. Each canto represents a respective part of His transcendental body. The first two cantos are His lotus feet, the Third and Fourth His calves, the Tenth His smiling face, and so on. When people hear this, they understand why we cannot break the sets. Also, the set is arranged in a particular order and should be read progressively, in installments.

11. ŚRĪMAD-BHĀGAVATAM IS NONDIFFERENT FROM LORD KṚṢṆA HIMSELF

The *Śrīmad-Bhāgavatam* is the literary incarnation of Lord Kṛṣṇa, and those who read it with devotion will feel His presence on every page.

12. PURCHASING A SET OF BHĀGAVATAMS SUPPORTS THE CAUSE OF PRESERVING AND DISTRIBUTING VEDIC KNOWLEDGE.

As distributors of *Śrīmad-Bhāgavatam* we work to revive and preserve Vedic knowledge. *Śrīmad-Bhāgavatam* is the essence of all the *Vedas,* and purchasing a set supports our efforts to both revive and preserve this important wisdom for the good of the world.

13. ŚRĪLA PRABHUPĀDA'S ŚRĪMAD-BHĀGAVATAM IS THE ONLY COMPLETE SET TRANSLATED INTO ENGLISH WITH WORD-TO-WORD TRANSLATIONS

With the BBT edition of *Śrīmad-Bhāgavatam* one can accurately pronounce the Sanskrit verses without knowing how to read Sanskrit. One can also see the word-for-word translations from Sanskrit to English. The English translations to each verse are clear. All of this allows us to better understand and transfer this knowledge to our children, who also may not know Sanskrit and who may respond better to English as a language of instruction. There is no other translation of the complete *Śrīmad-Bhāgavatam* in English that also gives word-for-word meanings and includes commentary to explain each verse.

*

When presenting sets of *Śrīmad-Bhāgavatam* for sale to those who have little or no prior knowledge of the Vedic tradition, we emphasize that *Śrīmad-Bhāgavatam* offers readers the opportunity to study and apply the philosophy of yoga. Applying yoga philosophy will help readers improve their lives in a number of ways. For example, they will develop more sattvic habits, leaving them feeling happier. We also tell readers about the value of chanting mantras. Since the verses of the *Bhāgavatam* are mantras, readers will benefit from chanting them. And we explain that the stories in *Śrīmad-Bhāgavatam* are transcendental; by reading them, people can elevate their consciousness.

Śrīmad-Bhāgavatam sets are so unusually substantial and attractive that they almost sell themselves. Try showing a set of *Śrīmad-Bhāgavatams* and see for yourself!

CHAPTER TWENTY-ONE

The Monthly Saṅkīrtana Festival

IN HER BOOK *Lord Krishna's Cuisine,* well-known cook and author Yamunā Devī Dāsī reveals an age-old secret about rice, a staple for so many parts of the world. When rice is mixed with other foods, like beans, its interaction with that food creates a complete protein. Modern research confirms that although both foods are nourishing on their own, the blend is replete with a perfect balance of amino acids, making the combination a kind of superfood.

So it is with the staples of devotional service: hearing and chanting. When devotees mix hearing and chanting with the compassionate act of giving Kṛṣṇa consciousness to the public, the mixture's spiritual potency is exponentially greater than each individual practice. This is because hearing and chanting please Lord Caitanya. Giving what one hears and chants to others pleases Him even more. As Śrīla Sanātana Gosvāmī says while praising the devotional service of Haridāsa Ṭhākura:

> Some behave very well but do not preach the cult of Kṛṣṇa consciousness, whereas others preach but do not behave properly. You simultaneously perform both duties in relation to the holy name by your personal behavior and by your preaching. Therefore you are the spiritual master of the entire world, for you are the most advanced devotee in the world.[1]

Śrīla Prabhupāda considered distributing transcendental literature as enhanced hearing and chanting (*saṅkīrtana*). He writes, "[M]y *guru mahārāja's* opinion is that press is the *bṛhat mṛdaṅga,* or the biggest, or the greater *mṛdaṅga*. The sound of press goes long distance, long distant places, so the organization of press and literature and public sales should be our main business."[2]

Furthermore, when we come together to brainstorm plans and set goals, not only does the *saṅkīrtana* movement expand, but also all those who participate in it naturally gain unique or deepened insights into the process of devotional service. In his purport to *Bhagavad-gītā* 11.55, Śrīla Prabhupāda writes:

> The highest benefit one can render to human society is relieving one's neighbor from all material problems. In such a way, a pure devotee is engaged in the service of the Lord. Now we can imagine how merciful Kṛṣṇa is to those engaged in His service, risking everything for Him. Certainly such persons must reach the supreme planet after leaving the body.

In summary, when devotees hear, chant, and come together to share this process with others, both the distributors and the recipients are nourished by the superfood of such spiritual practice. Devotees know this secret and absorb themselves in thoughts of how to benefit people by devising ways to increase the distribution of the holy names all over the world.

Ṭhākura Bhaktivinoda, for example, devised a marketplace of the holy name – something akin to today's multilevel or network marketing – through which people could embrace the chanting of God's names and widely spread the process to others through dynamic promotion. He defined *dharma* as the showing of compassion to all living beings by distributing the holy names; and he showed by example how a busy householder with heavy professional duties could contribute significantly to Lord Caitanya's movement.

Today's interconnected world, brimming with innovative social networking systems and high-tech capacities for organizing people, provides more facilities than ever before for spreading Lord Caitanya's *saṅkīrtana* movement. Now is the ideal time, therefore, for spiritual entrepreneurs to advance Lord Caitanya's movement far and wide, completely nourishing and satisfying the souls of both the givers and the receivers.

The Monthly Saṅkīrtana Festival (MSF) is a proven way to bring people together for complete spiritual nourishment. In essence, it is a monthly gathering of devotees to unite them in spreading the *saṅkīrtana* movement. In this chapter I will share with you what I've learned by developing the MSF into a regular and festive event. Here's how it works:

Devotees choose a specific day each month to work as a team to distribute the holy name, *kṛṣṇa-prasāda,* and transcendental literature. To help as many devotees as possible participate, I started by choosing a weekend day.

Of course, the MSF can be as elaborate or as simple as time, place, and circumstance allow, but even in its humblest form – for example, with just a few family members or friends joining in – the MSF is always a success. Why? Because in the sincere attempt to cooperate and distribute Lord Caitanya's mercy, even the smallest effort results in immediate spiritual benefits to all who participate. Why? As we shall see, it's because such service not only pleases Lord Caitanya but also increases the devotees' capacity for service. And when the MSF matures and becomes a grand event that engages hundreds of devotees and state-of-the-art facilities, it is all the more blissful, productive, and pleasing to the Lord.

My friend Willy Jolley used to say, "Just as there's a recipe for baking delicious cakes and pies, there's also a recipe for success." The main ingredients in the recipe for a successful MSF are:

- a lot of people each doing a little.
- all the participants having fun together.
- everyone working together to meet fresh challenges.

A Lot of People Each Doing a Little

A large team of people working together – each doing a little – creates a sustainable effort, because when people contribute according to their ability and their capacity and see that their humble efforts are useful to the team, they feel encouraged and want to do more. As Franklin D. Roosevelt said, "Cooperation begins where competition leaves off."

In a symphony orchestra, every musician is given his or her part to play. Even the triangle player's role (tiny compared to the first violinist's) adds flavor to the symphony's crescendo. Similarly, the MSF gives all team members an opportunity to do their best according to their capacities and talents. By the law of synergy, each individual team member's results are increased, and through teamwork the members' combined efforts produce better-than-imagined results. Especially important: the more teammates work together to please Lord Caitanya, the more they discover unity in their diversity.

Here are three principles you can apply to attract a lot of people to participate in your MSF:

- lower the bar of expectations.
- emphasize teamwork.
- encourage and empower team members.

Many people are afraid to go out in public to introduce spiritual books. They worry they'll be rejected or embarrassed when they don't know what to say.

Lower the Bar of Expectations

One of the best ways to help people overcome fear of participating is to change the idea of what will be expected of them if they do. I highly recommend that team leaders allow beginners to join the *saṅkīrtana* team just to watch, learn, and have fun – and nothing else.

When I'm invited to introduce the MSF to communities that have never held one before, I repeatedly assure those new to *saṅkīrtana* that on our first day out in public no one is expected to distribute books or to perform in any way. Our only goal is to move the team out the door to the designated *saṅkīrtana* spot as efficiently as possible. This effort is actually more difficult than distributing books, but for most newcomers it seems less intimidating. I tell them that when we arrive at our spot we'll touch the pavement together, and by doing so we'll complete our goal for the day. Anything we do after that will be extra.

At first the group members think I'm joking. When they see I'm serious, they feel the burden of expectation lift and they become eager to join. There's an inverse relationship between expectation and performance, especially for beginners and newly formed teams. The lower the initial expectation, the more people feel like jumping in. When we set the bar of expectation ridiculously low, people often say, "Oh, come on, I can do more than *that*!" I've also found that when team members are freed from the fear of failure, they tend to use their natural genius to innovate and expand their efforts.

In contrast, when new people sense a high degree of difficulty from the start, they tend to feel nervous and even look for ways to avoid coming out for the MSF that day. No one likes to fail, especially while others are watching.

In summary, the first golden rule for attracting a lot of people to participate in your MSF is to make team members comfortable by keeping the initial goals and expectations outlandishly low.

Emphasize Teamwork

The next key ingredient for involving a lot of people in your MSF is to promote teamwork. In the worlds of sports and business there is a wealth of information about the benefits of teamwork – efficiency, morale, innovation, support. Henry Ford writes, "Coming together is a beginning. Keeping together is progress. Working together is success." Other experts also give plenty of useful tips on how to build effective teams, including clarifying vision and goals, building trust and commitment, and so on. One can study and use these methods to create a successful MSF.

Śrīla Prabhupāda repeatedly asked ISKCON members to work together, and he emphasized love and trust as the basis for doing so. "Our ISKCON should be taken as being a family based upon love and trust."[3] Working together is natural; in the spiritual world devotees absorbed in pure devotional service to Kṛṣṇa work within their own like-minded groups (*gaṇas*). The more we promote an atmosphere of love and trust, the more people will come forward to join us.

As teams form, at candid moments even those who have already joined them sometimes reveal that they hesitate to distribute books for fear of being looked down on if they don't do well enough. Emphasizing team achievement over individual success is a good way to remove this fear, for the dynamic inherent in any team is for its members to appreciate one another. When members contribute to the team goal, they gain self-confidence and gradually lose the inhibition caused by thinking they might underperform. Furthermore, to help promote a positive atmosphere for beginners, there should be no emphasis on who is higher and who lower. In such an atmosphere, new participants steadily develop courage and poise, and their results naturally increase as they gain maturity and skill.

In summary, lowering expectations and promoting teamwork are essential ingredients for building a successful MSF program.

Śrīla Bhaktisiddhānta Sarasvatī Prabhupāda, the son of Śrīla Bhaktivinoda Ṭhākura, developed our family business by establishing multiple printing presses and making available an array of transcendental books and other publications. He wrote more than sixty books and three hundred scholarly articles aimed at Western academics and the intelligentsia of his time.

Encourage Team Members

The next key ingredient is encouragement. In fact, the credo for setting up and building a solid MSF team is "Encourage the heck out of everyone!" Who doesn't need encouragement? In the material world, even the noblest soul has detractors (not to mention the cynical voice sitting on each person's shoulder saying, "Who do you think you are? You can't do this!").

Encouraged people are freer to do their best. I've found that after only one well-deserved dose of encouragement, remarkably, people can recover from their own low estimate of themselves and thrive for a month or even years. When people get a taste for serving in a place where encouraging others is the norm, they not only stay but also bring others onto the team.

In his best-selling book, *The One Minute Manager,* Kenneth Blanchard teaches leaders to "catch employees doing something right" and then to take a minute to praise them for their good work. Lord Caitanya, the perfect leader and teacher, took time to encourage His devotees. In *Śrī Caitanya-caritāmṛta* (*Madhya-līlā* 12.116–17), Kṛṣṇadāsa Kavirāja Gosvāmī gives as an example how the Lord inspired His followers as they worked as a team to clean the Guṇḍicā temple: "When He saw someone doing nicely, the Lord praised him.... The Lord would say, 'You have done well. Please teach this to others so that they may act in the same way.'"

In the Brahma-gāyatrī mantra, the word *pracodayāt* means to enliven, encourage, or inspire. Through the Gāyatrī mantra and other mantras devotees chant daily, they pray to the Lord and their spiritual master for encouragement on the path of devotional service.

Those who encourage others in divine service certainly follow in the footsteps of the Supreme Personality of Godhead, Śrī Kṛṣṇa, as shown in His dealings with His devotees. *Śrīmad-Bhāgavatam* (1.11.22) gives this image of the Lord encouraging His devotees: "The Almighty Lord greeted everyone present by bowing His head, exchanging greetings, embracing, shaking hands, looking and smiling, giving assurances and awarding benedictions, even to the lowest in rank."

A book distributor is an agent representing Kṛṣṇa. An agent follows the policies and examples of the one he or she represents. What better way, then, to become an agent of Kṛṣṇa than to encourage those who serve Him.

Śrīla Prabhupāda himself was an exemplar of encouragement. He wrote thousands of letters with encouraging words like these:

> So your work is the most important preaching work, may Kṛṣṇa bless you more and more.

> You are working so hard for broadcasting the glories of Lord Kṛṣṇa's lotus feet, and thus my *guru mahārāja* will be so pleased upon you.

> I am very pleased to hear that you are distributing many of my books, especially *Kṛṣṇa Book*. You are a very sincere girl. Please continue to engage wholeheartedly in Kṛṣṇa's service and there is no doubt that you may go back to home, back to Godhead.

Try following in Śrīla Prabhupāda footsteps by applying this useful and unifying technique: Look for people doing well and take a moment to voice your appreciation and encourage them. Or write encouraging notes, emails, or letters to those who are doing well and let them know they are doing a good job. You might be surprised at the results. One act of conscious approval can give recipients just what they need to turn their life around or to raise their service to the next level. What a positive place the world would be if everyone were to adopt this principle of encouraging the heck out of people.

Embedded in the word encouragement is the word "courage," which derives from the Latin, *cor,* "heart." Thus the heart is both the seat of courage and the target of encouragement. In *Śrīmad-Bhāgavatam* (1.2.17), Sūta Gosvāmī says that when devotees hear and chant, Kṛṣṇa helps them from within their hearts by removing unwanted desires, and when they hear and chant together, they feel more and more encouraged as their doubts and misgivings fade away.

Another way to invoke an encouraging environment, then, is to emphasize and schedule time for hearing and chanting among the members of your team. Kṛṣṇadāsa Kavirāja Gosvāmī notes that the sound of Lord Caitanya's voice, as He chants the holy names and pastimes of the Supreme Personality of Godhead, reassures everyone by scaring away the "elephantine vices" in the heart. "May that lion be seated in the core of the heart of every living being. Thus with His resounding roar may He drive away one's elephantine vices."[4]

As the vices in our heart subside, the bravery to cross over the material ocean grows and our eagerness to spread the *saṅkīrtana* movement steadily increases. Who wouldn't want to join a group of devotees bravely determined to go back to Godhead and to bring others with them?

In summary, the more one encourages the team, the more the respective capacities of the MSF team members expand.

Empowerment

Related to encouragement is empowerment, which is the final element that attracts people to join an MSF. Harry Truman, former President of the United States, expresses the attitude that forms the basis of empowerment: "It's amazing what you can accomplish if you do not care who gets the credit."

Śrīla Prabhupāda exhibits this mood when writing to one of his godbrothers in the fall of 1965, when he was all alone trying to jumpstart the Hare Kṛṣṇa movement in America. In a long letter to that godbrother dated November 8, 1965, we find an outstanding example of Śrīla Prabhupāda's humility and detachment:

> So here is a chance of cooperation between us and I shall be glad to know if you are ready for this cooperation. I came

> here to study the situation and I find it very nice and if you are also agreeable to cooperate with it, it will be all very nice by the will of Śrīla Prabhupāda. So I am writing you directly this letter to elicit your opinion. If you agree then take it for granted that I am one of the worker of the Śrī Māyāpur Caitanya Maṭha. I have no ambition for becoming the proprietor of any Maṭha or Mandir, but I want working facilities.

A leader who gives up attachment to the credit for his or her work, whose sole purpose is to please the Lord, becomes empowered to empower others. Movements and organizations grow when leaders empower their team members to take initiative by giving them authorship, credit, and control of their various projects. Lord Caitanya empowered and sent out Śrī Rūpa and Śrī Sanātana, asking them to write about devotional service and to reveal the holy sites of Vraja. He inspired Nityānanda Prabhu to capture Bengal. He elevated Haridāsa Ṭhākura to the post of *nāmācārya*. To the Kūrma *brāhmaṇa* and to everyone else He met, He gave the instruction to become a guru!

As Śrīla Prabhupāda expanded his team of devotees, he repeatedly used phrases such as "organize freely," "do the needful," and "do it!" In a letter to Karandhara Dāsa dated December 22, 1972, Śrīla Prabhupāda writes: "The Kṛṣṇa consciousness movement is for training men to be independently thoughtful and competent in all types of departments of knowledge and action, not for making bureaucracy." Great leaders are willing to let others shine. As empowered team members excel, the brilliance of their accomplishments reflects on the leaders who empowered them. Napoleon Bonaparte notes, "Soldiers generally win battles; generals get credit for them."

As you develop your MSF, look for people who show a keen interest. These are the people who show up and who are first to offer help and useful suggestions. It's our duty to look beyond externals, such as people's appearance, inexperience, cultural backgrounds, or sex. Instead, look to their potential and empower them.

For example, during a meeting to discuss the MSF, eager participants might suggest improvements. In reply, one can ask whether those persons are willing to help make their ideas come to life. If they agree, the leader should engage them as soon as possible in the service and give them the authority to accomplish it.

The first words Śrīla Bhaktisiddhānta spoke to Abhay – who later became the great world *ācārya,* His Divine Grace A.C. Bhaktivedanta Swami Prabhupāda – empowered him to carry Lord Caitanya's message to the West. What a great act of instant empowerment. The results couldn't be more obvious.

This is a classic example of how the system of disciplic succession works. Empowered teachers constantly see how to empower new teachers to spread Kṛṣṇa's message, inspiring them to carry it forward to the next generation. Thus in his purport to *Śrī Caitanya-caritāmṛta, Ādi-līlā* 10.160, Śrīla Prabhupāda also writes:

> It was the desire of Lord Caitanya Mahāprabhu that His cult be spread all over the world. Therefore there is a great necessity for many, many disciples of the branches of Śrī Caitanya Mahāprabhu's disciplic succession. His cult should be spread not only in a few villages, or in Bengal, or in India, but all over the world.

Śrīla Prabhupāda again emphasized this same truth as he spoke to his intimate followers, representatives of the GBC, just before he left this world: "One [who] can understand the order of Caitanya Mahāprabhu, he can become guru. Or one who understands his guru's order, the same *paramparā,* he can become guru."[5]

As early as 1968, Śrīla Prabhupāda emphasized the importance of his disciples' becoming learned from reading his books and taking the responsibility of initiating others into the line of devotional service. Śrīla Prabhupāda writes:

> Next January there will be an examination on this *Bhagavad-gītā*. Papers will be sent by me to all centers, and those securing the minimum passing grade will be given the title as Bhakti-śāstri. Similarly, another examination will be held on Lord Caitanya's Appearance Day in February 1970, and it will be upon *Śrīmad-Bhāgavatam* and *Bhagavad-gītā*. Those passing will get the title of Bhakti-vaibhava. Another examination will be held sometimes in 1971 on the four books, *Bhagavad-gītā, Śrīmad-Bhāgavatam, Teachings of Lord Caitanya,* and *The Nectar of Devotion*. One who will pass this examination will be awarded with the title of Bhaktivedanta. I want that all of my spiritual sons and daughters will inherit this title of Bhaktivedanta, so that the family transcendental diploma will continue through the generations. Those possessing the title of Bhaktivedanta will be allowed to initiate disciples. Maybe by 1975, all of my disciples will be allowed to initiate and increase the numbers of the generations. That is my program. So we should not simply publish these books for reading by outsiders, but our students must be well versed in all of our books so that we can be prepared to defeat all opposing parties in the matter of self-realization.

His Divine Grace also writes, "Our International Society for Krishna Consciousness is one of the branches of the Caitanya tree."[6] That branch will go on living and will remain vital only because its members continue to teach, empower, and connect new members to the spiritual family tree. As Kṛṣṇadāsa Kavirāja Gosvāmī explains, "From each branch of the tree have grown hundreds and thousands of subbranches of disciples and granddisciples."[7] Thus the MSF and the family tree of Lord Caitanya grows.

Tools of Empowerment

Now let's take a closer look at some of the tools the leaders of an MSF can use to empower team members.

Enlightened companies practice employee empowerment: they give workers decision-making authority and thus motivate them and increase their productivity. Moreover, when managers regularly consult and brainstorm with their employees – whose eyes are everywhere – they discover valuable information about how the company can improve its products, services, and policies.

Again, when everyone's ideas and contributions to the team, no matter how humble, are honored, team members feel freer to contribute ideas and bring forth useful and sometimes groundbreaking innovations.

Śrīla Prabhupāda encouraged his students to come together for regular group discussions of Kṛṣṇa conscious philosophy. He called them *iṣṭha-goṣṭhīs.* In a 1975 meeting with *saṅkīrtana* leaders in Vṛndāvana, Śrīla Prabhupāda pointed out that every devotee has creative potency, an inner genius, and that the qualification for pulling that genius out of oneself (and others) is a sincere desire to serve Kṛṣṇa.* So, in an atmosphere where innovation, open discussion, and fresh ideas are welcomed, devotees come up with amazingly useful ideas from that inner genius.

Meet with the team members before and after every MSF and discuss with them what's working well and where there's room for improvement. At ISV we call this method of continually capturing suggested improvements and then acting on them *always better service* (ABS). As we practice the ABS principle, teammates notice incremental improvements and become eager to do more. A well-known management rule says that when team members see that things are improving, they do more than expected. When they see that things are staying the same, they do just what they have to. When they see that things are declining, they quit.

One night after a Sunday program at ISKCON Potomac,

* This point came out in interviews I conducted with Brahmā Dāsa, Gopavṛndapāla Dāsa, and Tripurāri Swami, who were all present at this 1975 *iṣṭha-goṣṭhī* with Śrīla Prabhupāda. They all agreed that this is what Śrīla Prabhupāda said.

I met with a group of devotees to brainstorm ideas for increasing their *saṅkīrtana* and book distribution results for the year. We huddled in a small room and discussed possible improvements, taking suggestions from everyone present as one person wrote down all the ideas on a whiteboard. In a short hour we had collected forty-five fresh ideas for expanding book distribution, refining systems, procuring useful new tools, and improving the team's efficiency. Through consensus we prioritized the points and made specific, time-bound goals for the top ten ideas, assigning a devotee to see to the completion of each. The results were amazing. Working on only ten of their goals, the Potomac team tripled their book distribution in just a year and a half. Needless to say, the Potomac team is still growing, due to the devotees' strong optimism about their future.

As I write, ISKCON's communities worldwide are overflowing with multitalented, part-time participants who live in their own homes but regularly come to an ISKCON temple, eager for service and spiritual friendship. In the Eleventh Canto of *Śrīmad-Bhāgavatam* (5.38–40), Karabhājana Muni says that the pious souls in Satya-yuga "eagerly desire to take birth in this Age of Kali," knowing that they can achieve complete success by participating in *saṅkīrtana*. These devotees, the Muni says, will take birth in many places, but especially in South India. Now, because people move freely about the planet, these pious souls end up in various places around the world to help push on the *saṅkīrtana* movement. Five hundred years ago, Lord Caitanya said, "I order every man within this universe to accept this Kṛṣṇa consciousness movement and distribute it everywhere."[8] Thus according to scripture, the wave of sincere people from India and other parts of the world currently flooding the *saṅkīrtana* movement has been sent by the Lord's arrangement. Considering all this, don't be surprised when people become attracted to your *saṅkīrtana* team and take Lord Caitanya's order to heart. They may have taken birth to do just that.

As you build your MSF, you can start with a few willing people. And as you "encourage the heck out of them" and empower them, more people will join. At ISV we began with just a handful of devotees in 2006. By sticking to the recipe for MSF success, we've increased our results every year since then. Three years after our startup, more than a hundred devotees went out at a single MSF. These results have been duplicated in devotee communities from Laguna Beach to Baltimore and Toronto and anywhere else leaders have followed this recipe for success.

All the Participants Having Fun Together

The second main ingredient of a successful MSF is to have fun. People like to have fun, and they go everywhere from sporting events to shopping malls to places of natural beauty to look for it. Dale Carnegie, entrepreneur and author, writes, "People rarely succeed unless they have fun in what they are doing."

Devotees who work together toward a worthy goal in a spirit of cooperation naturally have fun. When Lord Caitanya organized His devotees to clean the Guṇḍicā temple, they formed a production line, working together to bring hundreds of pots of water to wash the temple inside and out. As they worked they communicated with one another only by saying the name of Kṛṣṇa. Meanwhile, Lord Caitanya worked alongside His devotees, setting an example that encouraged them in their service. The entire process became yet another joyous festival. The *Caitanya-caritāmṛta* (*Madhya-līlā* 12.85) recounts: "Śrī Caitanya Mahāprabhu washed and cleansed the temple in great jubilation, chanting the holy name of Lord Kṛṣṇa all the time. Similarly, all the devotees were also chanting and at the same time performing their respective duties."

In addition to cooperating and working toward goals, people need a social life. Without it, they become bored. As the proverb goes, "All work and no play makes Jack a dull boy."

Fortunately, the spiritual world and the *saṅkīrtana* movement are always festive.

The word *festival* derives from the Latin *festa,* "joyous." The spiritual world is an eternal festival, where every word is a song, every step a dance, and where Kṛṣṇa's flute captures the minds and hearts of everyone. Kṛṣṇa's eternal affinity for His flute means that He's "all play and no work." We never see a picture of Kṛṣṇa working in a factory; instead, we see Him playing with His cows, friends, family, and *gopīs.*

Kṛṣṇa goes out every day to play in the forest with his cows and cowherd friends, and every day there's a festival to greet Him when He gets back. Kṛṣṇa's mother and father, Yaśodā and Nanda, are so attached to Him that they follow Him out of the village. Only by reminding Nanda Mahārāja that he has to organize the decorating of the village for Kṛṣṇa's return can Kṛṣṇa convince His father to return home, because the source of Nanda's happiness or fun is in pleasing Kṛṣṇa with other devotees.[9]

Śrīla Prabhupāda comments in his purport to *Caitanya-caritāmṛta, Ādi-līlā* 5.22 that the residents of the spiritual world move about for "pleasure trips only." Even Lord Caitanya, the strictest *sannyāsī,* enjoyed festivals with His devotees during each season of the year: mango-eating, splashing and swimming in the Ganges, cleaning the Guṇḍicā temple, chanting and dancing all night at Śrīvāsa Ṭhākura's home, and so on.

After each of Mahāprabhu's pastimes of cleaning the Guṇḍicā temple, going to see Lord Jagannātha, or performing *saṅkīrtana,* He would sport with His devotees:

> There were many gardens near the Guṇḍicā temple, and Śrī Caitanya Mahāprabhu and His devotees used to perform the pastimes of Vṛndāvana in each of them. In the lake named Indradyumna, He sported in the water. The Lord personally splashed all the devotees with water, and the devotees, surrounding Him on all sides, also splashed the Lord. While in the water they sometimes formed one circle and sometimes

> many circles, and while in the water they used to play cymbals and imitate the croaking of frogs. Sometimes two would pair off to fight in the water. One would emerge victorious and the other defeated, and the Lord would watch all this fun.[10]

Locana Dāsa Ṭhākura called Mahāprabhu's method "simply joyful."[11] MSF planners should follow Lord Caitanya's example and think about how to make their local MSF a joyful experience. At one MSF, the *saṅkīrtana* team rode around the city on a double-decker bus, singing *harināma* and distributing books and *prasāda* at various stops. Devotees from every part of the *yātrā* showed up for that MSF because it was so much fun.

As Lord Caitanya and His followers had picnics, played games, and at times cleaned the temple together, so do His contemporary devotees, as part of their MSFs. After all, spirit souls are *ānanda-mayo 'bhyāsāt* – they just want to have fun. If we tax our brains to make our events fun for both adults and children, people will flock to our door and join the MSF.

When we invite people to sing, dance, and eat delicious food in the company of the all-attractive Person, they show up, because that's what everyone is really looking for. What's more, when they participate in a festival designed to share the bliss of *saṅkīrtana,* Lord Caitanya fills the hearts of all with happiness and satisfies their desires. Karabhājana Muni says that serving Lord Caitanya's lotus feet gives complete fulfillment of the innermost desire of the soul (*abhīṣṭa-doham*).[12]

Everyone Rising Together to Meet Fresh Challenges

The third main ingredient of the MSF is to always generate fresh challenges. Will McCoy, my old friend and a successful entrepreneur, says, "Goals are potent." The instant one sets a goal, one's mind begins to think about how to achieve it. Poet Robert Browning writes, "Ah, but a man's reach should exceed his grasp, or what's a heaven for?"

Newcomers may thrive when expectations are low, but seasoned team members thrive on facing fresh challenges and meeting goals. The first step in getting your MSF team ready for fresh challenges is to define your mission.

Earlier, in the chapter "You Must Organize," I elaborated on how to develop a mission statement and set goals. Here, I will discuss establishing principles.

The word *mission* comes from the Latin *mittere,* "to send," and has origins in the Christian idea of delivering the Holy Spirit into the world. For lack of a clear mission or goal, people become pessimistic and begin to wander in their lives. But in the words of W. Clement Stone, businessman and philanthropist, "When a person discovers his or her mission, he or she feels its demand and becomes filled with enthusiasm and a burning desire to get to work on it."

Without a mission, a community is merely a gathering of people without direction, because they aren't sure where to go. In fact, the word *community* is a back formation from the word "common"; a group of people with a common mission was originally called a community.

There's a famous line in the hit musical *South Pacific:* "If you don't have a dream, how you gonna have a dream come true?" A well defined mission that seems worthwhile naturally inspires people to join in. Spreading the *saṅkīrtana* movement is a most attractive mission, for not only does it have unlimited scope for expansion, but it also keeps devotees deeply absorbed in thinking about how to do good for others. Kṛṣṇa discusses in the *Gītā* (17.16) that the way to a satisfied mind is to make it austere. Śrīla Prabhupāda comments on that verse, "To make the mind austere is to detach it from sense gratification. It should be so trained that it can be always thinking of doing good for others."

People are naturally fascinated by noble and expansive goals, and when given a part in achieving them they feel uplifted and also excel in other aspects of their devotional lives. Śrīla Prabhupāda writes that an *uttama* devotee is one who constantly meditates on spreading the *saṅkīrtana* movement: "Always thinking of Kṛṣṇa, devising means by which to spread the holy name of Kṛṣṇa, he understands that his only business is in spreading the Kṛṣṇa consciousness movement all over the world."[13]

As I previously mentioned, ISV's mantras include "Always Better Service," "No books left behind," and "We serve all living beings by widely spreading the holy names of Kṛṣṇa."

Śrīla Prabhupāda told one of his top managers that he should "generate fresh challenges" so that the devotees in his community would be inspired to rise up and meet them. When your MSF team members set fresh goals for themselves each month, their capacity to fulfill them grows over time. Stretching a little more each month, the devotees gain superior strength and knowledge in Kṛṣṇa consciousness while rising to meet fresh challenges. To strengthen team members' determination to meet new challenges, MSF leaders should guide their teams to increase their hearing and chanting of Śrīla Prabhupāda's books.

When NASA builds a rocket bound for outer space, its technicians, engineers, accountants, and janitors all work as a team to accomplish the task. When the rocket finally blasts off, the team members then celebrate together because they have all done their parts to reach the goal.

What's most remarkable about the event is not the launch itself but what happened during the rocket's construction. Although the launch from Cape Canaveral is what makes front-page news, the more significant accomplishments go unnoticed by the public because they happen behind the scenes. The news behind the news is that the group's goal and the pressure of deadlines have driven the men and women of NASA forward cooperatively and allowed them to invent new technologies. In fact, the modern science of project management evolved in part from projects at NASA.

Why does the pressure of meeting a deadline and team goals bring out the best in people? It is due to the law of forced efficiency, which states that when people work toward a fixed deadline their productivity increases. It should be noted here that the terms "forced efficiency" and "fixed deadline" do not refer to the weight of quotas imposed in an authoritarian manner. Rather, when a team of devotees schedules an MSF and then participates in setting goals for themselves and their team, everyone involved, including the team leader, welcomes the pressure that comes from trying to meet their deadlines and the MSF's goals. In fact, rising to meet those goals, they find themselves with the capacity to do more and to get things done in newer and better ways. Combined with the devotional maturity that comes from strong *sādhana* and caring leadership, they find themselves craving more service and relishing the pressure. This relish acts as a catalyst for their internal exchange of service with Kṛṣṇa. As Śrīla Prabhupāda writes in his purport to *Śrīmad-Bhāgavatam* 1.2.6, "This relation of servant and the served is the most congenial form of intimacy."

Developing Themes for the MSF

At ISV we compose mind-catching themes to reflect the freshness of each MSF. The theme is then advertised ahead of time through postcards, posters, and emails. Here are examples of some of our themes:

The MSF of Steady Improvements: During this MSF, the devotees meet together to brainstorm and make lists of areas in which they can improve their personal *sādhana,* elements of the *saṅkīrtana,* and all kinds of temple functions, as well as the quality of their book distribution. After these planning sessions, the devotees go out together to distribute books and test the improvements they've made.

The MSF of Loving Exchanges: This MSF is based on the fourth verse of Rūpa Gosvāmī's *Nectar of Instruction* wherein he lists the six loving exchanges between devotees: "Offering gifts in charity, accepting charitable gifts, revealing one's mind in confidence, inquiring confidentially, accepting *prasāda,* and offering *prasāda* are the six symptoms of love shared by one devotee and another." The devotees study this verse and then increase these loving exchanges among the community's members. They then extend themselves by going out and sharing these same loving exchanges with the public.

The MSF of 30,000, an Occasion for Selfless Service: 30,000 is the number of books the ISV devotees decided to distribute during one December marathon. You can choose numbers according to the time and occasion. Big numbers capture the imagination of everyone in the community, and all kinds of people come forward to help realize the goal.

The MSF of Learning Foreign Languages: We choose a particular foreign language commonly spoken in our area. Team members learn how to say a few words in this language so they can present books to people in a way that accommodates them.

With these three main ingredients – a lot of people each doing a little; making the event fun; and devising regular, fresh challenges – you are ready to put together an effective MSF. Here are some more practical steps to help you proceed.

Plan Ahead

The further ahead you plan your MSF, the better. Ideally, you should sit with your team members at the beginning of the year and plan all the MSFs, writing the dates and themes into a yearly schedule and posting it where everyone in the community can see it. In busy Vaiṣṇava communities, devotees are engaged in many projects. To ensure the best possible attendance at the MSF, be sure that the dates are in harmony with other important scheduled events.

One way to harmonize the yearly schedule of MSFs is to plan them to coincide with auspicious days. In May, for instance, you might want to dovetail the MSF with Lord Nṛsiṁha's appearance day. Working toward that holy day, devotees can go out to distribute books while meditating on the mood of Lord Nṛsiṁha's great devotee Prahlāda Mahārāja, who laments for the fallen conditioned souls. Prahlāda doesn't want to go to a cave, doesn't want to stay away from the big cities and towns. Rather, he prays to live among the fallen souls and give them relief from *māyā,* helping to "lift the burden of material life from their heads."

Carrying out an MSF a week or two before a holy day gives devotees extra impetus to remember Kṛṣṇa as they distribute books. When the holy day arrives, a representative of the *saṅkīrtana* team can read out to the Deities, assembled devotees, and guests something that explains the theme of the MSF and how the goals were met, including book scores, individual triumphs, and unique obstacles that were overcome. What's more, when guests and members of the congregation hear these offerings, they become inspired to join future MSFs. Having worked hard together to meet their goals, devotees deeply relish hearing the team's offering to the Lord and His devotees.

Here's a sample offering from a December marathon, written and read before our Deities and all the devotees and guests present by ISV's fulfillment director, Rasika-śekhara Dāsa:

> Hare Kṛṣṇa! Dear devotees,
>
> Please accept my humble obeisances. All Glories to Śrīla Prabhupāda!
>
> Our annual book distribution marathon referred to as "The MSF of 25,000 Books, an Occasion for Selfless Service," began in the second week of October and was concluded yesterday, January 5. The main goal of this *saṅkīrtana* festival was to distribute at least 25,000 books – an initial goal, which was revised in early December to 30,000 books.
>
> This annual book distribution marathon turned out to be a historic event, with ISV devotees distributing thousands of

Śrīla Prabhupāda's books throughout the Bay Area and at distant spots, including other parts of the US, Europe, and India.

Book distribution occurred with much enthusiasm during practically all weekends of the marathon (MSF), during several *harināma* performances in Palo Alto, during special days marking festivals such as Dussehra and Diwali, on Govardhana-pūjā, Thanksgiving, World Enlightenment Day, the day marking the advent of the *Bhagavad-gītā,* the Christmas holidays, and on so many weekdays involving spontaneous and voluntary *saṅkīrtana* activity.

The highlight of this MSF was that by going door to door at large apartment complexes, devotees distributed hundreds of book packs, *Bhagavad-gītās,* and *Kṛṣṇa Books* all across the Bay Area. Both adults and children were active participants in door-to-door book distribution, including Sunday school kids, who organized their own *saṅkīrtana* with a goal of 2,500 books, and who succeeded in distributing 2,894 books.

In addition, numerous cases of *Bhagavad-gītā As It Is* and sets of *Śrīmad-Bhāgavatam* were distributed at temple programs, and hundreds of *Gītās* were shipped for placement in motels all across the US, with extensive devotee participation by MotelGita team members from different states. (The MotelGita team succeeded in placing more than 10,000 *Bhagavad-gītās* in this marathon).

During this MSF Śrīla Prabhupāda's books were also placed in libraries, distributed at weddings and special events, at Indian stores and other venues, and at nearby and distant temples. Book distribution continued through Smart Boxes placed in various establishments. The Smart Box team set a goal of opening new Smart Boxes. We are pleased to announce that by their untiring efforts they were able to open nineteen new Smart Boxes in the Bay Area alone.

The final results of the marathon can be summarized as follows:

- More than 150 devotees participated in book distribution.

- They distributed 31,099 books, surpassing ISV's MSF goal and setting a new record for book distribution, crossing the previous high of 23,581 books distributed during the previous marathon.

- ISV devotees raised $55,383, setting another new record, surpassing the previous high of $33,864 set also during the last annual marathon. The *lakṣmī* score includes donations, $27,309 of which was made to ISV MotelGita in this year's marathon.

We thank all participating devotees, including members of Team ISV and all donors and sponsors who contributed to the success of this MSF.

On behalf of Team ISV, MSF of 30,000 *kī jaya*!

Hearing the results of their team effort read before Śrīla Prabhupāda and the Deities, the devotees cheer and feel great satisfaction knowing that they have given their life energy to serve Kṛṣṇa. In fact, an offering like this to the Deities of the results of one's devotional service is one of the items Śrīla Rūpa Gosvāmī lists in his instructions on how to discharge devotional service:

> When the Deity is coming out, the servitors in the temple put forward the daily accounts before Them: so much was the collection, so much was the expenditure. The whole idea is that the Deity is considered to be the proprietor of the whole establishment, and all the priests and other people taking care of the temple are considered to be the servants of the Deity. This system is very, very old and is still followed.[14]

Śrīla Prabhupāda confirms the importance of making a substantial offering: "But simply a festival of flowers and fruits does not constitute worship. The one who serves the message of the guru really worships him."[15] And in a letter to Satsvarūpa Dāsa Goswami dated September 2, 1974, Śrīla Prabhupāda tells of his specific appreciation for an offering of book distribution results:

> Your letter is very much pleasing to me with the report of the book distribution. Whenever I get report of my book selling I feel strength. Even now in this weakened condition I have got strength from your report. You should know that in this work you have Kṛṣṇa's blessings.

Getting It Done

Here's a list of things you'll need or need to do in order to pull your MSF together:

***Saṅkīrtana* spots:** Assign someone to brainstorm and research where the team can go to distribute books. Every city or town has different opportunities and challenges. Discover what you can do with what you have. Until you try a spot, you won't know for sure whether or not it is good. I've seen devotees assume that some spots are not good and neglect them only to find out later that they are fantastic.

Most urban areas provide multiple arenas for *saṅkīrtana:* door-to-door, events, city streets, and so on. Some spots, like downtown areas, may require a permit. Other spots, like events, street fairs, vegetarian fairs, and so on, may require that you register in advance. When *saṅkīrtana* spots are arranged ahead of time, the MSF team members can go out confidently, knowing that they will be fully engaged.

***Saṅkīrtana* lunches:** In preparation for the MSF, a team works to make bagged lunches for all the book distributors to take with them. Someone hands them to each devotee as he or she leaves. After being out on book distribution for a while, devotees get new life from tasting *prasāda,* and those who lovingly cooked and packed the lunches relish transcendental bliss from having served the devotees.

Books: Obviously, team members need a variety of books to take out for distribution. When the books are made available well in advance of the MSF, devotees can pick up what they need without wasting time. Ideally, there should be a balanced mix of large, medium, and small books, along with foreign-language books.

Invest in BBT books and hold them sacred. Scripture is imported from the spiritual world. Stock up on a variety of books and keep them in a clean, temperature-controlled, well-organized space. Promote the idea that the space is as sacred as the Deity room.

Credit card acceptance devices: Nowadays, it's easy to accept credit cards while on *saṅkīrtana.* Square, PayPal, and others provide services and devices so that one can accept credit and debit cards on the fly. Since many people *only* use credit cards, having these systems and devices ready for your MSF team members is a must.

Sharing *prasāda:* *Prasāda* for distribution to the public should be thoughtfully prepared and packaged. For example, it should be hygienically packaged and labeled. With *prasāda* in hand, the devotees are confident that they have a "secret weapon" at their disposal as they go out to meet the public. Vaiṣṇavas become more eager to meet people, because giving out delicious food makes fast friends. First-class *prasāda* – for both the MSF team members and the public – thus completes a successful MSF. Śrīla Prabhupāda writes:

> By rendering a little service, even by eating *prasāda,* what to speak of chanting and dancing, everyone can be promoted to Vaikuṇṭha-loka. It is therefore requested that all our devotees in the ISKCON community become pure Vaiṣṇavas, so that by their mercy all the people of the world will be transferred to Vaikuṇṭha-loka, even without their knowledge. Everyone should be given a chance to take *prasāda* and thus be induced to chant the holy names Hare Kṛṣṇa and also dance in ecstasy. By these three processes, although performed without knowledge or education, even an animal went back to Godhead.[16]

Mantra cards: Devotees can liberally distribute cards with the *mahā-mantra* written on them as well as your temple's or the event leader's personal contact information, and gain an added sense of giving to the public and making the temple community and atmosphere more available to them.

Rallying the troops: On the MSF day, team members should first meet to hear, chant, and prepare for the day. As they start out the door to their preassigned spots, I've noticed that devotees are often laughing, smiling, and praying due to their feelings of anticipation and spiritual progress. Śrīla Prabhupāda writes about the life preaching brings: "Yes, the preaching work is giving you new life. My Guru Mahārāja Bhaktisiddhānta Sarasvatī used to say: *pran ache yar sei hetu pracar,* 'One can preach who has got life.' So one who is preaching this Kṛṣṇa consciousness movement means he has got real life."[17]

After-party: At ISV, after a day out on book distribution, we enjoy meeting up at the temple or someone's home to share stories of our adventures. To facilitate such get-togethers, team leaders can prompt their group members to recount what happened the day they went out. We have the devotees sit in a circle. Then we ask each person to express his or her experiences and realizations. We've found that by sharing these encounters, we feel bliss and learn valuable lessons.

Reporting scores: At ISV everyone reports their book and collection scores conveniently through a Google group. A devotee is assigned to tally the scores, report them to the "World Saṅkīrtana Newsletter," and get them ready for the offering to the Deities. Keeping abreast of the results in this way helps keep the team inspired.

The Good News Action Broadcast (GNAB): It's important for any expanding movement or enterprise to broadcast good news. As author Alexandre Dumas famously said, "Nothing succeeds like success." The GNAB is the passing on of good news from the *saṅkīrtana* field. When devotees go out on *saṅkīrtana,* amazing things happen. I have always encouraged participants to write down their experiences and post them to our Google group so the entire community can read them. Through the GNAB the devotees hear about breakthroughs, realizations, or sudden feelings of compassion their teammates relished while in the field, by Lord Caitanya's mercy.

Here's a sample of a GNAB that I wrote and posted on a Google group maintained by ISV:

> Dayānidhi Prabhu and I went together to Cash and Carry on Saturday. As soon as we set up our table, people at once began coming over to see what we had. Dayānidhi, although an experienced book distributor, had not been out on *saṅkīrtana* for many years. At first he mostly watched, but then he jumped in, head first. Really funny! The first man he spoke to argued with him for about ten minutes, giving many reasons why he didn't want to buy a book. The man also kept repeating, "I am God," to which Dayānidhi persistently replied, "You're a part of God." The man finally walked away. About twenty minutes later, however, he came back and said, "I'd like to take back my words. I've decided to buy a book." He gave Dayānidhi $20 and took a couple of books with him. Just see. You never know! Using the same kindhearted persistence, I saw Dayānidhi convince many people after that to also take books and give donations. And he left everyone with a good impression. He is a valuable new member of Team ISV! Please, everybody, welcome him to Team ISV and congratulate him for his efforts next time you see him. Go, Go, Go! With gratitude.

Because performing *saṅkīrtana* is a transcendental activity, the GNABs are very pleasing to hear, and they create a buzz about *saṅkīrtana*.

New Services and Teams Within Teams

As the MSF develops, more organization is required to handle the various activities as they are created. I've already discussed encouragement and empowerment as important ingredients for developing successful participation in the MSF. You also need to organize. So here is a better idea of how to develop the MSF with empowered "teams within teams." This is based on how the necessary service positions have evolved over the years at ISV to support the book distribution.

Fulfillment Director: The fulfillment director keeps the books flowing by liaising with the BBT. Someone must be assigned to order the proper ratio of books and make sure they are paid for, shipped, stored, and dispensed. This service includes good record keeping.

Packing/Stamping Director: Each book should be stamped with the contact information of the local temple, community, or event leader. A nice selection of books can then be bundled together so that people buy several books at a time.

Accounts Director: To take care of every penny collected, a team member should be assigned to keep careful accounts and then generate reports so that you can see how you are doing.

Communications Director: This position is extremely important. Keeping the devotees in touch with one another and broadcasting good news creates an enlivening esprit de corps in the community.

Cooking Team: An army runs on its stomach. You'll need a team to make memorable *prasāda* not only for team members but also for distribution to the public.

Design Team: Fliers, postcards, posters, and so on, all need good designs. This team brainstorms and produces attractive posters, cards, and other collaterals to promote the MSF.

Devotee Care Team: This team's goal is to make sure that devotees are getting what they need – spiritual guidance, counseling, rides, mediation, support during illness, job counseling, and help with time management and childcare – whatever it takes to keep the devotees grounded and happy. Because ISV is built around the principle of *saṅkīrtana,* and because *saṅkīrtana* is its mission, everyone in the community is part of the team no matter what their service.

The above list shows how preparing for an MSF opens service opportunities for everyone. When you open the MSF to everyone – mothers, children, parents, the seasoned, first-timers, and so on – everyone will serve according to his or her liking and capacity.

As more people join, you will be induced to expand your vision and capabilities. As newcomers join, you'll find you need to orient and tutor them. Pairing new people with veterans in an apprenticeship system to make sure first-timers have a good experience on *saṅkīrtana* is essential.

In 2006, when ISV held its first Monthly Saṅkīrtana Festival, we decided to schedule one weekend every month, during which everyone could go out on *saṅkīrtana* together. After our first outing the devotees were so euphoric from the experience that some of them said, "Let's do it every week!" But we didn't. We held steady at once a month. After we had performed the MSF for three months in a row, some devotees said, "Let's do it every *other* month." We didn't do that either. Holding to our original plan, by the time a year had gone by, everyone had become steady at performing the MSF once a month. As a result of the momentum, capacity, and taste gained over the years of performing the MSF, devotees now go out more frequently than once a month, even though we still have a designated MSF each month.

Śrīla Prabhupāda encouraged all the devotees in his temples to go out on *saṅkīrtana.* I participated in such an event while a resident of the *brahmacārī āśrama* on the top floor of ISKCON's twelve-story temple in New York City. It was there that I got my first lesson in the power of "a lot of people each doing a little." It was the summer of 1976 when the devotees of 340 West Fifty-Fifth Street in Manhattan came together to organize a one-day event that would engage everyone in our temple community in book distribution. Śrīla Prabhupāda had written a message to the devotees in Los Angeles on April 15, 1973, in his own handwriting, to inspire them: "Everyone should go with the *saṅkīrtana* party as soon as possible." On December 6, 1974, he also wrote in a letter to Śrī Govinda, "Regarding the temple management, one man can be left behind, while the others go out."

The devotees in that high-rise lived together and worked untiringly, each in their own unique ways, to serve Śrī Śrī Rādhā-Govinda. There were offerings to be cooked, pots to be washed, *āratis* to be performed, and so on. Getting everyone out the door – all on the same day – for the single purpose of distributing books, required sacrifice and smart planning.

From our community, a dozen devotees, most of them *brahmacārīs,* were going daily to the streets and airports around New York to distribute books. During that era, most devotees thought of book distribution as a full-time service that not everyone could do.

So, as we were preparing for the day when all the devotees in the temple would go out – women with children, cooks, *pūjārīs,* and temple leaders included – everyone was excited and a little nervous. Some were skeptical, thinking such an event might be a lot of work with only a small return.

But the devotees' smiles and vigor that morning as they left the building were telling. On my way out of the temple I held the front door wide open, allowing a group of devotees to exit with their arms full of books. Among them I noticed that a mother pushing a stroller had tucked copies of *Śrī Īśopaniṣad* and *Bhagavad-gītā As It Is* in with her baby. "A transcendental Trojan horse," I thought.

That day, even the temple president, busy as he was, left the management helm to lead the devotees onto the field of battle. As the proverb goes, "Not the cry, but the flight of the wild swan, leads the flock to fly and follow."

Amid the euphoria, no one had talked much about the results this excursion might bring. But the next morning when the book distribution scores were tallied and announced to the Deities, I was stunned. Over a hundred devotees had gone out to distribute that day, setting a new temple record for numbers of books distributed in one day. I marked this event permanently in my memory.

When it came time to organize our *saṅkīrtana* team at ISV, we brought Śrīla Prabhupāda's "everyone to go with the *saṅkīrtana* party as soon as possible" out of storage, dusted it off, and made plans to invite all the members of our congregation to join. Try it. It works.

REALIZATIONS

"The transcendental gardener, Śrī Caitanya Mahāprabhu, distributed handful after handful of fruit in all directions, and when the poor, hungry people ate the fruit, the gardener smiled with great pleasure."

ŚRĪ CAITANYA-CARITĀMṚTA
ĀDI-LĪLĀ 9.30

CHAPTER TWENTY-TWO

The Penny Principle

THE FOLLOWING PARABLE illustrates the Penny Principle. Once upon a time, a *brahmacārī* was going door to door to beg alms for his temple. From the threshold of one of the houses he could see a couple inside. They looked angry, as if they had just finished a heated argument. Having caught sight of the *brahmacārī* at their door, the irritated couple disdainfully gave him some ashes as a donation and shooed him away.

The wise *brahmacārī* carefully wrapped the ashes in his cloth, carried the bundle back to the temple, and asked the *pūjārī* to polish the Deity's brass paraphernalia with the ashes. Day by day the *pūjārī* polished the Deity's brass cups, bowls, and plates, and as he did so, he purified the hearts of the unkind householders who had given only ashes in charity.

Months later, as the *brahmacārī* was again making his rounds, he chanced to knock at the door of the same house. This time the couple opened the door and fell at his feet. They begged his forgiveness and plaintively asked how they could serve him.

The moral of the story is clear. The most insignificant donation given to Kṛṣṇa, even unknowingly or with malice, purifies the donors and begins their devotional lives.

In the summer of 1973, on my first day out distributing BTGs and collecting donations, my assigned coach, Bhakta Patrick, taught me this important principle: "Even if people give you only a penny, you should accept it gratefully, because their donations give them eternal benefit by starting their devotional service."

In America the smallest denomination of currency is a penny. Could it be that one who gives such a tiny amount to Kṛṣṇa gets such great benefit? The Supreme Lord, the scriptures, and the great souls all answer a resounding "Yes!" In the *Gītā* (2.40), for example, Lord Kṛṣṇa says, "In this endeavor [devotional service] there is no loss or diminution, and a little advancement on this path can protect one from the most dangerous type of fear."

To stress that everything we do for Kṛṣṇa or His devotees counts, Śrīla Prabhupāda says in his purport to this verse, "One percent done in Kṛṣṇa consciousness bears permanent results, so that the next beginning is from the point of two percent."

One may doubt that this verse and purport apply to those ignorant of what they are doing. But Śrīla Prabhupāda stresses throughout his teachings that a giver need not be fully aware of the significance of his or her donation; that is, the donor may not even know that it's for the Supreme Personality of Godhead. Indeed, the donor might not even know that there *is* a Supreme Personality of Godhead. Even one so ignorant as that gets credit for giving.

Śrīla Prabhupāda confirms this eternal truth in numerous statements like this: "In *Bhagavad-gītā* (18.46) we find it is stated, *yataḥ pravṛttir bhūtānām:* if one decides to sacrifice for the supreme cause, even if he does not know that the supreme cause is Kṛṣṇa, he will come gradually to understand that Kṛṣṇa is the supreme cause by the sacrificial method."[1]

And on the point that one gets credit for giving the smallest denomination of money Śrīla Prabhupāda says:

> Yes. You save him from going to hell. Because a farthing* spent for Kṛṣṇa it will be accounted: "Oh, this man has given a farthing." This is called *ajñāta-sukṛti* [spiritual activity one performs unknowingly]. They are very poor in their thought. Therefore the saintly persons move just to enlighten him a little, to give them a chance to serve Kṛṣṇa. Giving them a chance to serve Kṛṣṇa. That is saintly person's study.... That is his duty.[2]

I've seen for myself over the years how practical and true such statements are. Countless times I've seen people with small beginnings in Kṛṣṇa consciousness – even those averse to it – eventually come to the full-blown practice of devotional service by giving a mere pittance in the beginning.

More often than not, the people who give aren't even aware of what they are doing. But Kṛṣṇa is so kind that He counts, records, and gives them credit for whatever they've done. Even though I cannot always see how Kṛṣṇa is doing this, I know that His divine hand is involved because He Himself, sacred scriptures, and saintly devotees throughout history all emphatically and repeatedly confirm His presence in everything – as further evidence in this chapter will verify.

Remembering Bhakta Roberto's words, heeding the sacred words of scripture and of the great souls, and being fond of simplifying philosophical concepts into mantras, I've coined a phrase – the Penny Principle – to describe this scriptural truth about the power of small beginnings in devotional service.

I like distilling principles into mantras because I find that such succinct, condensed slices of philosophy are easier for people to understand, recall, and become inspired by. The Penny Principle is meant, therefore, to convince devotees of

* A farthing is one fourth of a penny in the UK, although it was withdrawn from circulation in 1961.

not only how important it is to engage people in Kṛṣṇa's service but also how easy it is, by Lord Caitanya's grace, to help lost souls make a start on the path of pure devotional service to Kṛṣṇa.

To summarize the fundamental truths behind the Penny Principle, even the smallest contribution given to Kṛṣṇa or His devotees

- starts the giver on the path back to Godhead.
- is counted and recorded and thus never goes in vain, even if the giver doesn't know that Kṛṣṇa is the Supreme Personality of Godhead.
- brings eternal benefit to the giver.
- accumulates and grows.

What to speak of giving something to Kṛṣṇa or His devotees, the act of giving itself is generally good for living beings. Kṛṣṇa confirms this in the *Bhagavad-gītā* (12.11): "If, however, you are unable to work in this consciousness of Me, then try to act giving up all results of your work and try to be self-situated."

It's Better To Give Than to Receive

It's true, then, what all mothers teach their children: It's better to give than to receive. Here's some hard evidence that lends force to this traditional maxim. A team of researchers from Simon Fraser University in Canada polled 234,917 people from 126 countries and "found that respondents worldwide experienced feelings of well-being after giving to others." David Mielach from the *Business News Daily* reports on this study: "Giving really is better than receiving, new research confirms. That research found people in both rich and impoverished countries say they feel better about donating money to charity, spending money on others, or giving to others than they do about buying something for themselves."

Mielach quotes the lead author of this giving-versus-receiving study, Lara Aknin, as saying: "Our findings suggest that the psychological reward experienced from helping others may be deeply ingrained in human nature, emerging in diverse cultural and economic contexts."

Deeply ingrained, indeed. Lord Caitanya confirms that inherent within the heart of all living beings is the propensity to love Kṛṣṇa and to give themselves to Him in loving service. The bhakti scriptures confirm that the purpose of human life is to cultivate our love for Kṛṣṇa by the practice of giving; furthermore, as that love awakens, one gradually comes to the perfection of life by giving everything, including oneself, to Kṛṣṇa.

Sacrifice Is Valuable

Śrīla Prabhupāda elaborates on the value of giving, in his purport to *Bhagavad-gītā* 12.11: "Giving up the fruits of one's activities one is sure to purify his mind gradually, and in that purified stage of mind one becomes able to understand Kṛṣṇa consciousness."

And as Śrīla Prabhupāda says in his purport to *Śrīmad-Bhāgavatam* 1.5.17, "Once engaged in the devotional service of the Lord, one will continue the service in all circumstances."

In the *Gītā* (3.9–10), Lord Kṛṣṇa reveals that enlightened giving – giving that leads to full engagement in devotional service – begins with the practice of surrendering some of one's earnings to Kṛṣṇa. By such charity one becomes purified.

> Work done as a sacrifice for Viṣṇu has to be performed; otherwise work causes bondage in this material world. Therefore, O son of Kuntī, perform your prescribed duties for His satisfaction, and in that way you will always remain free from bondage.
>
> In the beginning of creation, the Lord of all creatures sent forth generations of men and demigods, along with sacrifices

> for Viṣṇu, and blessed them by saying, "Be thou happy by this *yajña* [sacrifice] because its performance will bestow upon you everything desirable for living happily and achieving liberation."

Śrīla Prabhupāda gives this practical advice about how people in the modern day can start the giving process:

> If one is a businessman, an industrialist, an agriculturist, etc., then one should spend his hard-earned money for the cause of the Lord. Think always that the money which is accumulated is the wealth of the Lord. Wealth is considered to be the goddess of fortune (Lakṣmī), and the Lord is Nārāyaṇa, or the husband of Lakṣmī. Try to engage Lakṣmī in the service of Lord Nārāyaṇa and be happy. That is the way to realize the Lord in every sphere of life.[3]

In the *Gītā* (3.15), Kṛṣṇa confirms that such giving connects one to Him when He says that the "Transcendence [God] is eternally situated in [such] acts of sacrifice." This means that from any position, one can advance in spiritual life, even to the point of feeling the presence of God, just by handing over some of the fruits of one's labor to a higher cause sanctioned in the *Vedas*.

When it comes to distributing Śrīla Prabhupāda's books, therefore, devotees dutifully ask people for donations in return for the books they distribute. The charity a person gives in exchange for one of Śrīla Prabhupāda's books is not ordinary. It is divine charity. In fact, Śrīla Prabhupāda recognizes such exchanges as expressions of love between Kṛṣṇa and the public:

> This Society was started single-handedly, but because people are coming forward and dealing with the give-and-take policy, the Society is now expanding all over the world. We are glad that people are donating very liberally to the development of the Society's activities, and people are also eagerly accepting whatever humble contribution we are giving them in the

shape of books and magazines dealing strictly with the subject matter of Kṛṣṇa consciousness.[4]

Divine Charity

Kṛṣṇa asks every living entity to surrender to Him completely. Such surrender bestows the highest good to the living entities in the material world; nonetheless, people are reluctant, to say the least, to surrender *anything* to Kṛṣṇa.

Kṛṣṇa's devotees know that even the tiniest gesture of giving puts a person on the auspicious path toward Kṛṣṇa, and so they ask people for monetary donations.

But why money? Anyone who has gone into a public arena to sell Śrīla Prabhupāda's books has surely been asked why devotees collect donations at all. Isn't a spiritualist supposed to shun money? Isn't the devotee's asking for money simply mundane business?

Hardly.

Distributors of Śrīla Prabhupāda's books are not motivated by material profit. They want only to do what in the *Bhagavad-gītā* (18.68–69) Kṛṣṇa says pleases Him the most: "For one who explains this supreme secret to the devotees, pure devotional service is guaranteed, and at the end he will come back to Me. There is no servant in this world more dear to Me than he, nor will there ever be one more dear."

Śrīla Prabhupāda indicates how an exchange with a book distributor may begin a person's loving relationship with Kṛṣṇa: "Love begins with this give and take. We give something to our lover, He gives something to us, and in this way love develops."[5]

In this way, those who voluntarily give to Kṛṣṇa through His devotees take a first step in their loving relationship with Kṛṣṇa. Considering the exchange to be sacred, book distributors accept people's donations joyfully and use them to serve Kṛṣṇa.

Money, although made of ordinary paper and metal, is a

token of one's life energy. Through hard work we give our life energy to earn money. Śrī Prahlāda Mahārāja confirms how important money is to people:

> Money is so dear that one conceives of money as being sweeter than honey. Therefore, who can give up the desire to accumulate money, especially in household life? Thieves, professional servants [soldiers], and merchants try to acquire money even by risking their very dear lives.[6]

Śrīla Prabhupāda elaborates on the benefits that accrue to people who give their hard-earned money for one of his transcendental books:

> **Gopī-kānta:** Śrīla Prabhupāda, what is the exact benefit if a person just takes a *Śrīmad-Bhāgavatam* on the street and gives some donation to help out with the printing costs or whatever?
> **Prabhupāda:** That is already explained. They will read. They will see the picture of Kṛṣṇa. Immediate profit is, they will ask, "What is this picture?" And you will say, "Kṛṣṇa." "Oh," they say, "it is Kṛṣṇa?" Then ... [laughter] From the beginning of the, what is called, cover, the benefit begins, because the uttering the word "Kṛṣṇa" is benefit. Then, if he reads ... Of course, if he pays for the book, he will read. So you give a chance to the person to know about Kṛṣṇa, their life becomes sublime.[7]

And in his purport to *Bhagavad-gītā* text 11.54, Śrīla Prabhupāda explains the importance of divine charity:

> As far as charity is concerned, it is plain that charity should be given to the devotees of Kṛṣṇa who are engaged in His devotional service to spread the Kṛṣṇa philosophy, or Kṛṣṇa consciousness, throughout the world. Kṛṣṇa consciousness is a benediction to humanity. Lord Caitanya was appreciated by Rūpa Gosvāmī as the most munificent man of charity because love of Kṛṣṇa, which is very difficult to achieve, was distributed freely by Him. So if one gives some amount of his money

> to persons involved in distributing Kṛṣṇa consciousness, that charity, given to spread Kṛṣṇa consciousness, is the greatest charity in the world.

Śrīla Prabhupāda further confirms that even one who is unaware that his charity is going to Kṛṣṇa still reaps the benefit: "This is called *ajñāta-sukṛti.* He does not know, but he is advanced one step to Kṛṣṇa consciousness. Anybody who is contributing even a farthing to you, he is advanced in Kṛṣṇa consciousness."[8]

The *Śrīmad-Bhāgavatam* (2.3.17, purport) goes as far as to say that one who gives in charity for *any* reason is never the loser; still, one who gives to Kṛṣṇa and His devotees gets the greatest benefit:

> Money given in charity to a suitable person is guaranteed bank balance in the next life. Such charity is recommended to be given to a *brāhmaṇa.* If the money is given in charity to a non-*brāhmaṇa* (without brahminical qualification) the money is returned in the next life in the same proportion. If it is given in charity to a half-educated *brāhmaṇa,* even then the money is returned double. If the money is given in charity to a learned and fully qualified *brāhmaṇa,* the money is returned a hundred and a thousand times, and if the money is given to a *veda-pāraga* (one who has factually realized the path of the *Vedas*), it is returned by unlimited multiplication. The ultimate end of Vedic knowledge is realization of the Personality of Godhead, Lord Kṛṣṇa, as stated in the *Bhagavad-gītā* (*vedaiś ca sarvair aham eva vedyaḥ*). There is a guarantee of money's being returned if given in charity, regardless of the proportion.

Accordingly, when I request a donation for a book, this is what I tell people: "It is an ancient tradition to give something in return for spiritual knowledge, because by that sacrifice one is connected to the previous teachers who have painstakingly passed this wisdom down to us over the ages."

Śrīla Prabhupāda spoke about this tradition in a lecture he gave on June 16, 1969: "Just like Nārada Ṛṣi is giving us good literature. He is instructing Vyāsadeva, 'Give this literature to the people.' We are taking advantage of *Śrīmad-Bhāgavatam*. Are we not debtor? We go to school, college, and pay so much fees to the teachers. Are we not debtor to Vyāsadeva and Nārada?"

When I am straightforward with people and tell them about this cultural tradition and how I am working on behalf of those who are saintly and renounced, I have noticed that they often nod in agreement, as if this were a principle that should be obvious to everyone.

Giving Grows

Book distributors who are well studied in scripture and who therefore know the validity of the Penny Principle sometimes ask people to give *at least a penny* in exchange for a book. They do this when people are hesitant to give, either because they think the book costs more than they can afford or because they are simply reluctant to give.

I have seen that reluctant donors often change their minds when asked for just a penny; many end up giving a lot more. This phenomenon reminds me of a dam that breaks and releases a sudden surge of water: people seem to exude goodwill once they have decided to give for a good cause.

For example, I once presented a book to a gentleman in Montreal, Canada. After I asked him for a donation, he hesitated, saying he couldn't afford the book. I told him that even if he didn't give I would gladly let him keep the book for free, but then I added that if he were to give even something small – even a penny – he would get spiritual credit. Apparently sensing my sincere intention the man went into his apartment, scooped some pennies out of a jar, and brought them back to me. I thanked him profusely and departed, leaving him with the book. Fifteen minutes later the man came looking for me.

He was eager to give more. From watching his body language I could make out that by giving the first donation the man had tasted something sweet and was inspired to give more, which he did.

Here's another story about how giving grows. Bhakta Kumar, one of our local book distributors, met a man at the door of an apartment and showed him a *Bhagavad-gītā*. The man wanted to keep it but was unwilling to give a donation. Bhakta Kumar told the man that to get the benefit of divine charity, he should give at least one penny. The man accepted Bhakta Kumar's proposal and went back into his apartment to find a penny. The man's wife found him rummaging through the drawers in their bedroom and asked what he was doing. He told her about the agreement he had made with the devotee at the door. As soon as she heard that her husband intended to give a volunteer only a penny for such a beautiful book, she insisted that her husband give Bhakta Kumar a more generous donation. A few moments later, the man handed Bhakta Kumar fifty dollars instead of the penny he had planned to give.

Very few people intend to surrender. But a kindhearted devotee can help by encouraging them to start their giving by donating the smallest thing to Kṛṣṇa. I once asked a woman to give a piece of fruit after she said she didn't have even a penny. She gave me an apple in exchange for a book. I took that apple back to the temple and gave it to the *pūjārī* to offer to Kṛṣṇa. Kṛṣṇa asks that one give Him at least a leaf, flower, fruit, or water.

I once observed Jayānanda Dāsa, while he was building the Ratha-yātrā carts in San Francisco, invite a man walking down the street to help him move a heavy beam. The man ended up staying to help out for the rest of the day. In this way, that man began his process of devotional service. When one gives something even insignificant to Kṛṣṇa, one's divine charity begins.

Another aspect of the Penny Principle is that even when

givers are unaware that they are giving to Kṛṣṇa, Kṛṣṇa still accepts their service. To illustrate this principle, Śukadeva Gosvāmī tells Mahārāja Parīkṣit the story of how King Satyavrata unknowingly did a small service for Matsyāvatāra. The Lord had appeared to the king as a helpless minnow and had asked the king to save Him from bigger fish. Although the king was unaware that the minnow was the Supreme Lord, he tried to help Him, and by so doing he attained the highest benefit. Śrīla Prabhupāda explains the significance of this story:

> Here is an example of giving service to the Supreme Personality of Godhead even without knowledge. Such service is called *ajñāta-sukṛti.* King Satyavrata wanted to show his own mercy, not knowing that the fish was Lord Viṣṇu. By such unknowing devotional service, one is favored by the Supreme Personality of Godhead. Service rendered to the Supreme Lord, knowingly or unknowingly, never goes in vain.[9]

Acts of Bhakti Are Special

That Kṛṣṇa favors people who knowingly or unknowingly serve Him is a display of His merciful nature as well as the supreme potency of devotional service, both of which are beyond the modes of material energy.

In *Mādhurya-kadambinī* (1.9–10), Śrīla Viśvanātha Cakravartī Ṭhākura writes that the path of devotional service is superior to the paths of karma and *jñāna.* Success on the path of karma requires exactness of procedures, and of *jñāna,* purity of mind. In contrast, advancement on the path of bhakti is independent of anything material. Even if one does not execute the practices perfectly or one's mind is not completely pure, if one incidentally or imperfectly gives something to the devotees engaged in serving Kṛṣṇa, especially if one chants the Lord's holy name, such service will take one forward.

About the advantage of devotional service over other processes, Kavi Yogendra states: "O King, one who accepts this process of devotional service to the Supreme Personality of Godhead will never blunder on his path in this world. Even while running with eyes closed, he will never trip or fall."[10]

In the same vein, *Śrī Caitanya-caritāmṛta* (*Ādi-līlā* 7.73) repeatedly acclaims the potency of direct devotional service, particularly the chanting of Kṛṣṇa's names, in statements like this one: "Simply by chanting the holy name of Kṛṣṇa one can obtain freedom from material existence. Indeed, simply by chanting the Hare Kṛṣṇa mantra one will be able to see the lotus feet of the Lord."

About the special efficacy of devotional acts, *Śrīmad-Bhāgavatam* (6.2.19) states:

> If a person unaware of the effective potency of a certain medicine takes that medicine or is forced to take it, it will act even without his knowledge because its potency does not depend on the patient's understanding. Similarly, even though one does not know the value of chanting the holy name of the Lord, if one chants knowingly or unknowingly, the chanting will be very effective.

And from the sixth chapter of *Kṛṣṇa Book:*

> It is concluded, therefore, that even a little energy expended in the service of the Lord gives one immense transcendental profit. This is explained in the *Bhagavad-gītā: sv-alpam apy asya dharmasya trāyate mahato bhayāt.* Devotional service in Kṛṣṇa consciousness is so sublime that even a little service rendered to Kṛṣṇa, knowingly or unknowingly, gives one the greatest transcendental benefit.

Śrīla Prabhupāda succinctly explains why acts of devotional service have such a special effect: "Devotional service to the Lord is not an activity of this material world; it is part of the spiritual world, where eternity, bliss, and knowledge predominate."[11]

Acts of devotional service, then, are special because they

are beyond the realm of the material world. They depend exclusively on Kṛṣṇa's oceanic mercy and incalculable generosity.

Kṛṣṇa is famous as supremely merciful and generous. For example, in dealing with the evil witch Pūtanā, who had come to kill Him, He awarded her the highest benefit by giving her an eternal place in His pastimes in the spiritual world. *Śrīmad-Bhāgavatam* 3.2.23, along with Śrīla Prabhupāda's purport, explains why Kṛṣṇa did this:

> Alas, how shall I take shelter of one more merciful than He who granted the position of mother to a she-demon [Pūtanā] although she was unfaithful and she prepared deadly poison to be sucked from her breast?
>
> Purport: Lord Kṛṣṇa accepted the motherhood of Pūtanā because she pretended to be an affectionate mother, allowing Kṛṣṇa to suck her breast. The Lord accepts the least qualification of the living entity and awards him the highest reward. That is the standard of His character.

It is well known that Kṛṣṇa gives much more than one can expect, even to those who make the slightest contact with Him for any reason. Kṛṣṇa is so kindhearted that when we take a step toward Him, He takes a thousand steps toward us. For that reason, one of His divine names is Vāñchātīta, "One who fulfills the desires of His devotees more than they can expect."

But someone might ask, "Pūtanā got the highest benefit because Kṛṣṇa was personally present before her. How do people get such benefit now, when Kṛṣṇa is not personally present performing His pastimes?" Śrīla Rūpa Gosvāmī answers this question in *Śrī Nāmāṣṭaka* (2–3):

> O Hari-nāma, all glories to You! Sung by all the sages, You are the supreme combination of syllables, and You bring transcendental bliss to everyone. If a person utters You but once,

> even disrespectfully, You still relieve his many extreme sufferings. O sun of the holy name, even a dim glimmer of Your splendor swallows the powerful darkness of materialistic life and gives those who are blind to the truth the vision to follow the path of pure devotional service. Who in this world, even if learned and pious, can fully describe Your transcendental glory?

That is to say, Kṛṣṇa is personally present in His holy name. He bestows benedictions on those who even now chant or hear His names from the lips of pure devotees, what to speak of those who read about Him in one of Śrīla Prabhupāda's books.

Śrīla Prabhupāda repeatedly stressed the potency of his books. He wrote this, for example, to Tamal Krishna Goswami on December 28, 1974:

> I am glad that you have understood the importance of my books. Therefore I am stressing it so much. Let everyone take these books. If he simply reads one page then he is getting something substantial, a real eternal benefit. Or if he hands it over to his friend and he reads one page the same result is there.

Elsewhere, Śrīla Prabhupāda comments: "[*The Bhāgavatam*] carries with it all the transcendental blessings of Lord Śrī Kṛṣṇa that we can expect from His personal contact."[12]

In *Śrī Kṛṣṇa-līlā-stava* (414), Śrīla Sanātana Gosvāmī writes, "I bow down to You [*Śrīmad-Bhāgavatam*], who are supremely blissful to read. Your every syllable pours down a flood of *prema*. You can always be served by everyone. You are Śrī Kṛṣṇa Himself."

The *Gītā-māhātmya* describes the *Bhagavad-gītā* to be the essence of all *Upaniṣads* and a veritable wish-fulfilling cow. It goes on to say that the words of *Bhagavad-gītā,* Kṛṣṇa's instructions, are like divine milk being distributed by the Supreme Lord Kṛṣṇa Himself, who is famous as a cowherd boy.

Arjuna is drinking this milk, and whoever is broadminded and advanced will attain all spiritual good fortune by drinking it too.

Kṛṣṇa's Devotees Are His Agents

But how will the people of the world receive this spiritually nourishing milk? Before coming to America, Śrīla Prabhupāda wrote a poem in Bengali called *Vṛndāvane Bhajan*. In it he explains how Kṛṣṇa distributes His favor through His devotees:

> Devotional service is causeless and self-manifesting;
> It is an eternally perfect substance but has become
> covered over.
> The *madhyama-adhikārī* Vaiṣṇava, being compassionate,
> Gives mercy to the innocent souls by awakening devotion
> in them.
> The Supreme Lord acts according to the will of the Vaiṣṇavas.
> Therefore by the mercy of the Vaiṣṇava the bewildered can
> be awakened.
> The Vaiṣṇavas can awaken the sleeping world.
> By their mercy the sinful can all become devotees.[13]

The *madhyama* devotees of Kṛṣṇa move about the world distributing transcendental books, the holy names of the Lord, and *kṛṣṇa-prasāda*. In this way they spread Kṛṣṇa's mercy around. Śrī Caitanya Mahāprabhu elucidates this point: "The root cause of devotional service to Lord Kṛṣṇa is association with advanced devotees. Even when one's dormant love for Kṛṣṇa awakens, association with devotees is still most essential."[14]

Śrīla Prabhupāda also gives us Bhaktivinoda Ṭhākura's conclusion on how people get their start in devotional service:

> Śrīla Bhaktivinoda Ṭhākura explains this point. Is this *bhāgya* (fortune) the result of an accident or something else? In the scriptures, devotional service and pious activity are considered fortunate. Pious activities can be divided into three

categories: pious activities that awaken one's dormant Kṛṣṇa consciousness are called *bhakty-unmukhī sukṛti;* pious activities that bestow material opulence are called *bhogonmukhī sukṛti;* and pious activities that enable the living entity to merge into the existence of the Supreme are called *mokṣonmukhī sukṛti*. These last two awards of pious activity are not actually fortunate. Pious activities are fortunate when they help one become Kṛṣṇa conscious. The good fortune of *bhakty-unmukhī* is attainable only when one comes in contact with a devotee. By associating with a devotee willingly or unwillingly, one advances in devotional service, and thus one's dormant Kṛṣṇa consciousness is awakened.[15]

Lord Kṛṣṇa Himself tells Uddhava about His plan to purify the world:

> With the dust of My devotees' lotus feet I desire to purify the material worlds, which are situated within Me. Thus I always follow the footsteps of My pure devotees, who are free from all personal desire, rapt in thought of My pastimes, peaceful, without any feelings of enmity, and of equal disposition everywhere.[16]

From the BBT purport to this text:

> Lord Kṛṣṇa thought, "I have established this strict rule that one can enjoy My transcendental bliss only through devotional service obtained from the dust of the lotus feet of My devotees. Since I also desire to experience My own bliss, I will observe the standard procedure and accept the dust of My devotees' feet." Śrīla Madhvācārya points out that Lord Kṛṣṇa follows the footsteps of His devotees in order to purify them. As the Lord walks along behind His pure devotees, the wind blows the dust of the Lord's feet in the front of His devotees, who then become purified by contact with such transcendental dust. One should not foolishly look for material logic in these transcendental pastimes of the Lord. It is simply a question of love between the Lord and His devotees.

Kṛṣṇa's pure devotees want nothing more than to please Him. Thus to fulfill His desire, they go out to give people transcendental books, the holy names, and *kṛṣṇa-prasāda.* And as they plant the seeds of bhakti in the hearts of conditioned souls, the devotees themselves become delighted by watching the smiles blossom on people's faces as they engage in acts of devotion, surprised by their own happiness. Such expressions often arise as delayed reactions or arrive in roundabout or unusual ways. Somehow or other, silently, invisibly, the seed of bhakti fructifies.

The following story illustrates the Penny Principle by showing how even those who give their pennies in a hostile mood can become purified. In 1974 devotees began prolifically distributing books at Chicago's O'Hare airport. Sarvopamā Dāsa used to go each day to the Rotunda in the middle of the airport, where passengers departed and arrived on (the now defunct airline) TWA.

As he distributed books each day, each day an airport employee named Mark harassed him. Mark was a gigantic young man who pushed passengers in need by wheelchair to and from the arrival and departure gates. Each time Mark passed Sarvopamā, he would stop nearby, speak some unkind words to him, pull out a penny or nickel, and fling the coin at him. The coins usually bounced off Sarvopamā's chest or skidded across the floor to his feet. More often than not, these incidents happened just as Sarvopamā was selling someone a book.

Although Mark intended to disturb Sarvopamā by interrupting his book sales, each time Mark let fly with a coin, Sarvopamā stopped what he was doing, retrieved the coin, and held it up with a smile, as if Mark had intended to donate it, and placed it in his pocket along with the rest of the day's collections. If Sarvopamā was talking to someone when the coin landed, he would politely excuse himself, pick up the coin, and then return to his customer as if none of this was unusual.

This harassment went on for months. But one day it ended abruptly when, to Sarvopamā's surprise, Mark put his arm around him and said, "You know, you're OK."

From that day on Mark was Sarvopamā's friend. He gave Sarvopamā compliments and encouragement each time he passed, and defended Sarvopamā whenever anyone bothered him as he distributed books.

Mark certainly didn't intend to give donations, but nonetheless his act of contributing and Sarvopamā's association softened his heart.

In the sixty-ninth chapter of *Kṛṣṇa Book,* Śrīla Prabhupāda explains how this kind of miracle happens:

> Anyone who attentively hears the narrations of the Lord's pastimes in Dvārakā *or supports a preacher of the Kṛṣṇa consciousness movement* [emphasis added] will certainly find it very easy to traverse the path of liberation and taste the nectar of the lotus feet of Lord Kṛṣṇa. And thus he will be engaged in Lord Kṛṣṇa's devotional service.

That is why Śrīla Prabhupāda repeatedly makes such statements as this: "Śrī Caitanya Mahāprabhu's mercy is so powerful that it acts automatically. If a person renders loving service to Kṛṣṇa, it never goes in vain. It is recorded in a spiritual account, and in due time it will fructify."[17]

Bhakti Credit Accumulates

When the Supreme Lord wanted to teach the world by His own example how to be a perfect devotee, He descended as Śrī Caitanya Mahāprabhu. Playing the role of a devotee, Lord Caitanya went about India inducing people to take up devotional service. Kṛṣṇadāsa Kavirāja Gosvāmī explains how expert Mahāprabhu was in engaging even the unwilling in acts of devotion without their even knowing what they were doing:

> Prakāśānanda Sarasvatī, however, caught Śrī Caitanya Mahāprabhu personally by the hand and seated Him with great respect in the midst of the assembly.
>
> Purport: The respectful behavior of Prakāśānanda Sarasvatī toward Śrī Caitanya Mahāprabhu is very much to be appreciated. Such behavior is calculated to be *ajñāta-sukṛti,* or pious activities that one executes unknowingly. Thus Śrī Caitanya Mahāprabhu very tactfully gave Prakāśānanda Sarasvatī an opportunity to advance in *ajñāta-sukṛti* so that in the future he might actually become a Vaiṣṇava *sannyāsī.*[18]

In the *Gītā* (6.44) Lord Kṛṣṇa says that those who take to devotional service do so because they have accumulated bhakti credits from past lives: "By virtue of the divine consciousness of his previous life, he automatically becomes attracted to the yogic principles – even without seeking them. Such an inquisitive transcendentalist stands always above the ritualistic principles of the scriptures."

Similarly, in *The Nectar of Devotion* (p. 43), Śrīla Prabhupāda recounts Śrīla Rūpa Gosvāmī's statements about the continuity of devotional service from one life to the next:

> Devotional service is a continual process from one's previous life. No one can take to devotional service unless he has had some previous connection with it. For example, suppose in this life I practice devotional service to some extent. Even though it is not one-hundred-percent perfectly performed, whatever I have done will not be lost. In my next life, from the very point where I stop in this life, I shall begin again. In this way there is always continuity.
>
> This relishing of transcendental mellow in discharging devotional service cannot be experienced by all classes of men, because this sweet loving mood is developed only from one's previous life's activities or by the association of unalloyed devotees. As explained above, association with pure devotees is the beginning of faith in devotional service.

And in the famous story of Ajāmila, Śukadeva Gosvāmī tells how the degraded Ajāmila unknowingly accumulated *bhakti-sukṛti* by chanting his son's name, which also happened to be the Lord's holy name, Nārāyaṇa. Śrīla Prabhupāda comments on this pastime in his purport to *Śrīmad-Bhāgavatam* 6.1.26:

> The Supreme Personality of Godhead is kind to the conditioned soul. Although this man completely forgot Nārāyaṇa, he was calling his child, saying, "Nārāyaṇa, please come eat this food. Nārāyaṇa, please come drink this milk." Somehow or other, therefore, he was attached to the name Nārāyaṇa. This is called *ajñāta-sukṛti.* Although calling for his son, he was unknowingly chanting the name of Nārāyaṇa, and the holy name of the Supreme Personality of Godhead is so transcendentally powerful that his chanting was being counted and recorded.

Finally, the Penny Principle goes beyond monetary exchange. Persons who express appreciation for Kṛṣṇa, Kṛṣṇa's devotees, or the process of devotional service, also build up spiritual credit.

As a startling example of this truth, in a room conversation Śrīla Prabhupāda tells some devotees that the Russians have already imperceptibly joined the *saṅkīrtana* movement because they have praised his books. He goes on to say, "In East Germany also they have placed order. So this is joining."[19]

Queen Kuntī says in her prayers that anyone who simply appreciates the devotional service of others makes advancement in spiritual life: "O Kṛṣṇa, those who continuously hear, chant, and repeat Your transcendental activities, or take pleasure in others' doing so, certainly see Your lotus feet, which alone can stop the repetition of birth and death."[20]

With great enthusiasm to see the people of the world receive the benedictions of Śrī Caitanya Mahāprabhu, Śrīla Prabhupāda penned this memorable purport in relation to Śivānanda Sena's giving his mercy to a dog, which later attained Vaikuṇṭha by the grace of Śrī Caitanya Mahāprabhu. Śrīla Prabhupāda's purport perfectly encapsulates the Penny Principle:

> This is the result of *sādhu-saṅga* – consequent association with Śrī Caitanya Mahāprabhu and promotion back home, back to Godhead. This result is possible even for a dog, by the mercy of the Vaiṣṇava. Therefore, everyone in the human form of life should be induced to associate with devotees. By rendering a little service, even by eating *prasāda,* what to speak of chanting and dancing, everyone can be promoted to Vaikuṇṭha-loka. It is therefore requested that all our devotees in the ISKCON community become pure Vaiṣṇavas, so that by their mercy all the people of the world will be transferred to Vaikuṇṭha-loka, even without their knowledge. Everyone should be given a chance to take *prasāda* and thus be induced to chant the holy names Hare Kṛṣṇa and also dance in ecstasy. By these three processes, although performed without knowledge or education, even an animal went back to Godhead.[21]

Knowing the powerful effects of distributing Śrīla Prabhupāda's books, the holy names, and *kṛṣṇa-prasāda,* may we distribute these to as many living entities as possible so that they can make their way back to Godhead. "Even a person with no knowledge can immediately acquire all knowledge simply by the benediction of Śrī Caitanya Mahāprabhu. Therefore I am praying to the Lord for His causeless mercy upon me."[22]

CHAPTER TWENTY-THREE

The Thoughtfulness Principle

IN THE PREVIOUS CHAPTER, "The Penny Principle," I discussed *ajñāta-sukṛti* and showed how a living being who even coincidentally or accidentally serves Kṛṣṇa or His devotees gets eternal spiritual benefit. In this chapter I discuss how book distributors can increase the possibility that people will have the chance to perform *ajñāta-sukṛti* – or, better yet, to offer service aware of what they're doing – by the devotees' making their presentations of Kṛṣṇa consciousness more relatable to their audience. We might wonder, if devotional service is so powerful, why does making one's presentation of it relatable matter? We have just read that if one simply hears Kṛṣṇa's name or touches a transcendental book, even if one has no knowledge of Kṛṣṇa consciousness, he or she is purified. So shouldn't *any* presentation of Kṛṣṇa consciousness work equally well? This question reminds me of an ad I once saw for a veterinarian who also offered taxidermy services. The tagline read, "Either way, you get your dog back."

So in this chapter I discuss what I call the Thoughtfulness

Principle, by which I mean that it's important for book distributors to be thoughtful about how they approach people. Yes, it's true that people are imperceptibly benefited if they somehow or other hear Kṛṣṇa's holy names or receive or even touch a transcendental book; but it's also true that they receive even more benefit if they appreciate or understand what you are giving them. The Thoughtfulness Principle, then, is about *yukta-vairāgya* and the kind of careful discernment devotees develop when they sincerely desire to help people. Such discernment compels them to present Kṛṣṇa consciousness in ways that take into consideration the cultural and intellectual sensibilities of their audience.

This topic has actually sparked a lot of important discussion among devotees. The heart of the discussion centers on the difference between what the *śāstra* refers to as unchangeable principles and adjustable details: how do we protect the pure, unchanging, eternal message even as we adjust the ways in which we present it? Is it safer and more loyal, for example, to stick exactly to the format and style of presentation Śrīla Prabhupāda used in the 1960s and '70s or to adjust our style to the needs of the people we are addressing today?

Devotees were aware of this issue even when Śrīla Prabhupāda was physically present. Think of the controversy that surrounded taking Śrīla Prabhupāda to the Mantra Rock Dance in 1967. Was it appropriate to chant Hare Kṛṣṇa in a place filled with raucous music and thousands of drugged hippies? And yet seeing the potential to glorify the holy name, Śrīla Prabhupāda chose to go. Later, he remarked, "That was no place for a *brahmacārī*." And yet he was not afraid to use the opportunity to serve Kṛṣṇa.

Devotees have looked at other examples from Śrīla Prabhupāda's preaching life, too, in order to see how he maintained the balance between unchangeable principle and adjustable detail. I have heard some devotees call Śrīla Prabhupāda's presentation "strict" – some have even said "ultraconservative" – while others call it "lenient" or "liberal." Which is correct?

Is it possible that it was both? That is, that he maintained the traditional values of the *paramparā* in *what* he taught, but adapted *how* he taught to make those principles easier for his audience to embrace?

It's clear that Śrīla Prabhupāda followed his spiritual master's mood in this regard. For example, Śrīla Bhaktisiddhānta Sarasvatī is famous for his strict practice of *sannyāsa* and his insistence that his disciples do the same. His strictness was not, however, the rigidity of a bigoted fundamentalist; rather, everything was meant for serving Kṛṣṇa, and Vaiṣṇavas should use everything in His service and take nothing for themselves.

In a letter dated April 25, 1933, Śrīla Bhaktisiddhānta Sarasvatī listed sixteen items Gauḍīya Maṭha *sannyāsīs* should avoid in the strict practice of bhakti – an attempt on his part to warn certain *maṭha* residents against the loose behavior he saw developing among them. On his list were items like bragging, foppery, deceit, and accepting service from others. He also said that whatever *sannyāsīs* did for their own gratification "should be done by going barefoot, never using shoes or conveyances."[1] (Shoes and conveyances were not part of the renunciant's code; if the *sannyāsīs* hoped to maintain their *āśrama* strictly, these were to be used only for service.)

Of course, as I mentioned, Śrīla Bhaktisiddhānta Sarasvatī's strict following of *sannyāsa* is legendary. Before starting his preaching mission he once vowed to chant one billion names of Kṛṣṇa. To complete this vow he chanted 192 rounds a day over a period of nine years, all the while living in a grass hut near the Yogapīṭha. During that period he used only what he needed to keep life and soul together; he was so *sādhu*-like in his appearance that he could have been walking off the pages of the *Caitanya-caritāmṛta*.

Yet once he began his preaching mission, he became the first *sannyāsī* in India to ride in motorcars and wear shoes and a jacket. He did these things when preaching to dignitaries and scholars; at home in the *āśrama* he maintained his simple dress. And he encouraged his *sannyāsī* disciples to do the same – to use what was helpful in their preaching and *only* when it was helpful in their preaching. He did not himself claim any facility for his personal gratification, nor did he want his disciples to become personally attached to the facilities they were using – therefore his warning against "foppery" and "deceit."

We can ask the same question about Śrīla Bhaktisiddhānta Sarasvatī Ṭhākura that we asked about Śrīla Prabhupāda: was he liberal or conservative in how he practiced and presented Kṛṣṇa consciousness?

Like Śrīla Bhaktisiddhānta Sarasvatī, Śrīla Prabhupāda was a strict *sannyāsī*. He lived almost penniless in Vṛndāvana for nearly a decade as he planned his mission to take Kṛṣṇa consciousness west. Like his guru, he strictly followed the rules of his *sannyāsa-āśrama* throughout his preaching career. Yet like his guru he wasn't afraid to bend some of the strictures of his *āśrama* in order to help the people in front of him. For example, to help his young disciples build a solid foundation for a life in Kṛṣṇa consciousness, he conducted their marriages. No *sannyāsī* had ever performed weddings before. He explains why he did it:

> Should a *sannyāsī*, who is in the renounced order of life and who has given up his family relations, encourage the marriage ceremony? The Lord says here that any sacrifice which is meant for human welfare should never be given up ... A *sannyāsī* may perform a marriage ceremony to help his disciple in the advancement of Kṛṣṇa consciousness. If one renounces such activities, it is to be understood that he is acting in the mode of darkness.[2]

The fact is that pure devotees engaged in spreading Kṛṣṇa consciousness, following in the footsteps of Lord Caitanya, are able to be both conservative and liberal – that is, they are able to maintain the essential teachings of bhakti yet make those teachings accessible according to time, place, and person –

because doing so serves their goal of elevating people to Kṛṣṇa consciousness.

Śrīla Prabhupāda told his disciples that knowing the difference between a detail and a principle requires spiritual intelligence. We get such spiritual intelligence from Kṛṣṇa, who gives it to those who sincerely pray for it and who look for it by systematically reading Śrīla Prabhupāda's books and sincerely trying to understand and apply their teachings. Once endowed with such spiritual intelligence, thoughtful devotees become empowered to spread Kṛṣṇa consciousness according to time, place, and circumstance. This is *yukta-vairāgya*. Śrīla Bhaktisiddhānta Sarasvatī was willing to put aside the stricture that a *sannyāsī* should not wear sewn cloth or drive in any kind of conveyance, but only if riding in cars or wearing a coat allowed his audience to better hear his pure presentation of Kṛṣṇa consciousness. Śrīla Prabhupāda made a number of adjustments in order to facilitate the Western mindset, even as he instilled in his Western audience the essential practices and cultural values of the bhakti tradition. For example, seeing that in the West men and women mixed freely, he provided separate living facilities for young women in his Western centers and, after their brahminical initiation, allowed them to go onto the altars of his temples to serve the Deities, even though in India women traditionally do not serve the Deity on the altar. He writes:

> To broadcast the cult of Kṛṣṇa consciousness, one has to learn the possibility of renunciation in terms of country, time, and candidate. A candidate for Kṛṣṇa consciousness in the Western countries should be taught about the renunciation of material existence, but one would teach candidates from a country like India in a different way. The teacher has to consider time, candidate, and country. He must avoid the principle of *niyamāgraha;* that is, he should not try to perform the impossible. What is possible in one country may not be possible in another. The *ācārya's* duty is to accept the essence of devotional service. There may be a little change here and there

as far as *yukta-vairāgya* (proper renunciation) is concerned. Dry renunciation is forbidden by Śrī Caitanya Mahāprabhu, and we have also learned this from our spiritual master, His Divine Grace Bhaktisiddhānta Sarasvatī Ṭhākura Gosvāmī Mahārāja. The essence of devotional service must be taken into consideration, and not the outward paraphernalia.[3]

A Legacy of Thoughtful Vaiṣṇavas

The sages at Naimiṣāraṇya were curious to know from Sūta Gosvāmī what would bring the greatest good to the people of the world, and they asked Sūta to teach them in "an easily understandable way." Sūta obliged by reciting *Śrīmad-Bhāgavatam.*

The sages' request for an understandable explanation is important. In fact, all the great Vaiṣṇava *ācāryas* think not only of how to widely distribute Kṛṣṇa consciousness but also how to present it in a way that people can best grasp it. Śrīla Kṛṣṇa Dvaipāyana Vyāsa spelled out the sometimes enigmatic meanings of the *Vedas* when he compiled the *Purāṇas,* the *Mahābhārata,* and finally *Śrīmad-Bhāgavatam* to make the Absolute Truth easier for sincere souls in this age to comprehend.

The Third Canto of *Śrīmad-Bhāgavatam,* for example, contains a chapter called "Calculation of Time, from the Atom," which appeals to those with a scientific mind. In an array of topics sure to attract all kinds of people, Dvaipāyana Vyāsadeva writes of kings like Pṛthu Mahārāja, sages like Ṛṣabhadeva, and even prostitutes like Piṅgalā. *Śrīmad-Bhāgavatam* is filled with romance, chivalry, heroism, vivid battle scenes, and more – perennial topics relevant and attractive to the people of any century and any culture. Because people's tastes vary, Vedavyāsa compiled supplements to the *Vedas* in order to attract all kinds of readers, weaving the conclusions of the *Vedas* into a tapestry of teachings that could accommodate anyone's interests and frame of reference. Thus he systematically leads us to Kṛṣṇa's pastimes in the Tenth Canto. Even Kṛṣṇa's pastimes are full of philosophical truths meant to guide readers

His Divine Grace A. C. Bhaktivedanta Swami Prabhupāda expanded our family business internationally. He translated into English and commentated over eighty books of Gauḍīya Vaiṣṇava teachings and organized his followers to translate his books into all the languages of the world. To date, his books have sold over half a billion copies throughout the world.

toward understanding Kṛṣṇa's identity as the Supreme Personality of Godhead, such as we find in the Tenth Canto's many prayers, and especially in the eighty-seventh chapter, "Prayers of the Personified *Vedas*."

In the *Mahābhārata,* which many find an absorbing read because of its many plots and subplots, Vyāsadeva inserts Vedic philosophy amid the intrigue between the Pāṇḍavas and the Kurus, and then includes the *Bhagavad-gītā* in the text, giving readers of *that* work essential instructions on spiritual life.

Imagine if Vedavyāsa had left the original *Vedas* in code form, even though so few people would have been able to decipher them. How many people in this age would have been able to find their way into a life guided by Vedic ideals? It was out of immense compassion that he made clear the meanings of the Vedic aphorisms to accommodate the harried people of Kali-yuga. In *Śrīmad-Bhāgavatam* (1.4.24–25), Śaunaka Ṛṣi says, "Thus the great sage Vyāsadeva, who is very kind to the ignorant masses, edited the *Vedas* so they might be assimilated by less intellectual men. Out of compassion, the great sage [Dvaipāyana Vyāsa] thought it wise that this would enable men to achieve the ultimate goal of life."

These verses go on to say that Vyāsadeva compiled "the great historical narration called the *Mahābhārata* for women, laborers, and friends of the twice-born." We know, too, that he thoughtfully arranged the eighteen *Purāṇas* into three groupings of six, each group aimed at those affected by one of the three modes of nature.

Lord Caitanya and the Thoughtfulness Principle

Of course, the incarnation that best exemplifies the Thoughtfulness Principle is Śrī Caitanya Mahāprabhu. Kṛṣṇadāsa Kavirāja writes: "Even a person with no knowledge can immediately acquire all knowledge simply by the benediction of Śrī Caitanya Mahāprabhu. Therefore I am praying to the Lord for His causeless mercy upon me."[4] He goes on to describe

Lord Caitanya's ruminations on how to best present Kṛṣṇa consciousness according to the time and circumstances He faced:

> The impersonalists, fruitive workers, false logicians, blasphemers, nondevotees, and lowest among the student community are very expert in avoiding the Kṛṣṇa consciousness movement, and therefore the inundation of Kṛṣṇa consciousness cannot touch them. Seeing that the Māyāvādīs and others were fleeing, Lord Caitanya thought, "I wanted everyone to be immersed in this inundation of love of Godhead, but some of them have escaped. Therefore I shall devise a trick to drown them also."[5]

This means that even Lord Kṛṣṇa, playing the role of His own devotee, devised ways to attract all kinds of people to devotional service. Here we see Him considering people's perspectives and deciding how to capture their interest. In His meeting with the Māyāvādī scholar Prakāśānanda Sarasvatī in Benares, Mahāprabhu chose to capture Prakāśānanda Sarasvatī by a display of humbleness, so instead of entering the room and sitting as an equal among the revered Māyāvādī *sannyāsīs,* He sat in the area where people washed their feet. Moved by the Lord's humility, Prakāśānanda Sarasvatī caught Śrī Caitanya Mahāprabhu by the hand and pulled Him into the assembly of *sannyāsīs* with great respect. Lord Caitanya's actions had softened Prakāśānanda Sarasvatī's heart, making it possible for him to hear Lord Caitanya's words. In a purport to this section of verses Śrīla Prabhupāda writes:

> The respectful behavior of Prakāśānanda Sarasvatī toward Śrī Caitanya Mahāprabhu is very much to be appreciated. Such behavior is calculated to be *ajñāta-sukṛti,* or pious activities that one executes unknowingly. Thus Śrī Caitanya Mahāprabhu very tactfully gave Prakāśānanda Sarasvatī an opportunity to advance in *ajñāta-sukṛti* so that in the future he might actually become a Vaiṣṇava *sannyāsī.*[6]

This pastime contains a lesson for all those who teach Kṛṣṇa consciousness: how we teach is as important as what we teach. The way we approach people can cause their appreciation of bhakti to either wither or bloom. When peoples' appreciation is aroused, their hearts open and the teacher can pour in extensive amounts of mercy. On the other hand, an uncouth or inconsiderate presentation can stifle a person's interest and delay his or her advancement in Kṛṣṇa consciousness.

What if Caitanya Mahāprabhu hadn't displayed such humility in order to open the hearts of the Māyāvādī *sannyāsīs* of Benares? Would Prakāśānanda still have extended his hand to the Lord? Would he and the other Māyāvādī *sannyāsīs* have been able to assimilate the Lord's explanation of *Vedānta*?

Śrī Caitanya Mahāprabhu continued his humble approach with Prakāśānanda Sarasvatī when He answered Prakāśānanda Sarasvatī's initial questions with "My guru considered me too much of a fool to study *Vedānta*." But once He had won them over and they were willing to hear from Him, He spoke directly about the *Vedānta-sūtra* and especially Śaṅkarācārya's interpretation of it. If He had started with a direct criticism of Śaṅkarācārya, it is unlikely that the Māyāvādī *sannyāsīs* could have heard his words with an open heart and come to the point of surrender.

As previously mentioned, Mahāprabhu's acceptance of *sannyāsa* to attract those who had been resistant to His message was also part of a thoughtful presentation of Kṛṣṇa consciousness. With this external adjustment even the stubborn agnostics, who had previously avoided Him, accepted His message and took to devotional service. Śrīla Prabhupāda writes:

> The *kutārkikas, nindakas, pāṣaṇḍīs,* and *adhama paḍuyās* all avoided the benefit of Śrī Caitanya Mahāprabhu's movement of developing love of Godhead. Śrī Caitanya Mahāprabhu felt compassion for them, and it is for this reason that He decided to accept the *sannyāsa* order, for by seeing Him as

> a *sannyāsī* they would offer Him respects. The *sannyāsa* order is still respected in India. Indeed, the very dress of a *sannyāsī* still commands respect from the Indian public. Therefore Śrī Caitanya Mahāprabhu accepted *sannyāsa* to facilitate preaching His devotional cult, although otherwise He had no need to accept the fourth order of spiritual life.[7]

Discussion of the Absolute Truth, if not presented carefully and maturely, can be volatile and can easily cause eruptions of misunderstanding. We have seen throughout world history how those bent on misapplying religion for their own selfish purposes misapply spiritual principles in ways that endanger innocent people and don't open the heart to love of God. Instead, compulsively inflexible presentations create more hate and fear than love. Lord Caitanya was careful to take into consideration people's contrary dispositions and moods. This was His compassion. He showed us how to be perfect preachers. Rather than condescend, His approach soothed and built bridges of spirituality between people instead of sectarian walls. In this way He freed people from the speculative philosophies rampant in His day.

> O ocean of mercy, Śrī Caitanya Mahāprabhu! Let there be an awakening of Your auspicious mercy, which easily drives away all kinds of material lamentation by making everything pure and blissful. Indeed, Your mercy awakens transcendental bliss and covers all material pleasures. By Your auspicious mercy, quarrels and disagreements arising among different scriptures are vanquished. Your auspicious mercy pours forth transcendental mellows and thus causes the heart to jubilate. Your mercy, which is full of joy, always stimulates devotional service and glorifies conjugal love of God. May transcendental bliss be awakened within my heart by Your causeless mercy.[8]

We should be careful, then, not to become dogmatic crusaders when we are speaking to people. "A man convinced against his will is of the same opinion still." Lord Caitanya did not use strong-arm tactics to win people's faith and love and neither should we. He gave the pure Absolute Truth directly and compassionately in a way that opened people's minds and hearts with His sublime beauty, His humility, and His presentation of the joyful process of devotional service.[9]

As Lord Caitanya's loyal followers, we would do well to study His mood and methods for spreading Kṛṣṇa consciousness and apply them in our own lives and presentations, according to our capacity. Then we too will learn to charm people's hearts and open their minds. Those who ignore their audiences' needs, interests, and concerns, who are careless or insensitive in presenting Kṛṣṇa consciousness, are not following the mood of Mahāprabhu and cannot represent Him well. Recognizing this principle, Śrīla Prabhupāda writes:

> Śrī Caitanya Mahāprabhu, however, as a preacher, turned the minds of the Māyāvādī *sannyāsīs.* They were melted by the sweet words of Śrī Caitanya Mahāprabhu and thus became friendly and spoke to Him also in sweet words. Similarly, all preachers will have to meet opponents, but they should not make them more inimical. They are already enemies, and if we talk with them harshly or impolitely their enmity will merely increase. We should therefore follow in the footsteps of Lord Caitanya Mahāprabhu as far as possible and try to convince the opposition by quoting from the *śāstras* and presenting the conclusion of the *ācāryas.* It is in this way that we should try to defeat all the enemies of the Lord.[10]

The Key Principle: Relevance

When Śrīla Prabhupāda began his mission in America, he told his followers that he was following in Lord Caitanya's footsteps. Upon his arrival in America he studied the American culture and habits and then adapted his mood and presentation methods to accommodate them without watering down Lord Caitanya's message. He sometimes rode the subway to the end of its route and back simply to study the people and the way they did things. He explains why he did this: "An *ācārya* who comes for the service of the Lord cannot be expected to conform to a stereotype, for he must find the ways and means by which Kṛṣṇa consciousness may be spread."[11]

When he was living in the Bowery loft, he attracted guests by cooking for them and serving them *prasāda*. He offered Sanskrit classes. He sang *kīrtana* and offered to teach his guests how to play the instruments. He also told them about Kṛṣṇa and taught them a little philosophy from the *Bhagavad-gītā*. He lived as an ideal Vaiṣṇava even in the midst of the Bowery derelicts. Seeing his diligence, erudition, and sweet Vaiṣṇava mood, his guests soon came to appreciate him. It wasn't long before they wanted to help him. Eventually, some of them became so attached to him and to performing devotional service that they became devotees themselves. There's an adage that speaks to how Śrīla Prabhupāda taught: "People don't care how much you know until they see how much you care."[12]

One example of his finding the ways and means to connect with Westerners was his inauguration of the Sunday love feast. Sunday was the perfect day for a Kṛṣṇa conscious gathering of Americans, since in those days, few people worked on Sundays. The phrase "love feast" also appealed to the youth of that time, who had adopted the word "love" as a symbolic expression of their goals and philosophy – think of the Beatles' "All You Need is Love" and the slogan "Make love, not war." Śrīla Prabhupāda could have named his weekly program something incomprehensible to Americans, something in Sanskrit, perhaps. But accepting the suggestion of one of his American disciples, he molded the name to fit the frame of reference of the people he was teaching. Of course, cultural trends change over time, and Kṛṣṇa conscious teachers need to note these changes in order to keep their communications relevant.

Śrīla Rūpa Gosvāmī, citing a verse from the *Padma Purāṇa*, teaches the key to relevance: people should somehow or other think of Kṛṣṇa. In the *Bhakti-rasāmṛta-sindhu* he writes, "Kṛṣṇa is the origin of Lord Viṣṇu. He should always be remembered and never forgotten at any time. All the rules and prohibitions mentioned in the *śāstras* should be the servants of these two principles."[13] Śrī Rūpa's verse advises teachers of Kṛṣṇa consciousness that it is their duty to find the ways and means to help people fix their minds on Kṛṣṇa. All other rules and prohibitions are subservient to this rule.

As early as 1968, Śrīla Prabhupāda explained how he was applying this verse in his own outreach:

> I am just introducing one after another, little by little, but those who are practicing this Kṛṣṇa consciousness in India, there are so many rules and regulations. Somebody says that "Swamiji is very conservative. He has got so many rules and regulations," but I have not introduced one percent. One percent. Because it is not possible to introduce all those rules and regulations in your country. My policy is following the footstep of Rūpa Gosvāmī. He says that somehow or other, let them become first of all attached to Kṛṣṇa.[14]

"Dress ... Then Address"

In our presentation of Kṛṣṇa consciousness, dress and behavior matter. People notice our dress, mannerisms, and behavior well before they tune into what we are teaching. And first impressions last.

Lord Caitanya was careful how He behaved, especially in public. If as a *sannyāsī,* the natural leader of all the other divisions of society, He were to breach social etiquette and people were to find fault with Him, they would become degraded for criticizing a *sannyāsī,* not to mention criticizing the Supreme Personality of Godhead. Thus when Mahāprabhu's devotees asked Him to meet King Pratāparudra He refused, explaining that according to *śāstra* a *sannyāsī* should not meet a materialist, so people would criticize Him if he met with the king. He told Rāmānanda Rāya, "I must fear public opinion in three ways – with My body, mind, and words."[15]

Śrīla Prabhupāda too maintained a high standard in how he dressed and behaved, and he asked his followers to "do as he was doing." He expected his disciples to behave impeccably and groom themselves like ladies and gentlemen. Giriraj Swami recalls: "In his room in Juhu in 1974, Śrīla Prabhupāda told me, 'There is a saying: One who is known as a *brāhmaṇa* doesn't have to wear a thread. So, people know you, and they like you also, but still you should dress nicely.' He also instructed me to 'Dress nicely, then address' and 'As the leader of the devotees you should dress nicely.'"

Badrinārāyaṇa Swami gives another example: "In 1970, Śrīla Prabhupāda was in Los Angeles for about six months working on *The Nectar of Devotion* and *Kṛṣṇa Book*. During that time, a party of devotees was going out on the streets to chant Hare Kṛṣṇa. One day when we were in Śrīla Prabhupāda's room, we showed him some photos of our chanting party. He first praised the devotees for their service, but then he added, "I understand that you are renounced, but for my sake please dress nicely."

Śrīla Prabhupāda also gave advice to book distributors on dressing for their service:

> Regarding the techniques for book distribution, it is all right if the devotees dress like the young people they are selling the books to. The main thing is that the innocent are given the books and the chance to become Kṛṣṇa conscious by reading them. You have to see that our book distributors are also reading my books and following all the regulative principles. Then it is all right selling in public in that way.[16]

Appreciation Opens the Heart

Here's another application of the Thoughtfulness Principle: In 1970 Śrīla Prabhupāda stopped the devotees in Bombay from performing public *harināma*. "Wait," someone might gasp. "Are you saying that Śrīla Prabhupāda *stopped* a *harināma* party from chanting in public?" That's precisely what he did. Up until that time, all over the world public street *harināma* accompanied by the distribution of BTG had been the primary method for Śrīla Prabhupāda to introduce people to Kṛṣṇa consciousness. However, he stopped the devotees from performing public *harināma* in Bombay in 1970 when he perceived that the public was getting the wrong impression of the devotees. Because in Bombay pseudo-*sādhus* typically earned their living by chanting in public, when Śrīla Prabhupāda heard that the people of Bombay were throwing coins at the chanting party, he temporarily stopped the *harināma* parties from going out into the public.

Giriraj Swami: "In late 1970, after we had been in Bombay for some weeks, Śrīla Prabhupāda told us that in India so-called *sādhus* chant in the streets to get money and that he did not want people to mistake us for such beggars – and that he wanted us to stop the *harināma* and engage in making life members instead."

Applying the Thoughtfulness Principle requires realization. Śrīla Prabhupāda defines realization in his purport to *Śrīmad-Bhāgavatam* 1.4.1:

> Personal realization does not mean that one should, out of vanity, attempt to show one's own learning by trying to surpass the previous *ācārya*. He must have full confidence in the previous *ācārya*, and at the same time he must realize the subject matter so nicely that he can present the matter for the particular circumstances in a suitable manner. *The original purpose of the text must be maintained.* No obscure meaning should be screwed out of it, yet it should be presented in an interesting manner for the understanding of the audience. This is called realization.

Realization awakens in the hearts of those who have sufficiently and properly heard and applied the *ācārya's* teachings and who have developed a deep, caring attitude for those they wish to help advance in Kṛṣṇa consciousness. Realization is a key element, then, in perfecting the great art of distributing Śrīla Prabhupāda's books. A realized book distributor takes the responsibility not only for selling books but also for awakening an appreciation for the book within the hearts of the recipients.

There's a saying: "Whatever one appreciates, appreciates." And Voltaire once said, "Appreciation is a wonderful thing: it makes what is excellent in others belong to us as well." In other words, whatever people appreciate in their lives and in others grows. Just as expert gardeners amend and cultivate the soil before planting seeds, so realized teachers of Kṛṣṇa consciousness hone their presentations to awaken people's appreciation of their message. Knowledgeable marketers consider the needs, interests, and concerns of their potential buyers, because marketing is not as much about the product as it is about how consumers perceive and receive the product.

When people appreciate a devotee's presentation of a book, or even better, when they appreciate the devotee who is presenting the book, they think favorably of the book they receive. Such appreciation opens their hearts for Kṛṣṇa's mercy to flow in without restriction. In this sense, we can think of appreciation as synonymous with faith. As we all know, devotional service is more easily practiced with faith than without it. Lord Kṛṣṇa confirms this principle in the *Gītā* (4.33, 17.28): "O chastiser of the enemy, the sacrifice performed in knowledge is better than the mere sacrifice of material possessions. After all, O son of Pṛthā, all sacrifices of work culminate in transcendental knowledge.... Anything done as sacrifice, charity, or penance without faith in the Supreme, O son of Pṛthā, is impermanent. It is called *asat* and is useless both in this life and the next."

The preoccupation of Vaiṣṇavas in general, then, and especially those connected to Śrī Caitanya Mahāprabhu, is to do good for others by awakening in them an appreciation for devotional service. Devotees who spread Lord Caitanya's mission, therefore, constantly think of the best ways to fan the spark of people's appreciation for Lord Śrī Kṛṣṇa and His devotees.

A Spoonful of Sugar

We can take guidance from Mary Poppins: "A spoonful of sugar makes the medicine go down in the most delightful way." The medicine of chanting Kṛṣṇa's names and hearing about Him may at first taste bitter to the conditioned soul. The "sugar" that allows people to swallow the medicine, then, is the teacher's refined approach to giving it.

The painstaking work and thoughtful consideration devotees go through as they present to the public *hari-nāma, kṛṣṇa-prasāda,* and Śrīla Prabhupāda's books in aesthetically pleasing ways never goes in vain. Each of these items plays an integral part in the transmission of the transcendental vibration. Śrīla Prabhupāda worked hard to ensure that his books were free of mistakes and attractively presented. *Śrī Caitanya-caritāmṛta* records how Mahāprabhu handpicked his singers, responders, and dancers, appointing each to the tasks for which they were most suited. In summary, Mahāprabhu, Śrīla Bhaktisiddhānta Sarasvatī, Śrīla Prabhupāda, and our other *ācāryas* cared deeply about the ways in which they presented Kṛṣṇa consciousness.

Recently, we at ISV experimented with our setup in presenting public *harināma saṅkīrtana* performances. We looked for ways to make the atmosphere and appearance of our *harināma* and book distribution more attractive to the people of Palo Alto, California, which is a sophisticated cosmopolitan community next to Stanford, one of the top universities in America. Some of our improvements included well-designed signs, tents in which people could congregate, good lighting for nighttime *kīrtanas,* and attractive book displays. After making a few improvements with our audience in mind, we saw an immediate and marked increase in public participation. More people stayed to watch, more of them chanted and danced, and more of them bought books. We were chanting the same mantra, we were the same people, and we were in the same place, but because we made it easier for the public to participate and to relate to what we were doing, the people seemed to drink in the holy name and embrace Śrīla Prabhupāda's books more than before.

Another example of how devotees have made it easier for people to appreciate Kṛṣṇa consciousness and open their hearts to it is Kalachandji's, a popular devotee restaurant in Dallas, Texas, known for its excellent *prasāda* and soothing atmosphere, which the devotees have created by maintaining an open courtyard with trees and interesting seating arrangements. The restaurant has gotten excellent reviews and is always packed with customers, some of whom drive miles to eat there. Its entrance is right across the hall from a door to the temple room, where the devotees are worshiping Śrī Śrī Rādhā-Kalachandji. In the hallway between the restaurant and the temple room is a Smart Table prominently displaying Śrīla Prabhupāda's books. People who come to the restaurant are thus well aware that it's a Hare Kṛṣṇa establishment. In fact, over time many patrons, having discovered the beauty and sanctity of the temple room, spend some time there and then purchase books from the Smart Table. Recently I had the opportunity to stay with the devotees at ISKCON Dallas and go out with them to meet people door to door in neighborhoods not far from the temple. People were welcoming and friendly toward us because they knew and liked Kalachandji's. Their hearts were wide open to accepting Śrīla Prabhupāda's books. Creating such facilities, then, is a vital aspect of spreading the Kṛṣṇa consciousness movement.

The conclusion is that by our thoughtful and realized approach to presenting Kṛṣṇa consciousness, we help keep the world open to Kṛṣṇa's mercy. Wherever expert book distributors go, they make it their business to deal with each soul they meet with tender loving care so that those persons will leave with one of Śrīla Prabhupāda's books and appreciate it for the rest of their lives.

Sophocles once said, "There is no greater evil than men's failure to consult and to consider." Realized teachers of Kṛṣṇa consciousness take this concept to heart and apply it to their service. Those who consult and consider ways in which to thoughtfully administer Lord Caitanya's mercy to the people of the world leave a trail of footprints that lead the way back to the spiritual world.

CHAPTER TWENTY-FOUR

On the Other Side of the Door

RECENTLY, I WENT DOOR TO DOOR in Washington, D.C. to distribute Śrīla Prabhupāda's books. I knocked on five doors without getting an answer. When I knocked on the sixth, a woman called from inside:

"Who is it?"

"It's Vaiśeṣika Dāsa. We're delivering books."

"Sorry, we're not interested."

She didn't sound irritated. Her tone actually sounded a little sympathetic. She had a Hispanic accent. That I could discern all this in an instant after hearing her voice from behind the door is a small miracle. Have you ever wondered how a toddler learns a language just by hearing people speaking it? Toddlers are given no formal lessons in grammar and they sit in no classrooms. They do get some coaxing. But they learn many of the nuances of their native language simply by hearing it spoken by others. This is the mystical property of a sound vibration: it carries the qualities of the speaker and informs us of objects, environments, and situations beyond what we can see.

So responding to the woman's voice, I called from outside her apartment door, "Where are you from?"

"Colombia," she said, after a ten-second silence.

"*Hola*!" I said. Greetings! "*¿Como estas*?" How are you?

"*Bien, gracias*."

Since we were still talking I decided to continue. "*Por favor, dame un minuto*." Please give me one minute.

Another twenty seconds of silence, maybe more. Then the door slowly swung open to a young couple, curious to connect my voice with a face. They turned out to be professionals – she a teacher and he an electrical engineer. Somehow, my voice, even heard through a door, had instilled enough trust to make them willing to meet me.

I showed them *Bhagavad-gītā Tal Como Es,* Śrīla Prabhupāda's *Gītā* in Spanish, and told them that the title means "Song of God." I also explained that according to scripture anyone who hears God's song will be filled with happiness and knowledge. After we spoke and I had answered a few of their questions, they accepted the *Gītā* and gave a donation.

Do you remember how at the beginning of this book – in the chapter called "The Ambassador of Goodwill" – my friend Richie Corsa went out of his way to bring a BTG to my door when I was in high school? He had never intended to keep it for himself; he bought it to give to me, an avid spiritual seeker. When he knocked on my door that day, I was busy praying to God to show me the way to know Him. The magazine Richie delivered changed my life so dramatically that a few months later I myself was out knocking on doors, asking people to read Śrīla Prabhupāda's books, a service I have continued throughout my life.

Two decades after joining the Hare Kṛṣṇa movement, I met Richie again and honored him as my *vartma-pradarśaka* guru. Embarrassed by my praise, Richie said, "You know, Willie, even if I never do anything remarkable in my life, I will always consider that I did at least one great thing by introducing you to your spiritual path."

I found his words both touching and significant. One does get immense spiritual benefit from connecting people to devotional service. Śrīla Prabhupāda wrote about this point in a May 6, 1977 letter addressed to the German devotees:

> Whoever gets a book is benefited. If he reads the book he is benefited still more, or if he gives the book to someone else for reading, both he and the other person are benefited. Even if one does not read the book but simply holds it and sees it, he is benefited. If he simply gives small donation towards the work of Kṛṣṇa consciousness he is benefited. And anyone who distributes these transcendental literatures, he is also benefited.

In the process of distributing Śrīla Prabhupāda's books, reading them, speaking about their contents, and encouraging others to do the same, I've seen how true Śrīla Prabhupāda's words are. As a conclusion to this book, therefore, I will share with you a few of my realizations about the power and importance of distributing Śrīla Prabhupāda's books. I hope you will find them useful.

Urgency

Śrīla Prabhupāda had absolute, unwavering trust in the potency of the *Śrīmad-Bhāgavatam* to make devotees and change the world, and he never deviated from working to fulfill his spiritual master's request to make transcendental books available and accessible in English and other languages. Śrīla Prabhupāda was *urgent* about book distribution. According to the dictionary, when something is urgent – from the Latin "to press hard, drive, impel" – it requires "immediate action or attention." Śrīla Prabhupāda pressed his followers hard to distribute his books. He drove and impelled them. He made distributing his books ISKCON's highest priority.

Book distribution was the spear tip of the Kṛṣṇa consciousness movement, the point through which ISKCON could push through into the world. Book distribution can bring people's attention to the goal of life, love of Kṛṣṇa. True, he promoted other programs, but also he told us that book distribution made all other programs successful. On January 5, 1973, Śrīla Prabhupāda wrote to Jagadīśa Dāsa, "As soon as I see that there is such increased book distribution figures, I take that to mean that all other programs are successful." Śrīla Prabhupāda consistently emphasized book distribution as foundational to the Kṛṣṇa consciousness movement. As he said in a letter to Balavanta dated October 4, 1976, "The main thing is to distribute books more and more."

Śrīla Prabhupāda also let disciples know that distributing his books was the best way to please him. In 1974, for example, as book distribution was on the rise, Śrī Govinda Dāsa, temple president in Chicago, wrote to Śrīla Prabhupāda about a debate he was having with a leading book distributor. This distributor stated that it was the temple president's duty to make book distribution the temple's top priority. The book distributor was also saying that distributing books was the best way to please Śrīla Prabhupāda. However, some temple residents, including Śrī Govinda, thought the book distributor's claims were exaggerated, so Śrī Govinda wrote to Śrīla Prabhupāda to settle the matter. Śrīla Prabhupāda replied on December 6, 1974:

> Regarding your question, actually it is a fact that ultimately everyone should preach and distribute books if they want to please me in the best way. Book distribution must be given stress always. He has spoken the right thing. If you do this sincerely, it is a fact that Kṛṣṇa will supply everything else required.... I blindly follow my *guru mahārāja*. I do not know what is the result. So I am stressing on this point of book distribution. He told me this personally.
>
> Book distribution is *bhāgavata-mārga* and temple worship is *pañcarātriki-viddhi*. Both are important for cultivating

> Vaiṣṇavism, but comparatively speaking *bhāgavata-mārga* is more important than *pañcarātriki-viddhi*. As far as possible both should go on in parallel lines but still *bhāgavata-mārga* is more important than the other.
>
> So you are all intelligent boys, so you should judge the desire of my *guru mahārāja* and help me in that way. Regarding the temple management, one man can be left behind to take care of the Deity, while the others go out.

So this is my first realization: By sustaining the kind of urgency to distribute books in the ever increasing quantities that Śrīla Prabhupāda personally promoted, we not only respect his mood and method but also maintain the foundation for a high standard of Deity worship, the building of new temples, the development of programs like devotee care and cow care, the development of strong educational programs for our children and ourselves, and almost any other program you can think of. For all that, we urgently need to distribute Śrīla Prabhupāda's books. Again, Śrīla Prabhupāda considered book distribution foundational to our movement's health and development. We should too.

Where Are the Results?

Realization number two: How did Śrīla Prabhupāda measure the results of book distribution? Decades of book distribution have filled the Kṛṣṇa consciousness movement to the rafters with great souls whose transcendental qualities are inventoried in and lauded by the scriptures. Where did all these great souls come from? They were brought to ISKCON by devotees who studied Śrīla Prabhupāda's books, gave them out to others, and then gave their association, based on the teachings in Śrīla Prabhupāda's books, to those who came. ISKCON's great souls sustain themselves by reading Śrīla Prabhupāda's books and, in the company of other great souls who relish hearing Śrīla Prabhupāda's books, continue to advance in devotional service.

Worldwide ISKCON now has at least five hundred temples and who knows how many *saṅgas,* all growing Vaiṣṇava communities set on attaining pure devotion to Kṛṣṇa. Where did these communities come from and how do they maintain their spiritual health and stature? Their members read Śrīla Prabhupāda's books and follow what they teach. ISKCON has a long list of triumphant firsts: Ratha-yātrās – festivals of *all* kinds – celebrated worldwide by people from all walks of life; gorgeous Deity worship in countries that at the start of Śrīla Prabhupāda's mission had never even heard of Kṛṣṇa; massive *prasāda* distribution and *prasāda* restaurants as well as cooking classes that teach people how to offer their food and why; Vaiṣṇava schools (some government-sponsored), academies, and adult education courses; a swelling tide of public *harināma saṅkīrtana* parties that are attracting all kinds of people. Somewhere in the world, at every hour, a *maṅgala-ārati* is being performed and devotees and guests are bowing their heads at Rādhā-Kṛṣṇa's feet.

And we can look around the world for less direct results too. Vegetarianism is becoming more and more common in many first-world countries. The word *bhakti* is now in the American English dictionary. *Kīrtana* has become popular, with people all over the world joining in the singing.

On October 11, 1974, Śrīla Prabhupāda wrote Rāmeśvara Dāsa about ISKCON's astounding string of achievements: "Whatever progress we have made, it is simply due to distributing these books. So go on and do not divert your mind for a moment from this. I have full confidence in you."

"I have full confidence in you," Śrīla Prabhupāda wrote. We can ask ourselves, Do I have the same confidence in Śrīla Prabhupāda's instruction that he had in his guru's instruction: that the printing and distribution of books is the best way to spread Kṛṣṇa consciousness? Do I have full confidence in Śrīla Prabhupāda's statement, "Whatever progress we have made is simply due to distributing these books"?

I can almost hear devotees asking, "But we've distributed half a billion books. Where are the measurable results?"

Śrīla Prabhupāda just gave us the answer: "*Whatever* progress we have made, it is simply due to distributing these books."

So let's celebrate our successes. We have many. But let's also be forward-looking and self-critical and never rest on our past achievements. ISKCON needs to remain a dynamic, vital movement if it is to remain relevant and attractive and capable of helping people find their way to Lord Caitanya's shelter. Śrīla Prabhupāda has given us the means to accomplish that: read, follow the teachings, and distribute his books.

Refining Our Approach

In 1976, a group of sincere devotees questioned ISKCON's all-out push to distribute Śrīla Prabhupāda's books. Had we become too intrusive? Perhaps there was another way to advance the Kṛṣṇa consciousness movement. Perhaps we should focus more on public relations than on book distribution, so as not to risk turning off the public. After all, they said, by having sent out such young and enthusiastic devotees with their sometimes too-passionate approach to distributing books, were we being seen as too aggressive toward the public?

Śrīla Prabhupāda addressed these doubts in a room conversation in Honolulu on May 3, 1976:

> Now, the public may take or not take, that is public's option. But my duty is – because spiritual master has said – I must try my best. Spiritual master has not said that "You must sell so many books daily, otherwise I will reject you." He has not said like that. So everyone may try his best, that's all. The public may take or not take, it doesn't matter. And if you ... want to please the public, public says that "You dance naked, I will be very much pleased, I will give you some money." So I'll have

> to do that. Then what is the use of taking a spiritual master? Public, they have got their whims how to become pleased. So we have to follow all these things? We have to follow our instruction of the spiritual master. That is initiation. Why do you manufacture, "The public will be pleased like this"?

Throughout *Our Family Business* I have emphasized that advanced devotees honor all living beings and engage them appropriately so that they will make spiritual progress. This includes leaving people with a good impression of the devotees, as I have detailed in "Mood and Method." Śrīla Prabhupāda stressed this point in a letter to Bali Mardana Dāsa as early as 1972:

> The real preaching is selling books. You should know the tactic how to sell without irritating. What your lecture will do for three minutes? But if he reads one page his life may be turned. We don't want to irritate anyone, however. If he goes away by your aggressive tactics, then you are nonsense and it is your failure. Neither you could sell a book, neither he would remain. But if he buys a book that is the real successful preaching. That is the certificate of my Guru Mahārāja, if someone, *brahmacārī,* would sell a one *paisa* magazine, if one of our *brahmacārīs* would go and sell a few copies, he would be very, very glad and say "Oh, you are so nice!" So distribution of literature is our real preaching. Now if you cannot handle the matter nicely, that is your fault. But the success of your preaching will be substantiated by how many books are sold.

People talk to their friends and families about their impressions of devotees. Customer service experts say that people are apt to tell many more people about an unfavorable encounter than a favorable one. Anyone can do the math and conclude that it is important for devotees to treat people with respect, to avoid a condescending attitude, and to make friends rather than enemies wherever possible. So in addition to stressing that we should distribute books, Śrīla Prabhupāda told us to learn "the art" of how to present his books in a way that people could appreciate them. From a letter to Śrī Govinda Dāsa, December 25, 1972:

> If we simply stick to describing how wonderful is Kṛṣṇa, then whatever we may lie or exaggerate, that will not be lie! But other things, lies, they will not help us to train ourselves in truthfulness. Lie to some, not to others, that is not a good philosophy. Rather the *brāhmaṇas* are always truthful, even to their enemies. There is sufficient merit in our books that if you simply describe them sincerely to anyone, they will buy. That art you must develop, not art of lying. Convince them to give by your preaching the Absolute Truth, not by tricking. That is more mature stage of development of Kṛṣṇa consciousness.

So because Śrīla Prabhupāda has given all his followers the responsibility to continually increase book distribution as well as to "handle the matter nicely," we are duty-bound both to increase the numbers of books we distribute annually worldwide and to continually improve the way we distribute them. After four decades of distributing Śrīla Prabhupāda's books, I have had the time to reflect on what that might entail. I have also had the privilege of meeting tens of thousands of people. This is what I have learned:

- Every person I meet is special.

- Every word I say to the people I meet, my body language, and every attempt at kindness I extend leaves an indelible impression on them. (And as mentioned above, people remember my rough edges even more than my kindnesses!)

- Because of this, my prime objective while distributing books and at all other moments in my day is to leave each person I meet with a good impression – my service is to somehow increase their appreciation for

> Kṛṣṇa. This ethic now guides my life and inspires my teaching of the art of book distribution wherever I go.

What are *your* realizations about how to increase book distribution and do it better? Let's talk about that as a Society and help one another refine our mood in distributing Śrīla Prabhupāda's books. Some devotees tell me that they hesitate to distribute books or go out on *harināma* because they are afraid that an unconsidered approach might alienate people rather than bring them closer to Kṛṣṇa. So we have to work together to design ways to happily engage all ISKCON devotees in *saṅkīrtana* as well as to awaken the public's appreciation with our more refined approach.

When we know and love people as spirit souls, parts and parcels of the Supreme Personality of Godhead, we can sincerely help them in ways they can appreciate. Motivated by a desire to expand Kṛṣṇa's name and fame – and free from the desire for personal name and fame – we become free to be compassionate as we consider how to best engage the persons we meet and to listen to them before trying to help them.

So those who give up the desire for profit, adoration, and distinction and who stay pure by following the rules and regulations of devotional service are effective in attracting people to purchase and read Śrīla Prabhupāda's books. The *Bhagavad-gītā* (17.15) recommends that to purify our speech we regularly recite the Vedic literature and speak words that are truthful, pleasing, beneficial, and that don't agitate others. Each of these practices helps one to maintain the right behavior while distributing Śrīla Prabhupāda's transcendental books and become a potent presenter of Kṛṣṇa consciousness.

Each person we meet is a walking temple of Kṛṣṇa, because Kṛṣṇa is in each person's heart. Those who hold onto this realization will find themselves eager to go out of their way to somehow engage every soul they meet in Kṛṣṇa's service.

Of course, engaging people appropriately includes making distinctions between them. Sweet words are not always the appropriate response in every situation. Once, my friend Prema Kishore Dāsa and I, in dhotis and tilaka, went to distribute books on New York City's Canal Street, a rough-and-tumble district crammed with tourists and street hustlers selling knockoff Rolexes and Gucci handbags. I approached a young man wearing loose-fitting jeans riding low on his hips, a baggy T-shirt, and a baseball cap pulled slightly askew. He was sucking at the end of a straw stuck in an enormous McDonald's milkshake cup. As if sensing my approach, he lifted his gaze and, as if flicking a bug at me, said cavalierly, "I don't give to beggars."

In the *Śrīmad-Bhāgavatam* (11.23.3), Lord Kṛṣṇa tells Uddhava: "Sharp arrows which pierce one's chest and reach the heart do not cause as much suffering as the arrows of harsh, insulting words that become lodged within the heart when spoken by uncivilized men." I didn't hesitate. "I'm no beggar and I don't need your money. We have plenty of our own. Actually, I'm trying to do you a favor by allowing you to make some spiritual advancement today. We don't need you, but you need us."

The young man was visibly taken aback and apologized. I had stood up for what I was doing as a representative of my spiritual master, but without malice or even taking his words to heart. My approach affected the young man positively and changed his attitude. So being sensitive to the people you meet and true to yourself in how you respond to them are also aspects of a refined approach to book distribution.

As we push forward the next huge wave of book distribution, we should carefully consider all of Śrīla Prabhupāda's instructions on the matter and, using common sense, apply both the letter and spirit of what he told us. Yes, we must leave people with a good impression, but we must also increase the distribution of his books in every way we possibly can. The mass distribution of Śrīla Prabhupāda's books and being kind to the people we meet are not at odds. As I've already stated, book distribution is not disturbing to most people, although immature distributors sometimes are. And some people have already decided to dislike Kṛṣṇa consciousness, and are already naturally disturbed. Śrīla Prabhupāda's śāstric, realized opinion was that the eternal benefit people accrue by coming in contact with transcendental books outweighs any temporary inconvenience they may feel when approached to buy a book: "[E]ven if there is some complaint, they are getting the real thing from our books. They're forgetting the aim of life. Somehow or other, we have to give them the real thing."[1]

Have Faith in Good Seeds

Giving people the real thing and being able to measure the results of that gift, despite what I said earlier in this chapter, is not always easy in a world awash in negativity and malefic sound vibration. It's natural to expect, for example, that after years of book distribution, people should be flocking to our doors. That we successfully hold Ratha-yātrās around the world or that our movement has grown up enough to run schools the government will approve of are not small accomplishments, but they are not necessarily the accomplishments we are looking for when we think of books going out by the hundreds of millions.

So we simply have to keep faith in Śrīla Prabhupāda's words that even if people don't immediately respond after buying a transcendental book – even if they don't respond in this lifetime – the effect of their having taken a book will never be lost to them. Lord Kṛṣṇa affirms this in the *Gītā* (6.44): "By virtue of the divine consciousness of his previous life, he automatically becomes attracted to the yogic principles – even without seeking them. Such an inquisitive transcendentalist stands always above the ritualistic principles of the scriptures." Nonetheless, ISKCON still needs to develop robust follow-up systems if it wants to accommodate and cultivate the many millions of people who have been touched by Śrīla Prabhupāda's books.

We just can't know when Kṛṣṇa will manifest the mercy they have received and they will begin to practice bhakti. We also don't know who in a person's circle of influence will actually benefit from a book he or she receives. Perhaps it will be someone else in his or her family, as in the story of the Italian mother who gave her son a *Kṛṣṇa Book* for his birthday. Or a friend – I got my first piece of Kṛṣṇa conscious literature from a friend who didn't want it but was willing to pass it along. Perhaps it will be the person who picks up an abandoned book from a park bench, or finds it on the shelf of a used bookstore. Perhaps a person will have read one line that touched his or her heart and made an even imperceptible shift in his or her life because of something Śrīla Prabhupāda said. We might never see any of these people at a Sunday feast; they might never even speak to a devotee. That doesn't mean they aren't getting profound spiritual benefit by purchasing, reading, or even seeing one of Śrīla Prabhupāda's books. Who can actually measure these effects of book distribution except Lord Kṛṣṇa? So as we continue to increase the distribution of Śrīla Prabhupāda's books and those books touch people's lives across the generations, we can expect Kṛṣṇa consciousness to spread exponentially.

Successful gardeners place their faith in good seeds. These gardeners may not know precisely how their seeds germinate, but they trust that they will. If gardeners continue to garden season after season, they learn what soil and water and light conditions result in the best fruits. Robert Louis Stevenson said something apropos: "Don't judge each day by the harvest you reap but by the seeds that you plant." In the *Gītā* (2.40), Lord Kṛṣṇa tells us that the tiniest connection a person has to devotional service gives him or her a start on the transcendental path. In a letter to Jagadīśa Dāsa dated February 2, 1975, Śrīla Prabhupāda again confirms the value of giving people transcendental books: "Try to increase the book distribution as much as possible. This is our business – to put our books in the hands of intelligent men of America. If they read even one page, the influence will be so great."

Śrīla Prabhupāda knew that the mass distribution of his books would give rise to a blossoming of an auspicious atmosphere throughout the world, even if people did not immediately join his movement: "Your book distribution program is very much encouraging to me. The more such literatures are read and distributed, the more auspicity will be there in the world. Please continue this program with ever-increasing enthusiasm."[2]

Aboard a train bound for the Kumbha-melā in 1977, Śrīla Prabhupāda said more about the general effects of distributing his books and also predicted to his BBT secretary (who wrote Śrīla Prabhupāda's words down in his diary as he was speaking them) that historians would some day mark the time when his books were published as a turning point in the world. In the same conversation, His Divine Grace said that by the mass distribution of his books we would soon see an awakening of spiritual and religious sentiments in people all over the world and that distributing his books would cause a revolution in people's thinking. These people would then expose and defeat speculative, atheistic science and replace it with a theistic worldview. We have seen the fall of Communism in the USSR since Śrīla Prabhupāda made that prediction, and an explosion in the number of full-time devotees in all the countries that once comprised the Soviet Union. What else have we seen around the world?

For those who are impatient to see the distribution of books cause a systemic change in the world, Śrīla Prabhupāda gives yet another way to remain encouraged about the success of book distribution:

> You are having some doubts whether or not the mass of people will be able to appreciate Kṛṣṇa consciousness. Yes, it is a fact that most people cannot approach Kṛṣṇa consciousness. Just like a rare gem. Only a few men can purchase a rare emerald or diamond, so similarly only a few men may actually be capable of grasping the importance of Kṛṣṇa consciousness. It is confirmed in the *Bhagavad-gītā* (7.3):

manuṣyāṇāṁ sahasreṣu
kaścid yatati siddhaye
yatatām api siddhānāṁ
kaścin māṁ vetti tattvataḥ

"Out of many thousands of men, one may endeavor for perfection, and of those who have achieved perfection, hardly one knows Me in truth."

If just .01% of the world's population becomes Kṛṣṇa conscious, the whole situation on the earth will change. Just see what has happened. I started alone in 1966, and in just seven years now we are three thousand, and it is growing more and more.

So if the intelligent men of the world like yourself cooperate with this all-important mission of Caitanya Mahāprabhu, we can save the world from the state of misery and chaos that now prevails.[3]

In a similar vein he once told reporters in a 1973 interview:

Generally people are interested in eating, sleeping, mating, and defending. So how can we expect to find many followers? First of all it is not difficult to notice that people have lost their spiritual interest. Those who are actually interested are all being cheated by so-called spiritualists. You cannot judge a movement simply by the number of its followers. If one man is genuine, then the movement is successful. It is not a question of quantity but quality.

An important point to glean from these statements is that we must be patient. Ralph Waldo Emerson once wrote, "Patience and fortitude conquer all things."

Book Distribution Is Fun and Easy

There are a couple of myths that have grown up around the service of distributing Śrīla Prabhupāda's books. One of them is that it's difficult. While that may be true at first, once you commit to doing it, Kṛṣṇa helps you from within and without. From within He gives you courage, intelligence, and a taste of spiritual happiness. In a letter to Rāmeśvara Dāsa dated January 11, 1976, Śrīla Prabhupāda called book distribution "really intoxication."

From without, Kṛṣṇa sends sincere souls to take the books you are distributing. Even when people don't take books or they choose to ignore you, with time you will become more patient, detached, and determined. You will learn to become unflinching in your devotional service. When the cowherd boys in Vṛndāvana entered the mouth of Aghāsura (in the twelfth chapter of *Kṛṣṇa Book*), they told one another:

> "If we all at one time entered into the mouth of this great serpent, how could it possibly swallow all of us? And even if it were to swallow all of us at once, it could not swallow Kṛṣṇa. Kṛṣṇa will immediately kill him, as He did Bakāsura." Talking in this way, all the boys looked at the beautiful lotus-like face of Kṛṣṇa, and they began to clap and smile. And so they marched forward and entered the mouth of the gigantic serpent.

So when you go out to distribute books with friends, together you will laugh off the fear or disappointment, remind one another that Kṛṣṇa is protecting you, and, with the beautiful lotuslike face of Kṛṣṇa in your mind's eye, march forward to fight *māyā* together.

Wherever I go, I see that the devotee communities dedicated to distributing Śrīla Prabhupāda's books are unusually inspired. When devotees see people reading Śrīla Prabhupāda's books for the first time, they remember how sweet their own beginnings in Kṛṣṇa consciousness were, and how they too had a first discovery of the power of Śrīla Prabhupāda's books in their lives. What's more, devotees who go out to distribute books come back with a natural enthusiasm to hear and chant about Lord Kṛṣṇa and Lord Caitanya. They also dream of ways to increase book distribution and how to follow up with the people they are meeting: collecting the names and contact information for interested persons, keeping in touch with them, and inviting them to participate in Kṛṣṇa conscious programs that appropriately address their needs.

So let's distribute Śrīla Prabhupāda's books and, like the cowherd boys, laugh in the face of any apparent danger. Let's help Śrīla Prabhupāda further Lord Caitanya's *saṅkīrtana* movement and thus lift the world from its current state of degradation. You will feel a surge of Kṛṣṇa conscious enlivenment – the moment you pick up his books and start thinking of ways to distribute them, your mind and senses will come alive with spiritual energy, just as if you had touched a wire electrified by spiritual current.

When I meet with devotees who are nervous about going out to distribute books for the first time, I ask them to repeat the following mantra: "Book distribution is fun and easy." When they repeat the mantra, I can see some of them are still wondering if I'm serious.

Yes, I'm serious.

The Confident Path Back to Godhead

Another myth that has grown up around book distribution is that it is for neophytes. On the contrary, as I have described in depth in "Heavy Lifting," "Faith in God and Strength of Mind," and "Confidential Service," distributing Śrīla Prabhupāda's books – while consistently hearing and chanting from them – takes one to the higher states of Kṛṣṇa consciousness. In Kali-yuga, one cannot attain the highest state of Kṛṣṇa consciousness, Vraja-bhakti, without having one's heart purified by performing the *yuga-dharma* under the guidance of the *yuga-avatāra* Śrī Caitanya Mahāprabhu and His authorized representatives. This includes working hard to spread His *saṅkīrtana* movement. Teaching the *Bhagavad-gītā* is the activity that pleases Kṛṣṇa the most,[4] and that teaching is also best done while distributing Śrīla Prabhupāda's books. Śrīla

Prabhupāda consistently refers to book distribution as a self-realized activity: devotees absorbed in book distribution are actually in *samādhi* and can go back to Godhead by performing this activity.

> Prabhupāda: You are already self-realized. Otherwise how you can push on the books? You love Kṛṣṇa. Therefore you are taking so much labor for pushing on. And that is self-realization. If anyone tries to establish that Kṛṣṇa is the Supreme Lord, that is self-realization.[5]

> In our Kṛṣṇa consciousness movement, all our activities are concentrated upon distributing Kṛṣṇa literature. This is very important. One may approach any person and induce him to read Kṛṣṇa literature so that in the future he also may become a devotee. Such activities are recommended in this verse. *Kriyāsu yas tvac-caraṇāravindayoḥ.* Such activities will always remind the devotees of the Lord's lotus feet. By fully concentrating on distributing books for Kṛṣṇa, one is fully absorbed in Kṛṣṇa. This is *samādhi.*[6]

> So make this your important task, to print our books in French language and other languages, and distribute widely, and that will please my Guru Mahārāja. Never mind it takes little time to make progress, our process is slow but sure, and we are confident that if we continue in this way we shall go one day back to home, back to Godhead.[7]

Śrīla Bhaktivinoda Ṭhākura once defined the practice of Kṛṣṇa consciousness as *jīva-doyā kṛṣṇa-nāma:* compassion for living beings and chanting Hare Kṛṣṇa. The two are intrinsically linked. The combination of absorption in distributing Śrīla Prabhupāda's books while assiduously reading them and continually chanting Hare Kṛṣṇa is a potent mixture of practices that draw one into *samādhi* and fulfill all of one's spiritual desires.

Connected and Engaged

Another myth: distributing Śrīla Prabhupāda's books is a material activity – a service that's more like running a business than anything else and that can make us fall into materialistic consciousness.

Even if we put aside, for the moment, the understanding that Śrīla Prabhupāda's books are transcendental and of supreme spiritual value to their recipients, in order to accommodate this myth, let's consider the various services an *ācārya* like Śrīla Jīva Gosvāmī performed. Śrī Jīva was not only a pure devotee of Lord Caitanya, a scholar, and a prolific author, he was also a skilled manager and legal expert. He is known to have done extensive legal and executive work to assure the rightful protection and future maintenance of the invaluable properties and temples in Vṛndāvana established by his uncles, Rūpa Gosvāmī and Sanātana Gosvāmī.[8] Working with the material energy to expand the Kṛṣṇa consciousness movement, then, is something even pure devotees do. And, of course, Śrīla Prabhupāda himself did it. In his purport to *Bhagavad-gītā* 12.10 he writes:

> Every endeavor requires land, capital, organization, and labor to grow. Just as in business one requires a place to stay, some capital to use, some labor, and some organization to expand, so the same is required in the service of Kṛṣṇa. The only difference is that in materialism one works for sense gratification. The same work, however, can be performed for the satisfaction of Kṛṣṇa, and that is spiritual activity.

Everything in this world belongs to Kṛṣṇa and is to be engaged in His service. Using any kind of tool, technique, or strategy to spread the Kṛṣṇa consciousness movement, therefore, is both approved and fully transcendental. In his purport to *Śrīmad-Bhāgavatam* 5.16.3, Śrīla Prabhupāda offers an essential understanding of this point. I have quoted the full purport, but note the last paragraph, where Śrīla Prabhupāda directly addresses the printing and selling of his books:

> Mahārāja Parīkṣit had already been advised by his spiritual master, Śukadeva Gosvāmī, to think of the universal form of the Lord, and therefore, following the advice of his spiritual master, he continuously thought of that form. The universal form is certainly material, but because everything is an expansion of the energy of the Supreme Personality of Godhead, ultimately nothing is material. Therefore Parīkṣit Mahārāja's mind was saturated with spiritual consciousness. Śrīla Rūpa Gosvāmī has stated:
>
> *prāpañcikatayā buddhyā*
> *hari-sambandhi-vastunaḥ*
> *mumukṣubhiḥ parityāgo*
> *vairāgyaṁ phalgu kathyate*
> (*Bhakti-rasāmṛta-sindhu* 1.2.255–56)
>
> Everything, even that which is material, is connected with the Supreme Personality of Godhead. Therefore everything should be engaged in the service of the Lord. Śrīla Bhaktisiddhānta Sarasvatī Ṭhākura translates this verse as follows:
>
> *śrī-hari sevāya yāhā anukūla*
> *viṣaya baliyā tyāge haya bhūla*
>
> "One should not give up anything connected with the Supreme Personality of Godhead, thinking it material or enjoyable for the material senses." Even the senses, when purified, are spiritual. When Mahārāja Parīkṣit was thinking of the universal form of the Lord, his mind was certainly situated on the transcendental platform. Therefore although he might not have had any reason to be concerned with detailed information of the universe, he was thinking of it in relationship with the Supreme Lord, and therefore such geographical knowledge was not material but transcendental. Elsewhere in *Śrīmad-Bhāgavatam* (1.5.20) Nārada Muni has said, *idaṁ hi*

> *viśvaṁ bhagavān ivetaraḥ:* the entire universe is also the Supreme Personality of Godhead, although it appears different from Him. Therefore although Parīkṣit Mahārāja had no need for geographical knowledge of this universe, that knowledge was also spiritual and transcendental because he was thinking of the entire universe as an expansion of the energy of the Lord.
>
> In our preaching work also, we deal with so much property and money and so many books bought and sold, but because these dealings all pertain to the Kṛṣṇa consciousness movement, they should never be considered material. That one is absorbed in thoughts of such management does not mean that he is outside of Kṛṣṇa consciousness. If one rigidly observes the regulative principle of chanting sixteen rounds of the *mahā-mantra* every day, his dealings with the material world for the sake of spreading the Kṛṣṇa consciousness movement are not different from the spiritual cultivation of Kṛṣṇa consciousness.

Śrīla Prabhupāda states that those who propagate transcendental books like *Śrīmad-Bhāgavatam* "change the polluted atmosphere of the world" and as a result "people become sane in their transactions."[9] Śrīla Bhaktisiddhānta termed such propagation "extended altruism," because such propagation does good to "all beings in all countries at all times." Because *Śrīmad-Bhāgavatam* "uproots the threefold miseries," those who distribute it help others to the greatest possible extent.[10]

Book distribution is therefore not a material business that sinks its proponents into "pounds and shillings" consciousness. Rather, distributing books on the order of the spiritual master, extending the spiritual master's compassion to anyone one meets, being required to immerse oneself in the teachings the books contain and the deep realization that comes through prayer and grace and the willingness to become a conduit of Lord Caitanya's mercy – all of these ensure that a book distributor makes tangible spiritual advancement.

Śrīla Prabhupāda's Books Are the Basis

In ISKCON we hear devotees say "Books are the basis." Śrīla Prabhupāda himself used this phrase in a letter to Maṇḍali Bhadra Dāsa dated January 20, 1972: "My first concern is that my books shall be published and distributed profusely all over the world. Practically, books are the basis of our movement. Without them our preaching has no effect." He uses it again in a letter to Tuṣṭa Kṛṣṇa Swami (January 9, 1976): "Books are the basis of our movement. Whatever appreciation we are getting on account of our books, it is because we are following the path chalked out by exalted devotees."

So what does it mean that Śrīla Prabhupāda's books are the foundation – the basis – of ISKCON? We can begin to understand by reading the letter Śrīla Prabhupāda wrote to Dāmodara Dāsa on December 3, 1971:

> I'm especially pleased to hear that your distribution of our books and magazines has increased. Go on in this way, increasing more and more. Each time someone reads some solid information about Kṛṣṇa his life becomes changed in some way. These literatures are the solid ground upon which our preaching stands, so I want that they should be available to everyone, as many as possible. So please try for this.

It is interesting that Śrīla Prabhupāda uses the word "solid" twice in this letter. Before Śrīla Prabhupāda published *Bhagavad-gītā As it Is,* there were hundreds of translations of the *Gītā* in English, but almost none of them introduced Kṛṣṇa as the Supreme Personality of Godhead and encouraged readers to surrender to Him and attain the supreme goal of life, pure love of God. Consequently, after reading those translations, hardly anyone outside of India became a devotee of Kṛṣṇa – they did not read "some solid information about Kṛṣṇa" and so change their lives.

In stark contrast, as soon as Śrīla Prabhupāda's disciples began to circulate *Bhagavad-gītā As It Is,* hundreds and thousands of people in the West took up Kṛṣṇa consciousness seriously, as the text recommends, and many, many more took it up in India. Today, millions of devotees have heard the clarion call of *Bhagavad-gītā As It Is,* and more continue to do so daily. *Bhagavad-gītā As It Is* – and all of Śrīla Prabhupāda's other books – are "the solid ground upon which our preaching stands." These books change lives.

What makes them special? First, they undeviatingly and ceaselessly promote unmotivated, uninterrupted devotional service to the Supreme along with the practical means to attain it. Second, they precisely and authoritatively describe the name, form, abode, pastimes, and loving associates of the Supreme Personality of Godhead along with instructions on how to make one's way back to the spiritual world. Śrīla Prabhupāda's purports are not simply the musings of a single author; they are both authoritative and realized. This not only makes Śrīla Prabhupāda's books relishable, it makes them rare in the world of spiritual literature. As he wrote in the letter to Tuṣṭa Kṛṣṇa Swami I just quoted, "Whatever appreciation we are getting on account of our books, it is because we are following the path chalked out by exalted devotees."

The descriptions of the Lord and the spiritual world in Śrīla Prabhupāda's purports are enthralling. Here is one from his purport to *Śrī Caitanya-caritāmṛta, Ādi-līlā* 5.22:

> The residents of Vaikuṇṭha have brilliantly black complexions much more fascinating and attractive than the dull white and black complexions found in the material world. Their bodies, being spiritual, have no equals in the material world. The beauty of a bright cloud when lightning flashes on it merely hints at their beauty. Generally the inhabitants of Vaikuṇṭha dress in yellow clothing. Their bodies are delicate and attractively built, and their eyes are like the petals of lotus flowers. Like Lord Viṣṇu, the residents of Vaikuṇṭha have four hands decorated with a conch shell, wheel, club, and lotus flower. Their chests are beautifully broad and fully decorated with necklaces of a brilliant diamondlike metal surrounded by

> costly jewels never to be found in the material world. The residents of Vaikuṇṭha are always powerful and effulgent. Some of them have complexions like red coral cat's eyes and lotus flowers, and each of them has earrings of costly jewels. On their heads they wear flowery crowns resembling garlands.
>
> In the Vaikuṇṭhas there are airplanes, but they make no tumultuous sounds. Material airplanes are not at all safe: they can fall down and crash at any time, for matter is imperfect in every respect. In the spiritual sky, however, the airplanes are also spiritual, and they are spiritually brilliant and bright. These airplanes do not fly business executives, politicians, or planning commissions as passengers, nor do they carry cargo or postal bags, for these are all unknown there. These planes are for pleasure trips only, and the residents of Vaikuṇṭha fly in them with their heavenly, beautiful, fairylike consorts. Therefore these airplanes, full of residents of Vaikuṇṭha, both male and female, increase the beauty of the spiritual sky. We cannot imagine how beautiful they are, but their beauty may be compared to the clouds in the sky accompanied by silver branches of electric lightning. The spiritual sky of Vaikuṇṭhaloka is always decorated in this way.

Śrīla Prabhupāda's descriptions of the fascinating setting in which Śrī Kṛṣṇa's loving relationships take place against the backdrop of the sublime Vṛndāvana forest, with its cows and monkeys, its peacock and deer, Govardhana Hill and the Yamunā River, and the enchanting sound of the flute, draw readers to the Lord. Descriptions this distinct make it possible for readers to step away from their distant concepts of God and fall in love with Him. To find this kind of potency even in a religious book is rare.

Besides giving us descriptions of the Lord and the spiritual world, Śrīla Prabhupāda's books teach us how to develop an intimate, loving relationship with Kṛṣṇa as His servant, friend, parent, or lover as we advance from an awakening of faith to unalloyed love for the Supreme. Some of his translations offer us a glimpse into Kṛṣṇa's thinking, as does this translation from *Śrī Caitanya-caritāmṛta* (*Ādi-līlā* 4.15–26):

The Lord wanted to taste the sweet essence of the mellows of love of God, and He wanted to propagate devotional service in the world on the platform of spontaneous attraction. Thus He is known as supremely jubilant and as the most merciful of all.

[Lord Kṛṣṇa thought:] All the universe is filled with the conception of My majesty, but love weakened by that sense of majesty does not satisfy Me. If one regards Me as the Supreme Lord and himself as a subordinate, I do not become subservient to his love, nor can it control Me. In whatever transcendental mellow My devotee worships Me, I reciprocate with him. That is My natural behavior.

In whatever way My devotees surrender unto Me, I reward them accordingly. Everyone follows My path in all respects, O son of Pṛthā.' If one cherishes pure loving devotion to Me, thinking of Me as his son, his friend, or his beloved, regarding himself as great and considering Me his equal or inferior, I become subordinate to him.

Devotional service rendered to Me by the living beings revives their eternal life. O My dear damsels of Vraja, your affection for Me is your good fortune, for it is the only means by which you have obtained My favor.

Mother sometimes binds Me as her son. She nourishes and protects Me, thinking Me utterly helpless. My friends climb on My shoulders in pure friendship, saying, "What kind of big man are You? You and I are equal." If My beloved consort reproaches Me in a sulky mood, that steals My mind from the reverent hymns of the *Vedas*.

The major works Śrīla Prabhupāda chose to translate and commentate, particularly the *Bhagavad-gītā, Śrīmad-Bhāgavatam, Śrī Caitanya-caritāmṛta,* and *The Nectar of Devotion,* provide readers with a complete, inspiring, and balanced course of instruction on bhakti-yoga. His unparalleled purports display a level of compassion and faith in Lord Caitanya's mercy, in the process of devotional service, and in the power of the works themselves that is rarely seen in the world. Arguably, Śrīla Prabhupāda's purports have broken open the same storehouse of love of Godhead that Lord Caitanya and His associates plundered over five hundred years ago. Because the teachings in his purports are so down to earth and practical, beginners in spiritual life can follow them, but they also satisfy advanced practitioners who have learned how to read the layers of meaning they contain and thus find elucidations of the topmost devotional practices and sentiments. Śrīla Prabhupāda's purports – through their sensible, simple, clear, yet eloquent instructions on the proper execution of bhakti – can set people at all levels of spiritual development solidly on the path to pure devotional service.

His purport to *Śrīmad-Bhāgavatam* 2.9.36 is an example of both his deep compassion and his faith in the power of devotional service:

> Therefore there is no need to seek properly qualified candidates for discharging devotional service to the Lord. Let them be either well behaved or ill trained, let them be either learned or fools, let them be either grossly attached or in the renounced order of life, let them be liberated souls or desirous of salvation, let them be inexpert in the discharge of devotional service or expert in the same, all of them can be elevated to the supreme position by discharging devotional service under the proper guidance.

Sincere seekers, advanced practitioners, and especially those dedicated to expanding ISKCON can thus be confident in their study of Śrīla Prabhupāda's books, knowing that what he is offering, especially in his purports, will help them build a strong devotional foundation and progress safely to the goal of life. And they can be confident that by distributing these transcendental books, they are helping others to do the same. What's more, because Śrīla Prabhupāda strongly emphasized that all services connected to the *saṅkīrtana* movement are of equal value – *gurukula,* farming, scientific research, restaurants, Deity worship, and cleaning the temple room floor – those who have learned from Śrīla Prabhupāda's books have gone out and applied what they've learned in all kinds of ways, and people can now visit any ISKCON project and learn how to apply the knowledge in Śrīla Prabhupāda's books.

The Heart of ISKCON

As time passes, more and more ISKCON devotees are writing their own Kṛṣṇa conscious books. After carefully following the process of devotional service laid down by Śrīla Prabhupāda, a number of his loyal followers have profound Kṛṣṇa conscious realizations and then share them in writing, with Śrīla Prabhupāda's encouragement: "Realization means you should write. Every one of you. What is your realization? ... You write your realization – what you have realized about Kṛṣṇa. That is required."[11] From these mature devotee authors we now have stacks of published books. Some of them are brilliantly written. Given so much literature, devotees sometimes wonder which to read and distribute.

As it is important to emphasize Śrīla Prabhupāda's central position as the founder-*ācārya* and, therefore, the guiding authority of ISKCON for all time, consider how important it is to emphasize his books as the bedrock of ISKCON's literary canon. In fact, the leaders and members of ISKCON can keep Śrīla Prabhupāda "in the center" of ISKCON mainly by keeping Śrīla Prabhupāda's books in the fore. As ISKCON builds temples, communities, and outreach projects of all kinds, the books we display and sell from these places speak strongly to how we have aligned ourselves with Śrīla Prabhupāda as the founder-*ācārya* and center of this movement. It's not that we don't want or expect other books to be written. Besides writing his foundational books, Śrīla Prabhupāda trained, inspired, and empowered his disciples and followers to write their own authorized books.

Śrīla Prabhupāda's writings initiated a steady stream of books written by his loyal followers during and after his departure. These books cover a spectrum of subjects and genres – translations and commentaries on important Vaiṣṇava texts, biographies and memoirs, books on science, books on Vaiṣṇava culture, cookbooks, and books on various aspects of a devotee's life – that further elucidate Kṛṣṇa consciousness in a way that enable modern audiences of all kinds to connect with Śrīla Prabhupāda's foundational works.

The Bhaktivedanta Book Trust has particularly taken as its mandate to maintain in its own publications the high standard of translation and presentation followed in Śrīla Prabhupāda's books. The following excerpt by a distinguished scholar in the field of world religions shows how well Śrīla Prabhupāda trained his students to maintain the Bhaktivedanta Book Trust's unique position as the world's leading publisher of Gauḍīya Vaiṣṇava literature:

> There is a special significance to this publication over and above its making accessible to readers of English a Sanskrit classic of spiritual literature. This is the first publication by the Bhaktivedanta Book Trust of a major Vaiṣṇava theological text which disciples of the late Swami A. C. Bhaktivedanta Prabhupāda have accomplished without his immediate presence. It follows the widely disseminated versions of the *Bhagavad-gītā* in many languages and multivolume translations of the *Śrīmad Bhāgavata Purāṇa* and the *Caitanya-caritāmṛta,* each of which is accompanied by an elaborate commentary. These prior publications were substantially the work of Prabhupāda himself, with certain of his Sanskrit-trained devotees, including Gopīparāṇadhana Dāsa, serving as apprentices. The appearance of the *Bṛhad-bhāgavatāmṛta* thus marks a new phase of textual theological scholarship by members of the International Society for Krishna Consciousness. They have, as it were, come into their maturity as responsible for faithful transmission of the Caitanya Vaiṣṇava tradition of *prema-bhakti,* loving devotion to God Kṛṣṇa. What better way to assure fidelity to the words and spirit of Caitanya Mahāprabhu and his circle of immediate disciples than to enable devotees and attentive seekers to read, hear,

> and visualize the foundational texts of those very scholar-devotees who had experienced the charismatic presence of Kṛṣṇa-Caitanya himself! [12]

Professor O'Connell specifically appreciates the BBT edition of *Bṛhad-bhāgavatāmṛta* as a "faithful transmission," a publication accomplished without Śrīla Prabhupāda's "immediate presence," and a book that gives devotees and attentive seekers access to the "foundational texts" of Śrī Kṛṣṇa Caitanya.

These compliments for the BBT and its authors in truth glorify Śrīla Prabhupāda. The competence of BBT authors and the high standards they have maintained in their writing after Śrīla Prabhupāda's disappearance are consequences of Śrīla Prabhupāda's painstaking care in keeping his movement faithful to the examples and foundational writings of the previous *ācāryas* and in teaching his students to do the same.

Still, one may ask, which books must I concentrate on to be fully in tune with ISKCON's founder-*ācārya* as well as fully educated in the Gauḍīya Vaiṣṇava canon? Śrīla Prabhupāda answered this question when his disciples asked whether they could read books by the previous *ācāryas*. (And we can just as easily ask today, Can we read the books by realized contemporary devotees?) "Yes," he said, but "you first of all assimilate what you have got. You simply pile up books and do not read – what is the use?"

In the seventh chapter of *The Nectar of Devotion,* Śrīla Prabhupāda writes:

> And one should also not be very enthusiastic about constructing new temples, nor should one be enthusiastic about reading various types of books, save and except the ones which lead to the advancement of devotional service. Practically, if one very carefully reads the *Bhagavad-gītā, Śrīmad-Bhāgavatam, Teachings of Lord Caitanya,* and this *Nectar of Devotion,* that will give him sufficient knowledge to understand the science of Kṛṣṇa consciousness. One need not take the trouble of reading other books.

Fortunately, after reading Śrīla Prabhupāda's books and practicing their tenets, a number of his followers have written extensively about how to advance by following in his line of devotional service. One can reference these books as a complement to Śrīla Prabhupāda's teachings and thus stay solidly on the path.

Those who read Śrīla Prabhupāda's books are also naturally exposed to a number of other scriptures and authors, because he cites them profusely in his purports. He also points out other scriptures and recommends that we read them. For example, in his purport to *Śrī Caitanya-caritāmṛta, Ādi-līlā* 5.203, Śrīla Prabhupāda writes, "Śrī Sanātana Gosvāmī Prabhu, the teacher of the science of devotional service, wrote several books, of which the *Bṛhad-bhāgavatāmṛta* is very famous; anyone who wants to know about the subject matter of devotees, devotional service, and Kṛṣṇa must read this book."

Śrīla Prabhupāda was also pleased when his disciple Dr. Svarūpa Dāmodara wrote *The Scientific Basis of Kṛṣṇa Consciousness.* In 1976 in Detroit, he also asked Satsvarūpa Mahārāja to write a book about "how things fail without Kṛṣṇa." He then gave examples of what he meant, referring to several news items of the day that showed how worldly schemes collapse without Kṛṣṇa consciousness. So we can read books by devotee authors other than Śrīla Prabhupāda, but it is best to do so after assimilating, as far as possible, what he has given us. In that way we can more easily discern which books are in line with his high standard of accurately representing our *paramparā*. To say that none of his sincere followers who have read Śrīla Prabhupāda's books and practiced their tenets for decades could become qualified to write accurately, sweetly, and with realization about the science of Kṛṣṇa consciousness would be to belittle Śrīla Prabhupāda, the potency of his books, and the process he is teaching through them.

Rather, my point is that Śrīla Prabhupāda's books are *the heart of ISKCON*. The onus is on ISKCON's leaders, then, to promote His Divine Grace's books even before promoting the books of other authors; and ISKCON authors should feel the responsibility to use their writing to bring readers directly to Śrīla Prabhupāda's books. Śrīla Prabhupāda's books contain the distilled commentary of all the previous *ācāryas* illumined by his own realizations. It is through his books that Lord Caitanya's movement is expanded out into the societies of this age. More than anything, it is the authority of Śrīla Prabhupāda's books that hold his Society together. His books are the essential sound vibration of ISKCON, and if we are to follow Śrīla Prabhupāda and truly keep him in the center of ISKCON, we must stay intimately connected to his books, imbibe their lessons, and teach future generations who approach ISKCON for shelter to do the same.

In his paper, "Institutionalizing *Prema-bhakti,*" Joseph T. O'Connell defines an institution as a means to "transmit culture across time and geography." He particularly mentions that Gauḍīya Vaiṣṇavism transmits its culture – that is, its "ideas and feelings about what is most real, right, and valuable" – mainly through "soft institutions," symbolic means "of articulating loving devotion to Kṛṣṇa." These soft institutions, he writes, "may be shared throughout the community of devotees and across time," and the first on his list of such soft institutions related to Gauḍīya Vaiṣṇavism is the production and sharing of spiritual literature.

So in ISKCON, Śrīla Prabhupāda's books are not only irreplaceable; they are the primary means by which ISKCON devotees learn and disseminate the culture of Kṛṣṇa consciousness that Śrīla Prabhupāda gave us. One might say, based on O'Connell's perspective, then, that Śrīla Prabhupāda's books are an institution unto themselves. It was through his books that Śrīla Prabhupāda transmitted his "personal ecstasies," as he called his purports, his understanding of Kṛṣṇa consciousness, across the generations and worldwide. So while we have a number of important and necessary managerial structures in ISKCON, Śrīla Prabhupāda's books are the heart of ISKCON; they provide us with the text by which those managerial structures govern, and they articulate for our own generation and into the future the value of living a Kṛṣṇa conscious life. Śrīla Prabhupāda's books are the vessels in which we take Kṛṣṇa bhakti out into the world – across the globe and through time – sharing the heart of ISKCON and inviting others to join us.

Śrīla Prabhupāda said that our temples are bases from which we send out our devotees to drop hundreds and thousands of books into the laps of the conditioned souls. The more we organize around this principle, the more we will thrive.

Concluding Words

We've heard how Śrīla Prabhupāda came as an ambassador of goodwill; how he asked his followers to become ambassadors of goodwill; how those who apply the order of the spiritual master attain uncanny success; and how from its inception the main thrust of Śrīla Prabhupāda's mission was to print and distribute his books. We've heard about how those who apply Śrīla Prabhupāda's order to distribute his books become successful. We've discussed how Śrīla Prabhupāda established book distribution as the family business and financial engine of ISKCON. I've shared śāstric references from Śrīla Prabhupāda's writings to show how his books are spoken *kīrtana* and how by distributing them one fulfills the duties of the *yuga-dharma*. I've also shown how by working hard for Kṛṣṇa, especially to give mercy to others, one advances in devotional service, and how by facing obstacles for Kṛṣṇa one grows stronger in faith and learns to control one's senses. We've heard how book distribution is confidential service to the Lord.

I've also given you The Four Laws of Book Distribution: Your *Sādhana* Must Be Strong; Get Books!; The More You Show, The More You Sell; and You Must Organize. Following these laws guarantees that one will be successful in distributing Śrīla Prabhupāda's books.

I've encouraged and defined strong *sādhana* and presented

appropriate moods and methods of book distribution. I've also shown how to sell books door to door, how to sell sets of Śrīla Prabhupāda's books, and how to organize an MSF. And I have explained how devotional service is so powerful that if one gives even a penny to Kṛṣṇa, his or her devotional service begins. Finally, I wrote about how a thoughtful presentation of Kṛṣṇa consciousness opens people's minds and hearts and allows them to receive the highest benefit.

To know in truth how special it is to distribute Śrīla Prabhupāda's books, you have to try it for yourself. Those who distribute books know from experience how people light up when they come in contact with something of real spiritual value. They also see that well-mannered devotees who go out to give transcendental knowledge do not disturb the public; quite the opposite, the public is thirsty for this contact. Those who go out and give people transcendental knowledge are the best welfare workers.

Right now there are millions of special souls waiting to meet *Śrīmad-Bhāgavatam,* the *Bhagavad-gītā As It Is,* or any of Śrīla Prabhupāda's other books. Take some books out and look for those special souls. Lord Caitanya will help you find them. To illustrate the truth of this, let me introduce you to Jeff, a twenty-nine-year-old medical student who graduated from West Point Military Academy with a degree in physics and who recently came to Kṛṣṇa consciousness. Just a few days after Jeff began reading *Śrīmad-Bhāgavatam* he wrote:

> All of these books stand out in a kind of unusual way. For His Divine Grace Śrīla Prabhupāda to have translated so many texts at such a time and so accurately into such an alien language is itself a superhuman accomplishment. That alone is difficult to imagine doing, but that is not the strength of these books. The unique thing is the quality and detail that was put into the purports. They're not lip service like they would be in any other book of translation. It's obvious that his entire soul has been put into this writing, as if the ink is made of faith and philosophy and love, but love for Kṛṣṇa and for duty, not love

> for the feelings of the reader (the words are demanding and sharp, as they should be). You know how the word of Kṛṣṇa *is* Kṛṣṇa; it's of that same sort of caliber, he accomplished that, or as close to it as any spirit can. That's how powerful the devotional service was that he put into this task. It made the result transcendental to that degree.

Just see how Jeff received *Śrīmad-Bhāgavatam* and felt Śrīla Prabhupāda's compassion and personal association. Is he special? Obviously! But the truth is that there are untold numbers of people like Jeff waiting for these books. There are billions of others who don't have the level of spiritual qualification to respond to the *Śrīmad-Bhāgavatam* as Jeff has. Why not give those people a chance to grow too? Will they not get immense spiritual benefit from seeing Śrīla Prabhupāda's books, by touching them, by reading a few words from them, by meeting a devotee face to face? According to Śrīla Prabhupāda, they will.

In this world, people live behind closed doors. They need Lord Caitanya's devotees to knock on those doors and compassionately introduce them to Kṛṣṇa's voice in the *Gītā* and show them the light shining from the *Bhāgavatam.* Conditioned souls are in urgent need of the vibration contained in Śrīla Prabhupāda's books. People are crying out for this mercy. Śrīla Prabhupāda heard their cries and came to help them. Let's follow in his footsteps by tending to our family business.

Notes

FOREWORD

1 *Śrīmad-Bhāgavatam* 2.4.25, translation and purport.
2 *Śrīmad-Bhāgavatam* 9.10.20, purport.

INTRODUCTION

1 Lecture, Los Angeles, January 5, 1974.
2 Letter to Dayānanda Dāsa and Nandarāṇī Devī Dāsī, April 29, 1968.

CHRONICLES

CHAPTER ONE

1 *Śrīla Prabhupāda-līlāmṛta* vol.1, p. 233.
2 *Śrīmad-Bhāgavatam* 7.9.43.
3 *Mārkine Bhāgavata-dharma*, verse 4.
4 *Śrī Caitanya-caritāmṛta, Ādi-līlā* 9.39, 36.

CHAPTER TWO

1, 2 *Śrī Caitanya-caritāmṛta*, Concluding Words.
3 *Śrīmad-Bhāgavatam* 11.2.11.
4 *Aparādha-bhajana,* as quoted in *The Nectar of Devotion,* p. 295.
5 *The Nectar of Devotion,* pp. 3–4.
6 Letter to Boys and Girls, April 20, 1973.
7 *Śrīmad-Bhāgavatam* 11.2.12.
8 *Śrī Caitanya-caritāmṛta, Madhya-līlā* 7.128.
9 *Śrī Caitanya-caritāmṛta, Madhya-līlā* 24.255.
10 *Śrīmad-Bhāgavatam,* preface.
11 *Śrī Caitanya-caritāmṛta, Ādi-līlā* 9.39.
12 *Śrī Caitanya-caritāmṛta, Ādi-līlā* 9.34.
13 *Śrīmad-Bhāgavatam* 4.28.53.
14 *Kṛṣṇa: The Supreme Personality of Godhead,* chapter 37, pp. 355–56.
15 Lecture at Śrī Gauḍīya Maṭha, July 12, 1936, quoted in *Śrī Bhaktisiddhānta Vaibhava,* vol. 3, p. 113.
16 *Vṛndāvane Bhajan,* verse 25.

CHAPTER THREE

1 *Śrī Caitanya-caritāmṛta, Ādi-līlā* 7.95–96, purport.
2 Room conversation, Bhubaneswar, January 28, 1977.
3 *Śrīla Prabhupāda-līlāmṛta,* vol. 1, p. 104.
4 Room conversation, Gorakhpur, February 15, 1971.
5 Lecture, Gorakhpur, February 15, 1971.
6 *Śrī Bhaktisiddhānta Vaibhava,* vol. 1, p. 298.
7 *Śrī Bhaktisiddhānta Vaibhava,* vol. 1, p. 295.
8 Letter to Brahmānanda Dāsa, February 5, 1969.
9 *Śrī Brahma-saṁhitā* 5.54.
10 *Śrīmad-Bhāgavatam* 8.7.44.
11 Letter to Rāmeśvara and Co., September 1, 1975.

CHAPTER FOUR

1 *Śrīla Prabhupāda-līlāmṛta,* vol. 1, p. 522.
2 Letter to Hayagrīva Dāsa, November 18, 1968.

CHAPTER FIVE

1 *Śrīmad-Bhāgavatam* 10.80.34.
2 *Śrīmad-Bhāgavatam* 4.28.51, purport.
3 Letter to Śrī Govinda Dāsa, March 5, 1972.
4 Letter to Rāmeśvara Dāsa, January 9, 1973.
5 Letter to Rāmeśvara Dāsa, May 9, 1974.
6 Letter to Rāmeśvara Dāsa, August 13, 1974.
7 Letter to Tripurāri Dāsa, November 12, 1974.
8 *Śrīla Prabhupāda-līlāmṛta,* vol. 2, pp. 288–89.

CHAPTER SIX

1 Letter to Amogha Dāsa, September 29, 1972.
2 *Śrīla Prabhupāda-līlāmṛta,* vol. 2, p. 294.
3, 4 *Śrīla Prabhupāda-līlāmṛta,* vol. 2, p. 295.
5 "Checkmate: ISKCON's Victory in Russia," BTG, 42-02, 2008
6 Letter to Rāmeśvara Dāsa, October 11, 1974.

TENETS

CHAPTER SEVEN

1 *Lectures on Heroes,* p. 253.
2 Letter to Jayādvaita Dāsa, November 18, 1972.
3 Letter to Karandhara Dāsa, May 2, 1972.
4 "What Difference Can a Book Make? The Impact and Influence of the Genesis Flood," Michael Wagner, chalcedon.edu.
5 "James Chalmers and 'Plain Truth': A Loyalist Answers Thomas Paine," M. Christopher New, earlyamerica.com.
6 "Fidel Castro," *American Experience,* PBS Films.
7 *Bhakti-rasāmṛta-sindhu* 1.2.101.
8 Oxford Dictionary of English.
9 *Śrī Caitanya-caritāmṛta, Antya-līlā* 1.97.
10 Letter to Rāmeśvara Dāsa, December 12, 1974.

11 Letter to Tamal Krishna Goswami, October 30, 1976.
12 *Bhagavad-gītā As It Is* 4.42.
13 *Śrīmad-Bhāgavatam* 1.2.21.
14 *Śrīmad-Bhāgavatam* 3.26.32, purport.
15 *Vedānta-sūtra* 1.1.3.
16 *Vedānta-sūtra* 2.1.11.
17 *Vedānta-sūtra* 2.1.27.
18 *Śrīmad-Bhāgavatam* 1.7.6.
19 *Śrīmad-Bhāgavatam* 11.27.12.
20 *Śrīmad-Bhāgavatam* 1.3.40.
21 *Śrī Īśopaniṣad,* invocation, purport.
22 *Śrīmad-Bhāgavatam* 4.22.19, purport.
23 Vyāsa-pūjā offering, "Adore Ye, Adore Ye All the Happy Day," stanza 6.
24 "Books Don't Want to Be Free. How Publishing Escaped the Cruel Fate of other Cultural Industries," Evan Hughes, NewRepublic.com, October 8, 2013.
25 "Why People Still Read Books and other Fascinating News on the Web," Dave Pell, TIME.com, October 9, 2013.
26 "Nightclubs for literature? Why bookselling is booming in Taiwan," Johan Nylander, cnn.com, November 23, 2014.
27 *TKG's Diary: Prabhupāda's Final Days,* June 9, 1977.
28 Letter to Brahmānanda Dāsa, December 12, 1967.
29 Letter to Rāmeśvara Dāsa, August 3, 1973.

CHAPTER EIGHT

1 *Śrīmad-Bhāgavatam* 4.20.25.
2 Arrival speech, Vṛndāvana, May 17, 1977.
3 Room conversation, Bombay, November 7, 1970.
4 Founding document for the BBT, USA, May 29, 1972.
5 Room conversation, Johannesburg, October 16, 1975.
6 *Prārthanā, Hari Haraye Namaḥ,* verse 6.
7 *Śrīmad-Bhāgavatam* 1.2.3, purport.
8 *Śrīmad-Bhāgavatam* 1.2.3.
9 *Civilization and Transcendence,* chapter 12, "How to Love God."

CHAPTER NINE

1 *Śrī Caitanya-caritāmṛta, Ādi-līlā* 9.36
2 *The Science of Self-Realization,* p. 92.
3 *Śrī Caitanya-caritāmṛta, Ādi-līlā* 3.40.
4 *Śrī Caitanya-caritāmṛta, Ādi-līlā* 1.88–89.
5 *Śrī Caitanya-caritāmṛta, Ādi-līlā* 6.35.
6 Letter to Tamal Krishna Goswami, October 23, 1974.
7 Lecture, Māyāpur, February 21, 1976.
8 Letter to Ravīndra Svarūpa Dāsa, January 5, 1973.
9 Letter to Śrutadeva Dāsa, September 8, 1974.
10 Letter to Śrutadeva Dāsa, October 24, 1974.
11 Letter to Rāmeśvara, August 13, 1974.
12 Remembrances of Śrīla Prabhupāda, July 1976–77.
13 *TKG's Diary: Prabhupāda's Final Days.*
14 Letter to Śrutadeva Dāsa, May 19, 1975.

15 Room conversation, Bombay, December 31, 1976.
16 *Śrīmad-Bhāgavatam* 7.5.23–24, purport.
17 *Śrīmad-Bhāgavatam* 1.5.11.
18 *Śrī Caitanya-caritāmṛta, Madhya-līlā* 1.118–19.

CHAPTER TEN

1 *Śrī Caitanya-caritāmṛta, Madhya-līlā* 4.182, 185, 188.
2 *Śrī Caitanya-caritāmṛta, Madhya-līlā* 12.115.
3 *Śrī Caitanya-bhāgavata, Madhya-līlā* chapter 15.
4 *Bhakti-rasāmṛta-sindhu* 1.1.11.
5 *The Nectar of Devotion;* introduction, p. *xix*.
6 *Bhakti-rasāmṛta-sindhu* 1.2.295.
7 *Śrī Caitanya-caritāmṛta, Antya-līlā* 4.81.
8 *Bhagavad-gītā As It Is* 4.30.
9 *Śrī Caitanya-caritāmṛta, Ādi-līlā* 1.55, purport.
10 *Śrīmad-Bhāgavatam* 10.80.35–42.
11 *Śrīmad-Bhāgavatam* 6.3.25, purport.
12 Lecture, Los Angeles, January 5, 1974.
13 Letter to Lalita Kumāra Dāsa and Jāmbavatī Devī Dāsī, November 27, 1971.

CHAPTER ELEVEN

1 *Śrīmad-Bhāgavatam* 1.6.13, purport.
2 Lecture, Hyderabad, November 25, 1972.
3 *Bhagavad-gītā As It Is* 11.55, purport.
4 *Bhagavad-gītā As It Is* 3.29, purport.
5 *Śrīmad-Bhāgavatam* 7.7.51–52.
6 *Śrīmad-Bhāgavatam* 11.23.37.
7 *Śrīmad-Bhāgavatam* 11.23.42.
8 *Śrīmad-Bhāgavatam* 11.18.31.
9 *Śrī Bhaktisiddhānta Vaibhava,* vol. 1, p. 215.
10 Lecture, Washington, D.C., July 6, 1976.
11 *Śrīmad-Bhāgavatam* 7.9.43–44.
12 *Śrīmad-Bhāgavatam* 4.8.42.
13 *Śrī Caitanya-caritāmṛta, Madhya-līlā* 7.129, purport.

CHAPTER TWELVE

1 *Śrī Caitanya-candrāmṛta* 75.
2 *Śrī Caitanya-caritāmṛta, Antya-līlā* 3.52.
3 *Śrīmad-Bhāgavatam* 1.19.16, purport.
4 *Teachings of Lord Caitanya,* p. 278.
5 *Śrī Caitanya-caritāmṛta, Ādi-līlā* 1.4–5.
6 *Śrī Caitanya-caritāmṛta, Ādi-līlā* 7.18–19.
7 Letter to Uttamaśloka, December 11, 1975.
8 *Śrī Caitanya-caritāmṛta, Madhya-līlā* 2.87.
9 *Songs of the Vaiṣṇava Ācāryas, Sāvaraṇa-śrī-gaura-mahimā,* purport.
10 *Śrī Caitanya-caritāmṛta, Ādi-līlā* 2.2.

AXIOMS

CHAPTER THIRTEEN

1 *First Things First,* Steven Covey, p. 75.
2 Letter to Rajiblocan Dāsa, January 31, 1973.
3 *Śrī Caitanya-caritāmṛta, Antya-līlā* 20.22–26
4 *Śrīmad-Bhāgavatam* 11.2.42.
5 *Śrīmad-Bhāgavatam* 2.1.12, purport.
6 *Śrī Caitanya-caritāmṛta, Antya-līlā* 1.99.
7 Letter to Kīrtirāja Dāsa, January 11, 1976.
8 *Bhagavad-gītā As It Is* 5.18.
9 *Bhagavad-gītā As It Is* 6.29.
10 *Bhagavad-gītā As It Is* 13.28.

CHAPTER FOURTEEN

1 Lecture, Montreal, July 28, 1968.
2 *Śrīmad-Bhāgavatam* 7.5.23–24.
3 *The Nectar of Instruction* text 8, purport.
4 *Padma Purāṇa,* as quoted in *Śrī Caitanya-caritāmṛta, Madhya-līlā* 22.113.
5 *Śrī Caitanya-caritāmṛta, Madhya-līlā* 22.128.
6 *Śrī Caitanya-caritāmṛta, Madhya-līlā* 6.241.
7 *Bhagavad-gītā As It Is* 6.24, purport.
8 *Śrī Caitanya-caritāmṛta, Madhya-līlā* 22.133.
9 *Bhakti-rasāmṛta-sindhu* 1.2.8, commentary.
10 *The Nectar of Instruction,* preface.
11 *Śrīmad-Bhāgavatam* 4.25.25, purport.
12 *Śrī Caitanya-caritāmṛta, Madhya-līlā* 22.16.
13 *Bhagavad-gītā As It Is* 3.31, purport.
14 *Śrīmad-Bhāgavatam* 1.8.26, purport.
15 Lecture, San Francisco, September 12, 1968.
16 *Śrīmad-Bhāgavatam* 7.6.5, purport.
17 Letter to Citsukhānanda Dāsa, February 21, 1971.
18 Lecture, Gorakhpur, February 16, 1971.
19 Letter to Toṣaṇa Dāsa, February 20, 1972.
20 *Śrī Caitanya-caritāmṛta, Madhya-līlā* 8.70.
21 Letter to Haṁsadūta Dāsa, January 3, 1969.
22 *Śrī Śrī Ṣaḍ-gosvāmy-āṣṭaka,* verse 6.
23 *Eat That Frog!,* Brian Tracy, p. 94.
24 *Śrī Caitanya-caritāmṛta, Madhya-līlā,* 22.69.
25 *Bhagavad-gītā As It Is* 16.24.

CHAPTER FIFTEEN

1 *Bhagavad-gītā As It Is* 13.8–12, purport.
2 *Śrī Caitanya-caritāmṛta, Madhya-līlā* 22.14–15.
3 *Bhagavad-gītā As It Is* 18.61.

CHAPTER SIXTEEN

1 *Śrīmad-Bhāgavatam* 1.3.40.
2 Letter to Dāmodara Dāsa, November 12, 1970.
3 Letter to Bali Mardana Dāsa, November 4, 1970.

CHAPTER SEVENTEEN

1 *Eat That Frog!,* Brian Tracy, p. 109.
2 Letter to Brahmānanda Dāsa, February 20, 1968.
3 Letter to Satsvarūpa Dāsa, November 4, 1970.
4 Letter to Alex, Bob, Dṛḍhavrata Dāsa, Ṛṣabhadeva Dāsa, and Stan, January 24, 1977.
5 en.wikipedia.org/wiki/Community.
6 "Business Mission Statement," "The Community," Stephen R. Covey, stephencovey.com.
7 *Śrīmad-Bhāgavatam* 10.13.54, purport.
8 "Restate Your Church Vision Every 30 Days," Rick Warren, pastors.com, June 19, 2013.
9 *Bhagavad-gītā As It Is* 18.68, purport
10 *The Purpose Driven Church,* Rick Warren, p. 109.
11 *Art of the Start,* Guy Kawasaki, p. 3.
12 *Śrī Brahma-saṁhitā* 5.61.
13 Letter to Makhanlāl Dāsa, December 11, 1973.
14 *Eat That Frog!,* Brian Tracy, p. 14.

CHAPTER EIGHTEEN

1 *Śrī Caitanya-caritāmṛta, Ādi-līlā* 7.99, purport.
2 *Śrīmad-Bhāgavatam* 1.3.43.
3 *The Great Transcendental Adventure,* Kūrma Dāsa, p. 383.
4 *Śrīmad-Bhāgavatam* 1.1.2.
5 *Śrīmad-Bhāgavatam* 10.1.16.
6 *Śrī Caitanya-caritāmṛta, Ādi-līlā* 1.106.
7 Letter to Bali Mardana Dāsa, September 30, 1972.
8 *Śrī Caitanya-caritāmṛta, Antya-līlā* 20.90–91.

CHAPTER NINETEEN

1 "Discovering the Lord's Birthplace," BTG, vol.11, 03/04, 1976.
2 *Śrīmad-Bhāgavatam* 3.25.21, purport.
3 *Śrīmad-Bhāgavatam* 5.14.39, purport.
4 *Śrīmad-Bhāgavatam* 7.9.44, purport.
5 Lecture, Ahmedabad Rotary Club, December 8, 1972.
6 "What Your Clothes Might Be Saying About You," psychologytoday.com

CHAPTER TWENTY

1 "Our possessions, our selves: Domains of self-worth and the possession–self link," Ferraro, Escalas, and Bettman, "Science Direct," elab.vanderbilt.edu, August 30, 2010.
2 *Śrī Caitanya-caritāmṛta, Madhya-līlā* 20.122.
3 Lecture, New York, January 9, 1967.

CHAPTER TWENTY-ONE

1 *Śrī Caitanya-caritāmṛta, Antya-līlā* 4.102–103
2 Letter to Kīrtanānanda Swami and Hayagrīva Dāsa, August 23, 1968.
3 Letter to Īśāna Dāsa and Bibhavatī Devī Dāsī, September 21, 1970.
4 *Śrī Caitanya-caritāmṛta, Ādi-līlā* 3.31.
5 Room conversation, Vṛndāvana, May 28, 1977.
6 *Śrī Caitanya-caritāmṛta, Ādi-līlā* 9.18, purport.

7 *Śrī Caitanya-caritāmṛta, Ādi-līlā* 10.160.
8 *Śrī Caitanya-caritāmṛta, Ādi-līlā* 9.36.
9 *Śrī Bṛhad-bhāgavatāmṛta* 2.6.187, commentary.
10 *Śrī Caitanya-caritāmṛta, Madhya-līlā* 14.75–78.
11 *Śrī Śrī Gaura-Nityānander Dayā.*
12 *Śrīmad-Bhāgavatam* 11.5.33.
13 *The Nectar of Instruction,* text 5, purport.
14 *The Nectar of Devotion,* p. 54.
15 *Vaiśiṣṭyāṣṭakam* 3.25.
16 *Śrī Caitanya-caritāmṛta, Antya-līlā* 1.32, purport.
17 Letter to Brahmānanda Dāsa, September 2, 1972.

REALIZATIONS

CHAPTER TWENTY-TWO

1 *Bhagavad-gītā As It Is* 12.11, purport.
2 *Perfect Questions Perfect Answers,* pp. 59–60.
3 *Srīmad-Bhāgavatam* 1.5.32, purport.
4 *The Nectar of Instruction,* text 4, purport.
5 *Kṛṣṇa Consciousness: The Matchless Gift,* chapter 3, "Learning to Love."
6 *Śrīmad-Bhāgavatam* 7.6.10.
7 Room conversation, Melbourne, June 26, 1974.
8 Lecture, Los Angeles, November 29, 1968.
9 *Śrīmad-Bhāgavatam* 8.24.15, purport.
10 *Śrīmad-Bhāgavatam* 11.2.35.
11 *Bhagavad-gītā As It Is* 9.29, purport.
12 *Śrīmad-Bhāgavatam* 1.3.40, purport.
13 *Vṛndāvane Bhajan* 19.
14 *Śrī Caitanya-caritāmṛta, Madhya-līlā* 22.83.
15 *Śrī Caitanya-caritāmṛta, Madhya-līlā* 22.45.
16 *Śrīmad-Bhāgavatam* 11.14.16.
17 *Śrī Caitanya-caritāmṛta, Madhya-līlā* 14.16, purport.
18 *Śrī Caitanya-caritāmṛta, Ādi-līlā* 7.65.
19 Room conversation, August 3, 1976, New Māyāpur.
20 *Śrīmad-Bhāgavatam* 1.8.36.
21 *Śrī Caitanya-caritāmṛta, Antya-līlā* 1.32, purport.
22 *Śrī Caitanya-caritāmṛta, Madhya-līlā* 1.1.

CHAPTER TWENTY-THREE

1 *Śrī Bhaktisiddhānta Vaibhava,* Bhakti Vikāsa Swami, vol. 1, p. 102.
2 *Bhagavad-gītā As It Is* 18.5, 7, purports.
3 *Śrī Caitanya-caritāmṛta, Madhya-līlā* 23.105, purport.
4 *Śrī Caitanya-caritāmṛta, Madhya-līlā* 1.1.
5 *Śrī Caitanya-caritāmṛta, Ādi-līlā* 7.29–32.
6 *Śrī Caitanya-caritāmṛta, Ādi-līlā* 7.65 and purport.
7 *Śrī Caitanya-caritāmṛta, Ādi-līlā* 7.33, purport
8 *Śrī Caitanya-caritāmṛta, Madhya-līlā* 10.119.

9 "By His superexcellent beauty He subdues all the people of the age. In other descents the Lord sometimes used weapons to defeat the demoniac, but in this age the Lord subdues them with His all-attractive figure as Çaitanya Mahāprabhu. Śrīla Jīva Gosvāmī explains that His beauty is His *astra,* or weapon, to subdue the demons. Because He is all-attractive, it is to be understood that all the demigods lived with Him as His companions. His acts were uncommon and His associates wonderful. When He propagated the *saṅkīrtana* movement, He attracted many great scholars and *ācāryas,* especially in Bengal and Orissa. Lord Caitanya is always accompanied by His best associates like Lord Nityānanda, Advaita, Gadādhara, and Srīvāsa." (*Śrīmad-Bhāgavatam* 11.5.32, purport).

10 *Śrī Caitanya-caritāmṛta, Ādi-līlā* 7.99, purport.

11 *Śrī Caitanya-caritāmṛta, Ādi-līlā* 7.31–32.

12 Zig Ziglar.

13 *Bhakti-rasāmṛta-sindhu* 1.2.4, as quoted in *Śrī Caitanya-caritāmṛta, Madhya-līlā* 22.113.

14 Lecture, Los Angeles, December 2, 1968.

15 *Śrī Caitanya-caritāmṛta, Madhya-līlā* 12.50. Note: Śrī Caitanya Mahāprabhu did meet King Pratāparudra in private, when the king was disguised as a mendicant, because the king was actually a pure devotee.

16 Letter to Jagadīśa Dāsa, June 25, 1974.

CHAPTER TWENTY-FOUR

1 Letter to Śrī Govinda Dāsa, June 12, 1974.

2 Letter to Līlāvatī Devī Dāsī, March 26, 1972.

3 Letter to Ho Hon Pei, May 10, 1973.

4 *Bhagavad-gītā As It Is* 18.68–69

5 Room conversation, March 2, 1975.

6 *Śrīmad-Bhāgavatam* 10.2.37, purport.

7 Letter to Bhagavān Dāsa, November 5, 1972.

8 *The Caitanya Vaiṣṇava Vedānta of Jīva Gosvāmī,* Ravi M. Gupta, pp. 8–9.

9 *Śrīmad-Bhāgavatam* 1.5.11, purport.

10 *Śrī Bhaktisiddhānta Vaibhava,* vol. 1, p. 424.

11 Lecture, August 14, 1972.

12 Joseph T. O'Connell, Professor Emeritus, St. Michael's College, University of Toronto and Research Associate, Oxford Centre for Hindu Studies.